Contents

Part IV Soils and Biogeography

Part V Political Processes in Human Geography

Part VI Temporal Processes in Human Geography

Part VII Postscript

Processes in Physical and Human Geography

Processes in Physical and Human Geography
Bristol Essays

Edited by

Ronald Peel
Michael Chisholm
Peter Haggett

Heinemann Educational Books

Heinemann Educational Books Ltd
LONDON EDINBURGH MELBOURNE AUCKLAND TORONTO
HONG KONG SINGAPORE KUALA LUMPUR
IBADAN NAIROBI JOHANNESBURG
LUSAKA NEW DELHI

ISBN 0 435 35625 9
© University of Bristol 1975
First published 1975

Published by
Heinemann Educational Books Ltd
48 Charles Street, London W1X 8AH

Set in IBM Journal by
Preface Limited,
Salisbury, Wilts.
Printed in Great Britain by
Morrison and Gibb Limited,
London and Edinburgh

List of Plates

Preface

This collection of essays has been prepared to mark the fiftieth anniversary of the establishment in the University of Bristol of a separate Department of Geography, an event which occurred in 1925. All the contributors are, or have been, full-time teaching members of the Department during the period of Ronald Peel's Headship. The essays are grouped under major theme headings, but it will be apparent that within this framework several could have been classified in more than one way. Common to all the essays, however, is an emphasis on the processes that mould the surface of the Earth and its man-made environments, whether these processes can be directly observed and measured, or can only be examined by indirect and inferential means. A feature that also recurs is the modelling of these processes, whether in rigorous mathematical terms, or by the construction of conceptual frameworks for analysis.

In the primary division of the essays into those dealing with natural phenomena and those concerned with human creations, the reader will notice that two subjects receive particular attention. In the former, aspects of hydrology inspire many of the essays, ranging from atmospheric precipitation, through the modelling of surface and sub-surface hydrological systems, to the action of water in shaping landscapes. By contrast, the authors dealing with human affairs evince a strong concern with political decision-making in its widest sense, and its effects on various aspects of social and economic geography. These emphases reflect some of the main research interests of the Department over the period in question, but the varied approaches and conclusions are those of the individual authors. There has been no intention to offer any distinctive 'Bristol view' of geography. Should such exist, we leave it to be discovered by our reviewers and critics.

It remains for us as Editors to thank our colleagues, past and present, for giving so generously of their time and ideas to the preparation of the essays that follow. All either report original unpublished research, or present reviews of recent developments in their respective fields.

Bristol, November 1974.

Ronald Peel
Michael Chisholm
Peter Haggett

PART I

Bristol and its Region

Chapter 1

The Changing Role of Bristol in the Development of the South West

Allan Frey
Frank Walker

The recent publication of *A Strategic Settlement Pattern for the South West* (South West Economic Planning Council, 1974) reveals many of the difficulties facing regional planning in Britain today. Its authors recognise that 'the south west is in no way a fully integrated region in physical and economic planning terms [and that] because there are no strong connections between the main parts of the region, the option is not open for a regional strategy which might seek to divert growth from one area [in the South West] in order to secure better economic opportunities in another South Western area of greater need' (p. 20).

The study team recognise at least three areas of persistent and vigorous growth in that part of the S.W. region which adjoins trunk England. Therefore, what they say in effect is that the spread effect from these growth centres cannot be relied on to invigorate the less prosperous parts of the South West, and that help for these trailing parts of the region's economy must come from outside the region and be subsidised by the nation. The designation of Cornwall and West Devon as either Development or Intermediate areas demonstrates that the government shares the view that prosperity will not spontaneously spread there from the high enterprise corridor running from Gloucester via Bristol to Exeter. This may not reflect disbelief in spread effects *per se* so much as doubts about their ability to penetrate long distances, especially westwards into an attenuating and progressively isolated peninsula.

It is the purpose of this essay to examine the changing nature of growth in the Bristol/Severnside region, for long the leading sub-region of the South West and, in particular, to consider what significance this may have for a style of regional planning which aims to see the benefits of growth more widely distributed around the South West.

The historical perspective

It is remarkable how stable over time has remained the relative balance of prosperity between the constituent sub-regions of the South West. The strong influence of geographical position and resource endowment must have played an important part in this stability. As the largest city, Bristol has consistently been the most significant growth node within the South West, capable both of attracting a reasonable share of the nation's prosperity and of diffusing it to a substantial hinterland.

However, the city has been more than just the dominant node and surely qualifies for Richardson's (1973a) designation as a 'locational constant', an essential ingredient of economic growth. It is easy to see why Bristol should have early developed as a locational constant. Given the relatively small size of Britain and the difficulty of overland transport, sea-borne trade favoured the growth of towns with coastal sites. At the same time, the high agricultural fertility of trunk lowland England made it likely that major ports and cities would develop on the few large estuaries giving water access deep into that trunk. Searching for such a site on the Bristol Channel/Severn Estuary, attention would conventionally be directed at Gloucester, situated at the lowest effective crossing point and at the furthest estuarial penetration into the trunk. But navigation of the convolute Severn becomes treacherous long before Gloucester is reached, so a compromise site is necessary lower down the estuary. The south bank long formed a more prosperous hinterland than the Welsh north bank but the huge tidal range of the Bristol Channel means that all important settlements are found on the larger tributary streams. The precise site, upstream from the Avon Gorge, on which the small settlement of Bristol was initially established was largely determined by local circumstances which have already been documented by Jones (1946) but the town's rapid growth in importance after the eleventh century must be attributed in considerable measure to the fact that it lies on the first major south bank tributary downstream from Gloucester.

Bristol grew (Table 1.1) as a port-city serving from the west the axis of highest population density which ran east—west across southern England (Darby, 1936) until the industrial revolution caused a fundamental reorientation of this high activity axis. Access to foreign as well as coastwise trade was a powerful stimulant to growth, long ago recognised by Malthus: 'One of the greatest benefits which foreign commerce confers, and the reason why it has always appeared an almost necessary ingredient in the progress of wealth, is its tendency to inspire new wants, to form new tastes and to furnish motives for

TABLE 1.1

The approximate population of the Bristol urban area

Year	Population ('000)	Year	Population ('000)
1377	10	1801	68
1544	11	1821	98
1607	11	1841	143
1642	14—15	1861	176
1671/2	25—27	1881	242
1700	27	1901	369
1720	46	1921	412
1740	46	1931	435
1760	55	1951	496
1780	54	1971	520
1800	62		

Sources: Little (1954) for data to 1841.
Censuses of Population for later figures.

industry' (Malthus, 1836). Richardson (1973a) includes a region's ability to attract mobile resources from elsewhere as one of the qualifications for growth, so that the considerable variety of imported materials which entered Bristol allowed the development of a wide range of often interlinked industries. The necessary financial infrastructure, merchanting groups, risk capital and general urban concentration economies were all available in Bristol from an early date.

However, the agricultural prosperity of the hinterland and the vigour of Bristol as a port merely ensured the *regional* standing of the city and its tributary area. In terms of export base theory, to figure prominently in the life of the nation, the region has to have a good export performance. This was provided by the west country woollen industry, contributing an important part of the nation's wool and cloth production from mediaeval times until the nineteenth century, a period during which, as is widely recognised, the wool and cloth trade formed England's premier manufacturing and export activity. Furthermore, this activity in the West Country was regionally dispersed among a large number of settlements of varying size, so that, even though over time individual towns changed their rank order of importance, and even though London somewhat more than Bristol acted as the outlet for the trade, the whole region had access to the profits of the wool trade. This condition very well reflects Misra's (1970) observation that a growth pole is only possible when backed up by an hierarchy of intra-regional growthful centres.

Having begun life as a network of central places to serve a rich agricultural region, settlements around Bristol developed into an hierarchy of urbanised places contributing greatly to the growth of Bristol, England's second city until the eighteenth century. To a considerable extent, Bristol was the servant of its region until well into the Middle Ages, so making the economic fortunes of the port and its hinterland heavily interdependent, but the steady urban growth of the city, with its diversified trading and manufacturing functions, gradually saw it take on the role of growth pole leading the region. Strong parallels with the early development of North American regions and their cities can be seen particularly through the most interesting models of Meinig (1972), the regional analyses of Lithwick and Paquet (1968) and the factor mobility stages of Stöhr (1974).

Relative immobility of the factors of production, and especially of resources, labour and capital, encourages a system of dispersed regional markets. In the nineteenth century technological change gave these factors much greater spatial mobility but, in that it led to the replacement of water power by coal, it substituted a fundamentally new but still relatively immobile spatial pattern of industrial production for the old. The effect was to decimate the West Country woollen industry whose superfine broadcloths were eclipsed by the fashionable worsteds being mass-produced in Yorkshire (Walker, 1972). The dispersed West Country industry, though it did 'drain back' and concentrate in just five towns during the nineteenth century, was unable effectively to compete against the scale and external economies of the Yorkshire industry and so declined as the economic mainstay of the Bristol region's economy. The reorientation of the high-activity core region of England to the now familiar N.W.—S.E. coffin shape took developmental stimulus away from the port of Bristol, the basis of the city's economic life, as Liverpool began progressively to take over the role of western gateway to trunk England. Taking more than 75 years to decide on a suitable form of port improvement did not help the city and neither did the delay until the 1880s of the inevitable downstream migration of dock facilities to outports on the Severn. But these can be seen as symptoms of the massive uncertainty that must have faced the port authority at the time, caused by nothing less than a nation-wide revolution in trading patterns. With severe competition eroding the revenues of the port and the woollen industry, the two traditional bases of the local economy, the archaic and moribund decision-making apparatus of the city fathers was quite unable to cope. Robson (1973) not only highlights the importance of such decision-making competence in urban growth but demonstrates the importance of the spatial position of a city in relation to major growth stimuli, especially if it is to benefit from hierarchical and neighbourhood diffusion of technical innovation. Thus the nineteenth century brought an end to that phase of Bristol's development which had been almost entirely port-dependent and caused a painful diversification of the region's industry away from woollen manufacturing. It marked a major change of role for the port-city, reverting from one which had been of high importance to the nation at large to a more modest role as regional capital with now a smaller, though still well diversified, export base.

Twentieth-century developments

So well diversified were her activities at the turn of the century that Bristol was said to be largely immune to fluctuations in the trade cycle. However, the average size of firms was small and such inter-industry linkage as there was tended to take the form of a common dependence on the port. The twentieth century has seen a gradual reduction in the numbers of firms as the successful have been able to substitute internal economies of scale for a dependence on urbanisation economies and, at the same time, progressive amalgamation and take-over of firms has seen ownership and/or head offices move out of Bristol (Wright, 1967). Both these trends applied to the engineering industry in particular as it gradually agglomerated in space and reduced in numbers to specialise in a much narrower range of manufactures, especially aerospace activities. As a result of his enquiries in 1963, Britton (1967) was able to remark that 'for many industry groups intra-regional relations with other manufacturers are restricted in variety and importance', and that inter-industry linkages outside the region are more important than within. The input-output tableau constructed by Edwards and Gordon (1971) from consignment data for all Severnside's industries indicated a similar conclusion about the limited extent of internal linkages and the large flows to other, mainly adjacent, regions.

With fewer and larger firms, nowadays often controlled from outside the region or more vulnerable to national political decisions, there has been a considerable loss of manufacturing flexibility (Table 1.2).

TABLE 1.2

Percentage of all employees in the largest single manufacturing concern; figures in parenthesis show the 1971 census population ('000)

Over 30%		10–30%		Under 10%	
Keynsham	(19)	Tewkesbury	(9)	Bristol	(427)
Melksham	(10)	Chipping Sodbury	(4)	Bath	(85)
Dursley	(21)	Midsomer Norton	(7)	Gloucester	(90)
Chippenham	(19)	Trowbridge	(19)	Cheltenham	(74)
		Street	(8)	Stroud	(19)
		Bridgwater	(27)	Swindon	(91)
		Yeovil	(26)		
		Forest of Dean	(54)		

Sources: Walker (1972, 289).
1971 Census of Population.

Whilst it is probably true that the number of closures of Bristol branches of firms through rationalising decisions taken elsewhere has been matched by those selecting their Bristol branches for expansion (notably R.T.Z.), joining the E.E.C. threatens marginally located industries like those at Bristol somewhat more than those sited in England's industrial heartland. The aerospace industry, which now dominates Bristol's manufacturing employment, is a type-example of progressive amalgamation between national companies with a consequent loss of local opportunities for decision-making and, at the same time, it has become highly vulnerable to government policies, contracts and decisions. It is said that today one job in four in the city and its surroundings is linked directly or indirectly with aircraft.

If these trends in the manufacturing sector cause misgiving, then it is as well to recognise four grounds for optimism. The first arises from Britton's questionnaire finding that firms invariably quoted the availability of labour as the most powerful attraction of the Bristol region. The labour supply is constantly being supplemented, not only by a high rate of natural increase of the population but by the highest rate of net inter-regional in-migration in the country. The South West Planning Region showed a net gain of 20 700 persons in the 1965–66 sample census migration data (House, 1973, p 102) amounting to two-fifths of the total net migrational gain of all British regions, 90% coming from the South East, the West Midlands and the North West. Of this total net in-migration, over one-third was in the over-60 'retirement' group but this still leaves heavy net gains to the South West in the 25–44 age group (accompanied by their children aged 0–14) and in the 45–59 group, the only region where this latter 'mature' age group figures prominently. Of the total number of net inter-regional migrants in England and Wales between 1954 and 1971, almost 40% (366 000 persons) were accountable to the South West region (South West Economic Planning Council, 1974, p. 25). Part of this net inflow caused the population of the Bristol-Severnside sub-region to expand by 7.3% (60 000 persons) in this 17-year period compared with a natural increase of 9% (70 000 persons) making a total expansion of 16.3% (130 000 persons), quite easily the largest numerical (though not percentage) increase in the South West region. The equivalent figures for the whole Gloucester to Exeter corridor were expansions of 45% (149 000 persons) by net in-migration and 52% (117 000 persons) by natural increase. The motivation for this migration will be touched on later, but the result is clear; a steadily expanding workforce matched by a steady expansion in employment, though what exact relationship these two variables have is far from clear.

The second ground for optimism again arises from Britton's (1967) work, the finding that over 76% of the manufacturing labour force of the region is employed in industries that apparently are prosperous as demonstrated by employment expansion greater than the average for the nation. Some caution is necessary because of the crudity of the index and also because his data were collected during an expansive phase of the aerospace industry but the general growthfulness of Bristol-Severnside's industry is not in doubt, even to the extent that a possible cancellation of a major aerospace project would not, it is thought, give rise to more than shorter-term unemployment.

Thirdly, engineering industries, at first associated with wool and agriculture in settlements throughout the Bristol region, diversified during the nineteenth century and so took over from wool the role of dispersed yet important employers of the region's industrial workforce. Inevitably, there was some polarisation of this dispersed industry into Bristol, the paper making and boot and shoe industries providing good examples, but even today the relatively dense distribution of towns within the Bristol region and their extensive manufacturing activity is notable as Table 1.2 indicates. Moreover, the region has accumulated an impressive array of high-technology industry in fields like electronics and plastics, activities which are expanding ones for the future.

A fourth and major basis for optimism is to recognise that the part played by manufacturing in Bristol's total role has been progressively declining over the past half-century as the proportion employed in the tertiary sector has risen to something like two-thirds. Bristol has shared in the nation's growth of the service trades and, because this is essentially an urban phenomenon, has polarised service provision to a large west country hinterland. In the last five years however, Bristol has been accumulating not only functions which serve her own hinterland (which could hardly go anywhere else) but national footloose service activities which could go anywhere within a very wide indifference zone. Until the middle 1960s, such footloose activities would have followed the herd to London and their recent willingness to seek provincial locations marks a turning point in the balance of location factors which promises well for regional policies so often only successful when they reinforce rather than try to create trends.

The development of tertiary industries

As is well known, government regional policies in the post-war period have been preoccupied with causing expanding *manufacturing* industries to relocate, or establish new branches, in the assisted areas. Despite periods when this direction of industry was not very forcefully applied, and also taking into account that there had to be exceptional occasions when firms were allowed to expand *in situ*, these policies undoubtedly have had the effect of preventing manufacturing industries from locating in the Severnside region to anything like the extent that might have occurred spontaneously. Instead, the region has accumulated a plethora of tertiary service activities, wholesalers and factors, distributors, service depots, warehouses and the like, attracted by an expanding labour force and a rapidly developing motorway network. Even the Severnside lowlands, which represent one of the nation's few remaining reserves of large and well placed locations suitable for basic industries, have been invaded by these tertiary functions because of the absence of adequate planning controls.

In the developed countries of the world, it is the growth of employment in the service sector, characteristically housed in offices and including transport, distribution and public administration, that has been primarily responsible for the growth of metropolitan areas, especially in the post-war period. It is not surprising that, with the decline of the agricultural and industrial workforce consequent upon mechanisation and automation, the proportion of the total workforce in tertiary activities should increase so that, by 1961, one in five of England's workers was in an office. Total office employment in England and Wales increased by 15% between 1961 and 1966, though there was a strong spatial bias in favour of London and the South East where 39 000 of the 41 000 in-migrants in the period were office workers. Only the primate city can provide the contact environment necessary to sustain those kinds of office activities heavily dependent on information flows. These typically are firms spatially clustered so as to share external economies and whose decisions are said to be of the 'orientation' rather than the 'programmed' type (Thorngren, 1970). They may well face an uncertain market because of rapid changes in fashion, technology or demand, or because of intense competition, or the need for flair and highly specialised knowledge, or other similar sources of unpredictability. But, because of the lack of adequate controls and because an agglomerated site is always safer than a dispersed one in conditions of uncertainty, a vast array of other lower-level office functions gravitated towards the capital, so that in Goddard's (1973) opinion, only one-third of London's offices have good reason to be there on account of their need for external economies. Because of the importance of such tertiary activity in causing metropolitan expansion, not only is London subjected to excessive congestion effects but also the assisted areas, which all constitute rather poor contact environments, are starved of a growth-inducing mechanism in their towns.

The E.F.T.A. (1973) report identifies the territorial injustice caused by overlarge and undersized towns, and advocates policies which would lead to a more even distribution of city sizes basically by manipulating tertiary, especially office, employment opportunities. Manners (1974) uses similar arguments to advocate social engineering in American cities by more public control over office activities. In contrast, though well aware of the high social costs in large cities, Richardson (1973b) makes a powerful case against interfering too strongly with an hierarchy of places spontaneously responsive to social and economic needs, especially when goals are ill-defined and powers to achieve change so relatively weak.

Despite some office development restrictions in London and the Midlands, it could hardly be said that the British government has used *private-sector* office controls positively to bring help to the disadvantaged areas. However, by decentralising 64 000 civil service jobs from London since the war and creating 20 000 jobs in the provinces, it is already the case that 7 out of 10 Headquarters civil servants work outside London, well over half of them in the assisted areas. The recommendations in the Hardman Report (1973) for the decentralisation of a further 31 000 civil service jobs from London would have kept over a third of them in the South East region and sent little more than half to the assisted areas. The Labour government's decision of July 1974 goes much further in proposing that almost 90% of the dispersed posts should go to the assisted areas. Hardman's recommendations were calculated on the thesis that the considerable benefit to the receiving locations would heavily outweigh the inevitable but limited damage to civil service efficiency in London. The government's much more sweeping decision shows that perhaps at last the role of service activities in city-building is being recognised and manipulated and that the problems of the capital need stern measures to resolve even if civil service efficiency and *amour propre* suffer in the process. So far as the South West region is concerned, the proposals are nationally insignificant but regionally most revealing. Both Hardman and the government propose that just over 1000 D.O.E. jobs should augment the 4725 civil servants already in Bristol, neither an assisted area nor a city in need of growth stimulus; yet Plymouth, which is both these things and stood to gain 1560 jobs from Hardman, gets nothing from the government's decision (though the destination of 1610 Inland Revenue and 1540 Department of Employment jobs is still to be announced).

But it is the spontaneous arrival in Bristol of private-sector H.Q. offices in recent years which demonstrates the attraction of the region and helps push the eighth city in terms of population up to fifth rank in terms of number of office workers (after London, Birmingham, Manchester and Liverpool). The reason for this spillover from London cannot be fully identified but must include the increasing cost and difficulty of finding and keeping office staff in London, a growing realisation that 'programming' functions need not be located there, the availability of premises and labour in provincial cities now large enough to foster an office environment without being so large as to force firms to internalise some of the congestion costs, the attractiveness of high environmental amenity, and so on. By 1980, there are likely to be 52 000 office workers in Bristol and, if the employment multipliers are as effective as some claim them to be, the next phase of Bristol's development as a major national service centre will have begun.

Migration

Although in the past gross migration flows have been high, net flows from one region of the country to another have tended roughly to balance out so that the national settlement pattern has changed only very slowly. Trends revealed by recent census figures already indicate that net migration flows in the future might well lead to substantial re-location of the nation's population for reasons which are not fully understood but which must take account of increasing opportunities for mobility. As jobs become more standardised, workers are better able to include areal preference in their locational decisions. Easier access to more information has the effect of reducing distance-induced uncertainties which are probably the most serious barrier to longer distance migration. The number of locationally footloose workers is rising and so is the minority of workers who can afford to reside at a greater distance from their work.

Explanation of migration can be sought by establishing the relationship between migration and economic structure (Cordey-Hayes and Gleave, 1973) or by questionnaire enquiry among sampled migrants (Johnson, Salt and Wood, 1974). The former, using 1960—61 migration data rearranged into flows between 20 labour market areas, found that high figures for net in-migration (e.g. Southampton, Bristol, Weymouth, Norwich, Hull) were always the result of much higher-than-average gross in and out flows, i.e. high total migrational activity. Their conclusions also indicated that 'push' factors were of little consequence in migration compared with 'pull' factors and that 'pull' could be associated with 'intrinsic attractiveness', a term they tentatively defined as a combination of employment structure, the 'differential shift' components of economic growth, changes in basic and service employment and changes in activity and employment rates. Of these, changes in employment rates and in basic employment seemed to be the most promising. Though Richardson (1973b) suggests that many empirical studies favour employment opportunities as the key attracting force, Johnson et al (1974) found that only half of their sample households moved specifically for employment reasons, the other half moving in order to secure environmental improvement of some kind. However, inter-regional (and especially inter-labour area) migration is generally long distance and the study of Harris and Clausen (1967) revealed that 'work reasons' for moving became progressively more important with increased distance moved, peaking at 56.7% for moves of over 160 kilometres. Schwind (1971) came to the discouraging conclusion that, in the United States, the relationship between migration rates and factors like economic structure, social and demographic characteristics and personal welfare is weak and often anomalous. Perhaps this is the fault of aggregated statistics because towns can differ very widely in the kind of migrants they attract, their age, socio-economic characteristics and therefore motivation (Johnson et al, 1974, p. 216). When constructing a model of regional growth Richardson (1973a) found it necessary to include a locational preference function to help explain rates of inter-regional population migration though, since he gives prime importance to urbanisation and agglomeration economies, he must think of migration as being basically job motivated. Indeed, the extent to which perceived or actual job vacancies attract migrants, or whether firms follow in the same direction as net migration streams in order to tap surplus labour, is one of the considerable unknowns of regional policy.

To the year 2000

When, in 1964, it seemed likely that Britain's population would increase by 20 million to the end of the century, the government of the day commissioned feasibility studies of three estuaries (Tayside, Humberside and Severnside) to see whether they could absorb a useful proportion of this expected 40% increase in Britain's population. The last of the three studies appeared in 1971 disclosing that these estuarial regions were capable of absorbing an extra 1 million people in addition to the local trend growth without too heavy a stress; in terms of a national population emergency, the estuary regions would have absorbed no more than one-twentieth of the new population. Fortunately, extrapolation of more recent national population trends envisages an increase by the end of the century of less than 7 millions, a figure which can be comfortably absorbed by, indeed is being sought by, the two expansive core areas, the South East and the West Midlands. At the same time, the Severnside Study (1971, p. 19, para. 3.11) draws attention to a further 10 million persons likely to disperse from high density urban areas by 2001 and, though only a smaller proportion of these are likely to migrate over long distances, the South West is likely to be a preferred destination for many.

In view of the reduced population projections, the Severnside Study was officially shelved but, because the region still faces growth which will have to be accommodated, the Study lives on. The major disappointment of the Study was caused by its brief to report whether *low cost* development was feasible on Severnside. While it is perfectly proper for the government to seek to solve the nation's problems as economically as possible, it is equally the duty of regional authorities to bid for the best bargain for that region. For example, on an already growing Severnside, the Study discounted the need for a MIDA, a new port, an airport, a two-basin pumped storage hydroelectric scheme, a reservoir-cum-tidal electricity scheme with huge recreation potential, and so on. But without such schemes the estuary is being wasted; the two sides stay as divided as they have always been; no great water-based recreational opportunity is created and it could be deemed pointless to have chosen an estuary for study in the first place except as a low-protest haven for noxious industry. However, because of a generous physical endowment in terms of position and resources, Bristol and her region have always made minimum demands on the national exchequer. Even in the 1960s, when port development rarely took place without heavy government subsidy, Bristol had to forego container facilities, a railway freightliner depot, and to undertake her next major phase of port enlargement at Portbury (West Dock) from privately raised capital.

One major attitude which emerged from the Severnside Study survives into the 'Strategic settlement pattern for the South West' (S.W.E.P.C., 1974), the document with which this essay started. This is that development should not be allowed on an incremental basis over the whole region but should be concentrated in the three largest nodes; as 'fill-in' between Newport, Cwmbran and Pontypool, as new towns in the Gloucester—Cheltenham area, and as a huge eccentric city expansion on Bristol's N.E. side. The *Strategic Settlement Pattern* discards the new town style of development for Gloucester—Cheltenham but cautiously endorses Bristol's extension with a consequent restructuring of the Green Belt.

The Severnside Study used conventional sieving techniques to reveal that over half the Severnside area is of high environmental quality and the motive behind the suggested expansion of the three existing large nodes was to protect this environment from the intrusion that widespread incremental growth would have brought. So once again arises the welfare paradox that people like living at low density in pleasant scenery but are held to have impaired it if they are allowed to do so. More important, this concentration recommendation also discounts the long tradition of a dense scatter of vigorous smaller settlements in Bristol's hinterland while, at the same time, generating truly formidable physical planning problems in arranging for the massive expansion of Bristol.

Bristol's intra-urban problems

In common with other British cities, Bristol has tried to retain as many as possible of her urban service functions in the central area, including the major shopping area, entertainment, professional services, wholesalers and factors, major units of the health service and higher education, local and national government functions and offices of all kinds. All these functions depend on adequate access so that substantial road improvement schemes, including the construction of inner and outer ring roads, have carved up the urban area and at the same time led to the loss of a good deal of low cost housing stock. Fortunately, three long-term changes of land use have made space available in the central area to absorb some of this centripetal pressure, namely the out-migration of industry to the trading estates and peripheral greenfield sites, the run-down of the city docks and their attendant rail yards and warehouses, and wartime bomb damage, incredibly still not fully reinstated. But the inexorable expansion of the service sector has not only taken up much of this space but has occupied more land elsewhere in three main ways. Firstly, it has expanded concentrically into the housing zone often known as the decayed inner urban ring so eroding the stock of low price and rentable housing. Secondly, offices have been established in the fashionable Georgian town houses of Clifton and the Victorian houses of Redland. Thirdly, but only recently, speculative and purpose-built office blocks have appeared in suburban locations, usually along the major radial roads.

Because congestion has so badly reduced accessibility, some larger retail stores will no longer consider a central site; the wholesale vegetable market has moved out to Avonmouth; several applications for major out-of-town shopping precincts have been made but are still (late 1974) the subject of planning enquiry appeals; and the City's much vaunted municipal amenity area in the old city has had to be largely abandoned, partly at least in favour of offices.

City planning in Bristol has tended to follow somewhat rigid land-use zoning policies, though instances have occurred where office develop-ment in particular appears to have moved rather easily beyond zone boundaries. At the same time, policies have been transport-dominated in the sense that easing the flow of traffic throughout the city seems to have had some priority, though little specific action has been taken to facilitate the movement of public transport vehicles. A third pre-occupation has almost certainly been the maintenance of high rating revenues within the city. In these respects, Bristol has shared the experience of Southampton and Portsmouth described by Grant (1975) and faces similar social problems in consequence.

The loss of low cost and rentable housing, brought about by redevelopment and road construction and the inadequacy of a public transport system choked by increasing traffic congestion, bear most heavily on the less wealthy members of the community who do not use motor cars, whether or not they still live in or near the city centre. But everyone who lives, works or shops in the urban area is affected to some degree by what are becoming undesirably high occupation rates, by noise intrusion, and by the general over-use of the urban fabric, so that the newly constituted Bristol District Council is being confronted by widespread and growing demands for action to prevent further damage to the urban environment and to ameliorate the consequences of that which has already occurred. For example, advocacy planning, public protests and party political conviction may already have had the effect of turning the district council's policies away from transport-dominated planning if, as seems likely, ring-road construction has now been drastically curtailed.

Conflicts unresolved

However, since metropolitan status was not deemed appropriate for the former city and county of Bristol, its administration is now conducted by the lower tier Bristol District Council whose policies might be assumed to have purely local significance, particularly if they happen to conflict with policies of the higher tier Avon County Council. This may be true in the case of decisions which relate to the purely physical aspects of planning, but where decisions can have a vital effect on growth their consequences can hardly be entirely local. Thus the recent two-year moratorium on all new office building in Bristol represents a dramatic change of policy since, hitherto, planning permission had been given almost automatically to office applicants in the 'permitted' zone if they satisfied essentially technical requirements; this policy change could have an impact far outside the city itself. If tertiary activity is indeed the main metropolitan expansion force, and if growth-centre theory has real validity, anything which discourages the further movement of office industries to Bristol is of vital concern to the surrounding county and possibly to the South West as a whole. It would therefore not be surprising if Avon County Council continued to take the view that the growth of tertiary industries, and indeed growth in general in Bristol, should continue untrammelled. However, it seems to be an unpleasant but inevitable corollary of growth-centre theory that the social problems associated with growth are far more localised in the centres themselves than are the benefits of growth. Consequently, in a two-tier system of local government the solution of growth-induced problems tends to become both the direct responsibility and the preoccupation of the district council of the growth centre itself, whereas higher tier authorities and advisory bodies may perhaps be more concerned with the possibility of widespread advantages of growth. It seems logical that acceptance of the growth centre idea should ultimately lead to the view that metropolitan status could be justified for rather more centres than presently enjoy it.

For similar reasons, it is hardly surprising that at the regional level the *Strategic Settlement Pattern for the South West* (1974) should accept the inevitability of growth. But to advocate that 'the objective of structure planning over most of the region should be to accommodate population growth at the trend rate' (p. 20) reveals a lack of any substantive normative policies to ameliorate the region's problems by moderation of the trends themselves. Throughout the study runs the theme that development options are limited and that there is only marginal opportunity to modify trends, despite the fact that all sub-regions of the South West are gaining in population, some at substantial rates, and that these rates of increase are likely to accelerate. Nevertheless, most bodies in the South West concerned with welfare and conservation regard a 'trend' build up of population throughout the region as the most damaging outcome and they, like the authors of the

Severnside Study, and for the same reasons, would prefer a goal-oriented concentration of this new population.

Government regional policy in the past has been to diagnose sickness by the symptom of high unemployment and to inject doses of footloose manufacturing industry in order to create employment. How especially inappropriate the unemployment rate is as a diagnostic tool in the South West has already been demonstrated by Gordon and Whittaker (1972). It has to be decided whether priority for the receipt of such aid by the South West, whose problems are mainly ones of remoteness, a rural base and tourism, should rank higher or lower than other assisted regions in the nation whose problems are dominantly structural. It has been argued that employment both in services and manufacturing could be generated more effectively within the South West if remoteness could be reduced. Although Robson's (1973) analysis of the nineteenth-century British urban growth data did not demonstrate key growth points or a core-to-periphery diffusion of growth, or even the existence of persistent, region-wide, homogeneous growth, growth centre theory is now firmly embedded in regional policy. Accordingly, the question arises whether Bristol is the most effective node from which growth will diffuse to the whole South West, or whether the growth now taking place in Bristol should be re-allocated in some way to more effective diffusion nodes, say Exeter, Plymouth or Truro. The controversy to be resolved is whether only a Bristol-sized place can gather sufficient economies of scale and agglomeration to diffuse benefit widely, or whether such benefits can travel only short distances, so calling for the rapid build-up of selected more local and as yet smaller places in the South West. Though there appear to be no demonstrable thresholds in optimum city size (Richardson, 1973b), cities like London and Birmingham are well over that critical mass which guarantees continued growth, even though some of their activity is being diverted elsewhere, so Bristol, it is claimed, could surrender some activity for the benefit of the South West region.

Similar conclusions could, of course, be reached on welfare grounds. It could be argued that there are much greater extremes in the 'level of living' within urban Bristol than exist between different parts of the South West and that regional policy and aid might with greater profit be directed to overcoming the social problems of micro regions within the city rather than to encouraging further growth, which might exacerbate them. But here an element of paradox comes into the planning dilemma. Welfare and conservationist arguments appear to favour the concentration of growth rather than region-wide growth at the 'trend' rate; conversely, it is frequently suggested that activity is more economic when concentrated but that it brings more social justice when dispersed. Perhaps the real difficulties are those of deciding on what scale and in what localities the concentration should be, and of ensuring that local authorities, including those of the Bristol district in particular, are capable of accommodating it without social injustice or further damage to the urban environment.

Under these circumstances, the inter-relationships between the various tiers of government and between them and regional advisory bodies become charged with the possibility of conflict. It is a truism that party political allegiances are very different in urban and rural areas, so that in the two-tier system of local government ideological force may be added to the potential clash between growth centres and their rural surroundings. Moreover, in the South West the situation is complicated by the fact that important advisory reports have been prepared on different bases and from different briefs. The South West planning region has boundaries which ensure that it is not a nodal city region, not a functional region (Symanski and Newman, 1973), not a uniform homogeneous region and not an administrative region. The Severnside Study was concerned with an estuarine region which, though it could be regarded as an entity, overlapped sufficiently far into the South West planning region as to include its largest city and only major growth centre. Reports on both these regions were prepared by nominated or appointed advisory bodies, presumably aloof from conflicts of interest within their territories. Neither report really challenged the supposition that growth should occur and on the basic question of its location they have revealed diametrically opposed views which, in effect, leaves the most important principles to be determined at one level of government or another. The extent to which the advice of either of these bodies on broad regional policy is heeded will be decided by the central government on grounds which may involve some party political considerations. But, even if all such reports are shelved or ignored, decisions vitally affecting growth must be made continuously and almost from week to week by all planning authorities. At the local level, these are elected bodies whose political colour may depend in considerable measure on whether they represent urban or rural areas and this distinction may be vital when it comes to deciding which, if any, growth centres may control the fortunes of the South West.

REFERENCES

Britton, J. N. H. (1967). *Regional Analysis and Economic Geography: a case study of manufacturing in the Bristol region*, Bell.

Cordey-Hayes, M. and D. Gleave (1973). *Migration Movements and the Differential Growth of City Regions in England and Wales*, Centre for Environmental Studies, Research Paper I.

Darby, H. C. (1936). *An Historical Geography of England before 1800*, C.U.P., especially maps on pp. 209, 232, 438, 439, 524, 525.

Edwards, S. L. and I. R. Gordon (1971). 'The application of input-output methods to regional forecasting: the British experience', in Chisholm, M., A. E. Frey and P. Haggett (Eds.). *Regional Forecasting*, Butterworth, 415—430.

E.F.T.A. (1973). *National Settlement Strategies: a framework for regional development*, Geneva.

Goddard, J. B. (1973). 'Office linkages and location', in Diamond, D. and J. B. McLoughlin (Eds.) (1973). *Progress in Planning*, Vol. 1, Part 2, Pergamon.

Gordon, I. R. and R. M. Whittaker (1972). 'Indicators of local prosperity in the South West region', *Regional Studies*, 6, 299—313.

Grant, J. (1975). 'Urban transportation planning: a behavioural interpretation', (Forthcoming).

Hardman Report (1973). *The Dispersal of Government Work from London*, Cmnd 5322, H.M.S.O.

Harris, A. I. and R. Clausen (1967). *Labour Mobility in Great Britain 1953—63*, H.M.S.O.

House, J. W. (Ed.) (1973). *The U.K. Space: resources, environment and the future*, Weidenfeld and Nicholson.

Johnson, J. H., J. Salt and P. A. Wood (1974). *Housing and the Migration of Labour in England and Wales*, Saxon House.

Jones, S. J. (1946). 'The growth of Bristol', *Trans. Institute of British Geographers*, 11, 57—83.

Lithwick, N. H. and G. Paquet (1968). *Urban Studies: a Canadian Perspective*, Methuen.

Little, B. (1954). *The City and County of Bristol: a study in Atlantic civilisation*, Weiner Laurie.

Malthus, T. R. (1836). *Principles of Political Economy*, 2nd Edn., William Pickering, London. Reprinted by Augustus Kelley, (1968), 403.

Manners, G. (1974). 'The office in metropolis: shaping urban America', *Econ. Geog.*, 50, 93—110.

Meinig, D. W. (1972). 'American Wests: preface to a geographical introduction', *Annals*, Association of American Geographers, 62, 159—184.

Misra, R. P. (1970). 'The growth pole hypothesis re-examined', in Hermansen, T. *et al* (1970), *A Review of the Concepts and Theories of Growth Poles and Growth Centres*, U. N. Res. Inst. for Soc. Dev., Prog. IV, 233—53.

Richardson, H. W. (1973a). *Regional Growth Theory*, Macmillan.

Richardson, H. W. (1973b). *The Economics of Urban Size*, Saxon House.

Robson, B. T. (1973). *Urban Growth: an approach*, Methuen.

Schwind, P. J. (1971). *Migration and Regional Development in the United States 1950—60*, Research Paper No. 133., Department of Geography, University of Chicago.

Severnside: a feasibility study (1971). H.M.S.O.

South West Economic Planning Council (1974). *A Strategic Settlement Pattern for the South West*, H.M.S.O.

Stöhr, W. B. (1974). *Interurban Systems and Regional Economic Development*, Commission on College Geography Resource Paper 26, Association of American Geographers.

Symanski, R. and J. L. Newman (1973). 'Formal, functional and nodal regions: three fallacies', *Professional Geographer*, 25, 350—52.

Thorngren, B. (1970). 'How do contact systems affect regional development?', *Environment and Planning*, 2, 409—27.

Walker, F. (1972). *The Bristol Region*, Nelson.

Wright, M. (1967). 'Provincial Office Development', *Urban Studies*, 4, 258—275.

Chapter 2

Public Policy and Spatial Structure: Housing Improvement in Bristol

Keith Bassett
David Hauser

The study of the impact of local government policies is only just emerging as a theme in geographic research. However, the growth of public intervention in the urban economy of British cities, with important consequences both for physical and spatial structure and the distribution of real income among different social groups and areas, is likely to make this a theme of major significance in future urban studies. For example, the impact of local government activity is likely to be most obvious on the physical structure in the inner city, where urban motorways may be under construction and control over land use activities may be exerted through zoning powers linked to development plans. Inner residential areas are likely to be marked by an irregular pattern of redevelopment and improvement resulting from the shifting pattern of post-war planning goals and changing financial constraints on new building. Some areas may show the results of 'non-decision making' just as much as others show the results of purposeful decisions. The blight that affects certain zones results in this case from policy ambiguity and goal confusion that create a sense of uncertainty detrimental to the area. Although urban government does not have much direct power to redistribute income, Harvey has argued that over time the operation and implementation of urban public policies can have important redistributive consequences (Harvey, 1971). Urban policy-decisions can result in varying levels of service provision throughout the city and significant changes in the location of facilities, such as roads, houses, schools, parks and health centres that have important positive and negative externality effects. A particular package of policies creates a particular spatial pattern of service provision and service quality and an unequal distribution of costs and benefits for different neighbourhoods of the city.

To explain the distribution of these impacts requires an understanding of the urban public decision-making process which in turn involves an understanding of the nature of the relationship between local and central government and the extent to which power in the local community is concentrated in the formal structure of local government. For example, the traditional view that local authorities in Britain are simply the agents of central government has been rejected on the basis of empirical analysis by, among others, Boaden (1971), Davies (1968) and Dearlove (1973). On the other hand the borrowing of theories from the American tradition of community power studies (the so-called 'pluralist' and 'élitist' theories, for example) has not generally proved very successful; such theories, although offering some insights, accord a great deal more autonomy to the local urban community and place more emphasis on power groups and bargaining processes outside the formal structure of local government, than is generally justified in the British context (e.g. Miller, 1958a and 1958b; Newton, 1969). Recently, writers such as Hill (1972) and Brown, Vile and Whitemore (1972) have attempted rudimentary categorisations of urban political structures more relevant to the decision-making environment in British cities. The situation is made more complicated by the fact that the precise balance of national and local factors, and the number and relative influence of interest groups inside and outside the council chamber, will vary for different policies and policy areas. The study of urban policy making and its spatial impacts is obviously complex and is certain to involve the geographer in an interdisciplinary enquiry drawing upon political and sociological, economic as well as spatial theories.

This essay is concerned with the general question of housing policies and more specifically with the development and implementation of housing improvement policies in Bristol. To date, grant-aided house improvement has been little studied at the detailed spatial level within one city (but see Hamnett, 1973 and Watson et al, 1973). We will attempt to explain the changes in housing improvement policies within the context of overall housing policies for Bristol and to describe the spatial distribution of grant aid since the 1949 Housing Act. The study of government-financed improvement involves three levels of decision-making — national legislation, local authority implementation and the voluntary take-up of grants by individual households — and each of these will be considered. In this exploratory study, and especially given the nature of the available data, we are not able to discuss issues such as changes in the overall residential structure and effects on the distribution of real income for different groups of householders.

Central government policy:
post-war legislation on housing improvement[1]

In the two decades or so after 1945, the main concern of government housing policy was to construct new houses: the major burden was placed on local authority construction until the mid-1950s, after which time private building became predominant (see Figure 2.1). It is not surprising, therefore, to find that provisions for improvement in the 1949 and 1954 Housing Acts (see Table 2.1) had little impact. In the mid- and late-1950s, policy widened to include slum clearance. Although the 1959 House Purchase and Housing Act, which introduced the standard grant and relaxed earlier conditions for grant approval, resulted in a large increase in grant take-up (Table 2.1 and Figure 2.1), improvement remained essentially marginal to the main thrust of

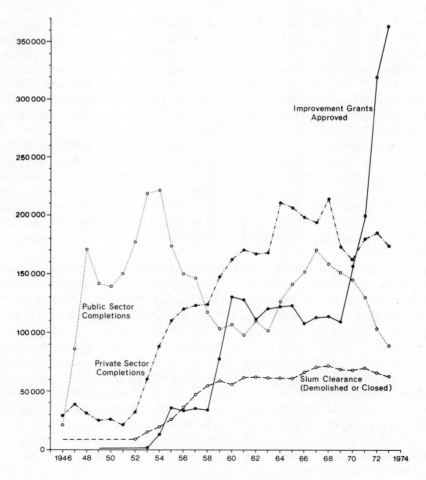

Figure 2.1   Post-war housing statistics, England and Wales.

housing policy, which continued to be the building of new houses and slum clearance.

But this approach was not to provide by any means the answer to housing problems. Increasingly apparent in the 1960s was the inadequacy of the slum clearance programme. The first plans in the mid- and late-1950s to cope with slums were based on local authority estimates, made in 1954, of 0.8 million unfit houses. Clearances rose to 60 000 p.a. by the early 1960s (see Figure 2.1), but the first of the Housing Condition Surveys (1967) estimated that there were 1.8 million unfit dwellings in England and Wales, and this despite the clearance of nearly 0.75 million houses in the period 1954–67. Such a figure represented over 10% of the housing stock, whose demolition would involve many years' work.

In any case, the nature of slum clearance was changing. The 1967 survey revealed that 0.7 million of the 1.8 million unfit dwellings were widely scattered, away from potential clearance areas. Further, as the areas of worst housing conditions were cleared, clearance areas came to include an increasing number of fit houses (5.6% in 1960, 9.8% by 1968), and higher proportions of owner-occupiers who were liable to voice more opposition to demolition than had been encountered formerly. Since there can be no absolute definition of what constitutes an 'unfit' dwelling, there was increasing room for argument over the number of houses requiring demolition.

At the same time as the case against massive slum clearance was hardening, the case emphasising rehabilitation was being strengthened. It had long been argued that the costs of social disruption caused by clearance were, in many cases, very high (e.g. Young and Willmott, 1957; Jennings, 1962). Now such disruption may well be justified in areas of extremely bad 'unfit' housing, but the surveys of the 1960s were also revealing unexpectedly large numbers of substandard houses. The 1967 Survey indicated the existence of 4.5 million dwellings (30% of the total stock) not classified as statutorily unfit but which required either a minimum of £125 spent on repairs, or which lacked one or more of the basic amenities, or both. Demolition provided no acceptable or practicable answer to the problems of these dwellings, whereas their continuing decline into obsolescence required immediate attention.

The mid-1960s also saw the publication of a number of feasibility studies that pointed to the escalating costs of redevelopment (studies of twilight residential areas in Bolton and Fulham indicated that private redevelopment was uneconomic), and to the desirability of rehabilitation (especially the Deeplish Study of a part of Rochdale, M.H.L.G., 1966a; see also Cullingworth's study of Lancaster, 1963). Accordingly, there was a strong weight of opinion which urged the need and potential for relatively cheap improvement. In 1968, the government published *Old Houses into New Homes* (M.H.L.G.), which recognised

TABLE 2.1

Post-war legislation on house improvement grants

	Individual dwellings			
	Type of work	Maximum grant possible	Area policy	Grant as % of expenditure
1949 Housing Act	Improvement; conversion (to 16-point standard). Expected life of 30 years. At discretion of local authority.	£300		50%
1952		£400		50%
1954 Housing Repairs and Rents Act	12-point standard. Expected life of 15 years.	£400		50%
1959 House Purchase and Housing Act	*Standard* 5-point standard.[1] 15-year life (8 years). Awarded 'as of right'. *Discretionary* Improvement; conversion — 12-point standard, 30-year life (15 years).[2] (Basis for these given in 1958 Housing Act.)	*Standard* £155 (£350 mainly when bathroom reqd. extra building). *Discretionary* £400 (£500 for conversion where 3 or more storeys).		50%
1964 Housing Act			'Improvement Areas'	

	Description	Amount	Area / provision	%
1969 Housing Act	*Standard* As 1959 *Special* Provision of standard amenities in multi-occupied dwellings at discretion of local authority. *Discretionary* As 1959; repairs eligible for grant, up to 50% of grant.	*Standard* £200 (£450) *Special* As standard *Discretionary* £1000 (£1200)	'General Improvement Areas'; environmental grant to a maximum of £50/dwelling.	50%
1971 Housing Act			Maximum grant raised to £100/dwelling	75% in Development and Intermediate areas. 50% elsewhere
1974 Housing Act	1. Improvement grant: good repair and all amenities. 30-year life (10 years). Approval subject to r.v.	£1600 (£1850 for 3 storeys).	'Housing Action Areas'; grant payable for 'external works'.	75% (discretion 90%)
	2. Intermediate grant: standard amenities. Good repair. 15-year life.	£350 for amenities £400 for repair and replacement.	'General Improvement Areas'.	60%
	3. Special grant: standard amenities in multi-occupied dwellings.	£350		
	4. Repairs grant: only available in H.A.A.'s and G.I.A.'s.	£400		50% elsewhere

Notes: [1] 5-point standard refers to the five standard amenities, viz.:

(a) a fixed bath or shower;
(b) a wash-hand basin;
(c) a sink (a ventilated food store before 1969);
(d) a water closet (preferably inside the dwelling);
(e) a hot and cold water supply at (a), (b) and (c).

[2] 12-point standard includes the five standard amenities, plus a good state of repair, freedom from damp, adequate heating and lighting, a proper drainage system, facilities for preparing and cooking food, and adequate fuel storage provision.

the force of these arguments, and the Housing Act of 1969 implemented the White Paper's proposals.

One basic aim of this Act was to place the economics of improvement in a much better relationship to those of redevelopment. As such, it represented a major shift in the emphasis of housing policy; the size of improvement grants was significantly increased (see Table 2.1). The Act also attempted to give more attention to areas of sub-standard housing, suggesting that local authorities direct their main efforts to the improvement of whole areas, not just individual houses. Whereas the various Housing Acts specified standards of improvement and gave local authorities increasing discretion in approving grants, the initiative for improvement remained with the householder. But it gradually came to be recognised that, for an improvement programme to be effective, whole areas of substandard houses needed to be improved, not just scattered dwellings, and that improvements to the external environment were, in many cases, just as important as internal improvements (argued notably in the 1966 Dennington Report, M.H.L.G., 1966b). Despite the success of towns like Leeds in pioneering such work (see Pepper, 1971, chapter 5), central government has been very slow to incorporate these ideas into its legislation. It is true that the 1964 Housing Act introduced the concept of the 'improvement area', but little use was made of the cumbersome legislative procedures (Spencer and Cherry, 1970, p. 5).

The 1969 Act introduced the 'general improvement area' (G.I.A.), stressing, by contrast with the 1964 Act, the importance of voluntary public participation, while reserving for local authorities wide powers for the acquisition of improvable properties. Grants were made available for area rehabilitation (Table 2.1). In theory, area rehabilitation was to be a very significant part of the improvement programme; in practice, however, the policy has failed to concentrate resources where need is greatest, and to a large extent since 1969 the improvement programme has continued to involve primarily the physical characteristics of individual dwellings.

The most recent Housing Act (1974) attempts to take account of this and other shortcomings in the 1969 Act. The blanket approach to improvement is replaced by much more explicit discretionary powers for local authorities to ensure improvement in areas of greatest need, notably 'stress areas' (Housing Action Areas) and more stable housing areas (G.I.A.'s) (details given in Table 2.1).

The local scale: factors influencing levels of housing improvement
The previous section has established the general legislative framework within which local authorities have had to operate. However, there is considerable evidence of variations between cities in the nature of local housing problems, the level of housing improvement activity and the

relative weight attached to improvement in overall housing policies (see, for example, the figures for 21 major provincial cities, 1967–1972, in Bassett and Hauser, 1974, and the case studies of individual cities by Muchnick 1970, Davies 1972, Pepper 1971, and Duncan 1973). The relative importance and impact of improvement activity also varies for different areas within cities. The level and distribution of improvement activity in a city responds to a complex interaction of factors which operate at different spatial scales and influence local authority implementation as well as voluntary take-up by households.

(a) The level and location of improvement activity within the city will reflect certain city-wide factors. Firstly, the rate of new suburban construction and the rate of filtering may be important in providing various ways for households to increase their consumption of housing services without improving their existing properties. Secondly, certain neighbourhoods may become especially favoured as residential areas through changes in locational advantage or through changes in their relative accessibility to essential urban services such as transport facilities, educational and leisure facilities, etc.

(b) The environmental characteristics of the neighbourhoods themselves will also be important determinants insofar as demand for improvement will reflect the level of local public services, the spatial externality effects of competing land uses and the quality and state of repair of surrounding houses. The operation of residential externality effects has been explained by Davis and Whinston (1961), and Rothenberg (1967), in terms of a 'Prisoner's Dilemma' type of game. An individual owner hesitates to improve his property if surrounding neighbours do not simultaneously improve their properties and his optimal strategy in the way of financial return can be shown to be a policy of undermaintenance relative to his neighbours. The outcome arrived at by optimal individual decision-making is sub-optimal at the community level, in the sense that the co-ordinated actions of all owners could make each better off through a general improvement or increase in maintenance throughout the neighbourhood. These externality effects operate to some degree in all areas but for various reasons, discussed by Davis, Whinston and Rothenberg, are likely to be of particular significance in areas of poorer housing quality.

(c) The characteristics of individual dwelling units are of major significance. The state of decay and deterioration and the structural and site possibilities for improvement or conversion are probably the key variables here.

(d) Characteristics of individual households, such as income level, tenure, size of household, and stage in family life cycle will be influential at the smallest scale of analysis (Kirwan and Martin, 1972).

(e) The actions of local authorities can influence the pattern of improvement activity both indirectly and directly at different scales. The implementation of land-use plans and policies in the city can influence the relative accessibility of different areas, the externality effects of different land uses, and levels of service provision in different neighbourhoods. More directly, the local authority can exert influence on the motivation of individual households and landlords to improve their houses through effective publicity of improvement schemes, and through G.I.A. policies can overcome important negative externality effects at the neighbourhood level by encouraging co-operative action and assuring a long-term future for the area. The actions of local authorities can thus operate to varying degrees on most of the factor levels defined previously, and these actions are in response to national and local political, economic and administrative factors.

Certain aspects are important enough to be examined in more detail, in particular the voluntary take-up of grants by different income and tenure groups, the explanation of variations in local authority implementation of improvement policies, and the effectiveness of local authority action to encourage co-ordinated areal improvement.

Tenure, income and grant take-up
Given the voluntary nature of improvement grants it is most surprising that until very recently virtually no attention has been paid to the demand for improvement as it varies between different tenure and income groups (Kirwan and Martin, 1972, are an exception). There is a need to look more closely at those tenure classes concerned with improvement — those living in rented accommodation, landlords and owner-occupiers — and, as the 1971 House Condition Survey has confirmed, particular attention needs to be paid to the owners of typical below-standard houses, small landlords letting one to two properties, and low income owner-occupiers.

The core of the substandard housing problem exists in the rented sector. The 1967 Housing Survey showed that 61% of all unfit dwellings were rented (cf. 30% owner-occupied) and that these constituted 33% of all rented accommodation. Similarly, 48% of dwellings lacking one or more amenities were rented, and these accounted for 56% of all rented accommodation (comparable figures for the owner-occupied sector were 33% and 18%). The general picture for England and Wales was largely confirmed by the 1971 House Condition Survey (although the number of unfit and substandard houses had been substantially reduced by this date): for example, 42% of all rented dwellings required a minimum of £250 to be spent on repairs, compared with 13% of owner-occupied houses. Although the rented sector accounts for well over 40% of all substandard housing, only about 20% of improvement grants have been for dwellings in this tenure group. By contrast, owner-occupiers took roughly 50% of approved grants. These proportions relate to the 1960s but have not been substantially changed since the passage of the 1969 Act. Furthermore, in certain areas (notably central London) most grants to landlords have been to convert dwellings into high-price flats: for example, in Islington, in only 15 out of 467 units converted with grant aid since 1969 was accommodation re-occupied by former tenants (Expenditure Committee, 1973, p. 553).

Of course, poor housing conditions associated with rented property have been common for decades. Much legislation to improve these conditions has appealed to the economic self-interest of landlords. Attempts to involve landlords in improving their properties have included the 1957 Rent Act; the raising of permitted rents by 6% of the landlord's share of the cost of improvement, through 8% in 1954, and 12½% in 1959; and the 1972 Housing Finance Act. But this, in itself, has turned out to be wholly insufficient; and allied to the low level of controlled rents and the poor tax position of landlords, these measures have given little economic incentive to improve.

It has become increasingly clear that legislation has too rarely considered the motivations of landlords, and has failed to distinguish the different problems faced by different types of landlords. For example, in areas of low demand for rented property, such as are found in many northern industrial towns, the typical landlord is over 65 years in age, with a low income, owning a couple of old terraced properties usually acquired by inheritance (see, for example, the Deeplish study and *New Life in Old Towns*, D.O.E., 1971), who regards 'management . . . as a burden which has to be borne' (Cullingworth, 1963, p.141), and has few resources for major improvements. Further, the tenants of such property usually have low incomes and can only afford low rents. Certainly the evidence is that in such areas very little is spent even on repairs and maintenance, let alone improvement: an average of £5–7 p.a. in Deeplish (M.H.L.G., 1966a, p. 26).

The situation is somewhat under-researched in areas of high demand for rented accommodation, but here too it would appear that improvement legislation is wide of the mark. In areas of social change and conversion to flats (predominantly central London, but also smaller areas elsewhere), improvement grants are essentially irrelevant when demand is high and inflation rapid (see Expenditure Committee, 1973, p. 435), and this seems to be true also where grants are used merely to convert dwellings for owner-occupation. Elsewhere, in areas of multiple occupation but with no real prospect of 'gentrification', there would appear to be little incentive for improvement, as this usually implies fewer dwelling units and thus less income for the landlord (see Rex and Moore, 1967, chapter 5); again, tenants are likely to be able only to afford relatively low rents.

The structure of rented housing in Bristol is unresearched, but it includes elements of all three 'ideal' cases presented above. Certain areas include small landlords owning few properties and little sharing of dwellings, whereas others, such as St. Pauls, are dominated by multiple-occupation (see Richmond, 1973, for an account of the additional problems caused here by racial discrimination in housing). Clifton shows evidence of conversions for owner-occupation using improvement grants.

Very little is known about the propensity of owner-occupiers to improve their properties: even studies of the demand for housing in general have produced very variable results (Clark and Jones, 1971). Indeed, the 1966 Deeplish Study (M.H.L.G., 1966a, p. 21) could claim that it was '. . . the first systematic inquiry undertaken into attitudes about house improvements since the improvement grant scheme started in 1949'. Certainly, virtually nothing is known about the income and price elasticities of demand for improvement on the part of low-income owner-occupiers, and it is this group, along with landlords, which typically owns substandard houses.

Evidence varies as to the level of improvement made 'indigenously' by low-income owner-occupiers in low standard houses. Some of it has been relatively optimistic. The Deeplish Study, for example, which had a seminal influence on the 1969 Act, noted (p. 26) a surprisingly high level of maintenance and improvements in the previous year, although very little in rented property. Comparable results were found by Cullingworth in Lancaster (1963, p. 169), and by Sigsworth and Wilkinson (1971) in a study of low quality housing in three Yorkshire towns. By contrast, the D.O.E. study of Nelson and Rawtenstall (1971) saw few grounds for optimism and found that reasons other than those relating purely to income were often quoted for not investing in improvement – including age of household, house not worth improving, fear of demolition, etc. It is of some interest to note that in all these studies the level of knowledge of the availability of improvement grants was remarkably low.

Perhaps the most comprehensive survey has been that of Kirwan and Martin (1972) who analysed improvements made by owner-occupiers in North East Lancashire over the period 1965–70. Despite low levels of statistical explanation (partly due to rather small variances in many of the variables), they suggest that high expenditure on improvement is associated with higher income levels, young adults with families, a recent move to a new address (confirmed for Dudley by Watson et al, 1973), and with housing not already in a poor condition. Accordingly, they assert that a high propensity to improve is related to relatively favourable housing and household characteristics. By contrast, social surveys have shown how those owning substandard houses tend to be small, settled, elderly households with low incomes. Their conclusion is that there would appear to be little scope for voluntary improvement for the benefit of low-income households in areas like the one they considered.

Now it is clear that all these findings have to be approached with some care, in that they are often rather restricted in the range of household types and housing areas considered. However, it would

appear that even allowing for the fact that maintenance and improvement expenditures by such households are perhaps somewhat higher
than may be expected, outlays are on average much too low to do other
than slightly reduce the rate of obsolescence (cf. Stone, 1970, chapter
8), average expenditure being usually less than half that required merely
for maintenance. Such substandard houses usually need substantial
capital sums spent on them at one time, whereas 'indigenous'
improvement is, by its nature, a slow and piecemeal process, to match a
household's flow of resources. In this context, a 50% grant towards a
lump sum total expenditure incurred at one time just is not adequate
and implies that the reduction in the cost of improvement works
afforded by the grant will induce a large increase in expenditure, an
unwarranted assumption so far as low-income groups are concerned.
Not only that, but as Kirwan and Martin point out (p. 33), a relative
improvement in the housing conditions of such households requires an
increase in the demand for housing, and thus in income, by such groups
relative to higher income groups — and yet it is these latter groups, with
a much higher elasticity of demand for housing and improvement,
which have been able to benefit more from the improvement grant
schemes.

Accordingly, it is difficult not to agree with Kirwan and Martin that
the demand for improvement among low-income households has been
seriously over-estimated. One reason for this may well be due to the
lack of clarity with which the objectives of improvement policies have
been enunciated. There has always been a basic conflict between
physical objectives, relating to the improvement of houses to the
maximum possible standard, and the social aim, which is to give a
choice to households to raise their housing standards (see Duncan,
1973, chapter 2). Physical objectives have generally prevailed, and to a
considerable degree these have not been within the purview of
low-income households.

If the above analysis is correct, then successful improvement requires
a stronger demand in the housing market on the part of low income
households. At the individual house and household level, it would be
possible to change the percentage share of total expenditure met by
improvement grants. Certainly, the 1971 Housing Act introduced a 75%
grant for the Development and Intermediate Areas for a period of two
years (later extended to three), but this was 'at least as much for
employment reasons as for housing motives' (Expenditure Committee,
1973, p. xxviii); also, the 1974 Housing Act provides for rates varying
from 50% to 90%. But these figures do not appear to have been based
on any empirical studies of the demand for improvement. Perhaps a
better suggestion, and one which should help low-income groups
especially, is for a flat-rate grant (Kirwan and Martin, 1972, p. 143).
Certainly, a much more flexible approach is needed to the provision of
finance for improvement.

Local authorities and areal improvement

Another solution, recognising that substandard houses tend to be spatially concentrated within cities, moves away from policies aimed exclusively at individual houses towards policies which concentrate on co-ordinated areal improvement of houses and environment. In the period before the 1969 Housing Act, the legislative emphasis was largely on the voluntary take-up of grants on an individual household basis wherever physical improvement was justified. Local authorities were largely restricted to the role of publicists for grant availability. However, although there was little legislation available to local authorities to effect areal improvement, a number of the major authorities did seek in different ways in the 1960s to direct the level and pattern of improvement within their urban areas. Birmingham, for example, used considerable discretion within the existing legislation to encourage short-term patching of houses due for eventual demolition. Leeds combined an energetic use of existing legislation with a local Corporation Act (1966) to pioneer an area-by-area approach to improvement, concentrated within its large tracts of old, terraced housing (Pepper, 1971). Newcastle, on the other hand, in its ill-fated Rye Hill scheme, attempted to go outside the existing legislation in seeking a compulsory purchase order for comprehensive area improvement (Davies, 1972). These approaches can be contrasted with that of Liverpool, where the emphasis was on demolition and redevelopment within the central areas with only passing regard for improvement programmes (Muchnick, 1970). These variations in the type and degree of direct local authority involvement in housing improvement reflected a variety of local factors such as the nature of the local housing stock and housing needs; the resistance or pressure exerted by local owner-occupiers and landlords; the party political and professional attitudes towards the alternatives of improvement and redevelopment; the relative power of different departments with respect to each other and to the politicians; and a variety of factors such as the competency, drive and organisation of local departments charged with housing research and administration.

Since 1969, the increasing emphasis upon the co-ordinated improvement of house and neighbourhood through G.I.A. policies has placed greater weight upon the actions of local authorities. However, local authorities can still exercise considerable discretion in the use of these policies and a recent survey by Duncan (1973) of the attitudes of 92 local authorities to the G.I.A. legislation suggested a continuation of the pattern of marked local variability in response and implementation, with many local authorities still relying heavily upon a relatively undirected voluntary take-up. The 1974 Housing Act extends the powers and options of local authorities in the housing and environmental improvement field and arguably the greater flexibility allowed will result in even more marked local variations in response.

After a slow start, the number of G.I.A.'s declared in England and Wales rose to 780 by the end of 1973, covering nearly 240 000 dwellings. But apart from some apparent successes the general consensus appears to be that the concept, one of areal improvement, has had little success so far. The rate of grant take-up initially within G.I.A.'s was very low, although this rate has accelerated recently. By the end of 1973, only 11% of dwellings had had grant work completed, although a further 14% had had work approved. It is not possible to be dogmatic about the reasons for this, largely because of the widely varying range of objectives that have been invoked in the designation of G.I.A.'s. As with general policy objectives of the improvement programme, little clear thought has been given to the aims which G.I.A.'s are supposed to achieve. Some local authorities have designated areas with the worst housing conditions, although it has been more common to select areas with considerable improvement potential. This is largely because a minimum lifetime of thirty years is required for properties in such areas. Accordingly, as Duncan puts it, G.I.A.'s have come to represent the 'élite' of the older areas (Expenditure Committee, 1973, p. 422). Since G.I.A.'s are small relative to the size of the substandard housing problem, there has often been a subtle form of gentrification in these areas (as, for example, in the Arlington G.I.A., Norwich), while other areas have remained 'in limbo'. Indeed, declaration of a G.I.A. can induce strong pressure on houses in areas adjoining the G.I.A. Accordingly, in many cities the areas with the worst housing conditions have not been declared G.I.A.'s; and in other places, changing social function has gone hand-in-hand with G.I.A. designation (although the direction of the causal link is often by no means clear).

However, even if the areas of worst substandard housing were declared G.I.A.'s, it is not apparent that such declaration would lead to marked improvement. We have already seen that the rate of grant take-up even within G.I.A's has been rather low. This is partly due to the fact that the standards of improvement required are very high. Since there is usually a wide range of housing conditions within G.I.A.'s, and it is expected that all properties reach a high level of improvement, then this implies that the greatest expenditures have to be made on the worst and cheapest properties (see Duncan, 1973, pp. 86–87). Such expenditures are beyond the means of the likely owners or tenants of such houses. Further, the mere designation of an area as a G.I.A. does not necessarily involve the improvement of any dwelling within it. The execution of environmental improvements will not by itself induce improvement of dwellings. As Kirwan and Martin (1972, pp. 126–127) point out, environmental quality is likely to be a necessary rather than a sufficient condition for rehabilitation: they see little ground for the hope that a better environment in poor housing areas induces a significant increase in the demand for improvement. Indeed, following our earlier argument, such an increase in demand is only likely with an increase in income of households – thus, the changing social composition of households in some G.I.A.'s (which may partly explain the recent increase in grant approvals within G.I.A.'s). Indeed, some local authorities have stopped further declarations of G.I.A.'s on just these grounds, i.e. that adverse distributional effects have been caused (see evidence given to Expenditure Committee, 1973).

Another reason for the lack of success of G.I.A.'s, from the local authority point of view, is the stress given in the 1969 Act to the importance of the voluntary decision to improve. Now it may be argued that, given the effects of externalities, such a stress is quite inappropriate. (This is certainly the case with respect to dwelling maintenance, and possibly with respect to dwelling improvement.) It has been shown that government has had a somewhat vacillating approach to the degree of coercion required to effect improvements. The 1964 Housing Act implemented a measure of coercion, though only for rented property. But its signal lack of success resulted in the emphasis on voluntary take-up embodied in the 1969 Act. This, however, has caused crucial difficulties in areal improvement. Evidence presented to the Expenditure Committee examining improvement grants indicated that many local authorities felt that the 1969 Act was quite inadequate here, and it was suggested that powers to enforce improvement should be at the initiative of the local authority instead of the tenant. Some authorities (Liverpool, for example) have gone so far as to suggest that areal improvement can be achieved reasonably quickly only when ownership in an area is unified.

The impact of improvement policies in Bristol

Bristol's housing and housing policies
The previous section has emphasised the complexity of the factors influencing the type and level of a city's improvement activity within the context of its overall housing problems and policies. A full discussion of improvement policies in Bristol is particularly difficult for, with the exception of one or two good studies of redevelopment and the social problems of council estates (Jevons and Madge, 1946; Jennings, 1962; Spencer, 1964), the nature of Bristol's post-war housing problems and the evolution of its housing policies have been poorly documented and researched. In the empirical work that follows we concentrate on the changing role accorded to improvement in post-war housing policies in Bristol, the changing spatial distribution of grant aid over time, and the matching of grant aid to housing need as the result of changing national legislation and local policies. The nature of the data does not support sophisticated quantitative analysis and our results are presented simply in map and tabular form. .

To put Bristol into a national urban context, figures on housing characteristics and housing performance were collected for Bristol and the other twenty cities in England and Wales with populations greater than 200 000 in 1971 (excluding London). The 21 cities have populations ranging from 204 300 (Portsmouth) to 1 013 400 (Birmingham), Bristol being in sixth place with 426 000. The relative position of Bristol as regards housing conditions and housing performance are summarised in Table 2.2. Bristol generally ranks high in terms of the amenities provided for the different tenure classes of its housing stock (its lowest ranking is tenth for proportion of households renting furnished accommodation). It appears as a prosperous commercial city without the major problems of housing decay and obsolescence that exist in many northern cities. It has slipped down the ranking of cities in terms of council house building in recent years but has moved up the scale in terms of grant-aided improvement activity. In particular, it has moved upwards in terms of discretionary grant approvals per 1000 households (the bulk of improvement in some northern cities has been with the aid of standard grants) and significantly has taken the lead in conversions per 1000 households (see Bassett and Hauser, 1974, for more detailed comparisons).

Although the comparisons presented here are limited, they do point to some interesting features of Bristol's housing situation that demand further examination. Some aspects can be treated in more detail by looking at the changes in Bristol's housing policies since the war with particular reference to the role of improvement policy. Variations in the basic housing variables for Bristol are plotted in Figure 2.2 and can be compared with the 'national' (England and Wales) pattern shown in Figure 2.1. In many respects the patterns of variation are similar, although there are also significant divergences in the timing of peaks and the relative amplitude of swings (compare, in particular, the respective patterns of grant approvals).

The high level of local authority building in the city after the last war reflected the need to replace bomb-damaged property and to catch up on the back-log on the council-house waiting list. The building programme managed to reduce the council waiting-list from a peak of 26 661 in 1946 to 10 492 by September, 1954; in fact, over the period 1948—51 Bristol completed more new permanent dwellings than any other local authority outside London. Much of this new building took place on peripheral housing estates.

This high level of new construction continued for a year or so after the 1954 Housing Act but, in the late 1950s, the level dropped and work was concentrated more on slum clearance and redevelopment. Bristol returned an estimate of 10 000 unfit houses to the M.H.L.G. in 1955 and a further 25 000 were estimated to be substandard. Major inner city redevelopment projects were started in St. Judes in 1955, Redcliffe in 1957 (both adjacent to the city centre) and Barton Hill in

TABLE 2.2

Bristol: comparative housing conditions and performance

	1st ranking city		Bristol		Last ranking city	
Conditions						
% Households with all exclusive facilities						
Total	(Leeds)	85.7	(6)	81.8	(Leicester)	66.0
Owner-occupier	(Leeds)	91.4	(9)	85.6	(Leicester)	73.4
Renting unfurnished	(Southampton)	65.3	(3)	62.1	(Sheffield)	27.8
Renting furnished	(Plymouth)	65.0	(10)	35.2	(Sunderland)	25.4
Construction & Demolition						
Council dwellings built per 1000 pop. up to 1966[1]	(Sunderland)	141	(15)	92	(Coventry)	71
Local authority housing starts per 1000 households 1966—72[2]	(Manchester)	121	(19)	22	(Cardiff)	20
Dwellings demolished or closed per 1000 pop. 1955—65[1]	(Leeds)	44	(15)	12	(Cardiff)	4
Dwellings demolished per 1000 households 1966—72[2]	(Manchester)	152	(18)	7	(Plymouth)	3
Improvement[2]						
Grants (all types) paid per 1000 households 1967—70	(Sunderland)	56	(15)	13	(Cardiff)	6
Grants (all types) approved per 1000 households 1971—72	(Sunderland)	76	(13)	26	(Manchester)	7
Discretionary grants paid per 1000 households 1967—70	(Stoke)	31	(8)	8	(Derby)	0.2
Discretionary grants approved per 1000 households 1971—72	(Sunderland)	65	(7)	24	(Manchester)	2
Conversions paid per 1000 households 1967—70	(Sheffield)	2.6	(4)	2.0	(Derby)	0
Conversions approved per 1000 households 1971—72	(Bristol)	6.6	(1)	6.6	(Coventry)	0.2

Sources: [1] Dennis, 1970.

        [2] *Local Housing Statistics* (Quarterly).

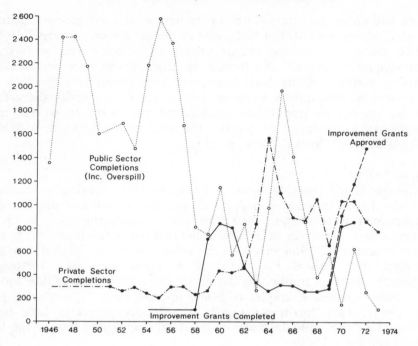

Figure 2.2   Post-war housing statistics, Bristol.

1958 (Jennings, 1962), involving the clearance of nineteenth-century terraced housing and its replacement largely by apartment blocks.

Local authority construction rose again in the mid-1960s, following the return of the Labour Party to power in Bristol in 1963 (after a gap of three years), and nationally in 1964. In fact, in the Bristol election Labour had campaigned on a promise to build 50% more council houses than the Conservatives had in their three years of office, although the housing situation was not a major issue in the election (Sharpe, 1967).

The state of the Bristol housing stock in the 1960s was briefly considered in the 1966 *Development Plan Review*. In 1961, it had been estimated that 9000 of the 135 000 houses in the city were unfit, and the *Review* felt that these should all be demolished by 1981, at which time it was projected there would be an overall demand for 22 000 new dwellings. By combining three indices of accommodation, density and housing amenities, the *Review* was able to present a rough rank-ordering of the neighbourhood units of the city in terms of overall housing deficiency. These areas comprised an inner ring, forming a nearly complete band around the city centre, although concentrated towards its eastern side. In fact, in 1966 in two of the three worst areas, work had either just started on comprehensive redevelopment (Easton) or was in progress (Barton Hill). But in the third zone, Montpelier—St. Pauls, there was nothing except proposals for some very small-scale redevelopment. Indeed, the *Review* spotlighted this area for its poor housing conditions, its high immigrant population and the lack of long-term housing policy proposals: 'with the future national increase of the immigrant population, conditions are likely to worsen and clearly action is needed to improve the residential environment of this neighbourhood' (Bristol, 1966, p. 25).

Improvement
Although major redevelopment programmes were continuing throughout the 1960s in many inner-city areas, the Council and the Housing Department were at the same time also encouraging the take-up of improvement grants in areas not scheduled for redevelopment. A city news brochure of 1964 surveyed the achievements up to that date and claimed that Bristol had adopted a 'pioneering' and 'forthright approach' 'both in publicising details of the assistance available and in providing practical examples of house improvement' (*Civic News*, No. 81, 1964). This 'forthright approach' certainly seems to have been reflected in the rapid increase in grant take-up in the city in the late 1950s and early 1960s.

The same edition of *Civic News* also outlined the Housing Committee's view on the future use of improvement grants and identified areas — Bedminster, Totterdown, Horfield, Bishopston, Brislington and St. George — where houses were lacking in modern amenities but were basically sound. These areas form something of a band circling the inner zones of the city where the major redevelopment projects were then being carried out. However, the inner zone also contained areas of the worst housing in the city that were not then scheduled for redevelopment (Montpelier—St. Pauls, for example) and these areas were not referred to as target areas for improvement. It is probable that, at this time, clearance and redevelopment were still envisaged as the long-term solution to the problems of these remaining inner areas. Nevertheless, in the inner-zone Chessels area (Bedminster) the Housing Committee did recommend the declaration of an Improvement Area under the new legislation provided by the 1964 Housing Act, since the Chessels area was regarded as particularly favourable to this type of treatment, the houses lacking amenities but being basically sound.

However, the early impact of the 1959 Housing Act was soon lost, and grant completions were running at an annual level of about 300 by the mid- and late-1960s. Further, from the mid-1960s, the level of private and public house building in the city was declining as major redevelopment projects neared completion and as the national economic situation brought restraints on housing expenditure. Underlying the decline in new council building was the emerging belief, expressed in the *Report on the Work of the Housing Department, 1969,* that the majority of the unfit houses had been dealt with, that there was less need for new construction and that greater emphasis should now be placed on the repair and modernisation of the remaining stock of older houses (Bristol, 1969).

The 1969 Housing Act provided just the legislation needed to encourage a greater level of improvement and conversion in the city's older housing stock. Figure 2.2 shows the considerable impact that the higher level of grants and the greater publicity for improvement aid had on the level of grant take-up in the city. In addition, Bristol has made full use of the Act to improve its own local authority housing. The years 1967-69 saw the approval of 2090 grants for improving Bristol's older council houses, while the corresponding figure for 1970 to mid-1973 was 12 558. Since there are just under 15 000 pre-war council houses in Bristol, these figures represent a considerable volume of improvement in relation to the overall public housing stock. In fact, since 1967, the improvement of local authority dwellings has accounted for approximately 50% of all grants awarded in the city.

However, despite the publicity the Council has given the improvement grant legislation, Bristol has continued to act since 1969, as it did before, largely as a 'clearing house' for private grant applications. The voluntary take-up of grants by individual households has resulted in a very scattered pattern of improvement throughout the city. Indeed, Bristol's use of area policies has been less than that of many other local authorities. Only three G.I.A.'s have been declared, two of them adjacent to redevelopment areas, and involving a total of only 200 houses. Two further areas have been identified as potential G.I.A.'s, covering between them 650 houses, and both are bounded by redevelopment projects. It is apparent that areas that might have been considered as areas suitable for inclusion in a future redevelopment plan in the 1950s and 1960s were being reconsidered for long-term revitalisation in the new climate of the late 1960s and early 1970s.

With the aid of the new legislation, the Council also turned to the problems of Montpelier—St. Pauls and draft policy proposals for the whole area were approved by the Planning and Traffic Committee in 1970. Although some small-scale redevelopment projects had been carried out within the area, little in the way of future redevelopment was proposed. Montpelier—St. Pauls was divided into zones in which the houses were expected to have lives of either 15 or 30 years; *Civic News* claimed 'the object will be to mount a sustained and co-ordinated programme of action in which great stress will be laid on partnership between the Corporation and the owners and occupiers of these dwellings, to secure major improvements in housing conditions' (*Civic News,* No. 149, 1971). The St. Agnes G.I.A. covered part of the area but G.I.A.'s could not be declared in the extensive areas of fifteen-year life expectancy because they were likely to be needed in 1985 for completion of the city's urban motorway ring, the Outer Circuit Road. Redevelopment in the Easton area of Bristol had allowed for the line of this motorway; it is ironic that when Bristol finally tackled the problems of the St. Pauls area on an improvement rather than redevelopment basis, it had some of the necessary legislation in the 1969 Housing Act but could not use many of its more effective provisions because of the restrictions imposed by long term transport planning requirements.

An interim summary
What picture emerges of Bristol's approach to its post-war housing problems in the period up to 1972? The picture appears to be of a prosperous, expanding city with a considerable but not massive housing problem, tackling its housing situation with enough success to suggest that the major problems had either been solved by the early 1970s or could be solved within the near future. In certain important respects, for example, the level of immediate post-war building and the redevelopment of many of the worst housing areas in the 1950s and 1960s, Bristol has appeared as a vigorous and progressive local authority. As regards improvement, the city seems to have had a national reputation as a leader in its approach in the early 1960s, although the sharp increase in grants taken up after 1969 would probably have occurred anyway regardless of the activity of the local authority in declaring G.I.A.'s, etc. In fact, area improvement policies have been limited in their application and the local authority has seen itself in a publicity role, encouraging the voluntary take-up of grants by individual households on a wide scale throughout the city, and also encouraging improvement to the higher standards.

The distribution of improvement grants within Bristol [2]
Data on improvement grant applications and completions were available from the Bristol Housing Department. Information on dates of enquiry and completion, type of grant and amounts of grant aid expenditure were coded from 1954 (the date of the first grant) to mid-1973 (the date on which the research project was begun). In all, information on 8610 grants (approvals and completions) was collected and each address was allocated to one of 96 common zones (see Figure 2.3). Common zones were designed by the Planning Department for general comparative and statistical purposes and cover an average of 9—10 enumeration districts. Unfortunately, no data were readily available on the type of applicant or the precise nature of the work carried out with the aid of the grant.

In order to analyse the distribution of grants within Bristol, some measure of housing need was required. Ideally, for our purposes, such a measure should take into account the provision of household amenities,

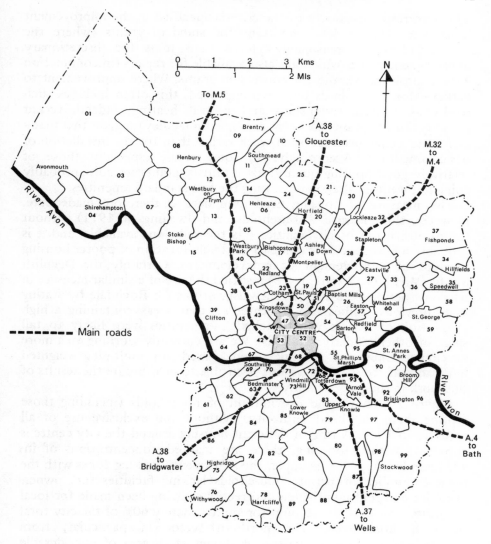

Figure 2.3   Bristol, the 96 zones.

obsolescence, structural defects, environmental characteristics, and the potential for improvement (as suggested by Duncan, 1971). However, detailed surveys along these lines carried out within Bristol have been on a small scale for specific purposes in restricted areas. The Census, the only source of detailed information, only considers the availability of basic amenities, and this study is limited to these data. The 1961 Census indicates the availability of hot and cold water taps, a fixed bath and a water closet; the 1971 Census reports on hot water, a fixed bath and an inside W.C. Neither Census gives details of amenity provision which correspond exactly to the criteria specified in the improvement legislation. This is less important for standard grants (where the correspondence is reasonably close) than it is for discretionary improvement grants which are also available for repairs (in conjunction with improvement), and for conversion grants. Where improvement to Parker—Morris standards has been approved, this often includes such works as kitchen extensions and central heating; indeed, recent investigations of grant work (for example, in Dudley) suggest that many grants are being given for such work rather than for the installation of basic amenities. Accordingly, in some areas, especially those of relatively good housing quality, discretionary grants are quite probably going to dwellings already possessing the five standard amenities.

The measure of housing need used here is therefore inadequate. However, this measure — households (and dwellings in 1971) without the exclusive use of all facilities — is the only one available, and it is probably a fairly accurate guide to the likely location of poorer housing in need of improvement or redevelopment. Certainly the Deeplish Study (M.H.L.G., 1966a, p. 18) justified the use of a similar measure in its construction of a list of renewal priorities for Rochdale by stating that 'previous studies had indicated . . . that areas containing a high proportion of houses which lacked . . . amenities were likely to fall short of other modern standards'. We are currently working on a more developed index of housing need, based on multiple, weighted indicators of stress but have not been able to incorporate the results of this work in the present study.

Figure 2.4 shows the distribution of households (including those renting from the local authority) without the exclusive use of all facilities in 1961. A ring of deficient housing around the city centre is apparent. Within the ring, there are marked concentrations of inadequate housing: for example, the first twenty ranking zones with the highest number of private households lacking facilities (i.e. owner-occupier and renting privately, corrections having been made for local authority households), account for approximately 60% of the city total of such households. The northern sector in particular, from Montpelier—St. Pauls to Easton, is shown as an area of considerable housing need.

Changes in the definition of basic amenities make a strict comparison between 1961 and 1971 impossible. However, allowing for this change of definition and the fact that the number of households lacking facilities (as defined in the Census) fell from 34% of all households in 1961 to 18% in 1971, the spatial distribution in 1971 is essentially similar to the 1961 pattern. The first twenty ranking zones in 1971 include sixteen of those occurring in 1961, and these twenty account for 62% of all private households lacking the exclusive use of all amenities. The 1971 Census also provides information on the number of dwellings lacking amenities: this pattern is similar to the 1971

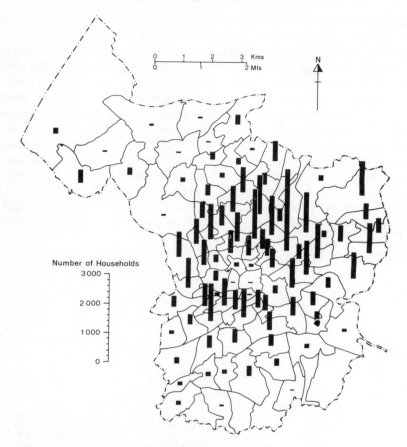

Figure 2.4   Households without the exclusive use of all amenities, 1961. Under 20 not mapped.

household deficiency distribution, with the major differences in areas of high multiple-occupancy. The twenty zones with the highest number of deficient dwellings include fifteen of those in the twenty given by the 1971 household definition (although the internal ranking is different), and account for 60% of total private dwellings lacking at least one amenity.

Household tenure
Before analysing the actual distribution of improvement grants, it is important to give some indication of the structure of household tenures in Bristol, because, as already noted, there is a strong relationship between tenure, housing characteristics, and grant take-up. Unfortunately, it was only in 1971 that the Census first published details of the

household amenities of different tenure groups; before then, recourse had to be made to the tenure pattern for all households.

In 1961, nearly 50% of Bristol's households were owner-occupiers, 30% rented from the Council, and the remaining households rented privately. Figure 2.5 shows the distribution of these households, by zones, using a triangle diagram to define combinations of owner-occupied, privately rented and local authority housing. With the same system of classification for 1971 some minor spatial changes can be noted. A number of peripheral zones, in the south of the city, changed classification from predominantly council-owned housing areas to owner-occupier or mixed council/owner-occupier areas as a result of new private house building on the urban fringe. To the east of the city centre (St. Pauls, Easton, etc.) changes of classification are related to the change from rental/owner-occupier to owner-occupier areas (zones

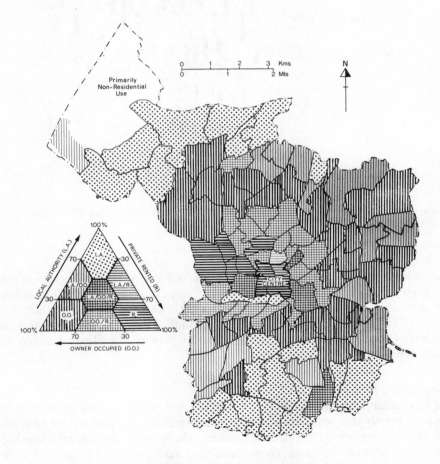

Figure 2.5   Household tenure, 1961.

31 and 51), or to the change from rental/owner-occupier to council or council/owner-occupier as a result of redevelopment or direct house purchase by the local authority (zones 26, 48, 54, 55, 95). Apart from these zones, the 1971 pattern remains substantially similar to that for 1961.

The 1971 Census indicates the tenure of households lacking the basic amenities. In Bristol, of 24 000 households (excluding Council tenants) that lacked the exclusive use of all facilities, 57% were renting privately (compare 43% owner-occupiers); put another way, 48% of all households renting private accommodation lacked one or more of the basic amenities, compared with only 14% of owner-occupiers. Figure 2.6 shows the distribution of the zones with the larger numbers and/or the greater concentrations of households lacking the exclusive use of all facilities: these zones account for 80% of all privately renting households and 70% of owner-occupiers so lacking. The predominant tenure pattern of these households is shown: a broad band of renting households to the west and north-west of the city centre gives way to a belt of owner-occupied and mixed owner-occupied/rented houses to the north and east, as well as to the south of the centre.

The distribution of improvement grants
Specially written computer programs aggregated the grant data for the common zones and printed out summary tables for each area and each year showing the number of grants by type, the amount of grant and expenditure, and average sizes and size distributions of grants and expenditures. It was decided to concentrate attention on aggregates for three time periods: up to 1958, 1959—68, and 1969 to mid-1973. This temporal division accords quite closely with the changes introduced by the 1959 and 1969 Housing Acts, and also enables comparison with the Census base years of 1961 and 1971. Aggregating data over such time periods leads to major problems of analysis, for changes in the levels of grants and expenditures reflect not only changes in legislation but also increases in the costs of labour and building materials for improvement work; the inflation of costs has been particularly acute since 1970. Accordingly, it was decided to deflate the values of grant and expenditure by an appropriate annual index of building costs. In the absence of a suitable local or regional cost index for the period being considered, a national index was used (1963 = 100; figures taken from D.O.E. *Housing Statistics* and *Housing and Construction Statistics*). All monetary totals presented here are therefore adjusted to the 1963 base year.

Any analysis of the distribution of grant aid needs to compare this distribution with that of need. The question may be asked: did grant aid go to the areas of housing need? This is a crucial question but very difficult to answer with the data currently available. The information to define areas of housing deficiency suitable for improvement is

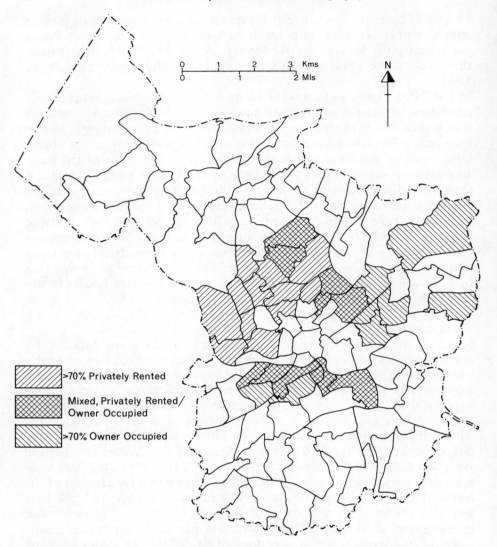

Figure 2.6   Tenure of private households without the exclusive use of all facilities, 1971. Includes zones with at least 400 such households, and also zones with 200–400 such households if they account for at least 35% of all households in the zone.

limited, and even if it can be shown that a large amount of aid went to such areas it cannot be said at this level of aggregation whether the individual houses with the greatest deficiencies or the households with the greatest need within the areas were the ones that received benefit. Indeed, in the case of discretionary grants it cannot even be said whether individual grants went to households lacking amenities (although this is not so for standard grants). However, despite these limitations, some general conclusions appropriate to the scale of data aggregation can be made.

To facilitate the comparison of distributions, a series of grant surplus/deficit maps was prepared. If grant totals and numbers of households lacking amenities within a zone are each expressed as a percentage of the respective totals for Bristol, then the difference between the two figures will represent the surplus or deficit within the zone. Such maps need to be interpreted with care, for the terms 'surplus' and 'deficit' refer only to a statistical relationship between areal 'need', defined for a particular point in time, and the subsequent flow of grants to that area. They do not take into account other possible changes in the population and housing stock that may modify the pattern of 'need' over time. For example, spontaneous, non-grant aided improvement may take place, although this is only likely to occur on any substantial scale in areas that have become relatively more favourable for investment by landlords or higher income groups. There is little evidence to suggest that such substantial improvement occurs in the poorest quality, lower-income housing areas of greatest need. Again, it is possible that a grant 'deficit' in an area reflects a greater concentration on redevelopment, or council purchase for rehabilitation, as a means of improving the housing stock and meeting household needs. However, little redevelopment took place in the city from the late 1960s onwards, and the areas of large-scale redevelopment at an earlier date have been indicated in the previous section. Extensive purchase of lower-quality housing by the council for rehabilitation appears to have developed on any scale only in the 1970s as a response to a failure to take up grants voluntarily in the poorest areas, and this factor does not substantially modify the conclusions stated here. Finally, a 'deficit' in a zone could also reflect an outward movement of households to other areas, or the clearance of houses for non-residential purposes such as roads. The population of central areas has certainly declined steadily and some households may have met their housing needs by moving to the inner suburbs, but clearance on any scale for roads has only been a factor in restricted areas of the city. When special factors appear to be important to the interpretation of 'surplus' and 'deficit' figures, these have been noted.

Completions, 1954 to mid-1973

Figure 2.7 shows the total number of grants of all types completed in each zone for the period 1954 to mid-1973. A band of grant-aided improvement around the city centre is defined, with a marked concentration of completions in the east and north-east sectors of the city but away from the central areas, and a smaller secondary area to the south-west, notably in Bedminster. Perhaps the most significant aspect of this map, when compared with Figure 2.4, is the very poor

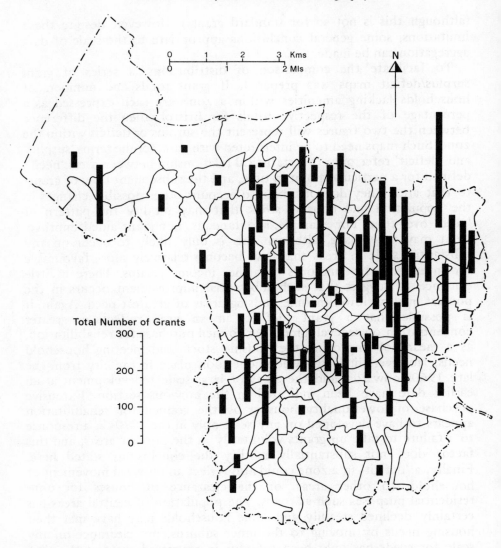

Figure 2.7   Total number of grants completed, 1954 to mid-1973. Under 10 not mapped.

showing of zones just to the north and east of the centre. Indeed, there is an inner ring of grant deficient areas when compared with the 1961 pattern of households lacking facilities, and eleven zones in this ring just to the north and east of the centre account for 30% of private households lacking amenities but for only 9% of grant numbers. Surrounding this ring is an outer area of surplus zones, concentrated especially to the east and south. This comparison, of course, takes no account of changes since 1961 in the pattern of households lacking facilities.

It must be remembered that Figure 2.7 is based on grant inquiries made between 1954 and mid-1973 and completed in that period. Since many inquiries in the early 1970s will have been completed after mid-1973, this map tends to underestimate that part of the pattern reflecting grants in the early 1970s. (For this reason, the analysis presented below of grants since 1969 will include both completions and approvals.)

Rather than discuss Figure 2.7 further, more detail can be gained by studying the different time periods separately. The years from 1954—58 are comparatively unimportant in terms of numbers and amount of grant, and tend to be characterised by a distribution pattern very similar to that for 1959—68. Accordingly, attention is turned first to the period between the 1959 and 1969 Housing Acts.

Completions, 1959—68
The 1959 Housing Act introduced the 'standard' grant, and over the period 1959—68 just under 60% of all grant completions were of this kind: however, the share of standard grants in total completions fell from 60—70% in the early 1960s to 40—50% by the late 1960s. Figure 2.8 shows the number of discretionary (1892 in total) and standard (2710) grants completed for which an initial inquiry was received between 1959 and 1968: concentrations to the north-east, east and south-west are clearly evident. Surplus/deficit zones are indicated in Figure 2.9.

The pattern shown in Figure 2.9 for all grants is, in general, true for both standard and discretionary grant distributions, although there are some interesting differences of detail. It is clear from Figure 2.8 that there is a much more widespread distribution of *standard grants* than there is of discretionary grants. Indeed, the surplus/deficit map of standard grants shows an almost uninterrupted outer ring of surplus zones surrounding a central deficit core which contained 55% of all private households lacking amenities in 1961 but attracted only 15% of all standard grants. (These households accounted for 60% of all households in the central area). In the absence of data on type of applicant, it is very difficult to give reasons for this pattern. Clearly, improvement using standard grants was being spread very widely over the city, and was least affecting those areas most in need (see Table 2.3). It is true that the measure of need used here — based on households — tends to overstate the deficit in some areas of multiple-occupancy, where single-person households share facilities in the same dwelling and where the standard grant is unlikely to be used; and also that some areas were zoned for redevelopment in the 1960s (see below). But these considerations only really affect the Clifton—Redland area and small zones immediately to the north-east of the city centre.

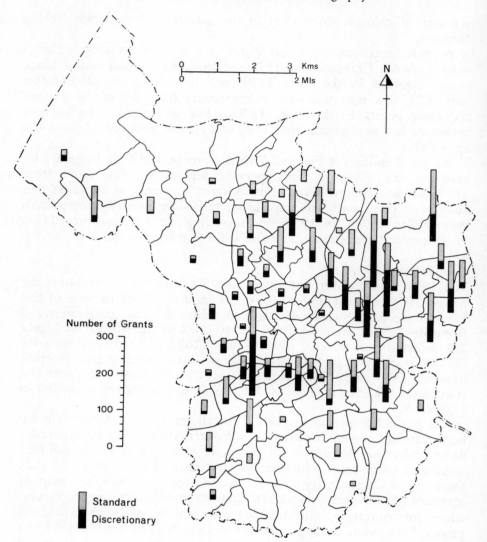

Figure 2.8   Total number of grants completed, 1959–68. Under 10 not mapped.

The zones of deficit extend well beyond these particular areas. The standard grant was introduced in 1959 to make it easier to raise household amenities to a certain minimum level without the need for further improvement. The clear implication of these findings is that such grants were utilised most in zones not in dire need, and – given the results of other research work – probably by owner-occupiers not on the lowest income level.

In discussing the distribution of *discretionary grants*, it needs to be

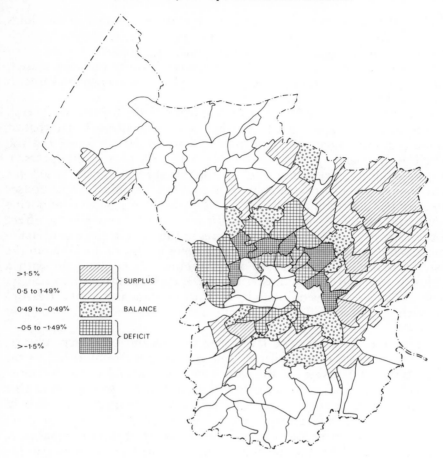

>1·5%

0·5 to 1·49%   SURPLUS

0·49 to −0·49%   BALANCE

−0·5 to −1·49%

>−1·5%   DEFICIT

Figure 2.9   Number of grant completions, 1959—68: surplus/deficit zones. Zones included are those with at least 1% of total households lacking one amenity or more and/or 1% of total grant completions. Where a zone has less than 1% on both counts, the difference between the two percentages must be 0.5 or greater for the zone to be included.

remembered that these are available either for the improvement of existing houses or for the provision of new dwellings by conversion. It thus seems reasonable to consider the two categories separately, especially as the distribution of conversion grants is likely to be related more to the demand for high-standard (12-point standard, see Table 2.1) flats, either for renting or for purchase, than to the measure of need used here. Accordingly, we will examine the pattern for all discretionary grants, and then with conversion grants excluded, and return in a later section to discuss conversions. In discussing the overall pattern, it has to be pointed out that grant numbers refer to the number of houses attracting grant, and not to the number of dwellings resulting from grant work. Accordingly, in areas where a high proportion of grants is used for conversions, the impact of grant work in terms of the number of new dwellings tends to be underestimated, since a grant for converting a house has resulted, on average, in three to four new dwellings.

With these provisos in mind, it is clear from Figure 2.8 that the overall pattern of discretionary grants is rather more concentrated than that of standard grants. Again, there is an inner core of deficit zones, but the deficit is not so large (see also Table 2.3), and nearly disappears in Clifton at least, primarily due to the number of grants used for conversions. Since conversion grants accounted for only 5.5% of houses affected by discretionary grants in 1959—68, the result of removing conversion grants is relatively insignificant overall. However, the effect in the Clifton—Redland area is to increase the deficit, since conversion grants were concentrated here. Surplus zones are highly localised in the east, in Eastville—Whitehall—Redfield (zones 27, 60, and 94 with a suplus of 8%) and in Bedminster (zone 63, a 6% surplus). Interestingly, these zones are in overall deficit in terms of standard grants. Reasons for such a pattern of surplus could not be adduced at this scale of analysis.

Figure 2.10 indicates the level of grant aid and total expenditure. The map suggests that the larger amounts of grant went either to the older terraced housing in the east and south-west, or to the more substantial Georgian and Victorian houses of Clifton. It is apparent that the expenditure pattern bears little relationship to that of number of grants: Clifton, for example, (zone 39) attracted under 1% of all grant completions, but over 5% of total grant aid. (Part of this discrepancy is, of course, due to the way in which grant numbers have been measured.)

Figure 2.11 shows expenditure surplus/deficit zones. Perhaps the most noticeable feature of this map is the surplus area of Clifton—Kingsdown. However, a high proportion of expenditure (70%) in this area was for conversions. Omitting grants used for conversions results in a surplus-deficit map rather similar to that for grant numbers. However, a disparity between grant expenditure and numbers still remains, and this reflects the relative proportions of standard and discretionary grants within zones and the average size of grants. Figure 2.12 shows the average size of grant per house for all grants combined; even when conversion grants are excluded, the average size of both discretionary and standard grants declines away from the area just to the west of the city centre, a decline reflecting to some degree the average size of house and the amount of grant-aided work per house.

Figure 2.11 also pinpoints the area of greatest deprivation in terms of grant aid — the band of housing immediately to the north-east of the city centre, stretching from Montpelier through St. Pauls and Easton to St. Phillips Marsh. This sector accounted for nearly 25% of the city's

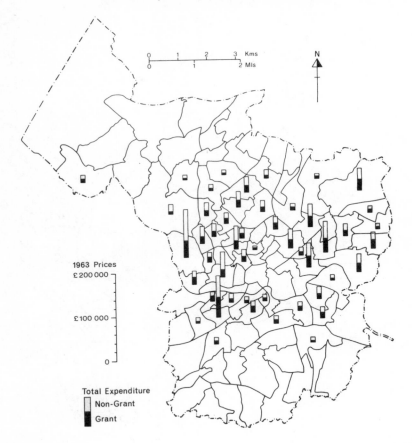

Figure 2.10   Grant and non-grant expenditure, 1959—68. Total expenditures under £10 000 are not mapped.

private households lacking facilities in 1961, and yet received only 6% of all standard grants, 10% of discretionary grants and 9% of grant aid.

Finally, the question may be asked: are grants going to zones with the greatest concentrations of housing deficiency? Table 2.3 shows the incidence of grants for zones with specified proportions of their households which lacked at least one amenity in 1961. It will be apparent that zones having in excess of 70% of their households lacking amenities attracted only 8—11% of grant expenditure in 1959—68 and yet accounted for about 26% of households so lacking. By contrast, zones in the 30—70% range appear to be roughly in balance with grant aid. Now, some of the worst housing areas in the city received very little in the way of grant aid proportionate to their general housing situation either because of population decline (zones 50 and 51) or

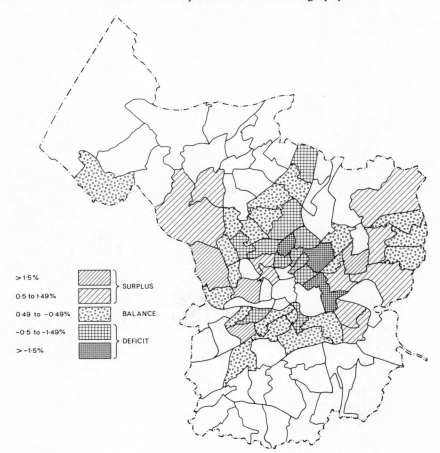

Figure 2.11   Grant expenditure, 1959–68: surplus/deficit zones. (N.B. See note to Figure 2.9.)

because of council action in clearing and redeveloping parts of these areas in the period 1961–1970: this applies especially to zones immediately adjacent to the city centre, in particular zones 46, 54, 95 and a part of 26. This implies, however, that there are several severely disadvantaged areas receiving benefit neither from council redevelopment nor from significant improvement (see zones listed in Table 2.3).

Three particular difficulties should be noted in the above empirical analysis. First, in both Figures 2.9 and 2.11, the surplus/deficit figures are based on all households lacking at least one amenity, including those renting from the local authority. Since this study excluded consideration of improvement to council houses, the inclusion of local authority households (necessary because of the format of the Census)

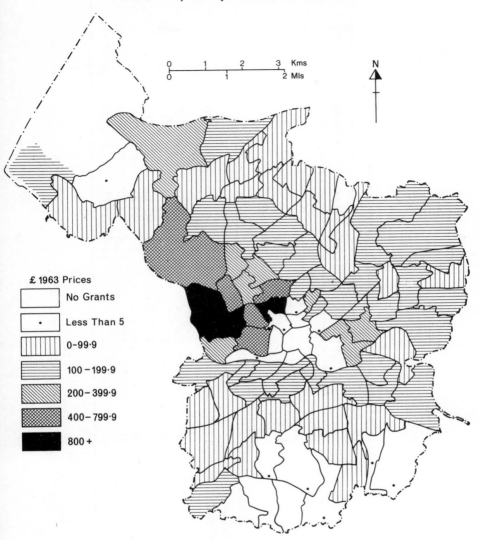

£ 1963 Prices

	No Grants
	Less Than 5
	0–99·9
	100–199·9
	200–399·9
	400–799·9
	800 +

Figure 2.12   Average value in £ for all grants, 1959–68.

has the effect of reducing the apparent grant deficit in deficit zones and increasing the surplus in surplus zones. However, this has little effect on the resulting overall pattern, and in the analysis of selected zones discussed in the text corrections could be made with the aid of enumeration district data.

Second, and more important, the specific results may depend on the shape and size of the statistical units employed, especially where there is a wide variation in zone size. This general point applies with equal

TABLE 2.3

The distribution of housing need and improvement grants by selected zones, 1959–68

	Private households lacking amenities (estimated)	% of total (figures in brackets exclude conversions)			
		Standard grants	Discretionary grants	Grants	Grant expenditure
Zones with given % of their private households lacking at least one amenity (min. of 300 households)					
+80% (50, 54, 95)	6	0.3	0.6 (0.6)	0.5 (0.5)	1.1 (1.5)
70–80% (19, 26, 31, 48, 51, 66, 72)	20	5.4	9.3 (9.8)	7.0 (7.1)	7.2 (9.2)
60–70% (45, 46, 57, 64, 70, 71, 94)	15	4.6	13.5 (13.6)	8.3 (8.3)	14.0 (11.5)
50–60% (23, 27, 41, 60, 63, 65, 73)	18	10.7	25.2 (25.8)	16.7 (16.7)	20.0 (22.3)
40–50% (18, 22, 38, 58, 69)	11	7.0	8.8 (8.2)	7.7 (7.5)	9.2 (8.0)
30–40% (16, 17, 39, 40, 59, 62, 93)	13	12.7	14.4 (14.0)	13.4 (13.2)	16.1 (13.6)

force to the study of any time period. In our case, we used the common zones to obtain comparability of the two census years. However, examination of the data for enumeration districts indicates that at this level of enquiry the common zones are reasonably homogeneous.

Third, the term 'household' can cover anything from, say, a single student or aged widow to a married couple with five small children. Any of these types may lack the exclusive use of all facilities, but clearly need differs widely. A measure of need based on households tends to overstate need for single-person households sharing facilities in a dwelling, and therefore to understate it for households in single dwellings lacking facilities. Thus, it can be said that for the period 1959–68 need has been somewhat overstated for the Clifton area, and understated elsewhere. Accordingly, analysis can be improved by utilising data on dwellings as well as households. The 1971 Census permits such an approach for the study of grants since the 1969 Housing Act.

Completions and approvals, 1969 to mid-1973
Figure 2.13 shows the total numbers of standard and discretionary grants (3466) for which an inquiry had been received between 1969 and mid-1973, and for which approval had been given (66% of the approvals had had work completed by 1973). Very few standard grants were approved (8.5% of all grants) as attention shifted towards discretionary grants. In terms of numbers, the overall distribution suggests a concentration in areas more to the north and west of the city centre than in the previous period. However, when the pattern is compared with private households lacking facilities in 1971 (and thus allowing for change since 1961), the overall surplus/deficit pattern remains similar to that for 1959–68. The major exception occurs in the Clifton Zone (39) where the number of grants used for conversions (one-third of grant numbers) changes this to a surplus zone. Another difference is that, unlike the earlier period, no zone has a surplus of grant numbers in excess of 1%. By contrast, several zones in the central core have deficits greater than 2%. There is, therefore, a wide scatter of grant effort at the expense of the central areas.

The comparison of grant numbers with *dwellings* lacking at least one amenity tends to highlight those zones with large numbers of single household houses. Zones with small surpluses (based on household numbers) on the eastern edge of the city have their surpluses reduced to near balance. By contrast, Clifton–Cotham–Redland, with a large amount of multiple-occupancy, is changed to an area of surplus, or to balance if grants used for conversions are excluded. However, both household and dwelling comparisons have two main deficit areas in common: the inner north-east sector, with 17% of private households lacking facilities and 20% dwellings, and only 10% of grant numbers; and a smaller deficit area just south of the city centre.

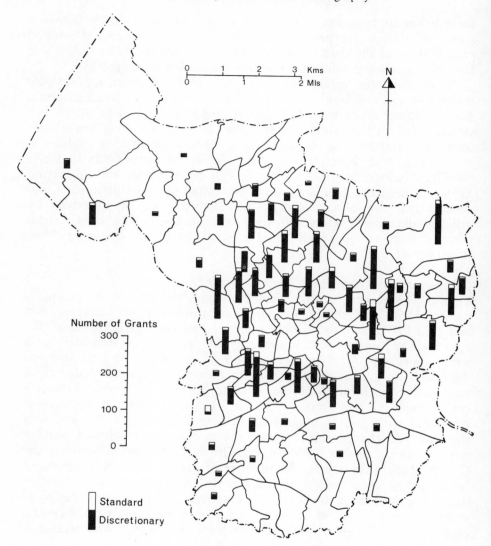

Figure 2.13   Total number of grant completions and approvals, 1969 to mid-1973. Under 10 grants not mapped.

Turning to grant *expenditure*, Figure 2.14 depicts grant and total expenditure for each zone: the concentration of grant aid in the north-west sector is immediately apparent. Figure 2.15 shows the surplus—deficit pattern when total grant aid is compared with house-holds lacking facilities in 1971. The dominance of Clifton—Kingsdown is clear, with the two zones 39 and 45 showing a combined surplus of nearly 10%. However, such a pattern is almost entirely due to

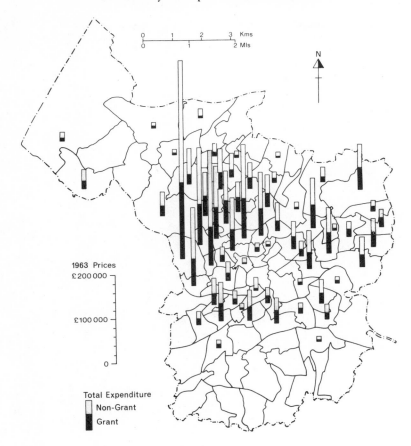

Figure 2.14   Grant and non-grant expenditure, for completions and approvals, 1969 to mid-1973. Total expenditures under £10 000 not mapped.

conversion grants (80% of the grant expenditure in these two zones), and the omission of such grant aid results in the eradication of the surplus in the inner north-west sector (with the exception of zone 39), the consequent broadening of the central deficit core, and the re-appearance of surplus zones to the east and south. As in the previous period, the average size of grant (excluding conversions) declines away from the Clifton area.

The comparison of grant aid and *dwellings* shows an intensification of the surplus in the zones to the north-west, from Clifton and Redland to Westbury Park (which have a combined surplus of 30% total grant expenditure), whereas the remainder of Bristol becomes a deficit area. The exclusion of conversions reduces the surplus in the north-west without eliminating it, and many of the remaining zones go into

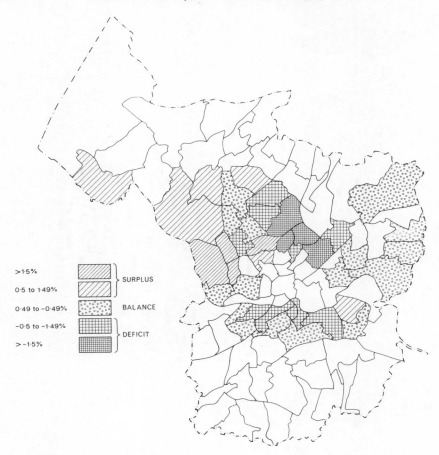

>1·5%   ▨

0·5 to 1·49%   ▨   SURPLUS

0·49 to −0·49%   ⁙   BALANCE

−0·5 to −1·49%   ▦

> −1·5%   ▦   DEFICIT

Figure 2.15   Grant expenditure (completions and approvals) 1969 to mid-1973: surplus/deficit zones. (N.B. See note to Figure 2.9.)

balance. As with grant numbers, both dwelling and household comparisons with grant expenditure indicate two main deficit areas: St. Pauls—Easton, with a deficit of 10% of grant aid, and Southville—Windmill Hill in the south.

Finally, as for the period 1959—68, it is possible to see how far grant aid went to zones with the highest concentrations of households or dwellings lacking at least one facility. It is clear from Table 2.4 that the worst household zones were receiving few grants relative to their need after 1969, as indeed they were before 1969, and this picture is intensified with the removal of conversion grants. The table also indicates the small amounts of grant aid going to zones with high concentrations of substandard dwellings: with the exception of zone

TABLE 2.4

The distribution of housing need and improvement grants by selected zones, 1969 to mid-1973

	% of total (figures in brackets exclude conversions)				
	Private households (dwellings) lacking amenities	Grant numbers		Grant expenditure	
Zones with given % of their private households lacking at least one amenity (min. of 300 households)					
+50% (19, 26, 31, 64, 72)	17.5	9.2	(8.5)	11.2	(9.7)
40–50% (23, 45, 46, 70, 94)	11.8	8.7	(7.5)	15.3	(8.9)
30–40% (18, 22, 27, 38, 40, 41, 60, 63, 69, 73)	30.0	25.8	(25.6)	26.6	(27.4)
Zones with given % of their private dwellings lacking at least one amenity (min. of 300 dwellings)					
+40% (26, 31, 72)	12.8	4.8	(5.1)	4.1	(5.6)
30–40% (19, 27, 60, 63, 70, 94)	22.4	17.1	(18.0)	14.4	(18.6)
20–30% (58, 69, 73)	7.2	7.2	(7.8)	4.8	(7.8)

Note: In 1971, 24 175 private households and 14 934 dwellings lacked at least one amenity.

19, the tenure of these dwellings is predominantly owner-occupied or mixed owner-occupied/rental (see Figure 2.6).

In discussing these disparities, a further component of Bristol's housing policies has to be taken into consideration: the increasing intervention by the Housing Department to purchase and improve properties itself, under the favourable terms of the 1969 Housing Act. This has occurred notably in the areas of poor housing conditions. For example, the area covered by the St. Pauls Plan (zones 19, 31, 51 and 50) includes the main multi-racial area of the city and some of the worst housing, and accounted for 10% of the city's deficient dwellings in 1971. Over the period 1969–73, 113 dwellings were acquired by the local authority, compared with the 157 grants approved for private owners (5% of total grant aid). By contrast, there were under ten such acquisitions in the Clifton–Redland–Cotham area. The inference can be drawn that, in the areas of the poorest housing not yet considered ripe for redevelopment, the failure of private owners to make substantial grant-aided improvements has necessitated Council intervention.

Conversion grants

We have already seen that Bristol, in relation to other British cities, ranks highly in terms of the use made of conversion grants per thousand households, coming first for approvals in 1971—72. Overall figures for grants paid in Bristol in the period 1967—70 indicate that 25% of all discretionary grants (measured in terms of *dwellings* resulting from grant-aided work) going to non-local authority applicants were for conversions (cf. just over 10% nationally), and that for approvals since 1970 the comparable figures are 30% for Bristol and 20% nationally (see D.O.E., *Local Housing Statistics*). Indeed, over the period 1959—68, conversions accounted for just over 20% of total grant expenditure and nearly 400 new dwelling units, rising to 40% of expenditure after 1969 and over 1000 dwellings either completed or approved by mid-1973.

Much of this conversion effort is concentrated spatially in the Clifton—Redland—Cotham area. Nine zones in this sector accounted for 66% of all conversion activity in Bristol since 1959; and within these zones, conversion has amounted to nearly 75% of all grant expenditure. Over time, the area subject to conversion has tended to spread towards the east, so that, for example, in St. Pauls (zone 19), one of the zones with the worst housing conditions in Bristol, 66% of grant expenditure has gone for conversions since 1969.

General improvement areas

The existing G.I.A.'s have not proved as successful as was first hoped in revitalising inner city areas. However, it is unlikely that the areas originally designated could have had much impact on the overall quality of housing in the inner city. The three declared and two potential G.I.A.'s between them only account for 839 houses. Duncan's survey of thirty-one county boroughs which had declared G.I.A.'s by 1971 revealed a total of 118 declared G.I.A.'s with a median size range of 200—299 houses (Duncan, 1973). The three Bristol G.I.A.'s declared by 1971 are all below this size range and two of them fall within Duncan's lowest size range of 0—99 houses. Only the potential St. Agnes G.I.A. is above the median range.

Moreover, within the G.I.A.'s the level of grant take-up has been uneven. A Housing Department survey carried out in late 1972 reported good progress in Barton Hill (zone 95: 17 grant-aided improvements completed and 39 houses acquired by the council), the Nursery (zone 63: 9 improvements completed and 28 houses acquired) and Armoury Square (zone 48: 3 improvements completed and 21 houses acquired). However, even taking into account grant aided work approved but not yet completed in these areas, the major factor in upgrading their housing quality appears to be council acquisition and council improvement rather than private improvement. Disappointing progress was reported in the two potential improvement areas. In Easton (zone 48), 18 improvements had been completed and 65 properties acquired out of a total of 273, and the report concluded: 'Properties continue to be acquired and improved but there is little or no interest in improvement by private owners'. In St. Agnes (zone 51), 14 grants had been completed and 36 properties acquired out of a total of 369 and the report concluded that despite the enthusiasm shown initially in public meetings 'in 216 cases out of 369 there was little or no prospect of house improvement'. It should be added that in both of the potential G.I.A.'s the council has followed the policy of not undertaking significant environmental improvements until a major response from the residents in the way of grant applications has been forthcoming (see Fleming, 1970, for a summary of the procedure). This is contrary to the policy of some other councils in using environmental improvement as an incentive to voluntary take-up.

Conclusions and implications

What conclusions can be drawn from these findings, and what are their implications? A number of themes can be isolated for further consideration and lines of research indicated.

1. The concept of housing need is complex and many-sided, and the type of need which is supposed to be solved by the use of grant-aided improvement is seldom spelt out with any precision as a policy objective. If the objective is to improve the physical quality of as much housing as possible in the city, then criteria of physical deficiency are needed. If, as is increasingly the case, there are broader social objectives as well as physical ones to be achieved, then more complex criteria of social and environmental deficiencies are needed. Whatever the policy objectives, the data on need available for Bristol refer largely to physical deficiencies and are inadequate even on this account. Nonetheless, despite these limitations, it is clear that there is a mismatch between need and level of grant aid. This mismatch appears to be acute in some of the worst housing areas — notably in the inner north-east sector — and cannot be explained by a greater reliance on redevelopment or council acquisition in those areas. (Indeed, our measure of need almost certainly underestimates the relative size of the housing problem in the north-east sector). By contrast, there are wide areas of Bristol away from the inner city which have attracted grants in excess of their relative share of need, and this has resulted in a diffuseness of effort at the expense of the central deficit core.

Accordingly, despite the impact of improvement grants in reducing the *overall* level of housing deficiency, the worst areas still remained very badly off in 1971: for example, zone 19 still had 60% of its households without exclusive use of the basic amenities, and in zone 31 the proportion was 50%. Indeed, in zone 19, 15% of households were living in shared dwellings which lacked at least one of these amenities. These zones, and others, are ones in which household tenure and income levels militate against the success of voluntary improvement.

Further analysis of the relationship between household need and grant take-up requires research at the level of the individual household. More detailed information is required on housing conditions and the determinants of the propensity to improve by households with different social and economic characteristics, and such information demands individual house condition surveys and household question-naires.

2. The use of conversion grants has been a significant feature of housing improvement in certain areas of Bristol. This use of such grants raises questions of the impact of improvement on the private rental sub-market and, through repercussions on other sub-markets, on the housing market as a whole. To trace the impact and repercussions necessitates further information on the type of house, the type of landlord and the type of tenant involved in housing conversion and the use to which the house is put after conversion. For example, to what extent are low-cost rental flats and bedsitters replaced by high-cost rental units, involving the displacement of the existing households? Are improvement grants an important incentive to convert property to higher-rental use in areas such as Clifton, or are market conditions such as to make them irrelevant? If low income or single person households are displaced, what pressure is exerted on other housing sub-markets as a result of the reduction in the stock of lower cost housing? Answers to these questions are important in considering the impact of improve-ment policies on the distribution of real income between different housing groups.

3. Finally, the relative failure to carry through G.I.A. policies on any scale in the city has important implications. In the light of the apparent loss of initial enthusiasm by residents in the proposed G.I.A.'s there is a need for more information on the interaction between council, planning department and residents in the area improvement process. This is important for the future, for the 1974 Act, with its Housing Action Areas (defined on the basis of social and economic factors), provides the basis for a more flexible approach to inner city housing problems. This in turn will demand a clearer statement of housing goals and objectives for different areas of the city and a clearer statement of priorities within an overall housing plan. To meet these goals and priorities a deeper understanding is needed of residents' responses to national and local government policy so that needs and resources can be matched for different groups defined on the basis of area, income, tenure or stage in life cycle.

NOTES AND REFERENCES

[1] For more extensive reviews of post-war legislation, see Cullingworth (1966), Pepper (1971), Spencer (1970), Spencer and Cherry (1970).

[2] We wish to acknowledge the financial assistance of the S.S.R.C. in carrying out this research, and the help provided by several research assistants.

Bassett, K. A. and D. P. Hauser (1974). *Spatial Impact of Public Policy in the City: improvement grants in Bristol*, Report to the Social Science Research Council.

Boaden, N. (1971). *Urban Policy Making*, C.U.P.

Bristol, City and County of, (1966). *Development Plan Review, 1966: Report of survey and written analysis*.

Bristol, City and County of, (1969). *Report on the Work of the Housing Department*.

Brown, T., M. Vile and M. Whitemore (1972). 'Community studies and decision taking', *Brit. J. Pol. Sci.*, 2, 133–153.

Clark, C. and G. T. Jones (1971). *The Demand for Housing*, University Working Paper 11, Centre for Environmental Studies.

Cullingworth, J. B. (1963). *Housing in Transition: a case study in the city of Lancaster, 1958–1962*, Heinemann.

Cullingworth, J. B. (1966). *Housing and Local Government in England and Wales*, Routledge and Kegan Paul.

Davies, B. (1968). *Social Needs and Resources in Local Services*, Michael Joseph.

Davies, J. G. (1972). *The Evangelistic Bureaucrat*, Tavistock Publications.

Davis, O. A. and A. B. Whinston (1961). 'The economics of urban renewal', *Law & Contemporary Problems*, 26, 105–117.

Dearlove, J. (1973). *The Politics of Policy in Local Government: the making and maintenance of public policy in the Royal Borough of Kensington and Chelsea*, C.U.P.

Department of Environment (1971). *New Life in Old Towns*, Report by Robert Matthew, Johnson-Marshall and Partners on two pilot studies on urban renewal in Nelson and Rawtenstall Municipal Boroughs, H.M.S.O.

Dennis, N. (1970). *People and Planning: the sociology of housing in Sunderland*, Faber.

Duncan, T. L. C. (1971). *Measuring Housing Quality: a study of methods*, Occasional Paper No. 20, Centre for Urban and Regional Studies, University of Birmingham.

Duncan, T. L. C. (1973). *Housing Improvement Policies in England and Wales*, Research Memoradum No. 28, Centre for Urban and Regional Studies, University of Birmingham.

Expenditure Committee (1973). *Tenth Report from the Expenditure Committee, together with the minutes of the evidence taken before the Environment and Home Office Sub-Committee in session 1972–73, appendices and index. Session 1972–73. House improvement grants*, 3 vols. H.C.349, I, II, and III, H.M.S.O.

Fleming, J. (1970). *The Central Areas of our Towns and Cities — recondition or renew?*, paper delivered to the Annual Conference of the National Housing and Town Planning Council, Brighton, October 1970.

Hamnett, C. (1973). 'Improvement grants as an indicator of gentrification in Inner London', *Area*, 5, 252–261.

Harvey, D. (1971). 'Social processes, spatial form and the redistribution of real income in an urban system', in Chisholm, M., *et al* (eds.), *Regional Forecasting*, Butterworth, 270—300.

Hill, M. (1972). *The Sociology of Public Administration*, Weidenfeld and Nicolson.

Jennings, H. (1962). *Societies in the Making: a study of development and redevelopment within a County Borough*, Routledge and Kegan Paul.

Jevons, R. and J. Madge (1946). *Housing Estates*, Arrowsmith, Bristol.

Kirwan, R. M. and D. B. Martin (1972). *The Economics of Urban Residential Renewal and Improvement*, Working Paper 77, Centre for Environmental Studies.

Miller, D. C. (1958a). 'Industry and community power structure: a comparative study of an American and an English city', *American Sociological Review*, 23, 9—15.

Miller, D. C. (1958b). 'Decision making cliques in community power structure: a comparative study of an American and an English city', *American Journal of Sociology*, 64, 299—310.

M.H.L.G. (1966a). *The Deeplish Study — improvement possibilities in a district of Rochdale*, H.M.S.O.

M.H.L.G. (1966b). *Our Older Homes: a call for action*, Report of the Sub-Committee on Standards of Housing Fitness (Chairman: Mrs. E. Dennington), H.M.S.O.

M.H.L.G. (1968). *Old Houses into New Homes*, Cmnd. 3602, H.M.S.O.

Muchnick, D. (1970). *Urban Renewal in Liverpool*, Occasional Papers in Social Administration, No. 33, Social Administration Research Trust.

Newton, K. (1969). 'City politics in Britain and the United States', *Political Studies*, 17, 208—218.

Pepper, S. (1971). *Housing Improvement: goals and strategy*, Architectural Association Paper No. 8, Architectural Association.

Rex, J. and R. Moore (1967). *Race, Community, and Conflict: a study of Sparkbrook*, O.U.P.

Richmond, A. H. (1973). *Migration and Race Relations in an English City: a study in Bristol*, O.U.P.

Rothenberg, J. (1967). *Economic Evaluation of Urban Renewal*, Brookings Institution.

Sharpe, L. J. (ed.) (1967). *Voting in Cities*, Macmillan.

Sigsworth, E. M. and R. K. Wilkinson (1971). 'The finance of improvements: a study of low quality housing in three Yorkshire towns', *Bull. Economic Research*, 23, 113—128.

Spencer, J. (1964). *Stress and Release in an Urban Community*, Tavistock Publications.

Spencer, K. (1970). 'Older urban areas and housing improvement policies', *Town Planning Review*, 41, 250—262.

Spencer, K. M. and G. E. Cherry (1970). *Residential Rehabilitation: a review of research*, Research Memorandum No. 5, Centre for Urban and Regional Studies, University of Birmingham.

Stone, P. A. (1970). *Urban Development in Britain: standards, costs and resources, 1964—2004*, Vol. I, C.U.P.

Watson, C. J. *et al* (1973). *Estimating Local Housing Needs: a case study and discussion of methods*, Occasional Paper No. 24, Centre for Urban and Regional Studies, University of Birmingham.

Young, M. and P. Willmott (1957). *Family and Kinship in East London*, Penguin.

PART II

Hydrology and Geomorphology

Chapter 3

Hydrograph Modelling Strategies

Michael Kirkby

A drainage basin is a complex combination of spatially distributed elements, many of which may be significant in their influence on the shapes of stream hydrographs from the basin. Its elements show great heterogeneity within small areas, but also reflect an erosional and hydrological history which has produced a functional whole, apparently organised towards efficient drainage of the basin. Precipitation falling on a drainage basin is transformed by these basin elements to an outflow hydrograph, by processes which are, at least in principle, deterministic.

The prediction of river flow is important in the science of hydrology, and has practical applications which are related to:

1. the immediate prediction of floods following rainfall;
2. the design of flood control works, bridges and spillways;
3. seasonal and annual water yield for water supply, reservoir design, etc.

In the first and third of these cases, it is usual to have some pre-existing records of both rainfall and runoff, so that a flow model can be 'fitted' to the record. In the second case it is common, particularly for small to moderate-sized catchments, to have no flow records, although applicable rainfall records may be available. It is therefore an advantage if the flow model takes some account of basin characteristics. Some physical basis for a model is also appropriate where changes are taking place in a drainage basin, for instance through urbanisation or afforestation, and it is desirable to predict changes in the runoff patterns that may result. A physical basis also facilitates cross-calibration between drainage basins, which greatly enhances the value of existing data.

Although a direct approach to flow frequency has been made by generating a stochastic sequence of river flows directly (Yevjevich, 1964; Matalas, 1966; Chow and Kareliotis, 1970), there is little possibility of fitting the stochastic generating function to basin characteristics, particularly as it contains elements of both rainfall and basin behaviour. Rainfall records contain strong serial correlations over both short and long periods (Hurst, 1951; Mandelbrot and Wallis, 1968). In the absence of serial correlation, the basin output would tend to be more normally distributed than the rainfall input, because the basin stores and accumulates the inputs. Serial correlation weakens this effect, so that outflows are almost as strongly skewed as inflows. The basin storage also introduces additional short-term serial correlations. Although there is also the possibility of considering the drainage basin's role as an operator on the correlogram or spectrum of rainfall events, our knowledge of hydrology does not yet allow an association of such an operator with basin characteristics. The difficulties of these stochastic models demonstrate that it is realistic to route rainfall through a set of stores which can be at least conceptually identified with zones of water storage in the catchment.

Attempts at producing a catchment model with a physical basis are faced with a dilemma. The drainage basin itself has a perplexing variety, which can only be represented by a very large number of parameters. Each parameter could in principle be measured, although the resulting work programme might be more time-consuming than installation and maintenance of a stream gauge for a year. On the other hand, exceedingly simple models with only two or three parameters can provide a very good empirical fit to the response of a particular catchment. Figure 3.1 shows that the goodness of fit of a particular model does not always reflect the number of parameters it contains, and that more recent models are not necessarily improvements on older ones. Such comparisons are only a little less than fair, depending as they do on the particular data period used, but authors seldom publish their least favourable examples! In some cases additional parameters are included in a model to give it greater generality, even though, for a particular catchment, they are more or less inoperative. The great differences in numbers of parameters do not, however, mainly reflect differences of this kind. It is inferred that a workable model should have no more than 5−10 parameters in the present state of the art.

With few exceptions, catchment models may be considered as a sequence of stores. Each store receives water from other stores and possibly from rainfall, and delivers water to other stores or to the basin outflow. The stores may be conceptual only, or may be identifiable with physical water bodies in the basin. They may respond linearly or not. There may be anything from one to an infinite number of stores. An alternative simple catchment model is based on the unit hydrograph (Sherman, 1932), but Dooge (1959) has shown that any unit hydrograph is equivalent to a sequence of linear stores in series and/or

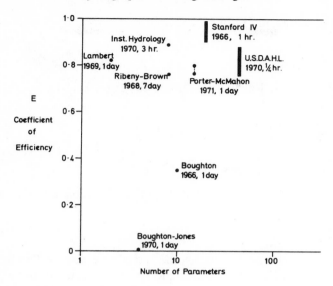

Figure 3.1 Progress in hydrological modelling. (Data from Aitken (1973) and Lambert (1969).)

$$E = 1 - \frac{\text{Residual SS}}{\text{Total observed SS}}$$

parallel, and *vice-versa.* There is convincing evidence that catchments do not respond linearly in detail (Amorocho, 1963; Hewlett and Hibbert, 1967; Weyman, 1974). Nevertheless, the near success of the linear model makes it a valid starting point for discussing the choice of appropriate catchment parameters.

Simple linear models
A linear store is defined as one for which the outflow, q, is proportional to the quantity of water stored, S (Dooge, 1959, p. 243).

$$S = kq. \tag{1}$$

If S and q have the dimensions of mm and mm/hr (spread over the catchment) respectively, then the constant k has the dimension of hours. The response of the store is determined by equation (1), when it is inserted into the mass balance (storage) equation for the store:

$$i - q = \frac{dS}{dt}, \tag{2}$$

where i is the rate of inflow in mm/hr
and t is time elapsed.

Substituting equation (1) in (2):

$$i = q + k \frac{dq}{dt}. \tag{3}$$

This is a first order linear differential equation for the outflow, with a general solution:

$$q = \frac{1}{k} e^{-t/k} \left\{ \int_0^t i(\tau) e^{\tau/k} \ d\tau + S_0 \right\}, \tag{4}$$

where S_0 is the storage at $t = 0$.

For a unit impulse of rainfall (1 mm applied instantaneously) at $t = 0$:

$$q = \frac{1}{k} e^{-t/k}, \tag{5}$$

an exponential decline following the initial jump at $t = 0$. The response of a linear system (in this case a single store) to a unit impulse at $t = 0$ is called its instantaneous unit hydrograph (IUH), and is written as:

$$u(t) = \frac{1}{k} e^{-t/k}. \tag{6}$$

Using this notation, equation (4) may be written in the form:

$$q = \int_0^t \frac{1}{k} e^{-(t-\tau)/k} \ i(\tau) \ d\tau + S_0 \frac{1}{k} e^{-t/k}, \tag{7}$$

or:

$$q = \int_0^t u(t - \tau) \ i(\tau) \ d\tau + S_0 u(t). \tag{8}$$

Equation (8) may be shown to be a general relationship for any IUH function $u(t)$, and is a convolution of the IUH with the rainfall sequence, $i(t)$ (Dooge, 1959, p. 243).

When two unequal linear stores are combined in series, the output q_1 from store S_1 becomes the input to the second store, S_2. If the stores have time constants k_1, k_2 respectively, then their mass balance equations are:

$$i = q_1 + k_1 \frac{dq_1}{dt} \tag{9}$$

and:

$$q_1 = q_2 + k_2 \frac{dq_2}{dt}. \tag{10}$$

For a unit impulse at t = 0; as before:

$$q_1 = \frac{1}{k_1} e^{-t/k_1}. \tag{11}$$

Substituting in equation (10), and solving as in (4) above for the second store:

$$q_2 = \frac{1}{k_2} e^{-t/k_2} \int_0^t \frac{1}{k_1} e^{-\tau/k_1} e^{+\tau/k_2} \, d\tau, \tag{12}$$

which gives:

$$u(t) = q_2 = \frac{1}{k_1 - k_2} (e^{-t/k_1} - e^{-t/k_2}), \tag{13}$$

which is the IUH for the two stores combined. It may be noted that this is symmetrical in k_1 and k_2, so that the order of routing through the two stores makes no difference to the combined response. This IUH has a peak at:

$$t_{pk} = \frac{k_1 k_2}{k_1 - k_2} \log_e(k_1/k_2), \tag{14}$$

and the peak discharge at this point is:

$$q_{pk} = k_1{}^{k_2/(k_1 - k_2)} / k_2{}^{k_1/(k_1 - k_2)}. \tag{15}$$

If equation (13) is standardised, so that the peak discharge occurs at t = 1, then the IUH becomes:

$$u(t) = \frac{\lambda \log \lambda}{(\lambda - 1)^2} \{ \lambda^{-t/(\lambda-1)} - \lambda^{-\lambda t/(\lambda-1)} \} \tag{16}$$

where $\lambda = k_1/k_2$.

This family of curves, which is illustrated in Figure 3.2a, allows a unit hydrograph to be fitted to a unimodal real form in respect of both time to peak and overall recession rate. Since real unit hydrographs commonly are unimodal, a good fit can commonly be obtained by the use of two linear stores, provided that the assumption of linearity is a reasonable one. However, the highest peak and most rapid recession rate occur at $\lambda = 1$, when the limiting value of the IUH is:

$$u(t) = t e^{-t}. \tag{17}$$

At this point the rate of recession is such that the discharge approximately halves in a time equal to the time to peak. If the recession rate is more rapid than this, the model of two unequal linear stores becomes unsuitable.

An alternative simple linear model with two parameters is one with n

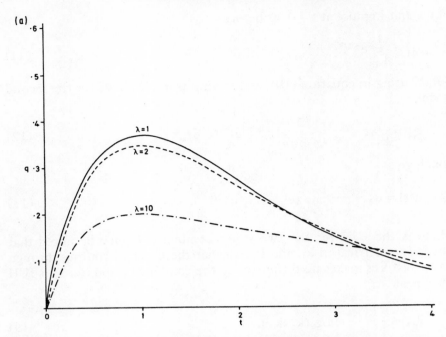

Figure 3.2a   Standardised hydrographs for two linear stores in series, for which $k_1/k_2 = \lambda$.

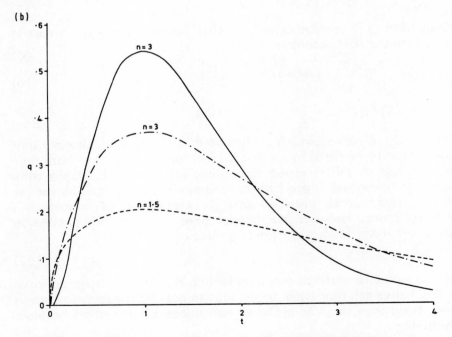

Figure 3.2b   Standardised hydrographs for n equal stores in series.

equal linear stores, each with time constant k. Applying the methods of equations (9) to (13) repeatedly, the following expression for the IUH is obtained, standardised to peak at t = 1:

$$u(t) = \frac{\{(n-1)t\}^{n-1}}{(n-2)!} \, e^{-(n-1)t}, \tag{18}$$

which is a Gamma distribution of order n. This family of curves is shown in Figure 3.2b, and it may be seen that for any whole number of stores ($\geqslant 2$) a series of sharply peaked and sharply receding hydrographs is obtained, complementing the spectrum of forms in Figure 3.2a. In the extreme case of an infinite number of equal stores, their combined effect is a simple delay with no attenuation of the input impulse. If fractional numbers of stores in the range $1 \leqslant n \leqslant 2$ are allowed, then a further series of curves can be obtained which closely match curves in Figure 3.2a. For example, the response of 1½ equal stores in Figure 3.2b is very similar to the response of 2 stores with time constants in the ratio of 10:1 in Figure 3.2a.

Identification of stores

It is argued that, insofar as a linear model is justifiable as an approximation, simple two-parameter models representing linear stores are commonly sufficient. The problems of non-linearity are considered below, but before abandoning linear models it seems crucial to attempt to identify the stores with physical water bodies. Figure 3.3 shows a schematic arrangement of stores in a catchment. Each soil layer is commonly considered as a store, with infiltration to the layer below, and downslope routing through a series of similar stores to the channel store. In a spatially distributed model, the stores are repeated for each spatial element of the basin, but most working hydrograph models lump the catchment at least as much as in Figure 3.3a. The Stanford/ Hydrocomp models for example typically combine each layer in a single non-linear store representing both the vertical and lateral slope flow components. In combining a large number of stores in this way, it is worth noting the effect obtained by combining several linear stores of different time constants, in a series chain. It is apparent that the stores with the longest time constants (k in equation (1)) have the greatest effect, so that the simplest two-store approximation will mainly reflect the properties of the two most slowly responding stores in the chain. To anticipate a little, it may be noted that if the stores are non-linear, and if k is understood to mean the average duration of water in the store, then the above result still holds, as has been shown by Wooding (1965). Furthermore, the most slowly responding store must be most accurately modelled in terms of its non-linearity, because the outflow discharge is less sensitive to the *form* of the second store,

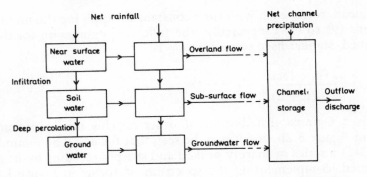

Figure 3.3a   Schematic arrangement of stores in a catchment.

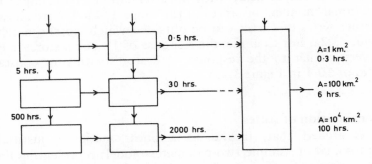

Figure 3.3b   Order of magnitude of stores' drainage times in hours for each direction (stores as in (a) above).

provided that an appropriate value of k is used for it. A linear approximation may, for example, be sufficient.

In Figure 3.3, a chain of stores in series can be followed through each layer. Although the time-constants for the various stores depend on soil and drainage basin characteristics, relative orders of magnitude may be estimated (Figure 3.3b). The value shown for each sequence of stores in the downslope direction is intended to indicate the total delay from the sequence. Estimates represent a large number of published infiltration curves, overland flow hydrographs and stream velocity values.

For the overland flow route, the duration of flow is likely to be critical only in catchments of 1 km² or less. In larger catchments, the overland flow may be treated as effectively instantaneous without appreciable loss of accuracy. It is, however, crucial to estimate accurately the *quantity* of overland flow, and the time at which it is *produced*. This involves modelling the infiltration capacity of the soil, and making use of the concept of partial contributing area, where this appears applicable. These topics are discussed below.

For sub-surface flow, both the infiltration process and the downslope flow are likely to be important, but the slower response of the downslope flow requires that its non-linearities are accurately modelled. Infiltration, on the other hand, needs to be modelled accurately in its *overall* timing, but the linearity or otherwise of the infiltration store is of less importance. This emphasis suggests that a full mathematical treatment of the infiltration phase is probably not justified in terms of increased accuracy in predicting basin discharge. The effect of the channel network probably becomes important for catchments of 20 km² or more, when the time-constants of the network compare with those of the infiltration phase, but for catchments of less than 1000 km², a *linear* network model may be sufficient. Similar arguments apply to lower soil levels and to groundwater. In the last case, the deep percolation process and groundwater lateral flow must be modelled, but infiltration and channel effects may be almost completely ignored. In comparing the three (or more) layers in the soil, it is also important to consider the relative peak and total rates of outflow from each layer into the channel system. It is clear that the proportions will vary widely. At one extreme, arid areas tend to show a high concentration of flow in the overland phase. At the other extreme many limestone areas show a preponderance of groundwater flow. A general model must allow for all three to be important, and be capable of distributing the flow between the layers. The groundwater component is clearly critical because of its long response time, but, because this is much longer than the typical flood event, and because experience has shown that groundwater has a response which is close to linear, an adequate approximation can commonly be made on the basis of:

1. a constant leakage rate from the soil water store, whenever there is any water in it;
2. a constant delay before reaching the groundwater store;
3. a linear groundwater store.

The soil water store and downslope flow within the soil must clearly be modelled with some care, and the physical description of this process needs perhaps to be the most comprehensive. The infiltration process and the associated near-surface store is also important, in three ways:

1. failure to enter this store is a failure to infiltrate, producing overland flow. It has been seen above that the timing and areal production of overland flow is very important;
2. water in the near-surface store can be roughly identified with water which is freely available for evaporation. A conversion of potential evapo-transpiration rates into actual rates is therefore associated with this store;
3. infiltration provides the inflow to soil water stores, and thus has a secondary effect on the hydrograph of soil water stores, particularly through its average timing.

Channel effects appear to become increasingly important in catchments of more than 10 km². In very large catchments, the effect of channel storage within the trunk stream becomes very important in attenuating flood peaks, but in drainage basins of less than 1000 km², the most important influence is probably that of the channel network pattern. Within the overall framework of the proposed composite model, it is important to keep a sense of proportion in the number of parameters used to describe each process. The following survey attempts, wherever possible, to suggest ways in which parameters might be obtained from basin measurements, and to keep within the suggested target of 5–10 parameters overall.

The infiltration process

Hydrological models have commonly considered entry into the soil in terms of the maximum rate at which water can enter the surface. This rate, the infiltration capacity, is commonly expressed as a function of time elapsed and initial soil moisture content. Functions used include the Horton (1939) equation:

$$f = f_\infty + (f_0 - f_\infty)\, e^{-\lambda t}, \tag{19}$$

the Philip (1957) equation:

$$f = A + B\, t^{-\frac{1}{2}}, \tag{20}$$

and the Green and Ampt (1911) equation:

$$f = A + B\, S^{-1}, \tag{21}$$

where f is the infiltration capacity,
      t is time elapsed from the beginning of infiltration,
      S is the total infiltrated so far
and f_0, f_∞, λ, A and B are soil constants.

Attempts to describe the infiltration process more fully, incorporating the effects of soil moisture hysteresis in particular, appear likely to give undue weight to the infiltration process if the number of parameters in the overall hydrograph model is to remain less than 10.

Concentration on the infiltration capacity emphasises the influence of rainfall intensity, but does not fit easily into the concept of soil water stores. As a result, it becomes difficult to assess the changes in infiltration capacity during a complex storm. The infiltration capacity approach differs from most hydrological store models by emphasising rate of *in*flow (or, strictly, maximum rate of inflow) rather than rate of outflow. It also emphasises Hortonian, or 'infiltration-excess' overland flow (Kirkby and Chorley, 1967), at the expense of 'saturation-excess' overland flow which arises when the soil can accommodate no more water, at which point overland flow can occur even at low rainfall intensities. An alternative model which overcomes some of these difficulties concentrates on the *storage* capacity of the near surface soil. If this store has water content S, capacity S_0 and outflow at rate $q = q(S)$, then although the infiltration capacity becomes meaningless, a value can be given for the total volume which can be infiltrated at a given constant rainfall intensity before overland flow begins. This value has meaning for both types of model, and may therefore be used as a basis for comparison. For the infiltration models of equations (19) to (21), infiltration is assumed to continue until $f = i$, the rainfall intensity (cf. Mein and Larsen, 1973). From equation (19):

$$t = \frac{1}{\lambda} \log_e \left(\frac{f_0 - f_\infty}{i - f_\infty} \right), \tag{22}$$

or:

$$V = \frac{i}{\lambda} \log_e \left(\frac{f_0 - f_\infty}{i - f_\infty} \right), \tag{23}$$

where V is the total volume infiltrating before saturation. From equation (20):

$$V = i \left(\frac{B}{i - A} \right)^2, \tag{24}$$

and from equation (21):

$$V = \frac{B}{i - A}. \tag{25}$$

For three simple storage models, the following somewhat different results are obtained, starting from an initially empty store:

1. If $q = 0$ (no leakage from store):

$$V = S_0; \tag{26}$$

2. If $q = q_0$ (constant leakage):

$$V = \frac{S_0 i}{i - q}; \tag{27}$$

3. If $q = S/k$ (linear store):

$$V = ik \log_e \left(\frac{ik}{ik - S_0} \right). \tag{28}$$

Figure 3.4 shows the relationship between the total volume infiltrated, V, and the rainfall intensity, i, for several of these equations. All are relatively simple, and differ most in their behaviour at high rainfall intensities. The choice of a particular equation is likely to depend on

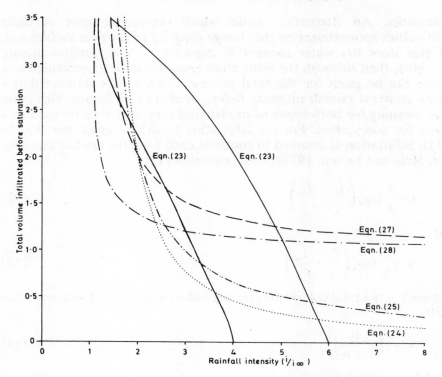

Figure 3.4   Total volume infiltrated as a function of rainfall intensity according to
a range of infiltration and storage models.
   Equation (23) = Horton infiltration equation
   Equation (24) = Philip infiltration equation
   Equation (25) = Green and Ampt infiltration equation
   Equation (27) = Store with constant leakage
   Equation (28) = Linear store

particular soil characteristics, but it is thought likely that the storage
type of model may be more appropriate for soils with well developed
horizons where the capacity of the 'A' horizon is a critical determinant
of overland flow (Carson and Kirkby, 1972, chapter 8). For this type of
soil the constant leakage model of equation (27) is thought to provide
an adequate and simple compromise which is suitable for modelling,
but the most appropriate form of curve can also be obtained directly by
field testing, using a spray infiltrometer.
    A modifying influence on the process of outflow from the infiltra-
tion store is concerned with delivery to the sub-soil store beneath. As
sub-soil water storage increases, the delay in reaching it decreases. This
influence may be modelled directly by using a variable delay, or else the
rate of outflow from the infiltration store may be coupled to the
contents of the subsoil store, since this rate affects the mean time to

reach the sub-soil. This second approach is computationally simpler, and it is suggested that the leakage, instead of being constant, may be treated as:

$$q_1 = q_1(S_2),\qquad(29)$$

where q_1 is the outflow from the infiltration store, and
$\quad$ S_2 is the storage in the sub-soil.

This approach is in keeping with the empirical finding of Laurenson (1964), who related lag time (proportional to $1/q_1$) to stream discharge (itself a function of S_2). He found that:

$$1/q_1 \propto q_2^{-0.27},\qquad(30)$$

so that $q_1(S_2)$ in equation (29) should be an increasing function of S_2. This function is considered below in the context of outflow from the sub-soil store.

The production of overland flow and evaporation

Any model with only a few parameters must necessarily simplify the spatial variation of moisture content over a drainage basin. For a given average moisture content, there is a wide range of possible spatial distributions, even if rainfall is always spatially uniform, as is assumed here. To predict the spatial consequences of an average moisture level, some assumptions must be made about the duration of the rainfall inputs. The simplest, which is adopted here, is to assume a time-independent steady state of net rainfall input, $\bar{\imath}$.

For a point in the catchment at which the area drained per unit contour length is a, the local slope angle is β, and the local lateral permeability is K, the discharge,

$$Q = (\bar{\imath} - q_0)a = KS \tan \beta,\qquad(31)$$

where S is the local soil storage level in rainfall equivalent units (e.g., mm).

Then

$$S = \frac{(\bar{\imath} - q_0)a}{K \tan \beta}\qquad(32)$$

The saturated area is then defined as the area for which

$$S > S_0, \quad \text{or} \quad \frac{a}{K \tan \beta} > \frac{S_0}{(\bar{\imath} - q_0)}\qquad(33)$$

Over the whole catchment, of area A, the mean water storage

$$\bar{S} = \bar{\imath}\,\frac{\displaystyle\int \frac{a}{K \tan \beta}dA}{A} = \frac{\lambda(\bar{\imath} - q_0)}{\bar{K}}\qquad(34)$$

where $\lambda = \bar{K} \dfrac{\displaystyle\int \dfrac{a}{K \tan \beta}\, dA}{A}$ is a constant of the catchment.

Combining equations (33) and (34), the saturated area is that for which

$$\frac{a}{\tan \beta} > \frac{\lambda K S_0}{\bar{K}\bar{S}} \tag{35}$$

The expression on the left hand side can readily be mapped for a particular catchment or sub-catchment. If K, the permeability, is assumed constant, then a single parameter, $\lambda K S_0 / \bar{K}$, relates the topographic distribution to the average storage level and saturated area. An example is shown in Figures 3.5a and 3.5b for a very small catchment of 0.052 km^2.

In a subsequent rainfall, the area obtained in this way may be closely identified with the concept of contributing area (Kirkby and Weyman, 1973), so that overland flow can be estimated as:

$$q_0 = i A_c, \tag{36}$$

where i is the instantaneous rainfall intensity, and A_c is the saturated contributing area, calculated from equation (35). Where A_c varies with S, a major source of non-linearity is introduced into the model for the first time. For the example shown in Figure 3.5, this non-linearity is very severe, but for many larger catchments the slope of the curve tends to be relatively low at low and moderate values of S, so that the condition for linearity (constant A_c) is more nearly satisfied.

The assumption of a finite store of near-surface moisture allows very simple estimation of evaporation. In each unit of time, new

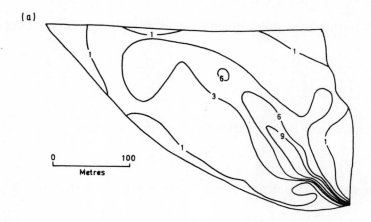

Figure 3.5a   Distribution of a/tan β in a part of the East Twin Catchment, Somerset. Values are in km.

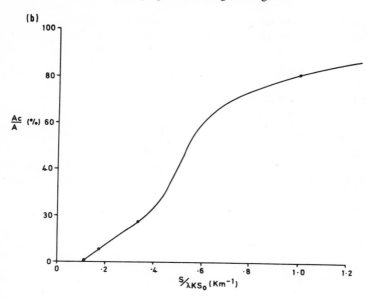

Figure 3.5b   Contributing area as a function of soil storage. Values derived from Figure 3.5a (dots correspond to contour lines).

rainfall is added to the store (which includes depression and interception stores). Overland flow, if any, occurs rapidly and so is satisfied first. The remainder must be allocated between downward infiltration and upward evaporation. It is reasonable to assume that both are satisfied at the full rate until the store is exhausted, and that there is no subsequent loss.

Subsurface soil storage and flow

Field observation and measurement (Whipkey, 1965; Weyman, 1971) suggest that flow within the soil is largely in the saturated phase, and that it occurs more rapidly in the more porous layers closer to the surface when these become saturated. In most cases levels of subsurface flow do not appear to back up to the surface, but this might provide an additional complication in some areas. However, the rate of response to infiltration is affected by the level of sub-surface flow, as has been outlined above.

If these assumptions are valid, then the spatial distribution of storages is much less significant than is the allocation of overland flow, so that a *single* store may be a reasonable basis for modelling. This viewpoint is reinforced by the commonly convex form of divides, which reinforces a near-linear behaviour for the soil water store, and tends to produce rather constant values for storage.

For saturated flow of varying depth within a single layer of constant permeability, the conditions for a linear store are closely met. In this case the flow can be described by equation (5) in the form:

$$Q = Q_0 e^{-t/K} \qquad (5a)$$

where Q is the discharge at time t = 0
and K is the constant for the linear store.

This is a classic form for recession curves for the various hydrograph components obtained by separate techniques. For the total flow, however, it is not generally a good fit to the falling limb of the hydrograph, which is commonly better fitted to an expression of the form

$$Q = \frac{Q_0}{(1 + \alpha t)^n}, \qquad (37)$$

where n is an exponent which is commonly close to 1.0.

If this equation is regarded as a solution to the mass balance equation (2) during a period of zero inflow:

$$-Q = \frac{dS}{dt} \qquad (2a)$$

Substituting equation (37):

$$S = \frac{Q_0}{n - 1} \cdot \frac{1}{(1 + \alpha t)^{n-1}} \propto Q^{n-1}/n \qquad (38)$$

or $\quad Q \propto S^{n/n-1} \quad$ for $n \neq 1 \qquad (39)$

and $\quad S = \dfrac{Q_0}{\alpha} \log_e (1 + t) = \dfrac{Q_0}{\alpha} \log_e (Q/Q_0) \qquad (40)$

or $\quad Q = Q_0 e^{\alpha S/Q_0} \quad$ for $n = 1 \qquad (41)$

These are the simplest forms for non-linear stores, and it may be seen that the linear store corresponds to the case of $n \to \infty$. Lambert's (1969) one store hydrograph model is based on the exponential store of equation (41), which is now analysed more fully.

For a steady inflow of intensity i, coming to a store of initial storage the outflow can be calculated from the mass balance equation (2):

$$i - Q = \frac{dS}{dt} \qquad (2)$$

For the exponential store, the storage–discharge relationship is:

$$Q = Q_0 e^{S/M} \quad \text{or} \quad S = M \log_e (Q/Q_0) \qquad (42)$$

Substituting for S in equation (2):

$$i - Q = \frac{dS}{dt} = \frac{M}{Q}\frac{dQ}{dt} \tag{43}$$

$$\therefore \quad -\int \frac{dt}{M} = \int \frac{dQ}{Q(Q-i)} \tag{44}$$

$$\therefore \quad -\int \frac{dt}{M} = \frac{1}{i} \int \left(\frac{1}{Q-i} - \frac{1}{Q}\right) dQ \tag{45}$$

$$\therefore \quad -\frac{it}{M} = \log\left(\frac{Q-i}{Q}\right) + \text{constant} \tag{46}$$

$$\text{or} \quad \frac{Q-i}{Q} = Ae^{-it/M} \tag{47}$$

$$\therefore \quad Q = \frac{i}{1 - Ae^{-it/M}} \tag{48}$$

Putting $Q = Q_1 = Q_0 e^{S_1/M}$ at $t = 0$:

$$A = 1 - i/Q_1 \tag{49}$$

$$\text{and} \quad Q = \frac{i}{(1 - e^{-it/M}) + i/Q_1 e^{-it/M}} \tag{50}$$

which reduces, as $i \rightarrow 0$, to

$$Q = \frac{M}{t + M/Q_1} \tag{51}$$

Figure 3.6 shows the response of an exponential store to increasing rainfall intensities. The non-linearity of the response is very apparent, and matches the response of many drainage basins. It can however be modified to

$$Q = Q_0 e^{S/M} - B, \tag{52}$$

for a constant B, to allow for two factors:

1. The exponential store predicts an infinite total flow following any input. This corresponds to the prolonged flow of several months during a dry period, with the exhaustion of deep moisture levels, but it may be desired to reduce this yield.
2. Basins differ in their non-linearity of response. An increase of Q_0, M and B tends to increase the linearity of the response more. At the limit, if

$$Q_0 = B = M/K \rightarrow \infty$$

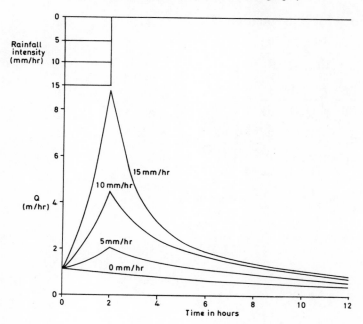

Figure 3.6   Response of an exponential store to rainfall of differing intensities $Q \propto e^{S/M}$ where M = 10 mm. Initial discharge, Q_1 = 1 mm/hr.

together, then the store behaves as a linear store:

$$Q = S/K \tag{53}$$

If an exponential soil store is coupled to an infiltration store with constant leakage, then equation (30) above suggests an appropriate form for the infiltration leakage, q_1. It is

$$q_1 \propto Q^\alpha \propto e^{\alpha S_2/M} \tag{54}$$

where α is a constant with a suggested value of 0.27 from equation (30). The value of α has a major influence on the responsiveness of lag time to rainfall intensity. A strictly linear response (constant lag time) occurs if $\alpha = 0$.

Flow from groundwater can be simulated within the framework of one or more exponential soil stores where there is no discrete aquifer system. Where the aquifers are well defined, an appropriate model must be added to the surface and soil models proposed, but it is not proposed to pursue this topic further here.

A slope flow model has been outlined above (Figure 3.7) to predict overland and subsurface flow to stream channels. By ignoring many of the soil and topographic differences within the catchment, it requires

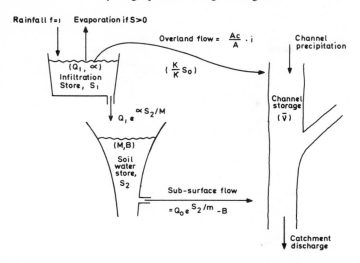

Figure 3.7 Schematic hydrograph model with seven parameters. (Symbols in brackets indicate non-topographic parameters.)

that the area be subdivided into more or less homogeneous units. All but one of the parameters refer to the hydrologic response of the soil. It is therefore of first importance to subdivide the catchment on the basis of major soil differences. These include influences of the organic horizons, so that land-use may also be a significant influence. Overland flow production also involves one parameter, so that areas of markedly different topography, especially stream head hollows, should also be sampled separately.

Within each area, some of the parameters can be measured directly. Q and S_0 can be measured by constant rate infiltration tests, and M by subsurface saturated permeability measurements. B, α and $K/\bar{K}$ cannot be measured directly but are likely to be conservative, with trial values of zero, 0.27 and 1.0 respectively. The remaining parameter, Q_0 is arbitrary, merely setting the zero-point on the scale of S_2 (which can take both positive and negative values).

Channel network flow

The response time of the channel is generally short (Figure 3.3), so that it is unlikely to be worth incorporating a non-linear model of network response for catchments of less than about 500 km^2. For smaller areas however, the network structure has an important influence on the magnitude of the peak flow. A given channel network can be described in terms of two distributions, as is shown in Figure 3.8. The first of these distributions is of the number of channels at a given distance up the network from the outflow point. The second distribution is of

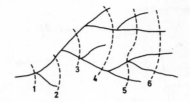

Figure 3.8a   Network map.

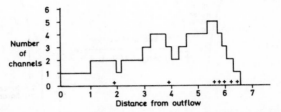

Figure 3.8b   Distribution of channel number with distance from outflow measured along network (+ = channel tip).

Figure 3.8   Production of channel frequency distribution.

stream heads, shown by crosses in Figure 3.8b. If stream velocity can be assumed to be spatially uniform, then the stream outflow may be obtained from two components:

1. convolution of slope-flow hydrographs with the channel frequency distribution, after converting distance to time units using an appropriate value for stream velocity, $\bar{v}$;
2. addition of suitably lagged hydrographs from stream head areas.

The first of these components (Calver, Kirkby and Weyman, 1972) has been shown to influence both the timing and peak value of the stream hydrograph. Stream networks, although very conservative in the Hortonian bifurcation structure, may be shown to differ appreciably from a mean form in a high proportion of cases, so that it is important to incorporate this distribution in the hydrograph prediction procedure. Where the sideslopes have been divided into sub-areas according to soil type or differing rainfall inputs, then the channel frequency distribution must be disaggregated into components corresponding to each sub-area.

In catchments of more than 500 km², the non-linearity of the network response must probably be taken into account, and a kinematic routing procedure adopted. The procedure described above is merely the linear case. The effect of a kinematic routing approach is to allow hydrograph peaks to go faster than low flows, so that the channel accentuates the typical skewed form of the hydrograph.

Conclusion

In searching for an economical hydrograph model with a maximum of physical reality, the notion of a fully distributed model has been rejected in favour of a model which divides the catchment into sub-areas, within each of which a two or three layer model is used. The layers are identified with unsaturated infiltration, saturated subsurface flow, and groundwater flow (if applicable). Sub-areas need to be defined on the basis of soil and topographic characteristics. The physical identity of the catchment is considered the most important in the following ways:

1. soil infiltration and permeability properties;
2. the relationship between mean near-surface storage and contributing area;
3. the channel network frequency distribution.

The second and third set of characteristics can be obtained unambiguously from topographic maps and survey, leaving a total of seven parameters in the proposed model. Four of these (Q_1, S_0, M, $\bar{v}$) can be estimated from short term hydraulic measurements, and the remaining three (α, B, $K/\bar{K}$) are thought to be conservative in value.

Although a model of the type proposed uses much less than all of the knowledge available from theoretical hydraulics, such a state-of-the-art model appears to be far from a practical reality. Given the poor return obtained from models with large numbers of parameters, it appears that the conservative tendencies of a catchment may be more realistically represented by the sort of hybrid model put forward here.

REFERENCES

Aitken, A. P. (1973). 'Assessing systematic errors in rainfall-runoff models', *J. Hydrology*, 20, 121—136.

Amorocho, J. (1963). 'Measures of the linearity of hydrologic systems', *J. Geophysical Research*, 68, 2237—2249.

Calver, A., M. J. Kirkby, and D. R. Weyman (1972). 'Modelling hillslope and channel flows', in Chorley, R. J. (Ed.). *Spatial Analysis in Geomorphology*, Methuen, 197—218.

Carson, M. A. and M. J. Kirkby (1972). *Hillslope Form and Process*, C.U.P.

Chow, Ven T. E. and S. J. Kareliotis (1970). 'Analysis of stochastic hydrologic systems', *Water Resources Research*, 16, 1569—1582.

Dooge, J. C. I. (1959). 'A general theory of the unit hydrograph', *J. Geophysical Research*, 64, 241—256.

Green, W. H. and G. A. Ampt (1911). 'Studies on soil physics: 1. The flow of air and water through soils', *J. Agricultural Soils*, 4, 1—24.

Hewlett, J. D. and A. R. Hibbert, (1967). 'Factors affecting the response of small watersheds to precipitation in humid areas', *International Symposium on Forest Hydrology*, Pergamon, p. 275–290.

Horton, R. E. (1939). 'Analysis of runoff plot experiments', *Trans. American Geophysical Union*, 20, 693.

Hurst, H. E. (1951). 'Long-term storage capacity of reservoirs', *Trans. American Society of Civil Engineers*, 116, 770.

Kirkby, M. J. and R. J. Chorley (1967). 'Throughflow, overland flow and erosion', *Bull. International Association for Scientific Hydrology*, 12, 5–21.

Kirkby, M. J. and D. R. Weyman (1973). 'Measurements of contributing area in very small drainage basins', Seminar Paper B3, Department of Geography, University of Bristol.

Lambert, A. O. (1969). 'A comprehensive rainfall-runoff model for an upland catchment', *J. Institute of Water Engineers*, 23, 231–238.

Laurenson, E. M. (1964). 'A catchment storage model for runoff routing', *J. Hydrology*, 2, 141–162.

Mandelbrot, B. B. and J. R. Wallis (1968). 'Noah, Joseph and Operational hydrology', *Water Resources Research*, 4, 909–918.

Matalas, N. C. (1966). 'Some aspects of time series analysis in hydrologic studies', *Proceedings, 5th Canadian Hydrology Symposium*, Montreal, Canada.

Mein, R. G. and C. L. Larson (1973). 'Modelling infiltration during a steady rain', *Water Resources Research*, 9, 2.

Philip, J. R. (1957). 'The theory of infiltration: 4, Sorptivity and algebraic infiltration equations', *Soil Science*, 84, 257–264.

Sherman, L. K. (1932). 'Streamflow from rainfall by the unit hydrograph method', *Engineering News-Record*, 108, 501–505.

Weyman, D. R. (1971), *Surface and sub-Surface Runoff in a Small Basin*, unpublished Ph.D. thesis, University of Bristol.

Weyman, D. R. (1974). 'Runoff process, contributing area and streamflow in a small upland catchment', in Gregory, K. J. and D. E. Walling (Eds.), *Fluvial Processes in Instrumented Watersheds*, Special Publication No. 6, Institute of British Geographers, 33–43.

Whipkey, R. Z. (1965). 'Subsurface stormflow from forested slopes', *Bull. International Association for Scientific Hydrology*, 10, 74–85.

Wooding, R. A. (1965/6). 'A hydraulic model for the catchment-stream problem'.

Wooding, R. A. 'I Kinematic wave theory', *J. Hydrology*, 3, 254–267.

Wooding, R. A. 'II Numerical solutions', *J. Hydrology*, 3, 268–282.

Wooding, R. A. 'III Comparison with runoff observations', *J. Hydrology*, 4, 21–37.

Yevjevich, F. M. (1964). 'Fluctuations of wet and dry years. II, Analysis of serial correlation', *Hydrology Paper No. 4*, Colorado State University.

Chapter 4

Some Statistical Approaches Towards Physical Hydrology in Large Catchments

Malcolm Anderson

The present inability to relate detailed hydrological process investigations in small catchments ($\leqslant 5$ km^2) to larger ones has meant that studies of physical hydrology at larger scales have frequently employed multivariate statistics and classical time-series models. Such an approach has limitations with regard to process inference since it represents a combination of system synthesis and system analysis. In the former case, a conceptual knowledge of the operating physical processes involved is assumed, whilst systems analysis makes no such assumption and frequently determines the transfer function between input and output (Brandsetter and Amorocho, 1970). The unit hydrograph is an example of a model employing both systems analysis and synthesis — the unit hydrograph being synthesised from analytically derived rainfall excess and storm discharge, and being represented by the linear convolution:

$$y(t) = \int_0^\infty h_1(s)x(t-s)ds \qquad (1)$$

where $h_1(s)$ = system response function
$\quad$ $x(t)$ = input
$\quad$ $y(t)$ = output

Since rainfall excess and storm flow relationships are non-linear (Pilgrim, 1966) and the unit hydrograph is time invariant and linear, the model combines non-linear synthesis with linear analysis. Solutions to equation (1) have been accomplished by the methods of least squares (Snyder, 1955) and harmonic analysis (O'Donnell, 1960). For the same catchments such methods have yielded slightly different unit hydro-graph results. Such differences have been previously accounted for by lack of uniformity in the precipitation field, although Amorocho and Brandsetter (1971) argue that a more likely cause is the fitting of a linear model to a non-linear process. The generalisation of equation (1) leads to a series of functionals (Amorocho, 1973)

$$y(t) = h_0 + \int_0^\infty h_1(s)x(t-s)ds$$

$$+ \int_0^\infty \int_0^\infty h_2(s_1, s_2)x(t-s_1)x(t-s_2)ds_1 ds_2 \quad (2)$$

where s = the variable of integration.

Such a model (equation (2)) has the attraction of being non-linear in the systems theory sense (Clarke, 1973). However, no relationship can be assumed between the components of the polynomial and physical processes, thus highlighting the problem of excellent model resolution combined with very poor or non-existent inferential capabilities. Such severe limitations of the unit hydrograph model are now well appreciated (Calver, et al, 1972) and more deserving of attention is the potential of time-series and related approaches in physical hydrology modelling and process inference.

Basic linear models

Many studies examining the controls of flood discharge at the larger scale have employed multiple regression methods having the general form:

$$Q_t = f(X_1, X_2, X_3, \ldots, X_n) \quad (3)$$

where Q_t is discharge of some recurrence interval and $X_1, \ldots, X_n$ are independent variables relating to basin topography, network pattern and precipitation factors. An example is provided by Rodda (1967) who, in a study of 26 basins in the United Kingdom, obtained the following relationship for the mean annual flood, $Q_{2.33}$, in cusecs:

$$Q_{2.33} = 1.08A^{0.77} \cdot R^{2.92} \cdot D^{0.81} \quad (4)$$

where A = basin area (sq. mls.)
R = mean annual daily maximum rainfall (ins.)
D = drainage density (mls./sq. ml.)

Such an approach does not provide a unique interpretation of the observed discharge phenomena. Moreover, since invariably spatial sampling is involved, and thus data from numerous basins are employed, interpretation is further complicated by the possibility of spatial autocorrelation of the residuals from the model. Although it has been observed that models of the form of equation (3) are widespread, few workers have examined the implications of spatial autocorrelation when attempting to assess causal factors accounting for flood variability. Benson's (1960) study of floods of nine different recurrence intervals in New England is an exception in this respect. Figure 4.1 shows the average ratios of actual to computed peaks for the nine flood recurrences when the model

$$Q = f(A, S, S_t, I) \tag{5}$$

is fitted, where A = basin area

     S = main channel slope

     S_t = % of surface storage area

     I = rainfall intensity factor.

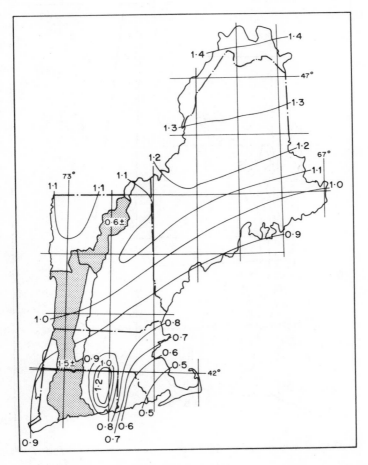

Figure 4.1 Map of residual error from model: $Q = f(A,S,S_t,I)$. (After Benson, 1960.)

Systematic under-prediction occurs in the north, whilst the southern part of the state demonstrates the reverse trend. The pattern is changed somewhat by the inclusion of a fifth variable, t, the average January temperature shown in Figure 4.2. However, when a further variable, an orographic factor, is included the pattern of the average ratios of actual to computed flows is random, and thus the final model takes the form:

$$Q = f(A, S, S_t, I, t, O) \tag{6}$$

The existence of more formal methods of spatial autocorrelation identification, necessitating the establishment of a contiguity matrix for the drainage basins, makes it inexcusable that such formal tests are not applied when models of the form of equation (3) are fitted. The spatial

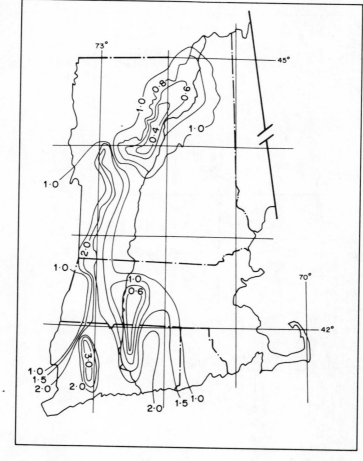

Figure 4.2   Map of residual error from model: $Q = f(A, S, S_t, I, t)$. (After Benson, 1960.)

selection of drainage basins rarely results in adjacent basins being chosen. The contiguity matrix is thus less easy to establish and more prone to ambiguity than in the 'county case' (Cliff and Ord, 1969), although theissen polygon methods provide one possible method for constructing the necessary matrix.

Autocovariance and cross covariance analysis

The most basic diagnostic procedure which is conventionally the prelude to stochastic model fitting of a series, as well as having inferential power, is the autocovariance function C(l) being defined as:

$$C(l) = \frac{1}{n-1} \sum_{k=1}^{n-1} (x_k - \bar{x})(x_{k+1} - \bar{x}) \tag{7}$$

where n is the sample size and l is the lag. The autocorrelation coefficient is given by:

$$r(l) = C(l)/C(O) \tag{8}$$

and may assume values in the range −1 to +1. Thus the autocorrelation coefficient enables the degree of linear association between observations that are l time units apart to be ascertained, and a plot of r(l) against l for $l \neq 0$ (the correlogram) reflects the structure of the time series. In physical systems which often preclude detailed investigation of the salient operating processes, for example in groundwater environments, the autocorrelation coefficient has been employed in an attempt to make inferences concerning the transfer function characteristics between input and output. Jackson *et al* (1973), examining groundwater discharge in an area of Manitoba, obtained the correlograms for groundwater, evapotranspiration and inflow rate, mean daily temperature and daily precipitation (Figure 4.3). The groundwater inflow rate shows the greatest persistence on account of the storage of the flow system, but of perhaps greater significance is the lack of coherence between the peaks in groundwater evapotranspiration (five days) and mean daily temperature (seven days), reflecting the importance of water table depth (Jackson *et al*, 1973).

Cross-covariance analysis provides the next logical step in such an analysis, enabling lagged association between different variables to be determined. The value of such an approach is that it allows a further dimension to be explored beyond the simple use of correlation structures, with the possibility of quantifying feedback effects as well as identifying transfer function characteristics, since relaxation times can be directly estimated. The karst system can be regarded for most purposes as a black box, since usually we possess knowledge of only the inflow and outflow and have little knowledge of the intervening processes. Brown (1973) outlined five possible types of flow within a

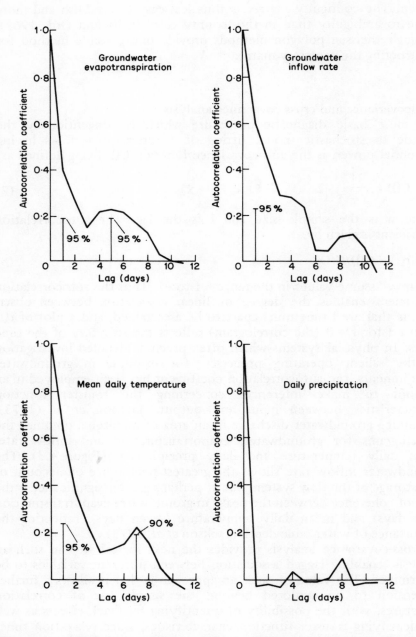

Figure 4.3   Correlograms. Percentage figures indicate confidence levels. (After Jackson *et al*, 1973.)

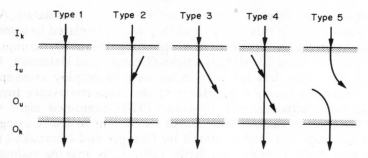

Figure 4.4   Five possible types of flow networks in karst. (After Brown, 1973.)

karst situation (Figure 4.4) and gave three hypothetical cross-covariance
plots under different conditions (Figure 4.5), these being estimated by:

$$C(l) = \frac{1}{n-1} \sum_{k=1}^{n-1} (I_k - \bar{I})(O_{k+1} - \bar{O}) \qquad (9)$$

Figure 4.5a indicates that the system takes a positive time to transmit a
wave, 4.5b that the system transmits the wave instantaneously, whilst
4.5c suggests that the output is dominated by an input other than the
one being monitored (situation shown in Figure 4.4 — type 2). Being
able to estimate the relaxation time in this manner allows elementary

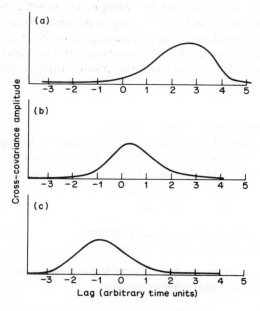

Figure 4.5   Hypothetical cross covariance of input-output in a karst system.
(After Brown, 1973.)

knowledge of the flow system (Figure 4.4) to be postulated. Assuming the two series, in this case I_k and O_k, to be correlated in some way, then the correlation between corresponding frequency components need not be the same for all frequencies (Granger and Hatanaka, 1964). It is this fact that has led certain workers to employ cross-spectral density functions (being a transform of the cross covariance function-equation (9)). Edwards and Thornes (1973) examined eight water-quality variables in the 570 km^2 Stour catchment in Essex using cross spectral methods outlined in detail by Granger and Hatanaka (1964), Jenkins and Watts (1968), and Kisiel (1969). By making estimates of the phase, $p^{(f)}$, at the annual frequency, f, between all pairs of variables they were able to construct a matrix giving the delay time $(p^{(f)}/2\pi f)$, from which it was concluded that peaks in pH and carbonate hardness occurred some nine weeks prior to the peak in discharge. The variables in this analysis were viewed as output from a highly complex chemical, hydrological and biological system. Dowling (1974), however, argues that only under comparatively stringent assumptions about the behaviour of the variables in the time domain can phase be interpreted as a simple lead or lag. Such an interpretation, Dowling argues, must assume that the two series are related in the following manner:

$$Y(t) = aX(t - t_0) \tag{10}$$

where t_0 = absolute delay time.

For all other linear input-output systems, phase in radians, or delay time in weeks or days, cannot be interpreted as reflecting an absolute delay time between the series, for a lag in physical time can be obtained from numerous distributed lag-generating models. It therefore follows that a more explicit model than equation (10) is required in the time domain to facilitate unambiguous phase interpretation (Dowling, 1974).

Harmonic and stochastic representation

Characterising many investigations in physical hydrology has been the study of travel times of flood pulses in river networks, initially taking the form of empirical relationships

$$t_d = 46.24_{\bar{q}_s}{}^{-0.301} \quad \begin{matrix} (r = -0.91 \\ n = 34) \end{matrix} \tag{11}$$

where t_d = log time to direct runoff (hours)
$\bar{q}_s$ = direct runoff (cubic feet/sec)

(Askew, 1970), numerous derivations have now been obtained, certain being based upon the Manning equation:

$$T_{ve} = 0.087_q{}^{2/5} \sum_{i=1}^{m} \frac{l_i n_i{}^{3/5} P_i{}^{2/5}}{s_i{}^{3/10} A_i{}^{2/5}} \tag{12}$$

where T_{ve} = time to virtual equilibrium (i.e. time in hours needed for flow to reach virtual equilibrium with a constant supply rate of long duration).

S_i = slope of the water surface of ith reach

q = uniform supply rate (inches per hour)

1_i= length of ith reach (feet)

P_i = wetted perimeter of the reach (feet)

A_i = basin area at upstream junction of the reach (sq. miles)

(Golany and Larson, 1971). The response from individual storm inputs in a given basin can thus be characterised, but additionally the memory properties of the complete discharge time series can be viewed (although aggregate in nature) as a response to climatic inputs and morphometric controls. It is in this latter context that correlogram analysis is generally a prelude to modelling the process being investigated, in that certain elements of the structure of the time series are depicted by the correlogram. Thus, in modelling discharge time series many authors have sought to identify a deterministic component (seasonality) and a stochastic component, and have then proceeded to model the components using harmonic and markovian models respectively. Such an approach attempts to represent the information in the time series more satisfactorily than the more aggregate measures of flow employed in models of the form of equation (3). Assuming monthly discharge data X_t, Roesner and Yevjevich (1966) obtained the series Z_t (being second order stationary) by effecting the transformation:

$$Z_t = \frac{X_t - M_\tau}{S_\tau} \tag{13}$$

where M_τ and S_τ are the mean and standard deviation of the month τ and where the monthly means of X_t are represented as a continuous function by the expression

$$M_t = \frac{1}{12} \sum_{\tau=1}^{12} M_\tau + \sum_{k=1}^{6} A_k \cos\frac{2\pi kt}{12} + \sum_{k=1}^{6} B_k \sin\frac{2\pi kt}{12} \tag{14}$$

and the standard deviation has a similarly defined continuous function S_t. The Z_t series thus obtained was stochastic and fitted by the autoregressive model

$$Z_t = \rho_1 Z_{t-1} + e_t \tag{15}$$

Analysing 137 drainage basins in the United States, Roesner and Yevjevich (1966) found $\hat{\rho}_1$ values to have a significant spatial pattern (Figure 4.6). The $\hat{\rho}_1$ values for precipitation series have been found by Roesner and Yevjevich to be considerably lower than those for discharge, and of the order of 0.05, the difference between the two being caused by the storage characteristics of the basin. The spatial

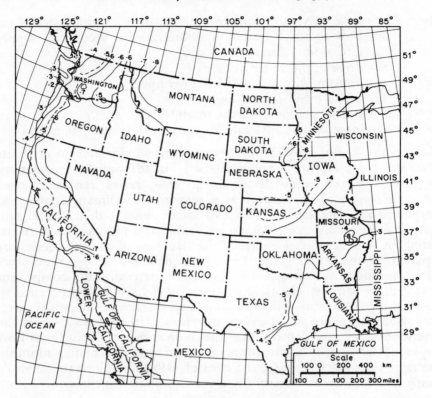

Figure 4.6   Areal distribution of $\hat{\rho}$, (equation 14) from Roesner and Yevjevich's (1966) study of monthly river flow series.

pattern of the discharge values of $\hat{\rho}_1$, reflecting both the broad precipitation distribution characteristics and basin storage, remains to be further investigated. Figure 4.7 shows $\hat{\rho}_1$ distributions from discharge series from both Roesner and Yevjevich (1966) and a study of 20 British basins using five-day mean data (Anderson, 1974). In seeking to identify the generating process in markov terms for slope profiles, Thornes (1973) has drawn attention to the effects of different sampling intervals. The differences in the means of the two distributions in Figure 4.7 therefore directly reflect the five-day mean and monthly mean sampling strategies employed in the two cases.

Studies attempting physical interpretation of the generating processes in the discharge series so identified have been few, and have been restricted to aggregate morphometric controls over the stochastic component (Anderson, 1973; Yevjevich personal communication), and yet such models have been extensively used by engineers for prediction purposes (Quimpo, 1968). Small sample bias in the estimation of $\hat{\rho}_1$ (Wallis and O'Connell, 1972) and the limited process information which

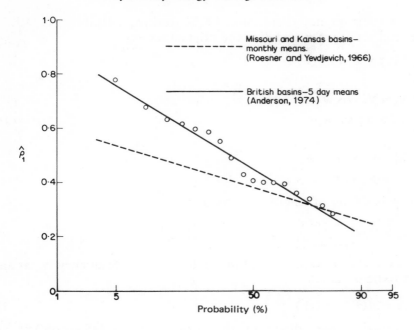

Figure 4.7   Comparative distributions of $\hat{\rho}_1$.

can be gained from such an approach will necessarily restrict such models to the category of exploratory rather than explanatory. However, such criticisms are premature in relation to the downstream analysis of channel width, depth and bed profile, since only recently have studies suggested that equally spaced readings along a stream channel allow a more sophisticated interpretation, of 'downstream' to be postulated when using time series techniques (Nordin and Algert, 1966; Thornes, 1974). Implicit in the model of equation (13) is that deterministic and stochastic elements in the series can be separated and correctly identified by the methods outlined. This is important since harmonic representation for a given frequency has a constant amplitude and phase. If the annual oscillation in discharge for given rivers, although always present, was found to vary in either amplitude or phase over a given period, models of the form of equation (13) would be meaningless since the stochastic and deterministic components would be mixed. Thus, just as simple regression methods yield the average relationship between two or more variables, on occasions masking significant thresholds in such relationships, harmonic analysis provides only average estimates of amplitude and phase. Although demodulation techniques enable changes in the amplitude and phase for a given frequency (W_0) to be determined (Granger and Hatanaka, 1964), applications to the study of precipitation-discharge relationships seem to be in their infancy (Anderson, 1975; Rodriguez-Iturbe *et al*, 1971). In general terms we may define the original series:

$$Y_t, t = 1, n$$

then

$$Y_t' = Y_t \cos w_o t$$
$$Y_t'' = Y_t \sin w_o t \tag{16}$$

and

$$Z_t' = F\{Y_t \cos w_o t\}$$
$$Z_t' = F\{Y_t \sin w_o t\}$$

where F is a filter of length 2 m and of the form

$$z_t = \tfrac{1}{2}m\left\{ \sum_{j=m+1}^{m-1} y_{t+j}' + \tfrac{1}{2}y_{t-m}' + \tfrac{1}{2}y_{t-m}' \right\} \tag{17}$$

and this allows an estimate of the amplitude A for frequency w_o at any time t to be obtained:

$$\hat{A} = 2((z_t')^2 + (z_t'')^2)^{0.5} \tag{18}$$

In practice, two filters of the form outlined (equation 17) are applied, the first of length k and the second of length p, where $k \gg p$. The choice of k and p is subjective, but the use of too narrow a window, whilst giving smoother estimates, will serve to increase the variance of the estimates. Figure 4.8 and 4.9 show monthly series for precipitation and discharge for the river Wye at Rhyader (O.S. grid reference SN969676 — basin area 167 km^2) and the river Blythe at Hamstall Ridware (O.S. grid reference SK109191 — basin area 162 km^2). The two precipitation amplitude series show a significant polynomial trend with the minima in the period 1945–48. The discharge for the Wye shows no low order trend in annual amplitude, the oscillations present merely reflecting 'noise' (Granger and Hatanaka, 1964). However, the discharge annual amplitude in the case of the river Blythe (Figure 4.8) shows a marked decline during the period 1952–54; the reason being that this period coincides with the impounding of the river upstream from the gauging site (Alexander, Trent River Authority — written communication). Such results clearly demonstrate that annual precipitation amplitude is a function of time, and samples could be analysed to evaluate spatial and temporal changes over large areas. The demodulated series for the Wye at Rhyader (Figure 4.9) demonstrates the situation where a significant trend in the precipitation annual amplitude is absorbed by the basin system, the discharge component being trend free. It is observations of this nature which serve to emphasise the gulf between small scale process investigations and large scale system behaviour. Moreover, increasing the sample size of observations, thereby ensuring better estimates, has

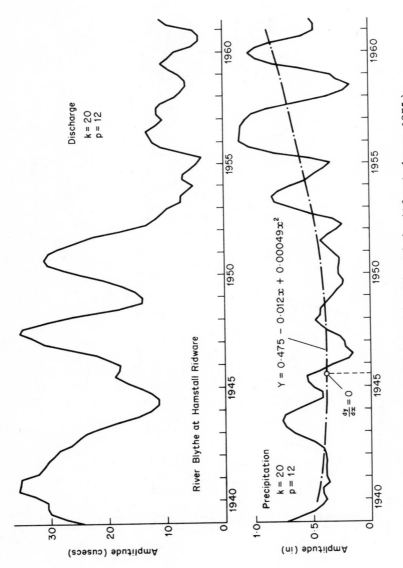

Figure 4.8   Demodulated series — River Blythe. (After Anderson, 1975.)

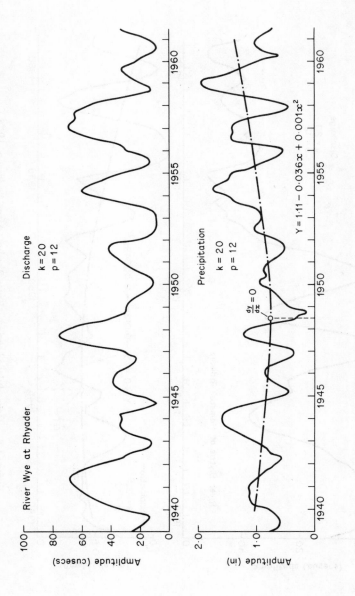

Figure 4.9   Demodulated series — River Wye. (After Anderson, 1975.)

the paradoxical effect of increasing the number of salient independent variables in the analysis. Thus, over a four-year period precipitation annual amplitude may be considered a constant, but over an eight-year period may prove variable. Investigations of this type have large exploratory potential in assessing adjustment of, for example, suspended sediment concentration to extreme natural events (floods, bush fires, etc.). In studying the effect of a bush fire in a New South Wales catchment, Brown (1972) found that the suspended sediment concentration returned to the pre-fire values four years after the event, although studies relating to demodulation and analysis in the frequency domain were not undertaken, despite their potential.

The Hurst phenomenon

Certain inadequacies in representing hydrological series by models of the form of equations (13) − (15), the generating process having been identified by correlogram and spectral methods, have been identified by Hurst (1951). Considering a Gaussian independent process (white noise), G(t), Hurst then defined:

$$G^*(t) = \sum_{u=1}^{t} G(u) \tag{19}$$

and $R_{(s)}$ at lag s as the difference between the maximum and minimum values of G^* (u) − (u/s) G^* (s), and $S_{(s)}$ as the standard deviation of the series $G(1)$, $G(2)$, ... , $G(s)$. Considering river flow data, for example, then the Hurst Range R is the storage required to maintain average discharge. Correlogram and spectral analysis of hydrologic records suggest such a series to be of short memory, i.e. when S is large X(t) and X(t + S) are independent (for example Hall and O'Connell, 1972; Quimpo, 1968). A plot of log R(s)/S(s) on log s for white noise should have a straight slope, H, of 0.5. For river flow data we would therefore expect H = 0.5. However, Hurst (1951) showed that this is not the case for some 1000 years of Nile flow data (Figure 4.10) nor for other phenomena such as annual tree-ring growth. Thus 'theory' anticipates an S^H relation, where H = 0.5, whilst Hurst demonstrated that on average $S^{0.7}$ holds empirically, and suggested the latter relation to be due to the correlation structure of the series. Series with H > 0.5 have been constructed (Wallis and Mandelbrot, 1969) being so-called fractional noises − the basis for self-similar models − where very distant observations continue to have an effect. The importance of H > 0.5 is clearly only relevant in understanding the very long term relationships of time series. Scheidegger (1970), however, observes that postulating models with H ≠ 0.5 is equivalent to postulating a priori a specific asymptotic behaviour for X(t). The classical Gauss-Markov model also makes such a postulate (i.e. ultimate independence), but in this latter case there is at least a physical reason for doing so, in contrast to the

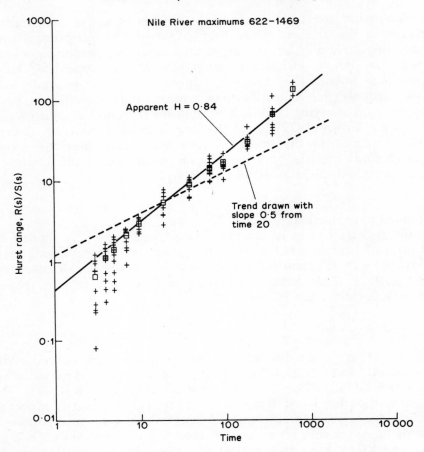

Figure 4.10   Log R(s)/S(s) versus log s for River Nile maximums. (After Wallis and Mandelbrot, 1969.)

current absence of a physical reason for the correlation characteristics engendered by processes with H ≠ 0.5 (Scheidegger, 1970).

Conclusions

The use of time series models in hydrology has been largely as an exploratory tool providing an aggregate picture of discharge character-istics. Such approaches must be seen as tangential to system synthesis approaches which have been successful in process interpretation at the smaller scale through attempting a process-response framework for study. Nevertheless, the behavioural characteristics of discharge and precipitation in demodulation terms have yet to be fully explored. A further factor which has ensured that such methods have not achieved their potential lies in the sampling procedures adopted by geomorphologists in their approach to physical hydrology. Despite dealing with spatial phenomena, the approach towards spatial approximations of different variables has been manifestly weak. Altitude measures, for example, have typically been of an index nature (Evans, 1972), thereby failing to embody the important spatial 'memory' properties of the original data (Anderson, 1973). Failure in this respect, combined with the strict requirements relating to multicolinearity, has ensured that multivariate statistical methods in general, and multiple regression in particular (equations (3) and (4)), have played a very restricted role in process-response modelling. However, in systems where detailed measurements are not possible, for example the karst system, input/output analysis using cross-covariance methods allows a broad interpretation of the response characteristics. Typically, it has been those areas of restricted data which have stimulated the greater amount of theoretical modelling, and karst conditions are now beginning to provide a focus for such activity, resulting currently in spectral-based models (Brown, 1973; Jackson et al, 1973). The longer term approach to inference at the larger scale is seen by some to involve delimiting areas of basins with similar 'characteristics' (hydrologic-response units) and attempting thereby to aggregate to the complete basin, having successfully modelled processes within such units (Striffler, Colorado State University — written communication). Inherent throughout the discussion has been the ambivalence in modelling between resolution of output and process-response interpretation. Adequate methods for comparing and evaluating the results of various stochastic models for streamflow series have yet to be devised (Rodriguez-Iturbe et al, 1971) and yet models of this type pose fewer potential problems from this standpoint than those of the process-response type to which geomorphologists aspire. Criticisms of the Stanford watershed model relating to the non-unique synthesis of an unknown system emphasise the very restricted rôle that statistical models of the type outlined can ultimately play. Time series and related models enable an insight to be gained into the structure of comparatively long term responses and occasionally of the whole basin system, and as such merely provide the source of one possible standard against which comprehensive process-response models of the basin hydrologic system can be judged.

REFERENCES

Amorocho, J. (1973). 'Nonlinear hydrological analysis', in Chow, V. T. (ed.), *Advances in Hydroscience*, **9**, Academic Press, 203—251.

Amorocho, J. and A. Brandsetter (1971). 'Determination of nonlinear functional response functions in rainfall-runoff processes', *Water Resources Research*, **7**, 1087—1101.

Anderson, M. G. (1973). 'Measures of three-dimensional drainage basin form', *Water Resources Research*, **9**, 378–383.

Anderson, M. G. (1974). *Analysis of River Discharge Characteristics and Associated Basin Forms*, unpublished Ph.D. thesis, University of Cambridge.

Anderson, M. G. (1975). 'Demodulation and streamflow series', (forthcoming), *J. Hydrology*.

Askew, A. J. (1970). 'Variation in lag time for natural catchments', *Proc. American Society of Civil Engineers, J. Hydraulics Division*, **HY2**, 317–330.

Benson, M. A. (1960). 'Areal flood-frequency analysis in a humid region', *Bull. International Association of Scientific Hydrology*, **19**, 5–15.

Brandsetter, A. and J. Amorocho (1970). 'Generalized analysis of small watershed responses', *Water Science and Engineering Paper*, No. 1035, Department of Water Science and Engineering, University of California.

Brown, J. A. H. (1972). 'Hydrologic effects of a bushfire in a catchment in south-eastern New South Wales', *J. Hydrology*, **15**, 77–96.

Brown, M. C. (1973). 'Mass balance and spectral analysis applied to karst hydrologic networks', *Water Resources Research*, **9**, 749–752.

Calver, A., M. J. Kirkby and D. R. Weyman (1972). 'Modelling hillslope and channel flows', in Chorley, R. J. (ed.), *Spatial Analysis in Geomorphology*, Methuen, 197–218.

Clarke, R. T. (1973). 'A review of some mathematical models used in hydrology with observations on their calibration and use', *J. Hydrology*, **19**, 1–20.

Cliff, A. D. and J. K. Ord (1969). 'The problem of spatial autocorrelation', in Scott, A. J. (ed.), *Studies in Regional Science*, Pion, 25–35.

Dowling, J. M. (1974). 'A note on the use of spectral analysis to detect leads and lags in annual cycles of water quality', *Water Resources Research*, **10**, 343–344.

Edwards, A. M. C. and J. B. Thornes (1973). 'Annual cycle in river water quality: a time series approach', *Water Resources Research*, **9**, 1286–1295.

Evans, I. S. (1972). 'General geomorphometry, derivations of altitude, and descriptive statistics', in Chorley, R. J. (ed.) *Spatial Analysis in Geomorphology*, Methuen, 17–90.

Golany, P. and C. L. Larson (1971). 'Effects of channel characteristics on time parameters for small watershed runoff hydrographs', *Bulletin*, **31**, Water Resources Research Center, University of Minnesota.

Granger, C. W. J. and M. Hatanaka (1964). *Spectral Analysis of Economic Time Series*, Princeton University Press.

Hall, M. J. and P. E. O'Connell (1972). 'Time series analysis of mean daily river flows', *Water and Water Engineering*, **76**, 125–133.

Hurst, H. E. (1951). 'Long term storage capacities of reservoirs', *Trans. American Society of Civil Engineers*, **116**, 770–799.

Jackson, R. E., J. A. Gilliland and K. Adamowski (1973). 'Time series analysis of the hydrologic regimen of a groundwater discharge area', *Water Resources Research*, **9**, 1411–1419.

Jenkins, G. M. and F. G. Watts (1968). *Spectral Analysis and its Applications*, Holden-Day.

Kisiel, C. C. (1969). 'Time series analysis of hydrological data', in Chow, V. T. (ed.), *Advances in Hydroscience*, **5**, Academic Press, 1–119.

Nordin, C. F. and J. H. Algert (1966). 'Spectral analysis of sand waves', *Proc. American Society of Civil Engineers, J. Hydraulics Division*, **HY5**, 95–114.

O'Donnell, T. (1960). 'Instantaneous unit hydrograph derivation by harmonic analysis', *International Association Scientific Hydrology*, 51, 546–557.

Pilgrim, D. H. (1966). 'Radioactive tracing of storm runoff on a small catchment', *J. Hydrology*, 4, 306–326.

Quimpo, R. G. (1968). 'Stochastic analysis of daily river flows', *Proc. American Society of Civil Engineers, J. Hydraulics Division*, HY1, 43–57.

Rodda, J. C. (1969). 'The flood hydrograph', in Chorley, R. J. (ed.), *Introduction to Physical Hydrology*, Methuen, 162–165.

Rodriguez-Iturbe, I., D. R. Dawdy and L. E. Garcia (1971). 'Adequacy of markovian models with cyclic components for stochastic streamflow representation', *Water Resources Research*, 7, 1127–1143.

Roesner, L. A. and V. Yevjevich (1966). 'Mathematical models for time series of monthly precipitation and monthly runoff', *Colorado Hydrology Papers*, 15, Colorado State University.

Scheidegger, A. E. (1970). 'Stochastic models in hydrology', *Water Resources Research*, 6, 750–755.

Snyder, W. M. (1955). 'Hydrograph analysis by the method of least squares', *Proc. American Society of Civil Engineers, J. Hydraulics Division*, 81, Paper 793.

Thornes, J. B. (1973). 'Markov chains and slope series: the scale problem', *Geographical Analysis*, V, 322–328.

Thornes, J. B. (1974). 'Speculations on the behaviour of stream channel width', *Discussion Paper*, No. 49, Graduate School of Geography, London School of Economics.

Wallis, J. R. and P. E. O'Connell (1972). 'Small sample estimation of ρ_1', *Water Resources Research*, 8, 707–712.

Wallis, J. R. and B. B. Mandelbrot (1969). 'Self-similar synthetic hydrology', in *The Use of Analog and Digital Computers in Hydrology*, Vol. 2, IASH/UNESCO, 738–755.

Chapter 5

Water Action in Desert Landscapes

Ronald Peel

Although the first civilisations arose along their flanks the great deserts have been among the last parts of the Earth to be systematically studied. Even fifty years ago large parts of them had barely been explored, and detailed investigations are mainly a product of the last three decades. Occupying a fifth of the non-Polar land area, and scattered through all the continents in middle and lower latitudes, the deserts display a wide range of geological build and history, a considerable variety of climates, and great contrasts in their natural scenery. Early interpretations of that scenery not unnaturally tended to be strongly influenced by the particular tract of desert penetrated, and we find an entertaining variety. C. Sturt, for example, struggling across the repellent 'Stony Desert' in east-central Australia that bears his name, felt that no familiar sub-aerial processes could have shaped its horrid surface, but that he must be traversing 'the floor of some vanished sea'. S. Passarge, on the other hand, viewing the endless burning plains of the Kalahari, was inclined to attribute their sculpture to solar heat shattering the rocks and wind removing the pulverised residues: ideas that also found favour with various early explorers of the hyper-arid deserts of North Africa and Arabia. That rainfall and streamflow could have made any significant contribution seems scarcely to have occurred to many of these pioneers, for these were phenomena seldom encountered in the extreme Old World deserts. Their introduction, and progressive elevation into the leading role, came mainly with the geological investigation of the American Far West; for in that huge region lofty rain and snow-catching ranges interweave with the semi-arid plateaux and markedly arid sunken basins in a varied and intricate network. In the mountains powerful rivers could be seen sawing out canyons, and seasonal floods continuing the dissection of the plateaux, while similar floods poured down occasionally into even the most desiccated basins. Almost everywhere the imprint of water-action was clearly visible; that of wind little in evidence outside the scatter of moderate-sized dune-fields. Basing his ideas mainly on studies made in this region, W. M. Davis (1905) accordingly had no hesitation in putting water-action, powerful even if intermittent, in the leading place in his theoretical model of how landscape evolves under aridity. Wind he relegated to a very minor supporting role until the phase of Old Age when, with diminished relief and rainfall, he conceded that it might become dominant. Passarge's *Inselberglandschaften*, Sven Hedin's central Asian yardang-fields, and the huge dune-complexes of the Sahara and Arabia, he presumably assigned to this phase of his scheme.

The great expansion of exploration and study of the deserts since Davis produced his paper allows us now to see matters in better perspective. It is apparent that the North American dry lands are by no means typically representative of the arid zones, and that much larger areas than Davis perhaps realised display the sort of characteristics he attributed to 'Old Age'. This is not to say, of course, that they necessarily acquired these by the evolutionary route he charted. As regards present dominant processes, however, we must accept that roughly a quarter of the more arid terrain on Earth is occupied by 'live' dune-fields or *ergs*, while wind has etched distinctive and sometimes deeply-cut patterns into the bedrock over substantial additional tracts of the more arid *Kernwüste*. In all these areas wind might today be held to be self-evidently in the ascendancy over water. At the other extreme, there are equally extensive areas where surface patterns and features leave no doubt that water is wholly dominant; but linking the extremes are huge tracts of pebble-desert (*reg*) and other surfaces where it is difficult to judge from surface appearances alone just where the present process-balance lies. In these zones of uncertainty current opinion generally inclines towards the dominance of water, largely because so many studies in semi-arid terrain have revealed remarkably high rates of water-erosion, the lower frequency and volume of water-flow events as compared with humid lands being more than counter-balanced by the reduction in vegetational protection. As aridity increases, however, the relative power and area of incidence of water-erosion must decrease, and that of wind increase, to some turnover point. Unfortunately we have at present quite inadequate observational data to determine this point for different deserts, and attempts to establish it empirically by inference from observed features are complicated by legacies from past periods of different climate. The identification and evaluation of these legacies present the desert geomorphologist with problems both in-triguing and intractable.

Palaeoclimatic legacies
Although studies are still very incomplete, it seems clear that the present deserts may vary considerably in age, but that all of them have experienced appreciable past oscillations of climate so that their present

landscapes are all in varying degree climatically composite. Even in the driest desert interiors residual mountains reveal abandoned water-cut erosion-surfaces, and are gashed by major canyons from which radiate outwards extensive drainage-channels, the whole being on a scale far greater than can be accounted for by the present restricted and episodic flow-events. The more distal portions of these old drainage-nets are today often part-obliterated, but are directed towards distant interior basins which commonly contain the dry beds of substantial former lakes. Great areas of the intervening plains are mantled by old alluvia, and debris transported by former flash-floods commonly fill the deeper tectonic basins to depths of thousands of feet. Many weathering features in the deserts, together with secondary superficial formations like the various duricrusts, are widely held to have required for their formation substantially more moisture than is available today, while the very sand of the great dune-fields is believed by the majority of students to have been brought together by water, and only sifted and built into dunes by the wind. Most of the relict features pointing to greater former humidity have been attributed to pluvial phases in the Pleistocene, but views differ widely on the number, duration, timing and spatial extension of such claimed pluvials. An equal diversity of opinion characterises ideas about their causation, their connections with the glacials and inter-glacials of higher latitudes, and the degree of climatic change involved. Attempts to quantify the last point have usually involved calculations of the degree of change in the present water-balance needed to restore inland desert lakes the size of Bonneville and Lahontan in the U.S.A., and Mega-Chad and the expanded Makarikari lake in arid Africa, both of which at their maxima matched the Caspian Sea in size. Unfortunately such calculations involve at least two unknown variables, precipitation and evaporation, and estimates of the change in climate necessary vary widely according to assumptions made about ruling temperatures, or rainfall, or both.

The possibilities of inheritances from earlier periods are not, however, confined to the Pleistocene and features carved or built in wetter conditions. All the evidence available seems to confirm the widely-held view that as aridity increases, so the overall rate of landscape change declines; and the logical conclusion would appear to be that, *ceteris paribus*, it is in the driest regions that we are most likely to find mummified relicts of former landscapes of the greatest antiquity. Consistent with this, claims for surviving Tertiary surfaces have been made on many occasions in the Sahara and elsewhere, and even Mesozoic survivals have been suggested (Birot, Capot-Rey and Dresch, 1955). To balance the inherited features of Pleistocene or earlier wetter phases, again, we have plenty of evidence of long periods of earlier aridity at least as severe as anything known today, and such evidence touches closely on the long-debated interpretation of the Qattara Depression and other major hollows as wind-excavated, and equally on the antiquity and palaeoclimatic relations of the great arcs of sand-stone yardangs in Borku (Peel, 1970; Mainguet, 1973). Consideration of these matters must introduce doubts about the validity of some schemes of 'climatic geomorphology', for as Stoddart (1969) has pointed out, we have no generally-accepted criteria for distinguishing geomorphic as distinct from climatic aridity. But case-studies of geomorphic interpretation in the deserts, and inferences drawn from them, are further complicated by the common lack of reliable evidence for dating. Without a certain base-line against which to measure features, and to infer process-rates, one is all too often left speculating whether an observed feature is to be wholly attributed to the present climatic regime, or regarded as a somewhat-modified residual from the Pleistocene, or from even earlier. This scarcity of reliable means of dating features, or phases, is certainly one of the major difficulties in desert work. But an equal handicap is imposed by the current sparsity of reliable measured data about the activities of the different processes at work today modelling desert landscapes, their respective contributions to landscape-shaping, and overall rates of change.

Present-day hydrology: general characteristics and available data

As commonly defined, aridity commences where mean annual precipitation is matched by evapo-transpiration, which in principle implies that there can be no general network of perennial sea-discharging rivers. Such perennial rivers as pass through the deserts are exogenous, drawing their waters from beyond the desert confines, losing water (often heavily) in their desert transects, and influencing landscape evolution only in narrow bands alongside their channels. Endogenous drainage-systems are periodic, intermittent, or episodic in their flow-regimes, and although in many deserts quite a number discharge to sea when in operation, a high fraction are arranged centripetally around enclosed interior basins. It has thus often been stressed that arid lands have 'no common base-level of water-erosion' (whatever the real significance of that may be), and that, until some may coalesce, each basin evolves independently. E. de Martonne (1927) computed that about one-third of the Earth's land-surface has endoreic (interior-basin) drainage, but the close agreement of this figure with Meigs' (1952) figure for the Earth's arid fraction is coincidental, for by no means all land drained endoreically is arid. Again, de Martonne's figure of 23% of the lands as areic, or lacking organised drainage-systems entirely, has been held to be excessive. Leaving these points aside, however, these characteristics of the dry lands present unusual difficulties for the measurement of regional erosion rates. Those relating to wind-erosion are beyond the scope of this essay, but as regards water-action a basic difficulty is that usually there are no major trunk rivers collecting the runoff and water-transported rock-wastes from large terrain divisions.

To obtain mean rates of material removal by the conventional methods would require sediment and solute load gauging on dozens of small independent systems for even one drainage-basin, and a repetition of the whole process for the next. The only alternative would appear to be micro-measurement of the rate of upward growth of the surface in the central playa, but even if practicable this would in all probability be most misleading since in most desert basins only the exceptional flood now reaches the central playa at all, while due allowance would have to be made for wind-removal from the playa in dry periods, and for compaction. But in addition to these intrinsic difficulties, there are the practical problems resulting from the intermittence of water-flows, and their brief and unpredictable occurrence. In the semi-arid fringing lands, channels and arroyos may flow several times a year and in roughly predictable seasons, but as aridity increases both regularity and frequency dwindle, until at the extreme channels still technically live may lie dry and inert for years on end, and then spring briefly into torrential life. In lands largely uninhabited, remote, difficult of access, and presenting formidable financial, logistic and often political problems for protracted visits, the practical difficulties of securing adequate quantitative data about short-lived water-events need no elaboration. Such data as are available not unnaturally vary a good deal in completeness and reliability, and are mainly confined to a scatter of more accessible locations.

Even in the basic matter of precipitation it is not always realised how limited is our information for the great deserts. In Britain the mean density of the recording-station network is roughly one observing-point for each 40 km^2. In the U.S.A as a whole, the figure is some 600 km^2, but is markedly higher in the arid south-west. For his important study of Saharan climates, however, J. Dubief (1959, 1963) could find only about 125 acceptable records scattered unevenly over an area larger than the entire United States, giving a mean station density of about one per 26 000 km^2. In some areas there were gaps of 1000 km between stations. The situation is not much better in some other deserts. Over much of the terrain we thus have no proven information on how much rain reaches the ground, while many records are deficient in details of rain-durations and intensities. We thus cannot locate with certainty the 'driest spot on Earth'. Various stations in the coastal Atacama desert, and in its continuation into southern Peru, have recorded periods of up to fifteen years between measureable rains, and in the driest parts of the Libyan Desert Bagnold (1954) estimated, from indirect evidence, that the mean recurrence-interval of rains sufficient really to moisten the ground might be as high as three decades; but we do not really know. Remote-sensing data from orbiting satellites may help to fill the gaps, for micro-wave sensors can yield data allowing some estimate of quantity of precipitation as well as occurrence. For the hot deserts, however, one must remember the rapid re-evaporation of falling rain as it enters the superheated air layers near the ground. Most desert travellers have experienced the curious sensation of standing under heavy rain visibly streaming from low clouds and not receiving a drop. This phenomenon must contribute importantly to the extreme desiccation of many desert lowlands and superheated basins.

Runoff generation

For assessment of the contribution of water to physiographic change in the deserts basic precipitation data are, however, only the starting-point. Light showers, below the runoff threshold, are significant only in maintaining moisture-supply to the slow processes of rock-weathering, and in that context may be augmented by night dews. In some localities, indeed, as in Namibia, the coastal Atacama, and (surprisingly) parts of the Negev-Sinai desert, annual dew precipitation has been measured to exceed that of rainfall. There are still great areas of uncertainty and argument about the relative importance of different factors and processes in desert weathering, and we have all too few reliable figures for rates. Such as exist point to perhaps the lowest rates in the world, and direct correlation with moisture-availability; a point which would support the trend of modern views in assigning a key role to moisture in the development of typical desert features like desquamation, case-hardening, the growth of weathering-pits and tafoni, surface vermiform markings, and the development of the various desert-varnishes. But for movement of materials away from the site of weathering, i.e. transportive erosion, water can only enter the picture if rainfalls exceed the local runoff threshold, and in conditions where potential annual evaporation may reach several metres, and large areas are blanketed by incoherent sands and gravel, one would expect such thresholds to be notably high. Slatyer and Mabbutt (1965) have indeed estimated that not more than 10% of the rains that fall within the arid zone produce any runoff at all. Yet a surprisingly large fraction of desert surfaces display patterns of recent water-flow, and deserts are notorious for their propensity to engender devastating floods.

As regards the former point, a few attempts have been made to assess the fractions of desert surfaces currently undergoing overland-flow action. Various studies in the sub-arid country of New Mexico and Arizona indicate that virtually all of the terrain there is currently being water-modified (and often remarkably quickly), but few of the major deserts seem to have been studied on these lines. For the Sahara, however, J. Dubief (1965) conducted a survey from maps and air photographs, and concluded that about one-third of that desert is today undergoing active 'ruissellement' on a scale sufficient to be recognisable on these media. He felt that perhaps another third is undergoing less frequent and copious water-action, insufficient to develop recognisable patterns on air photographs, while the remaining third is probably under dominant wind-control. Rain does, of course, occasionally fall over this last third, and Dubief illustrated recent rain-gullying on dune-flanks in the great ergs, but such traces would be very ephemeral. The conclusions reached by M. Teissier (1965) for the Algerian Sahara, based on ground evidence of the scale and frequency of flows in established wadi-systems, accord well with those of Dubief. The Sahara, however, is one of the driest of the great deserts, containing three-quarters of the 'extremely arid' country on Earth according to Meigs (1952). Most other deserts could be expected to show much higher fractions of ground under occasional water-action.

The flooding propensities of deserts are attested by a mass of evidence, although for fairly obvious reasons little of this is coldly scientific. Whole villages in arid lands have not infequently been washed away, as in southern Tunisia in 1969, while desert cities have also been invaded. A major flood damaged some quarters of Cairo in 1919, and Lima has also been severely hit. Dislocation of communications by floods in deserts is commonplace, and railroad records in the U.S.A. show that quite often more than half of the recorded track washouts occur in the driest States of the Union. Such events have led to a widespread belief that when it does rain in the deserts the falls are always of torrential intensity, but the available records by no means bear this out. 'Cloudburst' rains do, indeed, occur, even in the driest lands, at long and erratic intervals. Thus in 1925 at Lima, where the mean rainfall is 48 mm, 1524 mm of rain fell in a series of abnormal storms. Tamanrasset, in the Hoggar Mountains of the Sahara, received in May 1933 48 mm of rain in 63 minutes, while Aouzou, in Tibesti, received in May 1934 the astonishing quantity of 370 mm of rain in three days, its normal ration for about twelve years. In somewhat less arid terrain, Alice Springs, in central Australia, whose mean annual receipt is some 250 mm, has on a number of occasions received more than this in three or four days, as during the exceptional storms and floods of north-eastern Australia in January 1974. But such falls are distinctly abnormal, falling into the category of 'catastrophes' as defined by Wolman and Miller (1960). Slatyer and Mabbutt (1965) found that such abnormal rains are much more common round the margins of deserts than in their interiors, and detailed analyses in various deserts have shown that usually 50% or more of the rains received fall in gentle showers of very moderate intensity. For the whole of the Sahara, Dubief (1965), after a careful analysis, concluded that mean rain-intensities over the desert were little higher than those in France, and in the relatively well-documented American west the records indicate that even the heaviest summer falls seldom approach in volume and intensity the rains accompanying hurricanes striking the Gulf coast and the eastern seaboard. Major floods do, indeed, often appear to have as a contributory factor unusually widespread rains, especially if they should fall across a large concentrating catchment. The 'fifty-year' flood which swept down the Oued Saoura from the Saharan Atlas in April 1959 resulted from rains continued over several days which, although nowhere particularly heavy (maximum point fall recorded was 80 mm), nor particularly intensive (peak intensity recorded was 8 mm in 20 minutes), fell over an area as large as Western Germany, with a large fraction falling within the Bechar-Zousfana-Saoura catchment (Vanney, 1960). But we have plenty of recorded violent floods resulting from much lesser and more short-lived rains.

The effects of terrain characteristics
If the rapid generation of desert floods cannot be attributed to anything exceptional about desert rainfall, the answer must lie in characteristics of the terrain. This has long been believed by many students of the deserts and recent research in Israel has both confirmed and clarified the belief. Among many contributory factors two seem to be particularly important: the normally very slow rate of desert weathering, and the greatly reduced vegetational cover and quantity of edaphic life. Slow weathering rates, with physical disintegration predominating over more extreme chemical alterations, leave much of the terrain very thinly veneered with regolith, particularly on the steeper hill-slopes. Wind-deflation and periodic rain-wash sweep away the small quantities of fines developed, so that these slopes typically show a much higher proportion of exposed bedrock, scattered with coarse fragments, than do comparable slopes in humid climates. The scantiness of vegetation to hold loose material in place is no doubt a contributory factor. The permeability of these steeper rocky slopes naturally varies with lithology and structure, but many would appear to have rather low permeabilities, and to shed water freely once a fairly low threshold has been exceeded. On gentler slopes regolith and soil thickness will usually be somewhat greater, but here other factors come into play. The sparse vegetational cover provides little organic litter on the surface to absorb water, and only a slight feed-in of material to produce humus. Soils thus remain typically lithosols, almost entirely mineral, and often dense and compact in texture. Minimal disturbance by plant roots, and a greatly reduced soil animal population, contribute to this compactness, while on low ground dominantly upward soil-water movements commonly result in sub-surface deposition of salts, which may over long periods thicken up from scattered crystals or lime nodules to thick near-impervious beds of calcrete, silcrete or ferricrete. Detailed observations in southern Israel indicate, however, that the most important factor of all is surface crusting.

Attention has often been drawn to the tendency of desert surfaces to develop crusts of various types (Gerassimov, 1961), but the most widespread and important appears to be a mechanical crust developed by repetitive rain-beat and drying. Virtual absence of interception by vegetation allows rain to hammer the surface with maximum force, while fine particles are re-distributed by splash to lodge in pore-spaces. The process is analogous to puddling, producing a crust one or two centimetres thick, and with greatly reduced permeability. Studies at the Avdat Experimental Farm in the Negev have shown that whereas on disturbed ground infiltration rates may reach 10 mm/hour or more, where this crust exists the rate is reduced to about 2 mm/hour, and any rain at a rate in excess of this is likely to produce overland flow. Interestingly, it was found that the infiltration-rate appeared to vary directly with the density of stone-cover, for the small patches of soil below the stones were protected and did not form the crust. Air trapped in the layers below the crust could there escape, forming vesicular patterns and permitting faster infiltration. At Avdat it was found that by hand-picking all the surface stones off a patch of ground the permeability was quickly reduced after a few rains, and the runoff or water-yield appreciably increased. A further relevant factor is the fraction of swelling clays in the surface layers, for during dry spells these contract and crack, dividing up the crust and increasing initial infiltration at the next rain. As they moisten and swell, however, the clays seal the cracks, infiltration decreases, and runoff markedly augments (Shanan, 1974).

These conclusions from southern Israel offer clues to various phenomena that had long seemed puzzling. For example they confirm observations made elsewhere that low-angle slopes often seem to generate greater runoff yield per unit area than steeper slopes, slopes of 1–2° commonly yielding twice as much water as those at 20°. The explanation proposed is that on the steeper slopes particle mobility, removal of fines, and other factors inhibit the development of the low-permeability crust. Again, rain-intensities in excess of 15 mm/hour have been found to produce a lower runoff yield (proportionally) than those in the range 3–10 mm, apparently because the high-intensity rain damages and may break up the crust. The importance of this mechanical crust is further indicated by a study by A. Yair and others in a small catchment near Sede Boker in the Negev where it was found that a certain section of the ground persistently yielded less runoff, but more eroded fine sediment, than the remainder. Study revealed that this patch contained a particular plant whose roots seemed to be a popular food with isopods and nocturnal ground porcupines. Their diggings for the roots broke up the crust, and threw additional fine material up to the surface (Yair, 1973). This underlines a point made earlier, the significance of the total lack of earthworms, and a much reduced soil population, in the more arid areas. Equally, in the sparsely-inhabited open desert tracts the small number of larger surface-animals must lead to minimal disturbance of the crust by treading. The Israeli studies show substantially greater infiltration-rates in wadi floors than on open hill-slopes, by a factor of 3 to 5. This can presumably be attributed to the deeper layer of mobile materials on the wadi-floor and its more frequent disturbance both by floods, and by the hooves of animals. On the other hand in very remote and unfrequented desert wadis I have often noted a thin hard coating of fine sand and silt, lightly cemented, left by the static final evaporating waters of the last flow which, assuming it remained undisturbed, could well form a short-lived seal assisting the progression of the next flood by reducing immediate infiltration and preventing the egress of trapped air. In contrast to humid countries like Britain, where the antecedent moisture-state of the soil is a highly significant factor in determining whether overland flow develops or not, this factor is usually negligible in the deserts. Rains are separated by such long intervals that it would be most exceptional for the ground to be other than bone-dry prior to a new rain-event, and most rains penetrate the ground only to a very shallow depth. At Avdat it was found that even after an 8-hour wadi-flood the water had moistened the alluvia only to a depth of 8 cm. On open hillsides the wetting-depth seldom exceeds 1—2 cm, and with daily evaporation-rates of 3—5 mm the moisture is soon withdrawn again. These figures support the widely-accepted generalisation that in the arid lands surface water-flows are normally immediate and short-lived reflections of purely surface runoff with little if any longer-term base-flow from seepage. Very little of the normal rainfall over the low ground in the deserts makes any significant contribution to deeper groundwaters, which are often mainly fossil although mountain rains may afford small replenishments. Surface-flow hydrographs are thus typically of the exaggerated 'flash-flood' variety.

These observations and measurements from Israel confirm, and lend precision to, general conclusions that have emerged from various sources over the years. Thus Burmister (1952) published tables relating permeability to the percentage of fine particles in surface materials, and Schumm (1961) found this factor to be of prime importance in studies of sediment erosion and deposition in ephemeral washes in the south-western United States. Various studies by American geologists have indicated that infiltration-rates, and hence runoff-thresholds, show perceptible variations on alluvial fans in the dry country according to their ages, older Pleistocene surfaces being markedly more water-repellent than those more recently formed (Hunt et al, 1966). A higher degree of compaction and surface-crusting probably accounts for the difference. Much work on the infiltration-rates and water-absorbing capacities of different soils in Australia also supports the view that the physical composition of the upper skin of the regolith is the factor of prime importance in dry-land runoff-generation.

Runoff thresholds

The factors discussed would seem to hold the key to the apparently remarkably low runoff thresholds obtaining in many desert terrains, which allow rapid and copious flooding to develop from rains in no way exceptional; but conviction demands supporting quantitative evidence, and at present this is hard to find. In 1967 the I.G.U. Arid Zone Commission, at the author's suggestion, considered attempting to classify desert surfaces in terms of present-day hydrological activity by combining existing precipitational data with representative runoff threshold values for different kinds of terrain, but very few of the latter could be found (Peel, 1967). As early as 1935 L. J. Sutton (1935) estimated that on 'average ground' in Egypt runoff could be approximated by the formula:

$$E = 0.75 (R - 8)$$

where E is the expectable runoff, and R the day's rainfall, both in mm. Dubief (1965), from Algerian experience, concluded that on non-sandy terrain runoff could be expected to occur from any rain in excess of 5 mm, provided that the mean intensity exceeded 0.1 mm/minute. This is a value well above the threshold found to hold for crusted *reg* at Avdat. The extensive range of catchment studies that have been instituted in Israel in recent years are, however, beginning to provide some range of representative figures. On steep, debris-covered crystalline rocks in Sinai, Yair and Klein (1973) have reported observing runoff to start after 3 mm of rain had fallen with a minimum intensity of 1 mm in 3 minutes, this threshold being reduced if the rain started while the rocks were still wet. They found, however, considerable local variations with factors of geology, slope, exposure etc., and suggest that for more general application a fall of 5 mm within one day is likely to be the minimum required. Schick (1970), from a number of studies in the Negev and Sinai, concluded that 'conditions for incipient runoff seem to be satisfied by a variety of conditions of rainfall intensity, rainfall amount, and antecedent moisture', although (as mentioned above) in real aridity the last factor should seldom obtrude. It should perhaps be mentioned that although of the greatest interest and value to the geomorphologist, the Israeli study-programme has more practical primary objectives. Much of the information has come out of studies in connection with 'water-harvesting' for experimental cultivation in the Negev, while evaluation of flood-hazards at desert settlements and on key roads are other objectives.

It is not proposed to discuss the questions of spatial patterns and frequency-distributions of runoff-producing rainfalls further, important as these topics are, since reliable data are so few. It is commonly stated in textbooks that desert rains are 'notably spotty' in distribution, the majority of falls affecting only small areas for brief periods; but the author is not aware of any studies yet done that have produced convincing statistical demonstration of differences between desert and non-desert areas in these aspects of precipitation. They offer, however, an interesting field for study.

Forms of runoff and their effects

A number of general descriptions of arid-land water-flows have been given (e.g. Jahns, 1949; Lowdermilk, 1953; Hadley, 1968), and many terms employed, but the latter have not always been precisely defined. N. M. Fenneman early distinguished between 'concentrated' and 'unconcentrated' wash, the terms 'sheet-wash' and 'rill work' have been used freely, and Davis (1938) proposed a distinction between 'stream-floods' and 'sheet-floods', adopting for the latter form the term popularised by McGee (1897). In efforts to find an explanation for that very characteristic (though by no means universal) feature of the arid lands, the abrupt angular junction or 'knick' between low-angle pied-mont surfaces and the abrupt faces of mountains, a number of authors, notably L. C. King (1949), have postulated a change-over in the form of flow at this point: King suggesting that the turbulent flows down the mountain faces became laminar at this junction. Other observers have, however, contradicted this (and it seems highly improbable, given the velocity limits on laminar flow in water), while if advanced as an explanation of the genesis of the knick, it would appear to have transposed the hen and the egg. Apart from slowly-creeping moisture-films, all types of desert flow would seem to be at least semi-turbulent, observable differences being caused by variations in controlling para-meters. All no doubt grade into one another, but for descriptive purposes it may be acceptable to take Fenneman's distinction and apply it on two scales, dividing dispersed wash from rill-work, and stream-floods from sheet-floods.

Dispersed wash is a type of surface flow made up of a multitude of individually small and very shallow intertwining ribbons of water which commonly develops over the whole of gently-inclined surfaces when the infiltration-rate is exceeded. Individual threads of water tend to migrate laterally so that most of the surface gets worked over, and within the limits of its competence dispersed wash can transport large amounts of fine material. It would appear to be the main agency periodically removing accumulated weathering-fines from scarps and so assisting their retreat. In their studies of the Frijolles arroyo system near Santa Fe, New Mexico, L. B. Leopold and his collaborators (Leopold *et al* 1966) found that dispersed wash contributed by far the greater part of the sediment moving down the channel system, and many other studies have supported this. With the increase of volume downhill on long steeper slopes the sheet-wash may concentrate into *rills*, to give Fenneman's 'concentrated' form. Such rills may dig their channels a metre or more into the ground, but on the longer time-scale the rills may also migrate laterally, possibly by the sort of mechanism that Bryan (1940) suggested.

The *stream-flood* can be thought of as a macro-form of the rill-flow, in that it is normally generated in hilly or mountainous country and rushes down a confining canyon or wadi as an isolated event, often spaced out at long and irregular intervals. In a large canyon-system, with extensive catchment, the flood may pour down the previously-dry valley with a steep wave-like front, trains of succeeding waves or surges marking the contributions of tributaries. The discharge-curve leaps up from zero to a peak, perhaps followed by other peaks, before dropping back more slowly to zero. Durations of such flows can last from a few hours to days or even weeks, according to the size of catchment and duration of the rain. Their frontal waves advance with astonishing speed, and as wadi-beds and banks are usually copiously provided with loose materials they pick up vast quantities of rock-wastes and debris. The concentration of load may indeed reach such high figures that the flood becomes effectively a debris-flow. In such a flood in a wadi tributary to the Arava rift in southern Israel Schick (1971) recorded a mean flow-velocity at the peak of 7 metres/second, and mean sediment concentrations of 25%, with an estimated maximum of 50%. Such figures overlap into those of true mud-flows (Sharp and Nobles, 1953), and the vastly increased mean density and viscosity greatly increase the transporting-power of such floods. Particle settling-velocities are much reduced, and 'the submerged weight of a rock is reduced perhaps by over 60%' (Hooke, 1967), so that huge boulders can be transported and are sometimes carried out into the plains. During their spasms of activity stream-floods thus carry out a lot of physiographic work very quickly, but the shortness and variable timings and magnitudes of their flows offer little opportunity for the development of equilibrium conditions. Their valleys thus typically show marked irregularities in thalweg (particularly in the upper portions), while as weathering-rates are typically very low, valleys tend to remain gorge-like in cross-profile. Variations in lithology and structure, however, may combine to produce a wide variety of valley-forms.

Emerging from their canyons on to the piedmont zone stream-floods commonly break up into diverging distributaries, individually broad and shallow and liable to shifts of position, as the flood traverses the characteristic alluvial fan or pediment. Factors often cited to explain this change include the removal of the restraining canyon walls, the beginnings of reduction of discharge, some reduction of gradient, and consequent 'overloading' (sic), but the complete explanation does not appear to have been elucidated. Typical of this zone, however, is the relative shortness of the distance within which the flood changes over from being dominantly erosive-transportive, to being dominantly depositional. The critical transition-point, moreover, can migrate backward up the wadi-'estuary', or advance into the fan zone, with slight changes in the balance of conditions (Hooke, 1967). Fans and pediments, although distinguished in principle as respectively constructed and eroded, are often morphologically very similar, serve much the same hydrological purpose, and may grade into one another. Both still present problems of explanation, to solve which some students have felt it necessary to invoke climatic change, for example Lustig (1965) in relation to alluvial fans along the Californian edge of the Great Basin, and Oberlander (1972) to explain the classic Mohave Desert pediments. Some fans and pediments remain superficially remarkably smooth, but others currently display deep dissection by arroyo-like gullies. Studies by Cooke (1973) on the histories of arroyos in Arizona have shown how delicately-balanced hydraulic conditions can be in this transition zone, and how apparently trivial changes can locally swing water-flows from aggradation to erosion and vice versa.

Not all mountain-piedmont junctions, however, follow this pattern. In some areas where plateaux of massive sandstone rise from flattish plains, both wadis and wadi-piedmont junctions show intriguing relationships as described by Peel (1962) in western Tibesti, and Mainguet (1967) in western Ennedi. In both of these cases successive uplifts have elevated the Lower Palaeozoic sandstones, and the edges of the sandstone beds, almost horizontally-bedded and cut by several sets of near-vertical joints, have retreated to form steep cliffs. Detached outliers, in various stages of back-weathering and dissection, range from flat-topped mesas to tall slender rock-needles, while in the plateaux themselves almost vertical-walled *enneri* gorges have been deeply cut in patterns governed by the geometry of the joints and faults. In the steep walls of these valleys sub-vertical joints can be seen to have been eroded out deep below the plateau surface into a network of pipes, tunnels and caves, and in heavy rain on the plateaux most of the water flows down the opened joint-planes to gush out of the subterranean honeycomb at *enneri*-floor level. The main *enneris*, their floors mantled with sand, merge into the surrounding plains without the intervention of any perceptible fan or pediment, and the groups of isolated rock-needles also often rise from virtually flat surfaces with little or no pediment. The keys to this kind of development appear to be the permeability of the sandstone down its high-angle joints, and the fact that on weathering it produces no particles intermediate in size between large blocks and coarse sand. The extent of the development of subterranean drainage, to a degree normally thought to be confined to limestone, also deserves comment. In connection with this kind of sandstone plateau country, a further point of probable importance relates to the effects of rainfall seeping down through the strata to emerge close to the scarp-foot. Peel (1941) suggested this as a possibly important factor assisting scarp retreat and more recently Schumm and Chorley (1966) have emphasised it as well, in studies of scarp-retreat around the Colorado Plateau. Twidale (1967) and others have also appealed to the persistence of moisture, and hence a higher weathering-rate, to explain the sharp angular knick between domical inselbergs and their surroundings.

The fourth distinctive type of desert water-flow identifiable would seem to be the *sheet-flood*, which might be described as dispersed wash on the grand scale. The classic description of a sheet-flood in action was given by McGee (1897), while Jutson (1914, 1919) early described Australian examples. Subsequent descriptions are not, however, particularly common, for the phenomenon seems to occur somewhat rarely.

Intrinsically the sheet-flood appears to be a far-flung moving carpet of water spread out over a tract of desert, sometimes more than a mile wide, resulting from a sudden heavy downpour. A few descriptions in the journals of explorers speak of the entire landscape being inundated, but this must be very exceptional. In the case described by McGee the flood developed from a severe thunderstorm over an area of hills, and presumably was initially a stream-flood confined to their valleys, but spread abroad on emerging to flow over the pediment zone. It consisted of a network of interweaving shallow flows, several metres wide and up to 30 cm deep, above which minor hillocks and bushes emerged. Heavily charged with mud and debris, it advanced rapidly with a rolling motion exhibiting transverse waves and elongated patches of scour-and-fill. As the fluidity decreased the movement rapidly slowed, with numerous blockages and spurts, until it came to rest and all the water disappeared. Examination of their traces shows that sheet-floods can on occasion attain a width of several kilometres, and by repetition they must intermittently carry large volumes of detritus towards bolsons and playas. Earlier theories explaining the formation of pediments by their action seem, however, to be erroneous in that a fairly smooth low-angle slope must exist before water could flow across it in this fashion. Sheet-floods seem to grade into the related phenomenon of mudflows as described by Blackwelder (1928), but as they are difficult to catch and study in action we can only guess at their frequency-distributions from the traces they leave.

Magnitudes and erosional effects of surface flows

Having described the main kinds of surface water-action in the deserts it is frustrating not to be able to furnish more quantitative information about magnitudes, frequencies, and resultant erosional effects. A few illustrative figures may, however, be quoted.

In the central Australian floods of 1967 the heavy rains over the eastern Macdonnells and around Alice Springs sent huge volumes of water south-eastwards down the Todd, Finke, and Neales rivers. Water invaded the margins of the Simpson Desert and lapped between the dune-ridges, and some six weeks later a modest flow reached Lake Eyre via the Macumba channel, having travelled 650 to 800 km. Normally dry, the Finke river overtopped its banks to an average width of several kilometres, and was gauged at one point to be 6.95 metres deep. Its peak discharge was estimated at 1200 m³/second, and in its upper parts its peak mean velocity reached 3 m/second. Many bridges on the Port Augusta—Alice Springs railway were swept away, and communications severed for weeks over huge areas (Williams, 1970). In the 1959 flood in the Oued Saoura, Algerian Sahara, an estimated 2×10^{10} m^3 of water poured down the main channel into the desert, with peak flow on emergence from the mountains of 4000–5000 m^3/second. This had diminished to about 1000 m^3/second at Beni Abbes, 120 km downstream. Peak velocities were estimated at 2.4 m/second at Abadla, 3.1 m/second at Beni Abbes, and 3.4 m/second at Kerkaz, this downstream increase being attributed to constriction in the valley (Vanney, 1960). This flood ran some 400–500 km into the desert before coming to rest, and would seem to rank with major historical floods in this system. The longest flow on record reached some 800 km from the mountains (Dubief, 1965), but even this is only two-thirds of the distance to the sunken sebkhas of Tidikelt towards which the Saoura channel appears to be directed, and which were no doubt reached by Pleistocene floods. One point of interest about these major and far-travelled floods is how they survive to reach such distances despite the very high rates of water-loss. Dubief (1965, 1967) has suggested that a contributory factor could well be their generation of a protective micro-climate in the form of a blanket of near-saturated air above them preventing rapid diffusion and so reducing the evaporation-rate.

As regards the quantities of rock-wastes moved intermittently downhill within the deserts, and here and there exported to sea from them, by these various kinds of occasional water-flow, we have so far regrettably little information. In the last decade or two there has been a marked revival of interest in comparative regional or zonal erosion-rates in relation to factors of climate and, to some degree, of relief. Comparative tables and graphs on a world basis have been produced by Corbel (1959, 1964), Wolman and Miller (1960), Fournier (1960), and Strakhov (1967), plotting mean erosional-rates against climatic and relief criteria. That the correlations displayed vary somewhat between these tabulations is scarcely surprising, given the simplifications necessary and the limitations of the raw data, but all agree in claiming a markedly high rate of water-erosion to characterise the semi-arid lands, whereas in the really arid deserts the rate drops away rapidly to world minimal levels. The data for the semi-arid lands used in these summaries have been largely those available from the American South-West, and stemming from the field-studies of Leopold, Langbein, Miller, Emmett, Schumm and others in direct measurement of sediment-transport by arroyo flows, together with measurement of sedimentation-rates behind dams and in reservoirs. All the data indicate an astonishingly high rate of water-erosion in the form of suspended sediment, although relatively little solution-removal (Leopold *et al*, 1966; Langbein and Schumm, 1958). The accepted explanation has earlier been indicated: that up to a certain point, at least, erosion by water increases with increasing aridity, because the reduction of vegetational protection of the ground, with consequent increased erosional efficiency, more than compensates for the dwindling frequency, volume, and duration of water-erosional events. Beyond that point, however, the balance must begin to swing the other way, and some interest attaches to the 'turn-over' point. The graphs of Langbein and Schumm (1958) suggest maximum erosion at an *effective* rainfall level of about 300–380 mm (effective rainfall being defined as that which goes into runoff, after initial evaporative and other losses). The set of graphs later produced by Schumm (1965) suggest that for a mean annual temperature of 21°C maximal erosion should occur with a precipitation of around 600 mm. Most of the Sahara has a mean temperature in excess of 21°C, but the conventional boundaries of the desert fall within the 200 mm isohyet to the south, and march close to the 100 mm in the north. The whole of the Sahara is thus considerably too dry to be anywhere near the 'semi-arid maximum' defined by the authors cited; and indeed similar tests for other deserts suggest that all of Meigs' (1952) 'Arid' and 'Extremely Arid' divisions are in like case. Climatically, the belts of maximum erosional rate seem to lie within the semi-arid transitional lands, well clear of the deserts proper.

For the latter, measured rates of erosion and/or sedimentation are notably few. In enclosed basins north of Death Valley Lustig (1965) estimated sedimentation rates at between 3 and 6 mm/year, but these were in limited areas and under rainfalls varying from 75 to 300 mm. In the more distinctly arid Arava rift of southern Israel Schick, from measurements taken at a number of experimental catchments, has estimated that material is being water-transported from the whole area draining towards the rift valley on the western side at a mean rate of 0.3 mm/year, which would yield a mean aggradation-rate for the much smaller rift-valley floor of about 1 mm/year — a rate of surface rise which, as he says, just matches the rate of worldwide eustatic sea-level rise, and should thus prevent the progressive drowning of the rift-valley floor (Schick, 1971). A few other point-measurements could be quoted, but the data are far too few to tell us much. From the evidence outlined it seems reasonable to conclude that in terms of water-erosion all the deserts have mean rates well below world averages, and also considerable variations within themselves, with limited sections changing relatively fast, but huge areas undergoing very little modification at all under present conditions. For the drier areas, the devising of means to measure physiographic change-rates presents formidable problems. Indeed, standing on a horizon-wide carpet of level and wind-beaten *reg* in the middle of the Sahara, a gravel coating containing undisturbed Palaeolithic tools lying where their makers dropped them perhaps twenty thousand years ago, one has a feeling of unchanging timelessness, and a wonder whether human ingenuity will ever be able to measure the microscopic changes that are all that seem now to occur.

REFERENCES

Bagnold, R. A. (1954). 'Physical aspects of dry deserts', in Cloudsley—Thompson, J. L. (Ed.), *The Biology of Deserts*, Institute of Biology, London, 7—12.

Birot, P., R. Capot-Rey and J. Dresch (1955). 'Récherches morphologiques dans le Sahara central', *Travaux de l'Institut de Récherches Sahariennes*, 13, 13—74.

Blackwelder, E. (1928). 'Mudflow as a geologic agent in semi-arid mountains', *Bull. Geological Society of America*, 39, 465—84.

Bryan, K. (1940). 'Gully gravure: a method of slope retreat', *J. Geomorphology*, 3, 87—107.

Burmister, D. M. (1952). *Soil Mechanics*, Columbia University Press.

Cooke, R. U. (1973). Personal report on studies in progress.

Corbel, J. (1959) 'Vitesse de l'érosion', *Zeitschrift für Geomorphologie*, N. F. 3, 1—28.

Corbel, J. (1964). 'L'érosion terrestre, étude quantitative (méthodes — techniques-résultats)', *Annales de Géographie*, 73, 385—412.

Davis, W. M. (1905). 'The geographical cycle in an arid climate', *J. Geology*, 13, 381—407.

Davis, W. M. (1938). 'Sheetfloods and streamfloods', *Bull. Geological Society of America*, 49, 1337—416.

De Martonne, E. (1927). 'Regions of interior-basin drainage', *Geographical Review*, 17, 397—414.

Dubief, J. (1959 and 1963). *'Le Climat du Sahara'*, Vols. I and II, Mémoire hors serie de l'Institut de Récherches Sahariennes.

Dubief, J. (1965). 'Le problème de l'eau superficielle au Sahara', *La Météorologie*, VI, 77, 3—32.

Dubief, J. (1967) 'Les pluies, les crues, et leurs effets au Sahara', unpublished communication to International Geographical Union Arid Zone Symposium, Lima.

Fournier, F. (1960) *Climat et Érosion: la Relation entre l'Érosion du Sol par l'Eau et les Précipitations Atmosphériques*, Presses Universitaires de France.

Gerassimov, P. (1961). 'Self-defence of arid regions against processes of denudation', unpublished communication to International Geographical Union Arid Zone Symposium, Iraklion.

Hadley, R. F. (1968). 'Ephemeral streams', in Fairbridge, R. W. (Ed.), *Encyclopaedia of Geomorphology*, 312—14.

Hooke, R. le B. (1967). 'Processes on arid-region alluvial fans', *J. Geology*, 75, 438—60.

Hunt, C. B., T. W. Robinson, W. A. Bowles and A. L. Washburn (1966). 'Hydrologic basin: Death Valley, California', *U.S. Geological Survey Professional Paper*, 494 B.

Jahns, R. H. (1949). 'Desert floods', *Engineering and Science Journal*, 12, 10—24.

Jutson, J. T. (1914). 'Physiography of Western Australia', Geol. Surv. W. Australia, Bull. 61.

Jutson J. T. (1919). 'Sheet-flows or sheet floods and their associated phenomena', *American Journal of Science*, 48, 435—39.

King, L. C. (1949). 'The pediment landform: some current problems', *Geological Magazine*, 86, 245—50.

Langbein, W. B. and S. A. Schumm (1958). 'Yield of sediment in relation to mean annual precipitation', *Trans. American Geophysical Union*, 39, 1076—84.

Leopold, L. B., W. W. Emmett and R. M. Myrick (1966). 'Channel and hillslope processes in a semi-arid area, New Mexico', *U.S. Geological Survey Professional Paper*, 352 G, 193—253.

Lowdermilk, W. C. (1953). 'Floods in deserts', in *Desert Research: Proc. International Symposium*, Research Council of Israel Special Publications No. 2, 365—77.

Lustig, L. K. (1965) 'Clastic sedimentation in Deep Springs Valley, California', *U.S. Geological Survey Professional Paper*, 352 F, 131—92.

Mainguet, M. (1967). 'La bordure occidentale de l'Ennedi', *Travaux de l'Institut de Récherches Sahariennes*, 26, 7—65.

Mainguet, M. (1973). *Le Modelé des Grès: Problèmes Généraux*, Vols. I and II, Institut de Géographie National, Paris.

McGee, W. J. (1897). 'Sheet-flood erosion', *Bull. Geological Society of America*, 8, 87—112.

Meigs, P. (1952). 'World distribution of arid and semi-arid homoclimates', in *Reviews of Research on Arid Zone Hydrology*, UNESCO, 203—10 and maps.

Oberlander, T. M. (1972). 'Pediment formation in the Mojave Desert, California', in *International Geography 1972*, papers delivered at the 22nd International Geographical Congress, Montreal, Vol. I, 47—49, Toronto University Press.

Peel, R. F. (1941). 'Denudational landforms of the central Libyan Desert', *J. Geomorphology*, 5, 3—23.

Peel, R. F. (1962). 'Landforms of Western Tibesti', unpublished communication to International Geographical Union Arid Zone Symposium, Iraklion.

Peel, R. F. (1967). 'Surface runoff in deserts and its geomorphological significance', unpublished communication to International Geographical Congress Arid Zone Symposium, Lima.

Peel, R. F. (1970). 'Landscape sculpture by wind' *Papers, 21st. International Geographical Congress, India*, Vol. I, 99—104, National Committee for Geography, Calcutta.

Schick, A. P. (1970). 'Desert floods: interim results of observations in the Nahel Yael watershed, southern Israel, 1965—70', *IASH/UNESCO Symposium, Wellington, N.Z.*, UNESCO, 478—93.

Schick, A. P. (1971). 'A desert flood: physical characteristics; effects on man, geomorphic significance, human adaptation. A case study of the southern Arava watershed', *Jerusalem Studies in Geography*, 2, 91—155.

Schumm, S. A. (1961). 'Effects of sediment characteristics on erosion and deposition in ephemeral-stream channels'. *U.S. Geological Survey Professional Paper*, 352C, 31—70.

Schumm, S. A. and R. J. Chorley (1966). 'Talus weathering and scarp recession in the Colorado Plateaus', *Zeitschrift für Geomorphologie*, N.F.10.1, 11—36.

Schumm, S. A. and R. W. Lichty (1965). 'Time, space and causality in geomorphology', *American Journal of Science*, 263, 110—19.

Shanan, L. (1974). Communication to International Geographical Union Israel Symposium, March 1974, on Geomorphic Processes in Arid Environments, (unpublished).

Sharp, R. P. and L. H. Nobles (1953). 'Mudflow of 1941 at Wrightwood, Southern California', *Bull. Geological Society of America*, 64, 547—60.

Slatyer, R. O. and J. A. Mabbutt (1965). 'Hydrology of arid and semi-arid regions', in Chow, V. T. (Ed.), *Handbook of Applied Hydrology*, McGraw Hill.

Stoddart, D. R. (1969). 'Climatic geomorphology; review and reassessment', in

Board, C., R. J. Chorley, P. Haggett and D. R. Stoddart (Eds.), *Progress in Geography*, I, Arnold.

Strakhov, N. M. (1967), in S. I. Tomkieff and J. E. Hemingway (Eds.), *Principles of Lithogenesis*, Oliver and Boyd.

Sutton, L. J. (1935). *Rainfall in Egypt*, Survey Dept., Cairo.

Teissier, M. (1965). 'Les crues d'oueds au Sahara Algérien de 1950 à 1961', *Travaux de l'Institut de Récherches Sahariennes*, 24, 1–29.

Twidale, C. R. (1967). 'Origin of the piedmont angle as evidenced in South Australia', *J. Geology*, 75, 393–411.

Vanney J. R. (1960). 'Pluie et crue dans le Sahara Nord-Occidental'. *L'Institut de Récherches Sahariennes, Monographies Régionales*, No. 4.

Williams, G. E. (1970). 'The central Australian stream-floods of February-March 1967', *J. Hydrology*, 11, 185–200.

Wolman, M. G. and J. F. Miller (1960). 'Magnitude and frequency of forces in geomorphic processes', *J. Geology*, 68, 54–74.

Yair, A. (1973). 'Sources of runoff and sediment supplied by the slopes of a first-order drainage-basin in an arid environment (N. Negev, Israel)', International Geographical Union/Akad. der Wissenschaften in Göttingen Symposium, Göttingen (cyclostyled).

Yair, A. and M. Klein (1973). 'The influence of surface properties on flow and erosion processes on debris-covered slopes in an arid area', *Catena*, 1, 1–18.

Chapter 6

The Problems of Limestone Dry Valleys — Implications of Recent Work in Limestone Hydrology

David Ingle Smith

Landscape can be considered as the expression of a complex inter-relationship of climate, geology and process. The relationships are marginally easier to decipher if such studies are undertaken in regions dominated by a single lithology. The one widely occurring lithology on which distinctive landscape morphologies have for long been recognised is limestone. Limestone terrains are considered as a special case of rock dominance due to the relatively simple geochemistry of the weathering process, which is generally considered to be of a solutional nature. Early studies by Davies, Grund and Cvijic recognised the special nature of limestone landscapes and each of these workers outlined a sequential development for the landforms found in such regions. Subsequent work has elaborated this simple picture and, in keeping with the changing overall approach to landscape evolution, has shown that the differences that exist in the landscape between individual limestone areas are a result of climatic influences. Thus the morpho-climatic approach applied to general landscape evolution has its proponents in the more restricted case of areas developed solely on limestone lithologies. Lehmann (1936) considered that the observed differences in mor-phology of temperate and humid tropical limestone areas were due to differing climates. Later workers extended this approach to recognise distinctive limestone landscapes associated with more detailed climatic sub-divisions. For example, Tricart and Da Silva (1960) recognize a sub-humid karst in Brazil and Jennings and Sweeting (1963) a tropical semi-arid karst type in northern Australia. The situation arose where the geological factors in a limestone region were considered as generally similar and topographical differences were due to variations in process that were climatically determined. A simple relationship of limestone morphology to climatic conditions is, however, not sufficient to explain the observed landscape variations that occur within a single morpho-climatic region. Jennings (1971, p. 195) has summed up the current view of many limestone geomorphologists in the following manner: '. . . all efforts to distinguish climatomorphogenic systems other than those associated with climatic extremes must be regarded as tentative in terms of present knowledge.'

Turning to the actual landform elements that are responsible for the distinctive nature of limestone morphology, it is clear that we have only two consistently recurring major forms, namely dry valleys and enclosed depressions. Indeed, these two features are only commonly found in limestone regions and/or in regions of climatic aridity. The size and spatial organization of these two landscape elements can show very considerable variations, which are more likely to be determined by the structural and hydrological properties of the limestones involved than by the climate. An understanding of the relationships of the dry valleys to the subterranean drainage and its evolution would perhaps provide the key to the variations exhibited by limestone landscapes. The structural key may well be a more useful tool than its climatic counterpart. It is this relationship which will form the theme of this study.

Hypotheses for dry valley formation

Dry valleys occur in the limestone landscapes of every major climatic zone with the exception of areas affected by continuous permafrost. The origins of dry valley networks have been discussed for well over a century and the majority of the hypotheses for their formation were suggested many decades ago. These hypotheses can be divided into three major groups:

1. Differing climates in the past:
   (a) permafrost;
   (b) increased rainfall in the past.
2. Superimposition of the drainage net from non-limestone strata.
3. A fall in the level of the water table occasioned by:
   (a) a relative uplift of the land mass;
   (b) incision of the major valleys and therefore a lowering of the regional water table;
   (c) scarp recession.

Permafrost

This mode of formation was clearly described by Reid (1887) nearly a century ago, although the term permafrost is of later derivation. Reid was concerned with a study of the Chalk valleys and Coombe Rock deposits of the South Downs. He recognized that conditions in southern England during the Pleistocene:

'. . . would give a mean temperature in the south of England very considerably below freezing point: consequently all the rocks not protected by snow would be permanently frozen to a depth of several hundred feet. [Such freezing] . . . would modify the entire system of drainage of the country. . . all rocks would be equally and entirely impervious to water, all springs would fail . . . with consequent stoppage of all underground circulation in the south of England.' (Reid, 1887, pp. 369 and 370.)

That continuous permafrost has such effects is indisputable. The form of surface drainage in limestone regions with contemporary permafrost is indistinguishable from the drainage on juxtaposed non-limestone strata.

However, it must be realized that former periglacial conditions were not responsible for the formation of the valleys but only for their modification when surface flows re-occupied a pre-existing valley network. In many cases, as on the Chalk, the modifications are likely to have been of limited importance. Evidence presented by Findlay (1965) for the existence of fans of coarse, waterlaid gravels around the periphery of the Mendip Hills suggests that surface flow is likely to have occurred along the gorges of Mendip during the later cold phases of the Pleistocene. Such flows may have been responsible for the marked change in morphology of, for example, the gorge sections of the lower part of the now dry Cheddar Gorge valley system when compared to the morphologically different network of the upper section of the same catchment on the Mendip Plateau.

The contemporary effects of permafrost are confined to high latitude regions; the former extension of permafrost re-activated pre-existing dry valley networks with, in the main, only minor modifications to the landscape. Permafrost cannot be, in any way, an essential prerequisite for the formation of dry valleys, since dry valleys are found in all latitudes including those well beyond the maximum limits suggested for permafrost at any phase within the Pleistocene, or at any other time period.

Increased rainfall in the past
It is not surprising that such a simple explanation for dry valleys should occur in the early literature. Tylor (1875), for example, suggested that the Chalk valleys of England were best explained by postulating enormous increases in precipitation in the past. More recently, Dury (1954) has suggested a marked increase in run-off in Britain during the Pleistocene. He argued that such changes would have affected the Chalk valleys and that the present dry valleys are due to a subsequent

lowering of the water table '. . . due primarily to climatic change rather than to erosion'.

Superimposition from non-limestone strata
This suggested origin for limestone dry valleys has the advantage that the dry valley network would have been pre-determined by the evolution accomplished on non-limestone strata, but we are left with the problem of the disappearance of the surface stream network and its replacement by an underground system. A possible series of events has been suggested by Warwick (1964) for the dry valley network of the southern Pennines. The drainage pattern is thought here to have been superimposed from an overlying cover of Namurian shales.

A fall in the level of the water table
The major hypotheses were all well understood before the end of the last century and Reid could write in 1887 (p. 366) that '. . . other geologists have tried to overcome it [the formation of dry valleys] by an appeal to the former submergence and consequent rise in the level of the plane of saturation; or to a former higher level of the plane of saturation before the valleys had been cut to their present depth'. Reid penned these comments with respect to the Chalk, where the existence of a well formed plane of saturation (or water table) is a meaningful proposition.

The former case, which leaves a dry valley pattern when sea level falls with an associated drop in the height of the water table, has been particularly appealing to workers attempting to explain dry valley patterns developed on raised reefs. One such early example is afforded by the views of Harrison and Jukes-Brown (1890) for the dry valleys on the sequences of raised reefs which fringe the west coast of Barbados.

An ingenious application of the falling water table hypothesis appears to have been first described by Chandler (1909) and sub-sequently elaborated by Fagg (1923, 1954). Scarp recession lowers the altitude of the spring line which is situated, in Fagg's example, at the junction of the Chalk aquifer with the impermeable Gault Clay beneath. The decreasing height of the spring line with progressive scarp retreat causes a fall in the water table and consequently the valley system becomes dry. However, such a mechanism must be considered as a special case since it is necessary for the rocks involved to have a gentle uniclinal dip.

Dry valleys and hydrology
The worldwide occurrence of dry valleys in all forms of limestone and in virtually all climates demonstrates that none of the hypotheses outlined above can have a general application although all could have

exerted some influence in modifying the evolution and form of dry valleys in a local context.

The initial formation of a river network in limestone areas and its subsequent evolution into 'dry' valleys is undoubtedly closely related to the form and evolution of the groundwater hydrology. This is not exactly comparable from one limestone lithology to another. Groundwater movement is controlled by the porosity and permeability of the rock through which the water is moving. The porosity of a rock is a measure of the volume of the interstices and voids as a ratio of the total volume. This is normally expressed as a percentage and varies from values of less than 1% for the crystalline limestone typical of much of the British Carboniferous Limestone to well over 50% for recent coral limestones. However, the more important measure of porosity is that of 'effective porosity' which is expressed as the percentage of the total volume occupied by interconnected interstices suitable for the transmission of water. Effective porosity can, in some cases, differ greatly form porosity *senso stricto*. In clays, for example, the effective porosity is virtually zero while the porosity *senso stricto* can exceed 50%.

Permeability is most easily considered as a measure of the rate at which water can be transmitted through a rock. Further definitions are possible but for our purposes permeability will be used in this general sense, and the term hydraulic conductivity will be used to express the rate of water movement in metres per unit time. For a consideration of the definitions of the various groundwater terms in common usage reference should be made to Lohman *et al* (1972). The general case for permeability is described by Darcy's Law which can be expressed as:

$$v = K \frac{dh}{dl}$$

where v is the velocity of water movement, K the hydraulic conductivity and dh/dl is the hydraulic gradient.

Of particular importance to a study of limestone groundwater hydrology is the sub-division of permeability into primary and secondary permeability. Primary permeability can be determined in a laboratory on small rock samples by the use of various permeameter techniques. It is a measure of intergranular flow. However, it is clear that for massive crystalline limestones, particularly those affected by the solutional enlargement of bedding planes, joints and the like, the permeability relevant to field conditions will be very different from that obtained on small rock samples in the laboratory. Secondary permeability can only be found from field investigation and is a combination of both intergranular flow and fissure flow. In massive crystalline limestones the intergranular flow is likely to be only a very small fraction of the fissure flow.

In the British literature, a selection of which was reviewed above, much of the discussion of dry valleys is particularly concerned with areas of Chalk outcrop. The normal model portrayed for the ground-water circulation within the Chalk involves a water table. In such cases there is a distinct level of saturation which is normally mapped from the standing water level in wells. Considerations of water movement are generalized so that the rock is implicitly assumed to have true Darcian flow in a fully isotropic medium. For the water movement to obey Darcy's Law we have a situation where the field and laboratory determinations of hydraulic conductivity would be broadly similar and the flow would be fully laminar. This situation for Chalk aquifers is, as we shall see below, not strictly true although the assumptions of Darcy's Law and of isotropic flow form the working model for much applied study in such rocks. However, when massive crystalline limestones are considered there is considerable doubt whether the concepts of a general water table, laminar flow and near isotropism of the rock are of value in either an applied sense or in an academic consideration of the evolution of dry valleys.

The hydrology of the Chalk
Literature presenting good quantitative data on Chalk groundwater hydrology has, until recently, been rather sparse. An account of the permeability of the Chalk of England applicable to the dry valley problem was presented by Ineson (1962). Ineson produced a map of 'isotrans' for the area of the Chalk outcrop (reproduced here as Figure 6.1). An 'isotrans' is a line of equal 'transmissibility', a term which has now been largely replaced by 'transmissivity'. Transmissivity is itself defined as the product of the hydraulic conductivity and the thickness of the aquifer. The map of isotrans can, for our purposes, be regarded as a measure of the permeability. The map is based on information obtained from pumping test data on Chalk wells, the overall density of wells being about one per km^2.

Ineson also undertook laboratory determinations on the hydraulic conductivity of Chalk samples and obtained values of less than 0.1 m/day. These values are far too low to explain the large yields obtained from most Chalk wells in the area under consideration. Ineson (1962, p. 457) summed up his views on the groundwater flow of the Chalk as follows, '. . . the intercommunicating fissure systems are of paramount importance, and variations in flow pattern and in transmissibility must be examined from this respect . . . the ground-water flow through the aquifer takes place primarily through the fissure system.'

From Figure 6.1 it can be seen that there are zones in the Chalk where the values of transmissivity are particularly great. Further, these zones correspond to major valley systems most of which are now dry. The relationship between zones of high transmissivity and valleys argues for a common cause. As Ineson suggests, the initial river courses may have been controlled by the initial fissure pattern in the Chalk but an important consideration is that fluctuations of groundwater levels

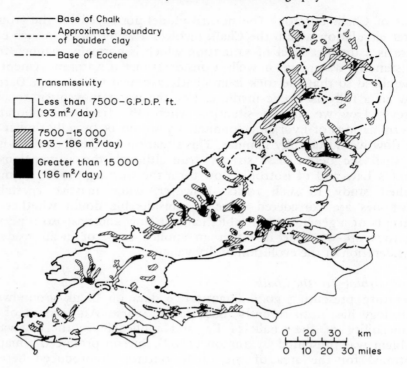

———— Base of Chalk

- - - - Approximate boundary
         of boulder clay

—·—·— Base of Eocene

Transmissivity

☐ Less than 7500–G.P.D.P. ft.
     (93 m²/day)

▨ 7500–15 000
     (93–186 m²/day)

■ Greater than 15 000
     (186 m²/day)

```
0   20  30    km
├──┼───┤
0  10  20  30 miles
```

Figure 6.1   Variations in the permeability of the Chalk in southern England.
(After Ineson, 1962.)

would have 'encouraged solution effects'. It is also worth noting that
similar branching networks of high transmissivity continue even where
the Chalk is covered by younger deposits of either Lower Tertiary
strata or Pleistocene glacial deposits.

The salient features observed by Ineson have, in general, been
reinforced by later work. Headworth (1972) presents a detailed study
of the data from twelve well recorders in the Hampshire Downs. For
nine of these wells the transmissivity values ranged from 43 m²/day to
nearly 3000 m²/day. The other three wells gave values of 5050, 10 100
and 28 600 m²/day but these are considered, for various reasons, to be
slightly inflated. Headworth also draws attention to the disparity in
hydraulic conductivity values obtained by Smith et al (1970) from
analyses based on measurements of natural tritium levels. These values
suggest that the vertical rate of seepage of water through the Chalk
above the water table is less than 1.0 m/yr. Headworth notes that the
response time of well levels to heavy rain suggests a seepage rate of
approximately 10 m/hr.

The results reported by Ineson have been verified in detail from a
local study by Edmunds et al (1973) from the Winterbourne valley near
Newbury. Detailed measurements from a borehole with a depth of

about 130 m show that '... the estimated bulk permeability of the Chalk aquifer and its intergranular permeability differ by many orders of magnitude'. The figures they present suggest a mean hydraulic conductivity for the intergranular flow of less than 0.001 m/day (with relatively little variation between vertical and horizontal values) and a bulk hydraulic conductivity of some 30 m/day, a difference of the order of some 30 000. A further fascinating addition to the techniques employed in studying the movement of water within the saturated zone is the use of borehole television. This method, and results obtained by its use, are described by Tate *et al* (1971). Briefly, borehole television pictures clearly demonstrate that water movement within certain zones below the saturation level is sufficient to move streamers and fine grained sediment and that the water at these points appears to be moving from distinct fissures that can be seen in the sides of the borehole.

Thus there is a marked range for the values of hydraulic conductivity in the Chalk. The Chalk areas of Britain, when compared to other limestone lithologies, have relatively few swallet streams. This may reflect either differences in hydrological properties between differing limestones, or the fact that in few localities is there an impermeable rock cover topographically higher than the Chalk. Small swallet streams have been described from South Mimms in Hertfordshire (Wooldridge and Kirkcaldy, 1937) where visual dye tracing methods showed a fast travel time between the swallets and the risings which were located some 15 km away. More recently, Atkinson and Smith (1974) have under-taken tracing studies from small storm water swallets in south Hampshire using sensitive dye tracing techniques and have shown the rate of flow to the springs to be about 1.6 km/day. Comparable results by Smith and Atkinson (unpublished) from studies of the hydraulic conductivity in Sussex, where pumping for abstraction has possibly interfered with the natural Chalk groundwater circulation, show rates of the order of 2 km/day. In this case, it was possible to trace the rates of flow by the injection of dye into Chalk wells and to recover quantities of the dye from several other wells in the region. In all three of these cases the rate of flow indicates that the water flows in fissures and that the mode of flow is turbulent.

Thus even in the Chalk, where earlier work suggested that laminar, Darcian, near-isotropic flow was a possible working model, there is a growing body of evidence that this is a considerable oversimplification. Ineson's comment that the groundwater flow consists of a dual system is thus adequately supported.

The hydrology of massive, crystalline limestones
If we consider the Chalk to represent one extreme in the spectrum of limestone groundwater hydrology, the other extreme consists of the circulation within massive crystalline limestones. These limestones are often cavernous and it is thus easier to envisage the circulation, in part

at least, as consisting of fissure or conduit flow of a turbulent type. This view is supported by the not infrequent reports that wells sunk at neighbouring localities exhibit vast differences in transmissivity and in some cases individual wells may be completely dry. Some workers have argued that the use of a water table model for such limestones is meaningless.

Numerous water tracing experiments attempting to link swallet streams to their re-appearance at springs have shown that the flow is fast. The figures given in Table 6.1 for the results of work on the Carboniferous Limestone of Mendip and the comparable massive White Limestone of north central Jamaica are typical of such results. Experiments of this kind have also, in some cases, yielded additional information on the nature of the groundwater flow within the limestones.

TABLE 6.1
Travel times from stream sinks to swallets for massive limestones

	Mean flow velocity (in km/day)	Standard deviation	Number of traces
White Limestone, Jamaica	3.45	4.05	40
Carboniferous Limestone, Central Mendip Hills	7.36	5.91	23
Carboniferous Limestone, Eastern Mendip Hills	6.00	1.68	16

It is not uncommon for the underground flow lines from neighbouring swallets to re-appear at springs in such a fashion as to indicate that the flow lines cross without mixing (Smith and Atkinson, 1973). Also, application of the pulse-wave technique detailed by Ashton (1966), and first used in the Malham area at the end of the last century (Howarth *et al*, 1900) shows that locally at least the linkages between swallets and springs can be regarded as analogous to a U-tube. Thus a storm or artificial pulse wave created at one end of the system causes a quick response at the spring, and the difference in time between the first arrival of the pulse, and of tagged water corresponding to the pulse, gives a measure of the volume of the flooded connecting system. In some cases, the groundwater circulation extends well below sea level which again conflicts with a simple water table model. Submarine springs in offshore locations in limestone regions are relatively common and were demonstrated by Drew, Newson and Smith (1970) in tracing work linking a surface stream swallet to the 'spring' encountered by the Severn Rail Tunnel at a level well below the estuary section of the

R. Severn. Further studies of the flow regime of large springs around the periphery of the Mendip Hills demonstrate that the hydrology, and the solute and suspended sediment characteristics, are very similar to those of neighbouring surface open channel streams (e.g. Smith and Newson, 1974).

Although most of the literature quoted above relates to the Carboniferous Limestone of the United Kingdom there is no doubt that the results are comparable for other massive crystalline limestones throughout the world. However, a word of caution must be sounded, for although fissure or conduit flow is of great importance in such limestones the dual nature of the groundwater system described by Ineson for the Chalk also applies to massive limestones. A detailed hydrological study by Atkinson (1971) for the Cheddar catchment assigns values to the proportions of the groundwater flow which follow various paths through the limestone mass. A series of flow diagrams presented by Smith, Atkinson and Drew (1975) illustrates the relative importance of these differing flow paths in differing limestone lithologies. An example of such a flow diagram for the Cheddar catchment is presented here as Figure 6.2. The situation is envisaged as similar to that described by Ineson except that the part played by fissure flow is greater and the intergranular movement is even less.

The Chalk and Carboniferous Limestone can be considered as representing opposite ends of a sequence but studies of other limestone types can also be given. For example, Downing and Williams (1969), in a detailed hydrogeological study of the Lincolnshire Limestone, suggest that fissure flow may be of significance in the groundwater flow. The Lincolnshire Limestone exhibits considerable facies variations but oolitic and shelly limestones typify much of the succession. Locally, swallow holes are developed as at Burton Coggles, and such streams are influent at times of relatively low discharge and effluent at times of high discharge. Work in progress by P. L. Smart, of the Bristol University Geography Department, has shown that water tracing on the Jurassic Oolite sequence in the catchment of the Bybrook, to the north of Bath, gives underground flow rates that are comparable to those obtained from swallets in the Carboniferous Limestone or the Chalk as described above. The Jurassic oolitic limestones thus can be considered as an intermediate case where fissure flow is greater than in the Chalk but less than in the Carboniferous Limestone.

The development of subterranean drainage

There is little doubt that in most limestone areas, but not all, the first phase is the development of a surface drainage network. It is the development of the underground flow paths that represents the heart of the problem, for as all limestones are noted for their solubility it is the links between the solubility and the opening up of the subterranean drainage paths that provide the key. This is relatively easily understood

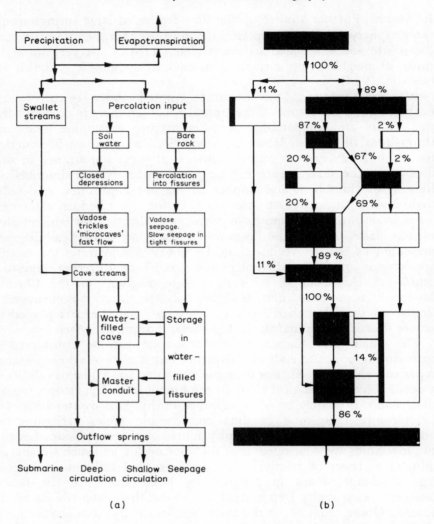

(a)   (b)

Figure 6.2a   Flow diagram for the hydrological cycle in limestone regions. (After Smith, Atkinson and Drew, 1975.)

Figure 6.2b   Flow in the Cheddar system during and immediately after heavy rainfall. The key is on Figure 6.2a. Percentage values show the proportion of total input, while the shading is diagrammatic. (After Smith, Atkinson and Drew, 1975.)

for the development of the classic stream sink where drainage from non-limestone strata passes over onto a limestone mass. The explanation that this water, which is usually markedly aggressive (i.e. is undersaturated with respect to calcium carbonate), will solutionally enlarge a joint or similar line of weakness in the stream bed, is generally accepted and provides a rational answer. In times of high discharge, the supply of water to such a swallet will often exceed the capacity of the underground drainage system and the flow will continue along the surface stream channel to be absorbed into the bed and into the underground drainage system at points further downstream. It is worth noting that classic swallow holes of this type are usually located at the margins of an area of limestone outcrop, e.g., the swallets in northwest Yorkshire, and those of Co. Clare, Mendip, etc. Such swallets are uncommon on the Chalk, which is rarely overlain by impervious material, but where this is present a very similar situation occurs. Such swallet sites are obviously ideal for rapid solution as the quantity of undersaturated water being delivered to the site is large and concentrates the catchment from a large area onto a very limited site.

To what extent is it possible to consider a similar mechanism developing in less favourable sites where the supply of water is from a very much smaller catchment? Studies concerning the initial enlargement of a joint by solutional processes are few and are bound to be of a theoretical nature. The basic study is by White and Longyear (1962) and was later developed by Atkinson (1968). The width of initial joint is assumed to be small, in the range of 10—20 microns, and the water flow is initially slow and laminar. Solutional erosion is thus restricted to a shallow depth, the 'penetration depth', which is attained when the saturation level with respect to calcium carbonate has reached the 90% level. However, the joint will slowly widen until its width becomes sufficient for the flow to become turbulent. White and Longyear in their calculations assume the onset of turbulent flow to occur at a Reynolds Number of 2000. They calculate that this figure will be exceeded at a width of about 0.5 cm. At this stage, the 'hydraulic jump point', White and Longyear suggest that the first channel to exceed a width of 0.5 cm will experience an increase of seven orders of magnitude in the effectiveness of solution. The first channel to reach this critical value will then evolve rapidly in width and could be termed a 'protocave'. Atkinson (1968), by substituting numerical values for the saturation levels for calcium carbonate observed in the field, gives an estimate of the time involved for these channels to reach a width that corresponds to turbulent flow conditions. The time for development from 10 microns to 0.5 cm is of the order of 50 million years, although from 100 microns to 0.5 cm takes only 1000 years. Atkinson then outlines possible mechanisms to reduce the very large time period involved in the initial evolution of the joint thickness under laminar flow conditions, including the consideration that the plane of the joint will not be geometrically smooth and that 'earth tide' and expansion/contraction effects could cause 'groundwater pumping' which could well enhance solution.

These studies have not, however, been directly aimed at obtaining exact time estimates for the development of subterranean drainage but rather to suggest a mechanism. The salient feature is that the mechanism involved links solution, flow type and the development of secondary, subterranean drainage paths. The model works in terms of planar surfaces and discontinuities but it is possible to extend it to take into account the secondary development of interconnected pores where a similar development from laminar to turbulent flow could be expected.

Putting together an hypothesis

Initially, the drainage on a limestone mass will commence in a similar fashion to that on neighbouring non-limestone strata. Details of drainage basin morphometry show that the same basic relationships occur on limestone lithologies as on neighbouring non-limestone\strata. This can be seen particularly clearly for the dry valley networks developed on the Chalk. It is possible that for some limestones this initial integrated drainage net never really becomes established. Three cases appear possible. First, some areas of Pleistocene or Recent coral reefs do not show a surface valley network (Fermor, 1972). The second case is for regions which have experienced an arid climate throughout the time available for their landscape evolution; Jennings (1971) considers the vast Nullarbor Plain of south Australia (an area of some 200 000 km^2) to fall into this category. The other possible case is that of cockpit karst. Tropical cockpit karst is invariably developed on massive limestone with low primary permeability but nevertheless displays no evidence of an integrated surface network of streams. It is difficult to decide whether the absence of evidence for a stream network arises from the removal by erosion of all traces thereof (Williams, 1972).

The solutional weathering of a limestone is concentrated at the soil/bedrock interface and in limestone regions throughout the world the general case is for the soil/bedrock junction to be extremely sharp. This solutional activity will slowly widen joints and similar lines of weakness in the manner suggested by White and Longyear (1962) and by Atkinson (1968). In the course of time the widening of the planes will become sufficient to enable the hydraulic jump to be attained and true groundwater circulation to commence. This then represents the development of secondary permeability within the limestones.

The form of the groundwater circulation will undoubtedly develop at differing rates and with variations in pattern from one limestone type to another. Marked enlargement of joints with a regular spacing will be the expected case for massive limestones. The form in this case is illustrated by the regular pattern of solutionally enlarged fissures exposed on the limestone pavements of the Burren and north-west Yorkshire. The pavements become exposed by the removal of the soil by later events.

Massive limestones exhibit four types of groundwater movement:

1. movement down a large number of solutionally enlarged fissures as described above;
2. the classic stream swallet developed at the edge of the outcrop;
3. closed depression drainage;
4. intergranular flow under laminar flow conditions.

Drainage of the kind envisaged in case 3 can be visualised as occurring at points of particularly well developed secondary permeability, as at cross joints (see Smith, Atkinson and Drew, 1972). An unpublished account by Smith and Smart, and initial studies by Drew (1968), demonstrate from dye tracing experiments that depressions of this kind (which do *not* have surface stream feeders) have rapid connections to neighbouring springs. Flow rates of the order of 1 km/day have been obtained. Such enclosed-depression drainage can extend to a situation where no signs of an original integrated valley network remain. This is typical of the Cockpit Country of Jamaica and parts of New Guinea (Williams, 1972).

It is important to realize that the system is continually evolving and this can only lead to the continued enlargement of the larger fissures, which will progressively take more and more of the flow. In such limestones the value of the water table model is limited. Indeed, many workers would consider it to be of no value. We have already discussed some aspects of the drainage in this type of rock that are difficult to reconcile with a water table model.

One or two further examples may make the proposed evolution clearer. In Co. Clare in western Ireland the River Aille crosses the line of a major cave system, the Doolin system (Tratman, 1969). The cave passage immediately beneath the river has a height of some 7 m. and contains a large stream, the roof of the cave at this point being separated from the bedrock floor of the river channel by about 6 m of massive limestone. At times of high discharge, the River Aille has a large surface flow over the line of the cave but only a small quantity of water leaks through from the river bed into the cave. Clearly, we have here a specific case in which the solutional enlargement of the joint planes in the limestone is still at an early stage of development. In this area, after periods of heavy rainfall, most of the caves are flooded to their roofs and stream swallets change from influent points to effluent. Further, as the fissure system fills with water it overflows to emerge at the surface at solutionally enlarged cross joints even where these are beneath a grass and soil cover. This pattern is repeated in many limestone regions under conditions of high discharge. During the major flood of July 1968 in the Mendip Hills many normally dry surface valleys became re-activated and '. . . . the peak discharge was that predictable from the dry valley density using empirically derived formulae' (Smith and Newson, 1974, p. 166). The underground drainage system is thus not sufficiently enlarged or adjusted in these regions to deal with major flood events. However, as the underground conduits further develop by solutional (and mechanical) erosion it is possible to arrive at a situation where the underground network is sufficiently enlarged to cope with the largest floods. This may well be the case with tropical cockpit karst where backing up of the subterranean water into the floors of the cockpit would appear to be unknown. If one wishes, it is possible to think in terms of a sequence of development analogous to the cyclic developments favoured by earlier workers for surface limestone forms.

Chalk underground drainage can perhaps be considered as developing in a similar fashion. In this case, the initial drainage network appears to be much better preserved, as is the case not only in the British Isles but in other climatic regions. Several workers have drawn attention to the very similar morphology developed on the Montpelier Chalks of Jamaica to those of western Europe, and to the complete contrast of the juxtaposed White Limestone with its fully developed cockpit landscape (Sweeting, 1972; Smith and Atkinson, 1975). Secondary permeability in Chalk is more likely to occur by an enlargement of interconnected pores than by the rectilinear fissure-controlled form associated with the more massive limestones. The development of enclosed depressions is much less evident in Chalk areas although features of this kind have been described by Prince (1962). Swallow holes are also less frequent, but where they do occur the flow rates are similar in all respects to those of the Carboniferous Limestone. The part played by the water table in Chalk is, however, more apparent. It appears possible that interconnected pore flow remains a more powerful process than purely fissure flow. Thus we have a water table which locally follows Darcian principles, but superimposed on this system is a network of fissure flow.

A modified water table with superimposed fissure flow appears to represent the best working hypothesis. However, the underground situation is still developing and it could be argued that as evolution proceeds there will be continued development of secondary fissure flow at the expense of intergranular flow. As with massive limestones, periods of high discharge cause the dry valley network to become re-activated, as is demonstrated in the many descriptions of winterbourne flow reported from the Chalk. This may represent the backing up of flow in the interconnected granular paths in addition to that of the fissure network.

Conclusion

Dry valleys, and associated enclosed depressions, are an essential element of the karst landscape found in all climatic zones except those underlain by permafrost. They can only be explained in terms of an origin of worldwide applicability, but the majority of the hypotheses seeking to explain their origin outlined in the earlier part of this paper demand special conditions at a local or regional scale. The results of recent hydrological studies, combining not only full water budgets but information regarding solute and sediment load, are sufficient to allow the initial formulation of an hypothesis of more general applicability. In brief, a combination of the solutional mechanism and the geohydrological properties of limestones, allows for a process that can encompass both the well ordered integrated surface dry valley networks of the English Chalk, the splendid grandeur of the gorges of the Carboniferous Limestone, and the bizarre but fascinating patterns exhibited by the cockpit landscapes of parts of the humid tropics. There is little doubt that if such an overall theory of origin is found acceptable, local circumstance and climatic change will suffice to explain variations in the pattern and mode of evolution.

REFERENCES

Ashton, K. (1966). 'The analysis of flow data from karst drainage systems', *Trans. Cave Research Group of Great Britain*, 7, 161—203.

Atkinson, T. C. (1968). 'The earliest stages of underground drainage in limestone — a speculative discussion', *Proc. British Spelaeological Association*, 6. 53—70.

Atkinson, T. C. (1971). *Hydrology and Erosion in a Limestone Terrain*, unpublished Ph.D. thesis, University of Bristol.

Atkinson, T. C. and D. I. Smith (1974). 'Rapid groundwater flow in fissures in the Chalk: an example from south Hampshire', *Quarterly J. of Engineering Geology*, Vol. 7, No. 2, 197—205.

Chandler, R. H. (1909). 'On some dry chalk valley features', *Geological Magazine*, 6, 538—9.

Downing, R. A. and B. P. J. Williams (1969). *The Ground-water Hydrology of the Lincolnshire Limestone*, Water Resources Board, Publication 9.

Drew, D. P. (1968). 'Tracing percolation water in karst areas', *Trans. Cave Research Group of Great Britain*, 10, 107—14.

Drew, D. P., M. D. Newson and D. I. Smith (1970). 'Water-tracing of the Severn Tunnel Great Spring', *Proc. University of Bristol Spelaeological Society*, 12, 203—12.

Dury, G. H. (1954). 'Contributions to a general theory of meandering valleys', *American J. Science*, 252, 193—224.

Edmunds, W. M., P. E. R. Lovelock and D. A. Gray (1973). 'Interstitial water chemistry and aquifer properties in the Upper and Middle Chalk of Berkshire, England', *J. Hydrology*, 19, 21—31.

Fagg, C. C. (1923). 'The recession of the chalk escarpment', *Proc. Trans. Croydon Natural History and Scientific Society*, 9, 93—112.

Fagg, C. C. (1954). 'The coombes and embayments of the chalk escarpment', *Proc. Trans. Croydon Natural History and Scientific Society*, 12, 117—31.

Fermor, J. (1972). 'The dry valleys of Barbados', *Trans. Institute of British Geographers*, 57, 153—65.

Findlay, D. C. (1965). *The Soils of the Mendip District of Somerset,* Memoir, Soil Survey of Great Britain.

Harrison, J. B. and A. J. Jukes-Brown (1890). *The Geology of Barbados,* Bridgetown.

Headworth, H. G. (1972). 'The analysis of natural groundwater level fluctuations in the Chalk of Hampshire', *J. Institute of Water Engineers,* 26, 107—24.

Howarth, J. H. *et al* (1900). 'The underground waters of north-west Yorkshire', *Proc. Yorkshire Geological and Polytechnical Society,* 14, 1—44.

Ineson, J. (1962). 'A hydrological study of the permeability of the Chalk', *J. Institute of Water Engineers,* 16, 449—63.

Jennings, J. N. (1971). *Karst,* A.N.U. Press.

Jennings, J. N. and M. M. Sweeting (1963). 'The limestone ranges of the Fitzroy Basin, Western Australia', *Bonner Geographische Abhandlungen,* 32.

Lehmann, H. (1936). 'Morphologische Studien auf Java', *Geographische Abhandlungen* (Stuttgart), 9.

Lohman, S. W. *et al* (1972). 'Definitions of selected ground-water terms — revisions and conceptual refinements', *U.S. Geological Survey Water-Supply Papers,* 1988.

Prince, H. C. (1962). 'Pits and ponds in Norfolk', *Erdkunde,* 16, 10—31.

Reid, C. (1887). 'On the origin of dry chalk valleys and of coombe rock', *Q. J. Geological Society of London,* 43, 364—73.

Smith, D. B., P. L. Wearn, H. J. Richards and P. C. Rowe (1970). 'Water movement in the unsaturated zone of high and low permeability strata by measuring natural tritium', in Ericson, A. (ed.), *Isotope Hydrology,* I.A.E.A., Vienna, 73—87.

Smith, D. I., D. P. Drew and T. C. Atkinson (1972). 'Hypotheses of karst landform development in Jamaica', *Trans. Cave Research Group of Great Britain,* 14, 159—73.

Smith, D. I. and T. C. Atkinson, (1973). 'Underground flow rates in cavernous and fissured limestones'. Groundwater Pollution, Conference Proceedings, Vol. 3, 71—75, The Water Research Association, Medmenham, Bucks.

Smith, D. I. and M. D. Newson (1974). 'The dynamics of solutional and mechanical erosion in limestone catchments on the Mendip Hills, Somerset', *Special Publication 6,* Institute of British Geographers, 155—67.

Smith, D. I. and T. C. Atkinson (1975). 'Process landforms and climate in limestone regions', in Derbyshire, E. (ed.), *Geomorphology and Climate,* Wiley.

Smith, D. I., T. C. Atkinson and D. P. Drew (1975). 'Hydrology of limestone terrain', in Ford, T. D. (ed.), *Spelaeology: the Science of Caves,* (forthcoming).

Sweeting, M. M. (1972). *Karst Landforms,* Macmillan .

Tate, T. K., A. S. Robertson and D. A. Gray (1971). Borehole logging investigations in the Chalk of the Lambourn and Winterbourne Valleys of Berkshire, *Water Supply Paper Research Report,* Institute of Geological Sciences, No. 5.

Tratman, E. K. (1969). *The Caves of North-west Clare, Ireland,* David and Charles.

Tricart, J. and T. C. da Silva (1960). 'Un example d'évolution karstique en milieu tropical sec: le morne de Bom Jesus da Lapa (Bahia, Brésil)', *Zeitschrift für Geomorphologie,* 4, 29—42.

Tylor, A. (1875). 'On the action and the formation of rivers, lakes and streams, with remarks on denudation and the causes of the great changes of climate which occurred just prior to the historical period', *Geological Magazine,* 2, 433—73.

Warwick, G. T. (1964). 'Dry valleys in the southern Pennines', *Erdkunde,* 18, 116—23.

White, W. B. and J. Longyear (1962). 'Some limitations on spelaeo-genetic speculation imposed by the hydraulics of groundwater flow in limestones', *Nittany Grotto Newsletter*, 10, 155—67.

Williams, P. W. (1972), 'Morphometric analysis of polygonal karst in New Guinea', *Bull. Geological Society of America*, 83, 761—96.

Wooldridge, S. W. and J. F. Kirkcaldy (1937). 'The geology of the Mimms Valley', *Proc. Geological Association*, 48, 307—15.

Chapter 7

River Patterns in the Bristol District

Allan Frey

'A river or a drainage basin might best be considered to have a heritage rather than an origin. It is an organic form, the product of a continuous evolutionary line through time'.
(Leopold, Wolman and Miller, 1964, p. 421)

In the days when landscape studies in British geomorphology were devoted to the geological objective of establishing a post-Cretaceous chronology of events, the reconstruction of drainage patterns across great sweeps of countryside was a fashionable alternative to *The Times* crossword. In the South West in particular, the early decades of the present century saw at least three attempts to identify the simple original form of the Bristol region's drainage pattern and the stages by which it had been fragmented into its present more complex form. These reconstructions, by Buckman (1900), Sanders (1918) and Varney (1921), well summarised by Bradshaw (1966), were all fairly quickly brought into question on sufficient points of detail to make them doubtful bases for further speculation. Yet it is the purpose of this essay to claim that some idea of the evolution of the regional drainage net is necessary if sense is to be made of both the meso- and the micro-features of the region. Just as micro-studies in process geomorphology need to be set in a *time* scale, often derived from outside the local areas, so they also need to be embedded in an *areal* context derived from larger region studies. It is precisely because local geomorphological studies in the Bristol region have lacked this more comprehensive areal frame that explanations like cavern collapse for the formation of Cheddar Gorge and glacial overflow to account for the Clifton gorge could survive for so long. If the general pattern is not known or hypothesised, local anomalies cannot be recognised.

There is a major difficulty in investigating stream patterns. Though eventually their study requires field work at key points within the area of interest, a general hypothesis of stream development can only be achieved by generalising the pattern over a large area using maps. The larger the scale of map the more valleys can be discovered upon it and *vice versa,* so that the vestiges of a stream pattern almost superseded by another could very well not be adequately featured on a small scale map. By the same token, the small scale map has already had a huge number of smaller valleys suppressed by the cartographer in the interest of clarity but perhaps to the geomorphologist's cost.

The durability of the drainage pattern

The great length of the geological time scale and the presumed inability of most contemporary erosional processes to cause rapid trans-formations of the British landscape induced a willingness on the part of many workers greatly to exaggerate the time scales needed to accomplish erosional tasks. In the last decade, especially with the gradual piecing together of events in the Pleistocene and the studies of catastrophic happenings and their recurrence intervals, has come a realisation that landscape change need not be the long drawn out process it once seemed to be. Linton (1957), writing directly on the theme of the 'everlasting' hills, could conceive of no pre-glacial topography surviving to the present day in areas where the precipitation was 2500 mm/year or more and Chorley (1962) makes the more general statement that 'in many, if not most, areas the condition is one of massive removal of past evidence and a tendency towards adjustment with progressively contemporaneous conditions'. If indeed landscape features rapidly become adjusted to contemporary energy flow conditions and this tendency is reinforced by the outstanding ability of high energy flows, such as those that have occurred in the Pleistocene, to obliterate previous forms, a morphological key to the past is hardly likely to unlock doors very far back in time. There is, however, one major exception to this picture of rolling destruction, and this is the pattern of stream courses which, once established, remains so tenaciously an imprint on the landscape that it provides enduring evidence of past conditions. Not only are stream lineaments difficult to eradicate, but they are in adjustment to such a wide range of forces that they provide a valuable window on the past. This is not to say that the pattern remains constant over time but rather that some elements of the pattern, especially the headwater elements and trunk streams, can survive over long periods of time and through extensive modification of the network. To establish the tenacity possessed by the orientation of stream pattern elements it will be useful to consider the events which can cause progressive alteration and final destruction of a river network. It has to be emphasised that, even at a late stage of alteration, sufficient of the original pattern may remain to provide fragmentary evidence of earlier conditions and, indeed, this claim is made for the Bristol region.

Change of base level

A negative change will rejuvenate streams in their existing courses and so will have the general effect of perpetuating the pattern. However, the increased vigour of flow will also have the effect of accelerating the adjustment of minor pattern elements to structure, a process that would take place anyway given sufficient time. On the other hand, encroachment of the sea upon the land will have two effects; of planation as the advancing sea cuts horizontally into the shrinking land area, and of deposition on to that part of the landmass now under water. If the positive change of sea level is large enough to flood over a substantial part of the land mass, deposition will begin to take place on this new sea floor. For some time the erstwhile sub-aerial topography of this new sea floor can persist, especially if major valley-ways are kept open by undersea currents or by the turbulence of water flows extending seawards from major rivers draining land as yet unsubmerged. But a combination of differential sedimentation into hollows and underwater slumping of sediments will eventually submerge and obliterate this one-time topography as it submits to sub-marine rather than sub-aerial processes. A distinction can be drawn between the essentially horizontal action, when erosional trimming of a landscape is accomplished by the waves of an advancing sea, and the essentially vertical action of deposition which blankets over a submerged landscape. A similar distinction can be drawn when considering the work of glaciation, the next kind of occurrence to be considered.

Glaciation

The predominant effect of glaciers and meltwater is to scour out and deepen pre-existing valleys. Some alteration to the drainage pattern is undoubtedly accountable to the diversion of streams from their original courses, watershed breaching, the creation of new pattern elements like spillways, sub-ice melt streams, reversals of flow and so on, but these aberrations are usually fairly easy to recognise in glaciated upland areas. Acting in a vertical direction, deposition from sheet glaciation often causes the infilling of pre-glacial valleys with till. Although by no means all such valleys are exhumed and reoccupied by post-glacial rivers, the shallower the till and the deeper the pre-glacial valleys, the more likely will reoccupation be.

Scarp retreat

The headwaters of one valley system often inter-lock into the headwaters of another system along a major escarpment. Retreat of the scarp line down the dip represents the victory of the scarp system over its dip counterpart and so, acting in an essentially horizontal plane, the more vigorous scarp slope system progressively captures and destroys the territory of the dip slope streams, eventually replacing the dip slope pattern with its own. This process can continue only so long as one pattern has an advantage over the other because of factors like a shorter distance to base level, higher rainfall, and steeper gradients. In practice, though one stream pattern might well hold the erosional advantage at first, an equilibrium condition is reached long before one pattern completely destroys another. Very good examples of rapid scarp retreat can be seen in the drainage pattern of the Bristol region.

Epigenesis
There are three particular cases of superimposition which can cause substantial alteration to the stream pattern in its downcutting process. All three occur when downcutting reveals a substantially different lithology from the one on which the pattern was initiated. The first occurs when a stream pattern, recently initiated on glacial deposits, regains and begins to exhume the pre-glacial landscape. In essence this situation is really only a special case of the second type of super-imposition which occurs when downcutting penetrates a massive uncon-formity and begins to expose a buried and partly formed earlier landscape whose lineations, strengths and weaknesses are totally different from those of the initiating landscape. A third case occurs when a stream pattern incises itself through non-limestone strata onto limestones whose behaviour in transmitting water and suffering erosion is significantly different from the non-calcareous rocks above.

It is to be emphasised that superimposition down through *congruent* strata, even though their facies may differ greatly, can lead to a change in stream pattern *density* but not in major orientation. Superimposition through major unconformities gradually opens up a terrain whose lineations are usually totally different from the initial surface but even so, though the alignment of subsequent or structurally guided elements of the pattern may change, the trunk streams can be expected to maintain their inherited orientations.

Earth movements
Examples abound of the maintenance of trunk stream orientations across the trend of rising folds by antecedence. Just as often, the orientation of subsequent tributaries adjusts rapidly to the rising relief. Far less predictable in its influence on a stream pattern is the collapse of strata in graben form across the course of a trunk stream; the Petrockstow fault basin provides a good illustration from the South West of England. For diversion to take place, the tectonic event has to be more rapid than the ability of the trunk stream to maintain its bed by downcutting and this is true whether the event be faulting, warping, tilting or folding.

The river patterns of the Bristol district

An important key to understanding the evolution of the drainage net in Western England lies in the Bristol district, where the eastward backwearing of the Jurassic and Cretaceous scarps is progressively exposing a pre-existing landscape of Permo-Triassic age. This old landscape consists largely of Silurian, Devonian and Carboniferous sediments which, having been thrown up into tight, dominantly east-west folds, were attacked during the Permo-Triassic, surely one of the longest periods of arid sub-aerial erosion that England has known. However, the great length of time (70 million years) has to be discounted by the infrequency of rainfall because, far from base-levelling the Hercynian upfolds, this erosional attack succeeded only in removing the less resistant Upper Carboniferous rocks from the anti-clinal crests and reversing the relief of only the western, most exposed, part of the Blackdown anticline (Frey, 1970).

This fossil and well articulated landscape is currently being exhumed by scarp retreat: consequently, there are two erosional provinces in the Bristol district; the emerging fossil Palaeozoic landscape to the west of the Oolitic escarpment and the belted scarp and vale of the Mesozoic dip slope to the east of this scarp. Not surprisingly, the drainage patterns of these two provinces are quite different. To the west the scarp streams show remarkable parallelism as they flow north-west to join the Severn Estuary (the Stroud Water, Little Avon, Bristol Avon, Blagdon Yeo, Axe, Brue, Cary and Parrett, shown in Figure 7.1a), while to the east there is a double pattern; the Thames headwaters flowing away to the east-north-east to drain the Jurassic (Figure 7.1b) and the Salisbury Avon and Test flowing away south to drain the Chalk into the English Channel (Figure 7.2).

However, the boundary between the two provinces is not entirely clearcut because, in the salient of high ground sandwiched between the emerging Mendip Hills, the retreating Oolitic scarp and the Jurassic outlier of Dundry Hill (marked S on Figure 7.2), the east-north-east direction of flow is still imprinted. Thus, the middle Chew, the Cam and the Wellow Brooks all rise on Keuper Marl from springs issuing from the foot of lower Jurassic slopes and flow east-north-east via increasingly deeply incised valleys *through* the Oolitic scarp before being intercepted on dip territory by the Bristol Avon and carried back through the scarp north-westwards to the Severn. Clearly, the Bristol Avon, a vigorous scarp stream, perhaps aided by glacial meltwater, has been able locally to push back the scarp and extend its headwaters sufficiently far into dip territory progressively to capture a series of Thames headstreams.

Figure 7.1b shows all those stream elements in the Bristol region which could support an hypothesis that the Thames once had its headwaters very much further to the west-south-west than is now the case. Such an hypothesis would require that at some later time the

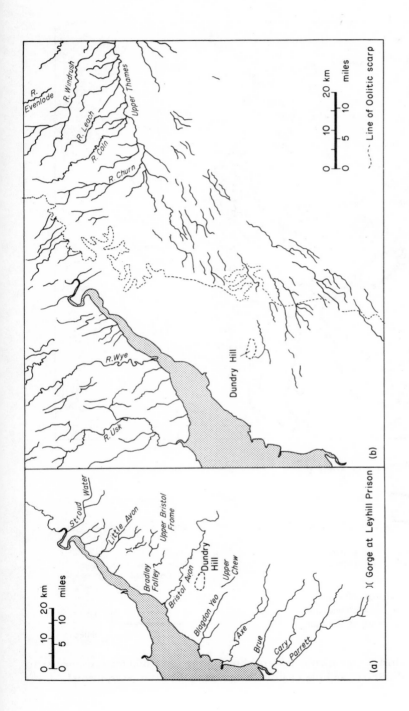

Figure 7.1 River pattern elements of the Bristol district.
a. North-west to the Severn.
b. East-north-east to the upper Thames.

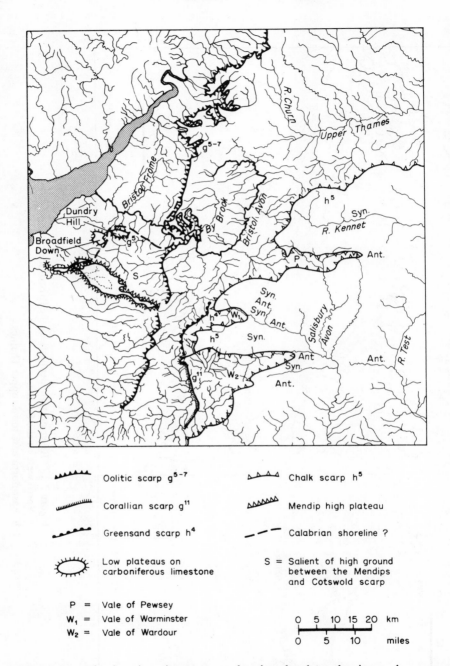

Figure 7.2   Bristol region river pattern showing the three dominant elements: to the Thames, the Severn and the English Channel, and the main escarpments.

ancestral Severn encroached eastwards into the territory of the upper Thames and beheaded its north bank tributaries. At the same time the south bank tributaries of the Thames were being attacked and turned westward by the intrusive attack of the south bank tributaries of the Severn (shown in Figure 7.1a).

Some writers (Wooldridge, 1961; Brown, 1960; Bradshaw, 1965) envisaged that the Severn and its tributaries might have been assisted by the encroachment of the Calabrian Sea flooding up the Bristol Channel against the Cotswold scarp and bevelling off the territory to the west of the scarp at around 185 m. An advantage of such a suggestion is that the north-west flowing tributaries of the Severn could then be initiated on an emerging sea floor. However, there is no depositional evidence for such a sea, the erosional evidence is ambiguous, and the hypothesis raises more difficulties than it solves; therefore, the parallel Severn tributaries will be explained by conventional river development and the controversy over the Calabrian Sea will be sidestepped.

Adjustments to structure
Although the main streams in both drainage provinces retain striking evidence of their dominant directions, there has been a great deal of adjustment to structure by secondary streams. On the Mendip Hills, apart from the Pleistocene innovation of the Cheddar system, most of the current drainage has faithfully reoccupied the old Triassic valleys. The Mells River that joins the Somerset Frome just north of the town of Frome (Figure 7.3) has eroded rapidly headward along the east-west strike of the Coal Measures, a prominent line of weakness, and so locally interrupts the pattern of north-east flow followed by its neighbours (the Cam and Wellow Brooks, Whatley Bottom, Nunney Brook and the Somerset Frome itself).

The Bristol Frome (Figure 7.2) has pirated north-eastwards not only because this direction lay along the strike of the Jurassic on which it originated but because it found itself, by chance, superimposed on the axis of the Trias-excavated vale along the syncline of the North Bristol coalfield. Expoiting this advantage, it has been able to capture not only a couple of minor scarp streams (Figure 7.1a) but to break into some of the headwaters of the Little Avon and turn them southwards. The minor gorge through the Carboniferous Limestone at Leyhill Open Prison marks the old course of this Little Avon headstream. Both the Boyd and the Westbury Trym flow along courses parallel to, but less successful than, the course of the Bristol Frome.

On the east side of the Oolitic scarp, the Bristol Avon has exploited the Jurassic strike between Bradford-on-Avon and Malmesbury to capture into Thames headwaters and turn them south then west just as, on a smaller scale, the By Brook has done (Figure 7.2). On the Chalk, the general east-west folds of the Miocene have been exploited by a series of tributaries of the Salisbury Avon and Test, some of them now dry

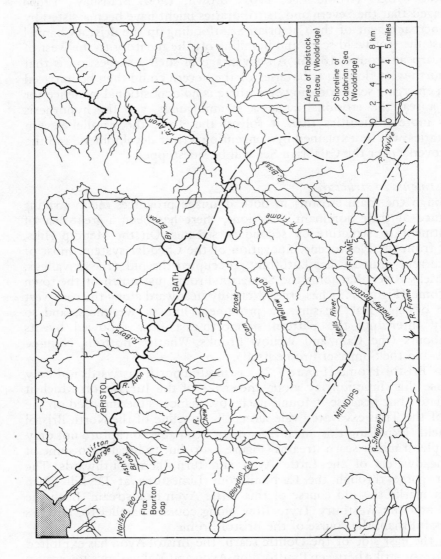

Figure 7.3 The river pattern of the Radstock Plateau.

Key within figure:
- ☐ Area of Radstock Plateau (Wooldridge)
- – – – Shoreline of Calabrian Sea (Wooldridge)

Scale:
0 2 4 6 8 km
0 1 2 3 4 5 miles

Labels: R. Avon, By Brook, R. Biss, R. Wylye, BATH, R. Boyd, Cam Brook, R. Frome, FROME, Wellow Brook, Mells River, Whatley Bottom, R. Frome, BRISTOL, R. Avon, Clifton Gorge, R. Chew, MENDIPS, R. Sheppey, Blagdon Yeo, Ashton Brook, Nailsea Yeo, Flax Bourton Gap valleys, so assisting in the unroofing of the three major re-entrant scarp vales; Pewsey, Warminster and Wardour (Figure 7.2).

Bearing in mind the hypothesis of two distinct drainage provinces, with the westerly province gradually encroaching on the eastern accompanied by adjustment to structure of the secondary streams, it is instructive to examine three recent geomorphological studies of the Bristol region in which the analysis depends, at least in part, on the evolution of the river system.

The Radstock Plateau

The first study, by Wooldridge (1961), seeks an explanation of the widespread concurrence of summit heights around 185 m. on the Radstock Plateau, an area between Bristol, Frome, Bath and the Mendips (see Figure 7.3). He proposes that the area was bevelled by the waves of the Calabrian Sea flooding in from the south-east via the narrow Wylye Valley and possibly joining up with an arm of the same sea flooding up the Severn Estuary. This sea not only provides for him an explanation for the accordance of summit heights but suggests to Bradshaw (1966) a possible reason for the breach of the Cotswold escarpment by the Bristol Avon. However, if the sea had sufficient power to create a widespread marine plane at around 185 m., it should also have eliminated the then existing drainage pattern of the area so that, when the sea retreated, a new pattern consonant with the inclination of the emerging sea floor should have been created. In fact, the majority of the streams in the area flow at right angles to the presumed inclination of this sea floor (the middle Chew, the Cam, the Wellow and the Somerset Frome). At the Calabrian stage these streams were likely still to have been tributaries of the upper Thames and therefore only weakly incised so that planation of the area would surely have eliminated them. This is our first example of a study in which insufficient attention to the drainage pattern invalidates the hypothesis being put forward.

The central Mendip Hills

Of considerable interest is our second example, a study by Ford and Stanton (1968) of the south-central Mendip Hills. They proposed that the stream pattern of their area was initially a radial one (though their diagram on p. 407 shows a general southwesterly rather than a radial pattern), later dismembered by capture along NW-SE lines. Imagining the circumstances in which this radial flow could develop on an upland *plateau* obviously presented them with considerable difficulty. They opt for the gentle updoming in the Miocene of a Rhaetic/Liassic-formed plateau buried under Mesozoic sediments. Their claim that a radial stream pattern was initiated on this modest dome ignores whatever stream pattern previously existed there and denies that old pattern the ability to maintain its lineaments by antecedence.

However, their radial pattern is implied to be part of a more general

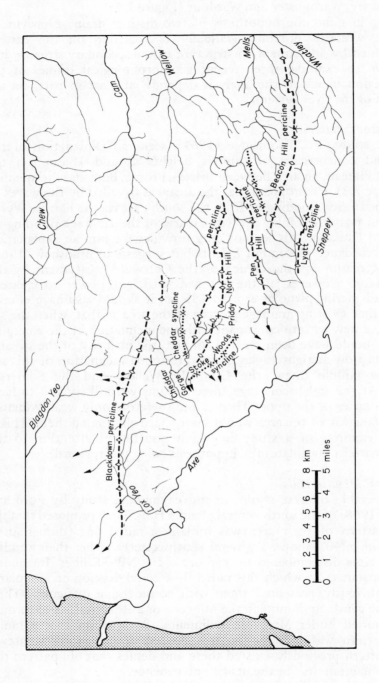

Figure 7.4 The valley pattern and major fold axes of the Mendip Hills.

net which, by the end of the Pliocene, had stripped most of the Mesozoics from the ancient Liassic plateau and had further trimmed it. A new cycle is claimed, without explanation, to begin in the Calabrian which progressively excavated the Mesozoic rocks from the area to the south of Mendip, so exhuming the steep southern flank of the Mendip upland, rejuvenating the south-west flowing streams and leading to a variety of captures on the upland plateau.

If we now look at this area in terms of the drainage hypothesis that is proposed in the present essay, the Mendip Hills today lie at the junction of streams flowing away to the north east (the middle Chew, Cam, Wellow and Somerset Frome) and those running north west to the Severn Estuary (the Axe and the Blagdon Yeo) (Figure 7.4). Since the hypothesis incorporates the view that the older and once more extensive east-north-east system is being dismembered by the attack of the north-westerly flowing Severn tributaries, we would expect the Mendip summit to show relics of WSW to ENE valley orientations. Figure 7.4 shows that the majority of central and east Mendip valleys do indeed have this *orientation* though it should be noted that the direction of flow is often to the west-south-west. Particularly important is the fact that the eastern headstream (now dry) of the Cheddar system trenches right through the unroofed North Hill anticline, so pointing to superimposition from the Mesozoic cover rocks which exist nearby in the form of the Harptree Beds.

However, there are three streams whose courses seem to be anomalous. The captures associated with the first of these, the Mells River, have already been mentioned. The course of the upper Chew will be dealt with later, so it is the middle reach of the Cheddar valley running south-east to north-west between Priddy and the head of the Gorge which provides the greatest difficulty. This valley needs to be explained as the course of a structurally guided secondary stream which allowed the ENE-WSW Cheddar Gorge stream to capture its next door neighbour to the east. The structural weaknesses along this line are easy enough to identify in terms of strike lines, the weakened crest of an anticline, and a minor syncline, but the general contempt that most streams on upland Mendip have for such weaknesses (and especially for the Lower Limestone Shale) does not generate confidence in this explanation. At least as big a problem is to know whether the capture took place before the Mendip summit was exhumed, when all drainage was to the east-north-east, or whether it happened later, caused by the greatly accelerated erosion and rejuvenation resulting from the attack by the north west streams especially in Glacial times. Arguing against the timing suggested in the second case is the fact that, in common with all Mendip-top valleys, this Gorge-to-Priddy valley is only weakly incised and does not look like the site of an important fluviatile battle. More work on this valley is obviously required though a possible explanation is suggested in Figure 7.5b and 7.5c.

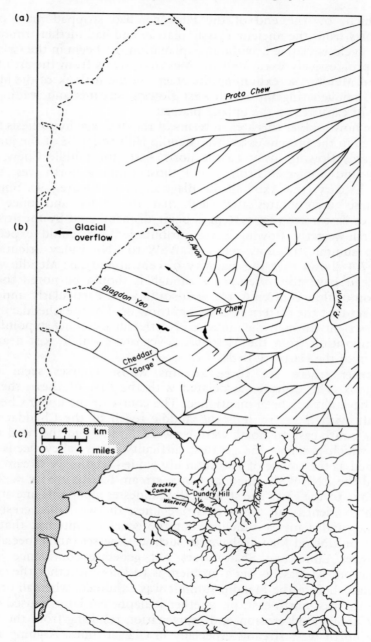

Figure 7.5   Stages in the development of the River Chew.
a.   Neogene-drainage, all to the Thames.
b.   Early Pleistocene: captures by Severn tributaries almost complete.
c.   Present pattern of valleys.

In summary, though their time scale of events is probably right, Ford and Stanton have taken too parochial a view of their study area to generate a valid solution to the problem of Mendip drainage.

The Clifton gorge and the course of the Chew

The third example of local geomorphological study dependent on the reconstruction of past river patterns is drawn from the work of Hawkins and Kellaway (1971) and Hawkins (1972). Their primary objective is to gain recognition for the fact that the Bristol region was glaciated and that there are deposits and drainage diversions to prove it. Unfortunately, while they must surely be right about a glacial interpretation for their deposits, the substantial glacial realignments of river courses they propose are not necessary to their thesis. The discovery of glacial material in the Flax Bourton gap to the west of Bristol prompts Hawkins to re-open the old controversy about the Clifton gorge. He supposes that the Bristol Avon originally flowed through the Flax Bourton gap (Figure 7.3) to reach the Severn but that an ice tongue blocked the gap, so impounding meltwater in the Bristol embayment until it overflowed north westwards to create the Clifton gorge. At the same time, ice is supposed to have diverted the Trym to cut the Blaise Castle gorge and create a new course to join the Avon, itself an overflow.

There is no reason why deposits which give evidence for the presence of ice should necessarily require the diversion of rivers in this most unlikely manner. The lower course of the Bristol Avon shows a remarkably consistent north westerly direction from Bath to Avonmouth and is strikingly parallel with the other Severn tributaries shown in Figure 7.1a. The Clifton gorge is formed where the Avon, by superimposition, finds itself flowing at right angles across a Triassic-unroofed and hitherto buried Hercynian anticline. The south east flank of the anticline is formed of resistant Carboniferous Limestone through which the Avon is forced by down-cutting to form a gorge. Upstream of the gorge lies a trough on the site of the Coal Measures excavated in Triassic times and, as the Avon has regained the Trias by cutting away the Mesozoic cover, this weaker formation has allowed a certain amount of migration of the Avon meanders, so locally creating a short east-west alignment which is further emphasized by the Ashton Brook, an Avon tributary. The Nailsea Yeo, also exploiting the Coal Measure vale, backs headwards on to the Ashton Brook, so creating the Flax Bourton gap. To propose that the Avon ever flowed through this gap must be regarded as absurd (see Figure 7.3).

More important for the elucidation of the regional drainage pattern is Hawkins' suggestion that the pre-glacial River Chew had its source 2 km south of Keynsham and flowed south west to join the Blagdon Yeo which then flowed north west to the Severn Estuary. The ice advance up the estuary is supposed to have blocked the Yeo valley and forced the Chew to overflow northwards into the Bristol Avon, a course it follows today. To controvert this unlikely suggestion it is necessary to reconstruct the possible stages in the development of the Chew in terms of the drainage hypothesis advanced earlier in this essay (Figure 7.5).

Figure 7.5a indicates an early stage of development, with the Thames headstreams flowing north eastwards across an unbroken series of Jurassic rocks forming a surface with a height of at least 300 metres, underneath which the fossil Triassic landscape still lies buried. Figure 7.5b shows that surface considerably dissected and reduced in height, its drainage pattern invaded and turned north westwards, and subsequent streams beginning to conform to the now emerging Triassic landscape. It is at stage 7.5c that the unexpected occurs. The River Chew, having been beheaded by the Blagdon Yeo (7.5b) is shown to have retaliated by capturing the headwaters of the Yeo. It is here that Hawkins' insistence on ice action can be invoked. The Rickford valley, cut across a protruding lobe of Dolomitic Conglomerate (illustrated on p. 282 of Hawkins and Kellaway, 1971), is clear evidence of marginal overflow and thus of the presence of ice in the lower Yeo valley. Ponding on the site of the present Blagdon Lake could only have resulted in an overflow to the north, so diverting the upper Yeo permanently into the Chew system. Even so, this still leaves the anomaly of the Winford Brook which, coupled with the valley of Brockley Combe, ought to be seen as one of the northwesterly flowing invaders parallel to the Yeo and the Bristol Avon, yet it flows in the wrong direction from the Bristol airport summit southeastwards to Chew Magna.

Enough has been said about the River Chew to demonstrate that it holds the key to the final problems of the regional river pattern.

Wider implications

It is now profitable to ask whether the drainage hypothesis for the Bristol district, which seems to offer a coordinated explanation within the region, is capable of extension to a wider area. On the basis of the orientation of selected river components, the upper Thames could be hypothesised to have had its early headwaters on the site of the Bristol Channel north of Minehead, collecting major tributaries in an arc from the River Tone, the east Quantock and north-east Exmoor streams, to all those streams in Wales east of a line running north-north-west from Cowbridge.

There is a long tradition of regarding the trunk rivers of southern England as having a dominantly west-to-east direction and Brown (1960, p. 267) summarises this thinking by illustrating three trunk rivers; the Trent, the Thames and the 'Solent'. The need for a 'Solent' river to transport the Dorset ball clays eastwards from Dartmoor is now realised to be unnecessary, so dispensing with a trunk river which ran in the opposite direction to the English Channel 'river'. As for the Thames, its course can be seen to comprise three distinct stretches. From its mouth upstream to Reading the lower Thames occupies the Tertiary London Basin, collecting tributaries like the Lea, the Colne and the Wey which have astonishingly strong north-south orientations. The middle Thames, allied to the Cherwell, has a prominent north to south course which makes a huge breach through the Cretaceous escarpment between the Chiltern Hills and the Berkshire Downs, the final incision being known as the Goring Gap. Both the upper Thames and the Kennet occupy lines of substantial weakness orientated roughly east-west, the upper Thames running along the strike of the Jurassic and the Kennet along the trough of a Miocene syncline. Both rivers collect as tributaries a large number of streams whose courses could be generally described as 'northerly-southerly' (rather than easterly-westerly).

The whole of the south-eastern quadrant of Wales and the whole of the South-west Peninsula are dominated by streams with north-south alignments. In South-east England, the dissection of the prominent anticlinorium of the Weald with accompanying adjustment to structure of the subsequent streams, is calculated to eliminate any *continuous* north-south drainage lines which might once have existed, though there are plenty of *local* north-south stream alignments to be seen today.

It is thus possible to think of the Thames as an intrusive element in southern England, taking advantage of the Tertiary London Basin, the Jurassic/Cretaceous strike, and Miocene fold axes to capture westwards into a series of trunk streams running south into the English Channel 'river'. An equivalent intrusion from the opposite direction by the River Severn has not only disrupted north-south streams in western England but has turned the tables on the piratical upper Thames. It is just as plausible to suggest that the early drainage of England was dominantly to the south as it is to claim that compound rivers like the Thames and Trent have been with us since the early Tertiary. The present courses of the middle Severn, the Cirencester Churn and the Salisbury Avon will be considered as a once continuous river in order to illustrate this point.

Today, the middle Severn from the Ironbridge Gorge to Tewkesbury and its tributary the Stourbridge Stour both follow a remarkably persistent course south-south-eastwards. (It is worth noting in passing that there is an array of south-east and south flowing streams even further north than the Wrekin and Cannock Chase, some of them tributaries of the intrusive Trent, which could be considered as headstreams of major south-flowing rivers like the Severn.) At Tewkesbury, the course of the River Severn is interrupted in two major ways. It is joined by the Warwickshire Avon, considered to be a glacial diversion of Saalian Age (Stephens, 1970), and it is captured by the lower Severn working back north-eastwards along the strike of the

Cotswold escarpment. The River Churn represents the beheaded former course of the Severn, trending southwards obliquely across the Jurassic dip before it, in turn, is captured by another Jurassic strike river, this time the River Thames. The former southerly extension of the Severn-Churn must have crossed the Marlborough Downs, just as the southward flowing upper Kennet does today as far as Avebury. But the middle Kennet is a structure-guided river which, in the post early-Miocene period, broke into and disrupted the old north-south alignments and so beheaded the Salisbury Avon, thus depriving it of its Severn-Churn headwater. Today the Salisbury Avon has to be content to employ its much more limited headstreams to unroof the Vale of Pewsey, a Miocene anticline (Figure 7.2). From its mouth at Christchurch to its source in Pewsey Vale, the Salisbury Avon follows a course transverse to structure, transverse to the regional dip, to the trend of the Miocene folds and to local strike lines. It surely played a major part in the breach of the southern Chalk rim of the Hampshire Basin between Ballard Down and the Needles.

Conclusion

The purpose of this essay has been to examine the enduring evidence of past events recorded by the different elements of drainage patterns. By looking first at the Bristol district, an erosional hinge-point in geomorphological studies, the history of the river pattern was hypothesised and then extended in a speculative fashion to a wider area. It is not claimed that this particular interpretation is necessarily correct; indeed, only extensive work in the field could test its veracity, but rather that such an hypothesis is an essential prelude to field study in that it focuses attention on key sites. Geomorphological studies on the basis of 'hard' evidence such as deposits and erosional facets alone, to the exclusion of the drainage pattern, ignore a most important key to the past.

REFERENCES

Bradshaw, R. (1966). 'The Avon Gorge', *Proc. Bristol Naturalists Society*, **31**, 203—20.

Brown, E. H. (1960). 'The building of southern Britain', *Zeitschrift für Geomorphologie*, 4, 264—74.

Buckman, S. S. (1900). 'Excursion notes: chiefly on river features', *Proc. Cotteswold Naturalists' Field Club*, 13, 175—92.

Chorley, R. J. (1962). *Geomorphology and General Systems Theory*, U.S. Geological Survey, Professional Paper 500—B, 1—10.

Ford, D. C. and W. I. Stanton (1968). 'The geomorphology of the south-central Mendip Hills', *Proc. Geologists' Association*, 79, 401—27.

Frey, A. E. (1970). 'Permo-Triassic erosion of the Mendip Hills', *Proc. Ussher Society*, **2**, 178.

Hawkins, A. B. (1972). 'Some gorges of the Bristol district', *Proc. Bristol Naturalists Society*, **32**, 167—85.

Hawkins, A. B. and G. A. Kellaway (1971). 'Field meeting at Bristol and Bath with special reference to new evidence of glaciation', *Proc. Geologists' Association*, **82**, 267—92.

Linton, D. L. (1957). 'The everlasting hills', *Advancement of Science*, **54**, 1—10.

Sanders, E. M. (1918). *La Région de Bristol*, thèses presentées à la Faculté des Sciences de Paris.

Stephens, N. (1970). 'The Lower Severn Valley', Chapter 5 in Lewis, C. A. (ed.), *The Glaciation of Wales and Adjoining Regions*, Longman, 107—24.

Varney, W. D. (1921). 'The geological history of the Pewsey Vale', *Proc. Geologists' Association*, **32**, 189—205.

Wooldridge, S. W. (1961). 'The Radstock Plateau: a note on the physiography of the Bristol district', *Proc. Bristol Naturalists Society*, **30**, 151—62.

PART III

Climatology

Plate 8.1

An example of modern weather satellite imagery in the visible region of the electromagnetic spectrum. This strip obtained from the Scanning Radiometer on Noaa-2 on 7th June, 1973, portrays clouds over much of the North Atlantic, as far north as the North Pole (illuminated in summer by the continuous polar day). (Courtesy U.S. Weather Bureau.)

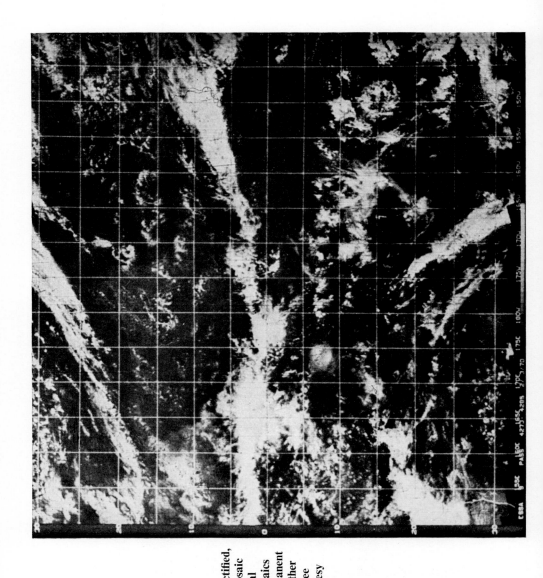

Plate 8.2
An Essa 9 computer-rectified, brightness-normalised mosaic of clouds over the tropical Pacific Ocean. Such mosaics comprise part of the permanent archive of American weather satellite cloud imagery (see also Figure 8.12). (Courtesy U.S. Department of Commerce.)

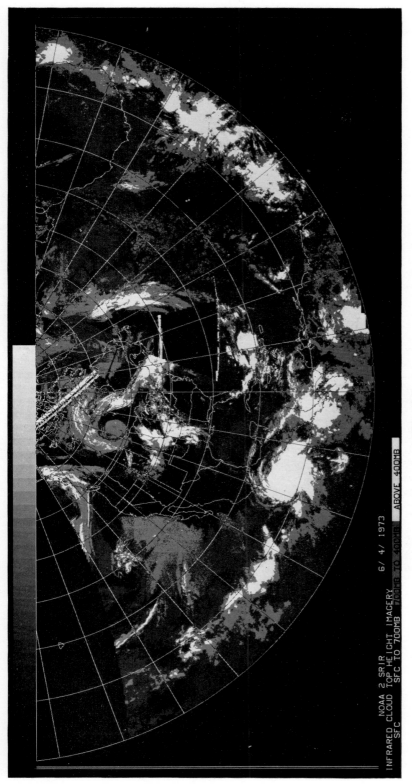

NOAA 2 SRIR   6/ 4/ 1973
INFRARED CLOUD TOP HEIGHT IMAGERY
SFC TO 700MB 700MB TO 400MB ABOVE 400MB

Plate 8.3

A 'three-dimensional nephanalysis' compiled objectively from Noaa-2 infrared Scanning Radiometer imagery. A range of cloud heights has been assigned
to the observed radiating temperatures of the cloud tops. Allowances have
been made for latitudinal variations in vertical temperature profiles.
(Courtesy U.S. Weather Bureau.)

Plate 8.4
This pair of images is derived from a single Essa mosaic for February 6th, 1970, by a Quantimet 720 analog computer. In the case of (a) a lower brightness threshold has been used than in (b). In (a), the cloudiness in the equatorial trough has a belt-like appearance; in (b) the brighter (deeper) clouds are isolated, revealing the underlying vorticity structure obscured in (a): a series of vorticity maxima are indicated, separated by neutral points (dark areas in the picture). This demonstration underlines the need for care in satellite image interpretation, and for more objective approaches to the analysis of the total information content.

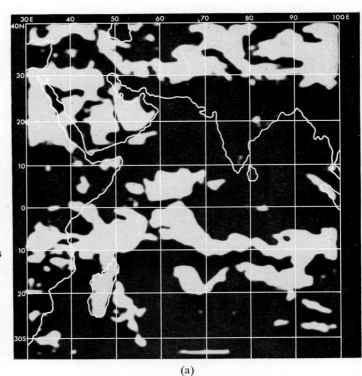

(a)

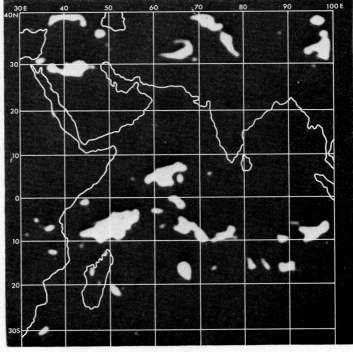

(b)

Briathar Dé mo Lóchrann

TREOIR OPAC

OPAC GUIDE

COLAISTE MHUIRE GAN SMAL

MARY IMMACULATE COLLEGE

FAILTE

WELCOME

OPAC : On-line Public Access Catalogue

The OPAC is available through any PC located in the library. It is also available through any PC in the college or outside at the following address:

http://136.201.111.1:8001/www-bin/www_talis32

OPAC will give you:

- Information on almost all of the Library's holdings of books, journals, e-journals, AV material, microfiche and microfilm.

- Information on the location and availability of material.

- Information on material ordered, but not yet received in the library.

    - An item marked *on order* has not yet been received.

    - An item without a shelf mark has not yet reached the library shelf and can be requested at the Issue Desk.

- Access to your borrower record, which can be used to check what material you have on loan and the due date. You can also check any fines due.

- A means to reserve material which is on loan.

- Access to lists of recommended books and articles placed on 4-hour loan by your lecturers.

Chapter 8

Analyses of Image Data from Meteorological Satellites

Eric Barrett

Until recently, climatology bore certain marks of middle age, most distressingly set ways, and a seeming lack of ambition. Today, meteorological satellites are prompting a timely rejuvenation, so much so that modern macro-climatology is vibrant with discovery, discussion, experimentation and innovation. Remote sensing, flourishing in many geophysical and environmental sciences, has proved particularly advantageous for studying the Earth's atmospheric envelope. It has been observed that 'The requirements of modern meteorology, hydrology and related geosciences . . . cannot be provided by any imaginable network of practical *in situ* sensors' (Yates, 1970). Fortunately, they can be met in large part by existing observatories in orbit. Modern methods of remote sensing permit the collection of data on a scale so uniform, with a coverage so frequent, that competition by conventional ('direct') means would be prohibitively expensive or otherwise virtually impossible for other reasons. Another invaluable bonus stems from the fact that the physical indications given by remote sensing data are often different from those implicit in conventional observations.

In Bristol, a team has concerned itself with the processing and analysis of weather satellite data, particularly with a view to the development and/or improvement of techniques suitable for routine application, but relying on a minimum of sophisticated equipment. With limited resources at our disposal it seemed impracticable to try to compete with the Americans and Russians at the higher levels of sophistication. However, it is our belief that few present or potential operational users of satellite data around the world are in a position to do so either. Since reviews of American and Russian research in satellite meteorology and climatology are numerous, this paper is concerned primarily with a review of our own work in Bristol. To some, it may seem a collection of unfinished studies and partly-developed ideas and techniques, but it will have achieved its object if it stimulates fresh ideas to further methodological or conceptual progress in climatology.

Climatic analyses

The advantages and disadvantages of weather satellite data in climatological studies have been discussed elsewhere. So, too, have been the principal problems associated with their routine use (Barrett, 1974a). The chief opportunities may be emphasised by listing the uses to which such data may be put. These include:

1. completing maps of climatological elements especially in regions of sparse conventional data coverage, e.g. maps of cloud cover across the tropical Pacific Ocean;
2. mapping climatological variables which were previously amenable to estimation alone, e.g. the pattern of the net radiation balance at the top of the Earth's atmosphere;
3. mapping variables previously unconsidered, e.g. radiation temperatures of cloud tops exposed to space;
4. classifying climates on new bases, e.g. in terms of net radiation balance, vorticity distributions and humidity regimes.

Until now, few techniques have been developed specifically to aid the study of climatology from satellites. However, as we move into the second decade of operational satellite activities (1975—84) there must be an upsurge of interest in this field as the runs of available data from satellites lengthen. In addition to the academic benefits derived from new inventories of atmospheric behaviour, practical benefits will surely multiply. Already some spaceflight operations are being planned using global cloud cover models based in part on satellite data (Salomonson, 1969). This is but one example of the many practical applications which spring to mind.

Cloud cover distributions

Many methods have been investigated for extracting cloud cover information from visible images, whether photographs or scanning radiometer photo-strips (Plate 8.1). These include freehand (Sadler, 1971), photographic (Kornfield et al, 1967) and computer-based (Taylor and Winston, 1968; Miller, 1971) techniques. Of these, the simplest and cheapest to undertake is the first. Amongst our earliest work was the preparation of sets of mean cloud maps from Essa satellite imagery, using a 2½° grid intersection sampling technique (Barrett, 1970a). Such maps could not be compiled either so quickly or so uniformly from conventional data sources. Although the maps are rather generalised (Figure 8.1), they are useful in revealing synoptic and sub-synoptic scale climatic sequences, even in quite remote regions of the world.

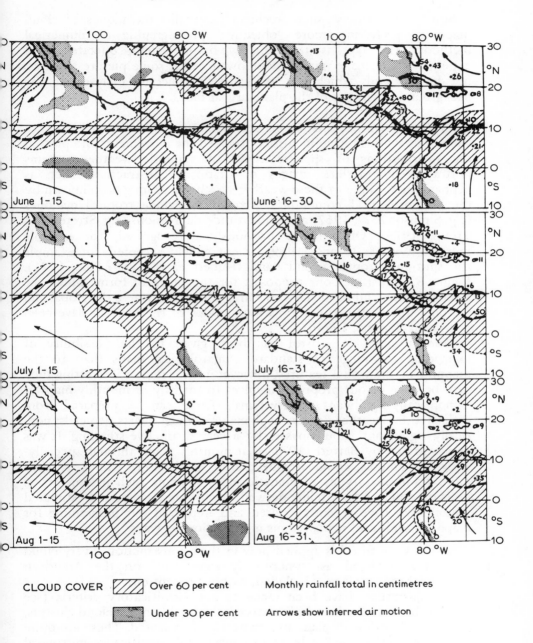

Figure 8.1   Maps of mean cloud cover, Central America and eastern equatorial Pacific for six successive half months, June—August, 1966, compiled from Essa imagery. Gross changes in the intertropical cloud band and the flanking tropical anticyclones can be followed. (After Barrett, 1970a; from Crowe, 1971.)

Some may criticise such freehand ('eyeball') techniques of cloud mapping, preferring more 'objective' photographic or numerical methods. The fact is that the eye-brain system, operated with experience, can make immediate allowances for some picture features, not due to clouds, which cause difficulties in objective analyses, e.g. the background brightness of the planetary surface.

Synoptically-significant cloud masses
Numerous workers have identified, tracked the movements and plotted the distributions of specific types of synoptic weather systems portrayed by satellite images or first-order abstractions such as nephanalyses. Some of these weather systems have long been known by the meteorological community. Examples include tropical cyclones (e.g. Simpson *et al*, 1967) and mid-latitude depressions (e.g. Streten and Troup, 1973). Others were previously unrecognised, for example inverted V-waves (Frank, 1969) or not widely accepted, for example the split intertropical cloud band (Hubert *et al*, 1969; Pike, 1971). Figure 8.2 illustrates our proposals for the range of forms which the intertropical cloud band (I.T.C.B.) may adopt. Elsewhere the global and seasonal distributions of the various modes of the I.T.C.B. have been portrayed (Barrett, 1974b).

More thought in Bristol has been given to the possibility of expanding the range of standard climatological maps than to the mapping of individual features, however unexpected or interesting they may be. One of our proposals involves fortnightly or monthly maps of 'synoptically-significant nephsystems'. These can be prepared from official U.S. Weather Bureau nephanalyses. Such charts depict 'synoptically significant' cloud masses by a very distinctive stippling. It was demonstrated by Barrett (1971) that monthly maps, through specially-designed symbols, could provide useful ('explanatory') links between more traditional types of climatic maps showing such parameters as pressure and winds, satellite-derived mean cloud cover, and estimated rainfall. We have recently revised and improved our programme for mapping significant nephsystems in the following ways:

1. no 'scale filter' is applied now in their construction. Every cloud area depicted as 'synoptically significant' on the American nephanalysis is now included, without exception;
2. adjustments have been made to the classificatory criteria (see Table 8.1) so that medium to small cumulonimbus cloud clusters, circulariform in plan, are separately represented. These are quite newly recognised as being of considerable significance in tropical climatology. They did not appear in our original scheme.

The principal purpose for which maps of significant nephsystems are compiled is to provide a dynamic view of the chief weather structures which contribute to monthly climatic patterns. A subordinate purpose

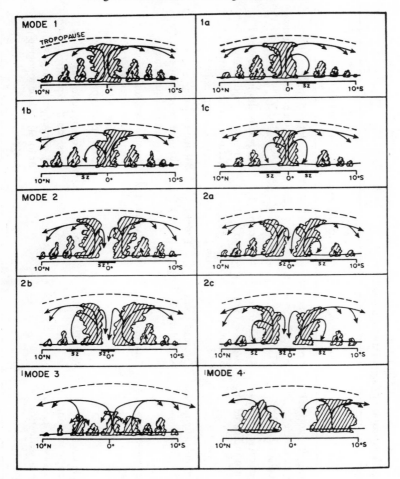

Figure 8.2 A comprehensive model of the intertropical cloud band in meridional section based on the evidence of satellite imagery. Of special interest is Mode 2, with its split I.T.C.B.'s. The existence of this mode was not known in pre-satellite days. (From Barrett, 1970c.)

is to illustrate the monthly distributions of certain individual classes of weather structures, e.g. tropical vortices or mid-latitude fronts. Since notable regional differences in the types and frequencies of neph-systems appear in such maps (see Figure 8.3, covering the Indian Ocean—Southeast Asian region in January 1970), it would seem worth investigating whether they might be used further to support new synoptic classifications of climate. Unfortunately, satellite data have been analysed and interpreted far too long in terms of already established climatological thought and practice. There is much to be

TABLE 8.1

Classification of significant nephsystems

Type	Form	Description	Dimensions	Length/breadth ratio	Synoptic interpretations
1.	Vortical	Circular or subcircular vortical cloudiness (vortex centre indicated on nephanalysis)	Vortical overcast circles $\geqslant$ (5° lat. × 5° long.)	From 1:1 to 1.5:1	Well-defined vortices of hurricanes or tropical storms
2.	Large circulariform	Circular or subcircular nephmass (vortex centre not indicated on nephanalysis)	Vortical overcast circles $\geqslant$ (5° lat. × 5° long.)	From 1:1 to 1.5:1	Large cumulonimbus cloud clusters, or moderately-defined vortices of tropical storms or depressions
3.	Small circulariform	Circular or subcircular nephmass	Overcast areas $<$ (5° lat. × 5° long.)	From 1:1 to 1.5:1	Medium to small cumulonimbus cloud clusters, or tropical disturbances
4.	Amorphous	Nephmasses lacking simple geometrical shape	Any size	Various and/or variable	Complex and/or various, e.g. poorly organised widespread instability and/or degenerations from other types
5.	Elongated (linear)	Relatively simple linear nephmasses, elongated along one principal axis (see Fig. 8.3 for subordinate classification by cloud type)	Any size	$\geqslant 2:1$	Various types of instability axes, most frequently caused by convergence (large scale or local) and/or topographic factors

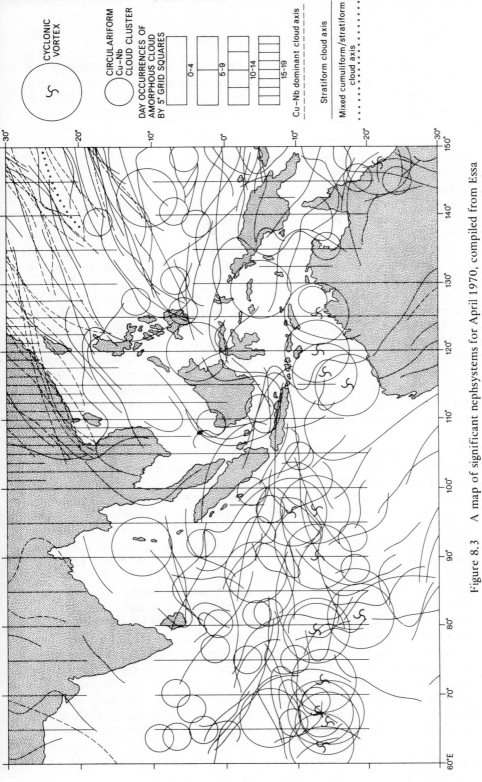

Figure 8.3   A map of significant nephsystems for April 1970, compiled from Essa nephanalyses. The distributions and forms of all the important weather-producing atmospheric organisations are revealed.

CYCLONIC VORTEX

CIRCULARIFORM
Cu—Nb
CLOUD CLUSTER

DAY OCCURRENCES OF
AMORPHOUS CLOUD
BY 5° GRID SQUARES

0—4

5—9

10—14

15—19

Cu—Nb dominant cloud axis

Stratiform cloud axis

Mixed cumuliform/stratiform
cloud axis

gained from viewing them in their own terms, or even — reversing the normal roles — as the primary reference data with which the others, now the conventional climatic statistics, should be compared. There is much scope for creative thinking in this area of climatology.

Meteorological and hydrological analyses

Patterns of wind flow

Linear or elongated cloud features are common in weather satellite imagery (Barrett, 1968, 1970a). Although, for well-known reasons, many such features are poor indicators of the direction of wind flow in any reasonably shallow layer of the atmosphere, there is general agreement that the more shallow nephlines are dominantly arranged in a downwind direction. Consequently, streamline maps can be constructed from carefully selected cloud evidence in images whose resolution is adequate. Although such maps have been superseded in low latitudes with the advent of geosynchronous satellites, smoothed nephline analyses still have a part to play in middle latitudes, particularly over open oceans. Within the tropics, wind mapping techniques based on cloud motion vectors (e.g. Fujita et al, 1969) are more satisfactory for short-term forecasting but beyond about 40°N and S of the equator foreshortening, due to the curvature of the globe, becomes an over-riding difficulty.

The displacement of bright nephmasses

In some regions, an analytical technique which can be regarded as a climatological counterpart of the meteorological method of cloud motion vector contruction may be employed to reveal the climatic nature and behaviour of certain air streams or air masses. The Indian Ocean, suitably data-remote in the conventional sense, provides an example. Figure 8.4a—f represents a crude Lagrangian view of horizontal motions through the greater part of the South Asian monsoon season of 1967 on a month-by-month basis (Hamilton, 1973, 1974). Although problems were caused by fission and fusion of some of the small, brightly-reflective cloud clusters ('nephmasses') which were tracked from day to day, and interpretation is complicated by some inevitable altitudinal blurring by circulations centred at different tropospheric levels, such maps do reveal interesting features of the macro-structure and behaviour of the summer monsoon. Note especially the patchy nature of convection cloud in the monsoon air-mass, its progressive expansion and retreat especially north of the equator, and the sparseness of clear evidence of widespread trans-equatorial air flow. On such a time scale as this, the long-awaited geosynchronous satellite over the Indian Ocean will probably reveal little more. Its important contribution will be to the study of the many very short-lived cloud clusters which we know survive for two days or less.

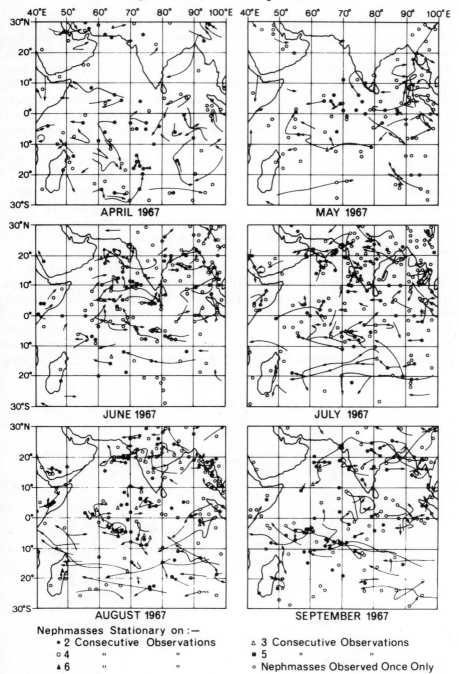

Figure 8.4 The lives and paths of discrete cloud clusters (minimum size one-fifth of a $10°$ grid square) observed over the Indian Ocean from April to September 1967 by Essa satellites. These reveal the convectively-bubbling nature of the South Asian monsoon, and its gross patterns of advance and retreat. (After Hamilton, 1973.)

Regional rainfall distributions

The author's interest in mapping and estimating rainfall from weather satellite data was aroused during a visit to Australia in 1969. Rainfall mapping in that region is hampered both in the continental interior and over the surrounding sea areas especially to the west and south by the sparseness or absence of conventional recording stations. Furthermore, it can be argued that maps of rainfall compiled from ground sources — with all their instrumentally and topographically-induced inhomogeneities — are not necessarily the best that can be conceived for input to computer models of the global circulation and the hydrological cycle. Consequently, an attempt was made to develop a method for the estimation of monthly rainfall from satellite neph-analyses or photographs. Resulting rainfall maps would benefit from the fact that one or two satellites can provide all the necessary evidence, and that a grid-intersection technique would smooth out the more abrupt local rainfall variations caused by surface relief.

Eventually, it was decided to analyse cloud fields for strength of cloud cover and cloud type. Different cloud families were accorded appropriate indices for their associated rainfall probabilities and intensities. The monthly compound cloud indices for a set of key stations were correlated with observed rainfall totals by regression techniques (Barrett, 1970b, 1971) and rainfall estimation maps were prepared for the tropical Far East (Figure 8.5). A similar technique was

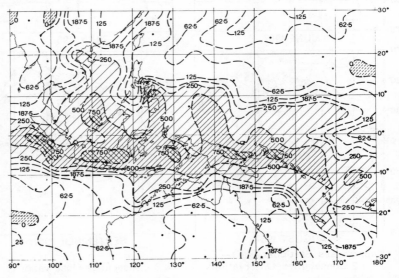

Figure 8.5   A map of rainfall across the tropical Far East, for January 1967, estimated from Essa satellite visible imagery by an indirect method which relates rainfall to cloud cover. The meridionally-orientated prongs of heavy rainfall between 5–15°N. are particularly striking. Similar patterns for this season were found by Leigh (1973) in humidity analyses of Tiros Medium Resolution Infra-red (M.R.I.R.) data. (From Barrett, 1971.)

applied later to individual stations in the Indian sub-continent (Hamilton, 1973).

Daily rainfall estimations

The monthly method for mapping rainfall was adopted and modified by Follansbee (1973) for estimating daily rainfall from satellite photographs for a wide range of localities including peninsular Florida, southern California, Arkansas, Louisiana and Mississippi in North America, as well as Zambia, India and the Mekong Basin in south-east Asia. Currently, the present author is evaluating a further derivative of the monthly method in semi-arid areas around the Persian Gulf. Although the results have been encouraging — in some cases the best available for hydrological forecasting purposes — a purpose-built daily technique may be preferred especially where estimates are required for very small basins, or even for forecasts for point locations. In the new model, it was proposed to identify, on a satellite nephanalysis, a quadrant which was upwind from the forecasting station, with a radius related to the speed of the approaching weather (see Figure 8.6). Cloud cover, rainfall probability and intensity indices were developed as before, and plots of rainfall estimates against rainfall measurements were used to prepare a nomogram of forecast rainfall by classes (cf. Figure 8.7). Over a trial period of six months a forecast accuracy of over 74% was achieved, good enough to warrant further developments of the basic method.

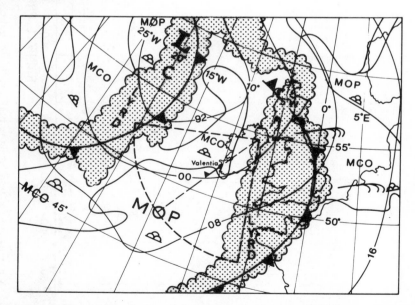

Figure 8.6   The nephanalysis quadrant (bordered by broken line) within which the satellite-viewed cloud cover for 18th July, 1970, was assessed to provide an appropriate. rainfall prediction index for Valentia in south-western Ireland. This can be translated into a rainfall forecast for the next 16 hours. (From Barrett, 1973a.)

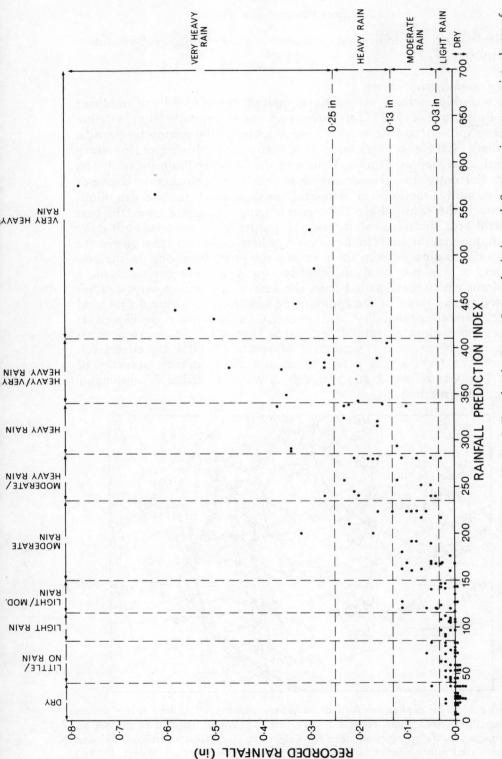

Figure 8.7   A nomogram for translating rainfall prediction indices for the Lower Parrett basin in south Somerset into appropriate classes of forecast rainfall for the following 24 hours. The plotted points indicate the observed relationships between rainfall prediction indices derived from satellite imagery and recorded daily rainfall through an evaluation period. The categories Light, Moderate and Heavy rain are equal sub-

Rainfall forecasts for river catchments

In order to expand the range of applications to which the satellite rainfall analyses might be put, recent tests have centred on a small catchment in south Somerset, namely the Lower Parrett (25 x 40 km) which drains into the Bristol Channel near Bridgwater. Mean daily rainfalls have been calculated from sixteen conventional stations through an evaluation period for which a forecasting nomogram was prepared (Figure 8.7). Using the mean precipitation over the basin, the influence of local anomalies is reduced. Further, such satellite estimates can be used directly in mean basin depth/area estimation for hydrological forecasting and river control. There are three other important procedural differences compared with the original Valentia method:

1. approaching weather is assessed on the basis of the Meteorological Office prebaratic chart for 24 hours ahead, not the 850 mb wind at the beginning of the forecast period;
2. in view of the greater confidence with which the appropriate clouds can be identified by means of 1 (above), the rainfall coefficient each day is calculated for a 30° segment astride the predicted line of approach of the weather, not a 90° quadrant as before;
3. shortcomings in the official U.S. Weather Bureau nephanalyses (e.g. their frequent failure to specify cumulonimbus in cold frontal and cold sector situations) are circumvented by the use of satellite photographs or visible scanning radiometer picture strips in preference.

Results for the initial trial 'forecast' period (July–December 1970) were good. The correct class of rainfall was obtained on more than 70% of all occasions for which the data were available. This level of success was achieved despite the lower range of daily rainfall totals in the Lower Parrett basin than at Valentia, and despite the sub-division for the first time of the 'heavy' rainfall category into subordinate 'heavy', 'heavy, or very heavy', and 'very heavy' categories, as shown in Table 8.2. For many hydrological purposes, such as hydrograph prediction for river management and flood control, the more extreme events are usually the more significant (Barrett, 1973b).

At present, we are investigating the scope for reducing the freehand components in this rainfall estimation/prediction method. One possibility is to consider the approaching cloud only along the predicted line of approach of the weather, analysing this with a one-dimensional microdensitometer (Figure 8.8). Another possibility is that indices of cloud brightness and texture established by semi-objective means might be combined to give an indication of the broad scale rainfall field (see Figure 8.9 and Table 8.3). Such an approach could be made more fully objective using a system like the Quantimet 720 analog computer applying a ground-cut technique to map cloud brightness, and a feature

TABLE 8.2

A check-list for the Lower Parrett basin, Somerset, relating satellite-evaluated rainfall prediction indices to classes of rainfall for 24-hour forecasts.

Rainfall category (Basic classes in italics)	Range (inches)	R.P.I. range
Very heavy	>0.25	>410
Heavy/Very Heavy	>0.14	340—409
Heavy	0.14—0.25	285—339
Moderate/Heavy	0.04—0.25	235—284
Moderate	0.04—0.13	150—234
Light/Moderate	0.01—0.13	115—149
Light	0.01—0.03	85—114
Little/No rain	0.00—0.03	40— 84
Dry	0.00	0— 39

TABLE 8.3

Observed relationships between satellite-photographed clouds analysed in terms of their brightness and texture. Category 1 is equivalent to (1) in Figure 8.9, categories 2 and 3 to (2), categories 4 and 5 to (3), and categories 6—10 to (4)

Cloud texture	Cloud brightness		
	Bright	Subdued	Dim
Smooth	1. CuNb with Ci anvils CuNb clusters NiSt	4. St Al St Ci shields	7. Ci Ci St Fog
Granular or striated	2. Scattered CuNb with Ci anvils Cellular CuNb Mixed CuNb/CiSt	5. Scattered CuNb and/or CuCg Low St—Cu sheets	8. Ci bands Al len Fair weather Cu
Rough	3. CuCg fields Monsoon clouds Broken cumuliform and/or stratiform patches	6. Dissipating cumuliform and/or stratiform patches Cellular St—Cu	9. Island wake eddies Other topograpically-induced cloud features 10. Cloud-free areas

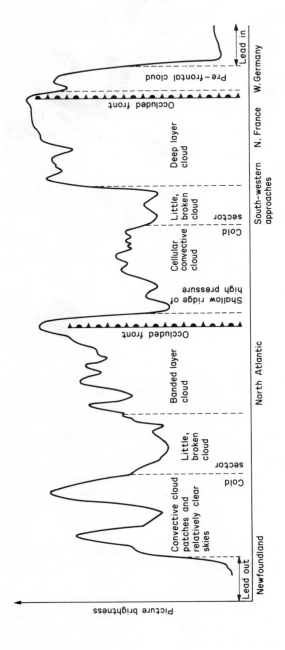

Figure 8.8 This microdensitometer trace of Essa-photographed cloud over the North Atlantic from western Germany to Newfoundland on 2nd September, 1970, clearly distinguishes a variety of synoptic-scale weather structures through the states of the sky.

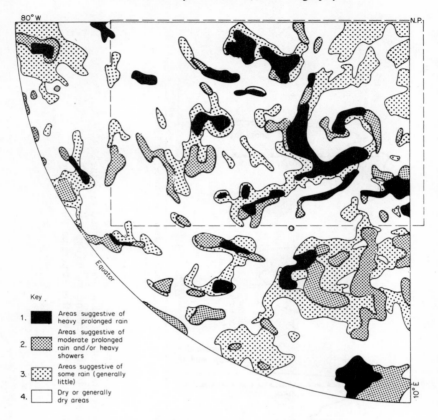

Figure 8.9   A combined brightness/texture map for a quadrant of the northern-hemisphere from Essa 8 visible imagery, 20th June, 1970. This was constructed from brightness information obtained by variably adjusting the image displayed on a suitable cathode ray tube, and a texture analysis obtained by using an appropriate capacitor as a band-pass filter to present the image in relief model form. Smooth, granular or striated, and rough areas were distinguished from one another by hand. Categories of cloud types set out in Table 8.3 were grouped in terms of types and intensities of rain. Unfortunately, it is difficult, using this approach, to allow for background brightness (e.g. over North Africa, in the south-east of the area covered by Figure 8.9) excepting by a final 'eyeball' assessment.

count to map cloud texture. Similar results might be achieved using Agfacontour film. This would have the advantage of relative cheapness but poses problems of calibration and quality control.

Other groups of workers are adopting different approaches to this problem, amply summarised by Martin and Scherer (1973). These include examination of image brightness, infrared data, and radar displays, in comparison with conventionally-measured rainfall. However, at the time of writing, none has given better results than the

Valentia/Bridgwater method. It is possible that ESMR (Electrically Scanning Microwave Radiometer) data of the type provided first by Nimbus 5 may eventually prove the most useful satellite data of all, though, for technical reasons, for sea areas only. From the Nimbus 5 ESMR data, maps of rainfall intensity have been produced in units of mm/hr. of rain (Wilheit *et al*, 1973). We might hope that quite accurate short-term forecasts of rainfall in sea and coastal areas could be derived from the integration of such intensities over appropriate forecasting segments, provided that, as in the Valentia and Bridgwater cases, the rainfall processes are advectional rather than convectional and little weather development is expected. Although the restriction of the utility of such methods to sea and coastal areas is in some ways unfortunate, it is precisely in these regions that rainfall forecasting by conventional means is most difficult. As in so many other situations, we see the satellite as a complement to, rather than a replacement for, the conventional weather observatory.

Operational cloud analyses

Satellite nephanalyses

The term 'nephanalysis' was already in everyday meteorological use in presatellite days, meaning the analysis of cloudiness, usually from the normal observing viewpoint on the ground. With the arrival of weather satellites, new forms of nephanalyses were quickly introduced. So one of the earliest, simplest, and most enduring methods of visible waveband imagery analysis has been the freehand compilation of schematic cloud charts, satellite nephanalyses (see Barrett, 1970c, 1974a). Figure 8.10 summarises the wide range of nephanalyses that have been considered, and the types of uses to which they have been put. Considering that general nephanalyses have been used widely in climatic research and are commonly the only form of satellite information supplied to the short-term forecaster in image form, it is surprising that there has been no generally accepted advance on the standard (general) scheme for nephanalysis construction for about a decade. Proposals for multispectral cloud-type identification methods using MRIR (Medium Resolution Infrared) measurements hold considerable promise for the future (Shenk and Holub, 1973), but single waveband methods will continue to monopolise the operational field for some time to come. Earlier studies mentioned in this paper alluded to shortcomings in the standard nephanalysis procedure. It seemed to us that there were several ways in which improvements could be made (Harris and Barrett, 1975). These included:

1. formalising the rules for nephanalysis construction;
2. increasing the information content;

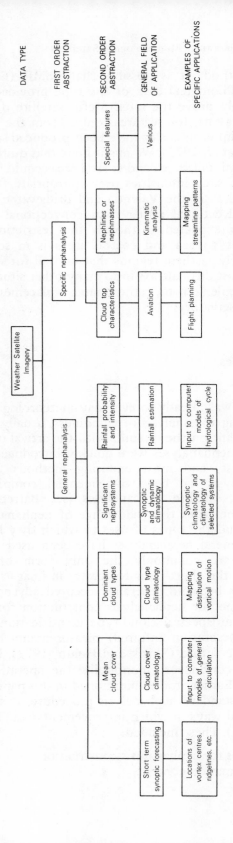

Figure 8.10 A diagrammatic summary of the range of analyses of satellite cloud imagery developed to date. Most are executed by long-hand ('eyeball') techniques. Most, if not all, should be amenable to automatic ('objective') techniques. Current work at Bristol is directed towards this goal.

3. increasing the frequency of coverage;
4. reducing the level of subjectivity in the construction process.

The first two improvements are possible using a freehand approach to visible imagery analysis. The third necessitates the use of infrared imagery in addition to, or instead of, visible imagery. The fourth involves automatic analytical techniques.

Improved freehand nephanalysis
In the construction of standard satellite nephanalyses, it seems that the analyst is free to go about the task as he pleases. Although there is a recognised code of nephanalysis symbols, there are no established rules governing the order in which different types of features should be sought. Not surprisingly, it is evident that the practice of nephanalysis construction differs from country to country and from one analyst to another. Different results may be obtained if, for example, one analyst draws his first boundaries around areas of uniform cloud type and another around areas of equal cloud cover. Figure 8.11 summarises the sequence of construction stages we would like to see adopted as standard practice.

Turning to the question of increased information content, the standard nephanalysis is open to criticism, partly on the rather limited range of synoptically-interpreted features it portrays, and partly on the range and detail of its cloud provinces. We would like to see included in the nephanalysis all features with an areal extent greater than 2½° square; as well as all linear features (e.g. cloud streets or striations) more than 5° of latitude or longitude in length (whichever locally is the shorter); and no cyclonic or anticyclonic rotation centres or vortical points should be omitted where there is reasonable certainty in their identification. A further proposal is that the range of cloud cover categories could be increased with confidence from four to five. This would be of benefit to the average user — especially if the standard notation for 'Open', 'Mostly Open', 'Mostly Covered' and 'Covered' conditions were dropped in favour of median values for five equal percentage classes. At a glance, the user could then obtain a meaningful estimate of the strength of the cloud cover.

An inevitable problem attending the proposed increase in the information content of the satellite nephanalysis would be the danger of overloading the chart. We estimate that our proposals would lead to an increase of between 3—5 times the standard information content. Our solution to the overloading problem is a sectionalised nephanalysis in three parts, as illustrated by Plate 8.2 and Figure 8.12 (Harris and Barrett, 1975). At the central forecasting/automatic picture transmission facility, the optimum arrangement is for the flanking charts to be printed in reverse on transparent material, so that they can be folded in as an overlay to the others. It would then be possible to examine each separately, or in combination with either or both of the others.

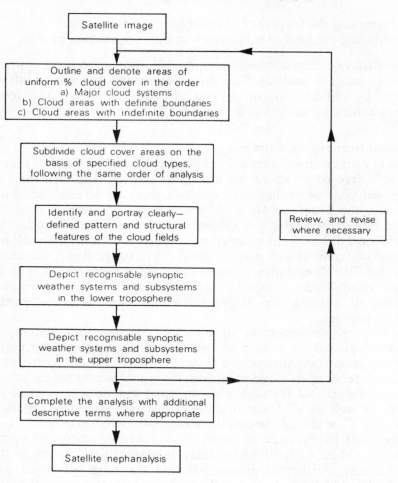

Figure 8.11   Flow diagram for long-hand nephanalysis. Standardisation amongst nephanalysts and between national weather bureaux has been lacking in the past. (From Harris and Barrett, 1975.)

For Mufax transmission to regional weather centres and other users, the three charts could be transmitted side by side. Despite the increased detail, the nephanalysis set can be compiled by an experienced analyst in an hour, within present 'real-time' forecasting requirements.

Infrared nephanalyses
The World Weather Watch plans for the middle and late 1970s provide for 4—5 geosynchronous satellites to give frequent data coverage in low latitudes around the globe, and a pair of low-orbiting satellites in polar orbits to observe middle to high latitudes at least twice daily. Thus, the scope for more frequent nephanalyses for the latitude of north-western

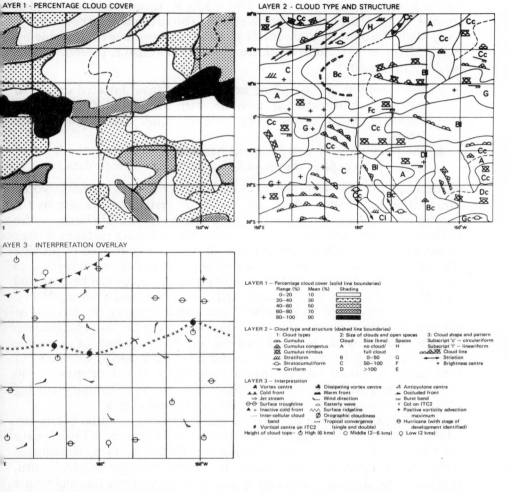

Figure 8.12   An example of an improved nephanalysis following the scheme outlined by Harris and Barrett (1975). This type of product should provide more information for short-term weather forecasters, whilst comprising a much more useful document for archiving. (From Harris and Barrett, 1975.)

Europe is comparatively limited, but better than the current once-daily coverage. To be increased at all, the nephanalysis programme must involve infrared imagery in addition to (or instead of) the visible imagery. The current family of operational weather satellites (Noaa) provides daytime visible, and daytime and night-time infrared imagery, by direct read-out to A.P.T. stations from scanning radiometers. The visible imagery is recorded within the $0.52-0.73\,\mu$m waveband (Plate 8.1), and the infrared imagery within $10.5-12.5\,\mu$m. At a planned spacecraft altitude of 1460 km, the scanning radiometers have a ground resolution of better than 4 km at nadir, and are capable of yielding radiance temperatures between 180°–330°K to an accuracy ranging from 4°K to 1°K at the respective limits (Stoldt and Havanac, 1973). Very High Resolution Radiometer (VHRR) images, newly available by A.P.T., have the excellent resolution of 0.9 km at nadir. It seems worth while to investigate:

1. the feasibility of compiling nephanalyses from infrared images to compare as directly as possible with those based on vidicon photographs or scanning radiometer visible waveband picture strips;
2. the possibility of compiling nephanalyses solely from the infrared imagery, to exploit the special characteristics of such data.

Although our studies in this field have only recently begun, it is worth noting the key issues which are involved. Perhaps the most useful feature of an infrared image is the fairly direct relationship between the radiation pattern and the temperature of the radiating surfaces. Either conventional or satellite spectrometer data can be employed to provide the necessary scale factors for converting the radiation temperatures into cloud top altitudes, so that coarse cloud top maps can be prepared (see Plate 8.3) from the infrared strips (de Cotiis and Conlan, 1971). Such maps could not be prepared from visible imagery on account of the much more complex physical indications given by cloud brightness. On the other hand, most if not all of the contents of a visible nephanalysis can be obtained from the infrared imagery. Certainly, at first sight, it would appear that a programme based on twice-daily infrared nephanalyses would be considerably better than one involving both daytime visible and night-time infrared cloud charts.

However, there is one problem in particular that must be overcome. Aloft, the radiation temperatures of cloud tops at selected levels vary very little from day to night. Nearer the Earth's surface, the diurnal temperature cycle becomes more and more strongly marked until, overland, the daytime radiation is much stronger than the night-time radiation, all other things being equal. This poses problems for detailed low-level cloud-top examination, but hinders little the processes of cloud cover mapping and cloud type identification. The self-evident advantages of being able to follow more closely on twice-daily charts the movements of very mobile weather systems, the development or dissipation of all significant cloud masses, and the diurnal rhythms of cloud growth and decay, need no elaboration.

Automatic image analysis

General considerations
As satellite data increase in quantity and improve in quality, the obvious shortcomings of longhand methods of analysis are forcing us to ask whether there might be relatively inexpensive ways in which more

'objective' products could be achieved automatically. Several commercial systems for image data analysis and display have ready applications in satellite meteorology and climatology. Those we have investigated include:

1. electronic scanning microdensitometers (e.g. Joyce Loebl Mk.III CS). Coupled with a suitable computer, one-dimensional density traces from satellite images can be combined into two-dimensional displays. Cloud features can be mapped, and analysed, in terms of brightness and texture, either statistically or by eye;
2. analog computers with a photographic input (e.g. the Quantimet 720). Cloud areas above a selected ('ground cut') brightness level (Plate 8.4), cloud shapes, and numbers of cloud elements can be rapidly assessed in selected regions;
3. image enhancers (e.g. the Datacolor 703). Black and white cloud images can be quickly rendered in selected colours for purposes of cloud identification and display.

We are of the opinion that, useful as such systems may be, the optimum data retrieval method is likely to be achieved by direct input of a tape-recorded signal from an A.P.T. facility into the computer (Horne, 1974). This may be justified as follows:

1. an input of photographic positives, using a vidicon camera and special interface hardware, is adversely affected by the high signal-to-noise ratio of vidicon cameras, the limited dynamic range of photopositives (approx. 20dB), and the difficulty of building effective hardware interfaces to relatively cheap low-speed digital computers from standard vidicon cameras with their high operating speeds;
2. an input of photographic negatives is subject to the same problems as 1, despite the fact that the dynamic range of the negatives is ~ 10dB greater: this is still much less than the dynamic digital range of a small computer such as the PDP-8E (approx. 63dB).
3. an input of tape-recorded A.P.T. scans for direct sampling is unaffected by the further processing which is carried out following final demodulation before application to facsimile machines. This produces a deliberate degradation of a signal from the point of view of computer input. Adopting the tape-recorded A.P.T. data as the input, two broad approaches to cloud mapping, analysis and recognition may be envisaged, using respectively analog and digital techniques.

Analog techniques
Perhaps the simplest task involves the compilation of brightness-contoured maps from visible image data, or temperature-contoured

maps from infrared image data. By electronic means, key points can be identified on each of the continuously-variable scan lines. These can be linked from line to line to give a two-dimensional display. If vertical scale factors are incorporated in the procedure as an additional type of specification, cloud top maps may be prepared, similar to that included as Plate 8.3. Figure 8.13 is a computer algorithm for this type of product.

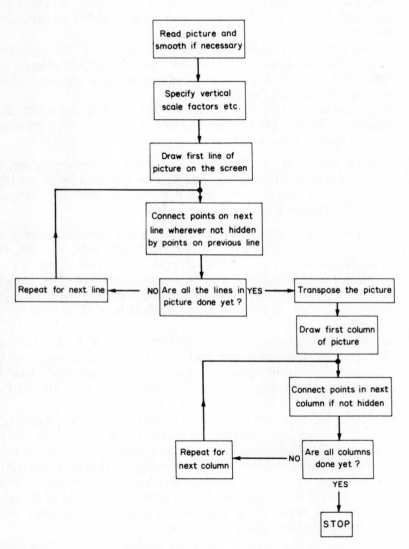

Figure 8.13   An outline of a computer algorithm for a program to produce three-dimensional (cloud height) analyses of satellite infrared imagery (see also Plate 8.3).

Digital techniques

We may examine two possibilities from the many that spring to mind. Both involve the two-dimensional Fourier transform. In the same way that a one-dimensional Fourier transform represents a time signal by a set of sinusoidal frequency components (the 'spectrum'), the two-dimensional transform produces a spatial-frequency specification of a two-dimensional space matrix. In the digital computer the two-dimensional Fourier transform has a counterpart known as the Discrete Fourier Transform (D.F.T.) which can now be computed very rapidly. Operations which were previously carried out in the space domain can now be carried out much more quickly in the frequency domain. The saving is in the order of $2N \log_2 N$ compared with N^2 operations, which is very considerable given that for a satellite picture matrix N would typically be 50 000 or 100 000. The D.F.T. might be used in the following ways to assist in objective pattern matching procedures, e.g. for classifying the contents of a cloud image in terms of its textural variations:

1. computing the D.F.T. of a selected area of a picture yields its spectrum. If this is segregated into a set of annular areas, an indication is given of the character of the picture sample by the set of total energies in the annuli. Applied initially to a series of type-example areas of different clouds, a 'fingerprint bank' may be built up by these means. For example, the 'fingerprint' for a strap of stratiform clouds will be very different from that for scattered cumuli. Operationally, each area of the unknown photograph would be matched against the key set and classified accordingly;
2. filter templates may be prepared from classical images, and with these new images may be matched. The D.F.T. of the unknown picture area is multiplied by the complex conjugate of the D.F.T. of the template picture. The resultant convolution plane contains peaks where the unknown image most closely resembles the characteristics of the template. Further analysis is then necessary before it can be said where the picture is similar to the matched filter, what proportion is similar, and how great the similarity is. Although the technique is more sensitive than 1 above, its use is complicated by rotational factors.

Unfortunately, such methods depart somewhat from the aim of establishing relatively cheap and simple techniques for satellite image analysis. However, a system can be envisaged wherein a small computer like the PDP-8 can be used for input to the digital world and output to the visual world (Horne, 1974); it combines the flexibility of a small low-speed machine with the capacity and speed of a main computer. Thus, even relatively sophisticated techniques may come within the reach of numerous operators. The next generation of polar-orbiting satellites after Noaa in the operational series will transmit data in digital, not analog, form. Thus the Tiros-N system now being derived from American DMSP (Defense Meteorological Satellite Program) configurations may lend itself particularly well to methods of this kind.

Many practical problems must be overcome before we can envisage operational applications of the more objective methods of weather satellite image analyses. Some stem from the nature and behaviour of the atmosphere itself: it is a fluid continuum whose visible tracers of state and motion can adopt an enormous variety of shapes, sizes, aggregations and patterns of organisation. To make matters worse, many clouds have diffuse, not sharp, margins. Consequently, many of the established pattern-recognition techniques are not amenable to weather satellite image analysis.

Summary and conclusions
Many years have elapsed since the first meteorologically-specialised environmental survey satellites were orbited. The stimulus weather satellites gave to atmospheric science is powerfully attested by the compendious literature which has grown up dealing with weather satellite data. Rather surprisingly, however, most published works have featured either processing and analytical techniques that could be carried out on a routine basis only by very large central facilities, or other techniques of rather local application, restricted or piecemeal in scope. The work at Bristol has been aimed between these two extremes, at the development of methods which could be applied broadly, with or without local modification, by technical means within the scope of any institution able to afford an A.P.T. receiving station for routine near-real-time work, or able to acquire rectified, normalised data from the archives in the U.S.A. for meteorological research and/or climatological studies. Without doubt, we have only begun to scratch the surface of this fascinating problem.

ACKNOWLEDGEMENTS

I would like to express my sincere thanks to satellite meteorologists around the world, but in the U.S.A. and Australia in particular, for their encouragement during ten years of research. My thanks are due especially to Mr. Vincent J. Oliver, Chief, Applications Branch, N.O.A.A., Suitland, Md., for keeping me in touch with new developments in the U.S. Weather Bureau. It has been stimulating to share my personal interest in this field with recent research students in the University of Bristol, especially Dr. M. G. Hamilton (now of the Observatory,

Edgbaston), Mr. R. J. Gurney and Mr. R. Harris; with Dr. D. Horne during his research at the University of Bath; and with numerous undergraduate students who have chipped away at problems in satellite climatology and meteorology in projects and dissertations.

REFERENCES

Barrett, E. C. (1968). *The Contribution of Meteorological Satellites to Dynamic Climatology*, unpublished Ph.D. thesis, University of Bristol.

Barrett, E. C. (1970a). 'A contribution to the dynamic climatology of the equatorial eastern Pacific and central America, based on meteorological satellite data', *Trans. Institute of British Geographers*, **50**, 25—53.

Barrett, E. C. (1970b). 'The estimation of monthly rainfall from satellite data', *Monthly Weather Review*, **98**, 322—27.

Barrett, E. C. (1970c). 'Rethinking climatology', Chapter 4 in Board, C., R. J. Chorley, P. Haggett and D. R. Stoddart (eds.), *Progress in Geography*, Vol. 2, Arnold, 154—205.

Barrett, E. C. (1971). 'The tropical Far East: ESSA satellite evaluations of high season climatic patterns', *Geographical Journal*, **137**, 535—55.

Barrett, E. C. (1973a). 'Forecasting daily rainfall from satellite data', *Monthly Weather Review*, **101**, 215—22.

Barrett, E. C. (1973b). *Satellite Data in Rainfall and Catchment Research*, British Association for the Advancement of Science, Section E. Paper 82, Canterbury.

Barrett, E. C. (1974a). *Climatology from Satellites*, Methuen.

Barrett, E. C. (1974b). 'Tropical climatology from satellites', *J. Brit. Interplanetary Soc.*, **27**, 48—65.

Crowe, P. R. (1971). *Concepts in Climatology*, Longman.

de Cotiis, A. G. and E. Conlan, (1971). 'Cloud information in three spatial dimensions using IR thermal imagery and vertical temperature profile data', *Proc. of the VIIth International Symposium on Remote Sensing of Environment*, May 17—21, 1971, University of Michigan, 595—606.

Follansbee, W. A. (1973). 'Estimation of average daily rainfall satellite cloud photographs', *NOAA Technical Memorandum, NESS 44*, U.S. Department of Commerce.

Frank, N. (1969). 'The "inverted-V" cloud pattern — an easterly wave?', *Monthly Weather Review*, **97**, 130—40.

Fujita, T. T., K. Watanabe and T. Izawa, (1969). 'Formation and structure of equatorial anticyclones caused by large-scale cross-equatorial flows determined by ATS-1 photographs', *J. Applied Meteorology*, **8**, 649—67.

Gurney, R. J. (1974). *Frequency Distributions of variables at Valentia, 1970, from Satellite and Conventional Measurements*, unpublished notes, University of Bristol.

Hamilton, M. G. (1973). *Satellite Studies of the South Asian Summer Monsoon*, unpublished Ph.D. thesis, Department of Geography, University of Bristol.

Hamilton, M. G. (1974). 'A satellite view of the South Asian Summer Monsoon', *Weather*, **26**, 82—95.

Harris, R. A. and E. C. Barrett (1975). 'An improved satellite nephanalysis', *Meteorological Magazine*, **104**, 9—16.

Horne, D. (1974). *Applications of Image Processing to A.P.T. Data,* unpublished notes, University of Bath.

Hubert, L. F., A. F. Krueger and J. S. Winston, (1969). 'The double intertropical convergence zone — fact or fiction?', *J. Atmospheric Sciences,* 26, 771—73.

Kornfield, J., A. F. Hasler, K. J. Hanson and V. E. Suomi (1967). 'Photographic cloud climatology from ESSA IV and V computer-produced mosaics', *Bull. American Meteorological Society,* 48, 878—83.

Leigh, R. M. (1973). *Tropospheric Relative Humidity and Cloudiness,* unpublished Ph.D. thesis, James Cook University of North Queensland.

Martin, D. W. and W. D. Scherer, (1973). 'Review of satellite rainfall estimation methods', *Bull. American Meteorological Society,* 54, 661—74.

Miller, D. B. (1971). *Global Atlas of Relative Cloud Cover,* U.S. Department of Commerce, U.S.A.F.

Pike, A. C. (1971). 'Intertropical convergence zone studied with an interacting atmosphere and ocean model', *Monthly Weather Review,* 99, 469—77.

Sadler, J. C. (1971). 'The analysis of cloud amount from satellite data', *Trans. New York Academy of Sciences,* Series II, 33, 436—53.

Salomonson, V. V. (1969). *Cloud Statistics in Earth Resources Technology Satellite (ERTS) Mission Planning,* NASA Report No. X-622-69-386, Goddard Space Flight Center, Greenbelt, Maryland.

Shenk, W. E. and R. J. Holub (1973). *A Multispectral Cloud Type Identification Method Using Nimbus 3 MRIR Measurements,* Conference on Atmospheric Radiation, Aug. 7—9, 1973, Fort Collins, Colorado. Preprint Vol. American Meteorological Society.

Simpson, R. H., N. L. Frank, D. Shideler and H. M. Johnson (1967). 'Atlantic tropical disturbances, 1967', *Monthly Weather Review,* 96, 251—59.

Stoldt, N. W. and P. J. Havanac (1973). *Compendium of Meteorological Satellites and Instrumentation,* National Aeronautics and Space Admin., N5SDC 73—02, Goddard Space Flight Centre, Greenbelt, Maryland.

Streten, N. A. and A. J. Troup (1973). 'A synoptic climatology of satellite observed cloud vortices over the Southern Hemisphere', *Q.J. Royal Meteorological Society,* 99, 56—72.

Taylor, V. R. and J. S. Winston (1968). *Monthly and Seasonal Mean Global Charts of Brightness from ESSA 3 and ESSA 5 Digitized Pictures, Feb. 1967—Feb. 1968,* ESSA Technical Report, N.E.S.C. 46.

Wilheit, T., J. Theon, W. Shenk and L. Allison (1973). *Meteorological Interpretations of the Images from Nimbus 5 Electrically Scanned Microwave Radiometer,* X-651-73-189 (Preprint), Goddard Space Flight Centre, Greenbelt, Maryland.

Yates, H. W. (1970). 'A general discussion of remote sensing of the atmosphere'. *Applied Optics,* 9, 1971—75.

Chapter 9

Bristol's Bridges: Microclimatology and Design

John Bailey

Until the Cumberland Basin Bridges Scheme in Bristol was opened in 1965, the Junction Lock Swing Bridge was, with the exception of the Clifton Suspension Bridge, the nearest low level road crossing to the mouth of the River Avon. It is subject to severe weight restrictions which limit its value as a crossing. The operation of the Swing Bridge to allow shipping movements on the River Avon into and out of the City Docks interrupted the heavy road traffic flows across the river at this point. The Cumberland Basin Bridges Scheme provided for a second swing bridge, the Plimsoll Bridge, and a road network arranged in such a manner that whenever one swing bridge was opened to allow shipping movements the other could carry road traffic across the river. Prior to the new scheme the journey times between the city boundaries varied between 18 minutes at off peak times when the bridge was not opened to 81 minutes at peak times when the bridge was opened (Wilson and Baldwin, 1965). It was intended that on completion of the scheme journey times would be around 18 minutes whatever the shipping movements. The whole scheme cost some £2 650 000, of which the Plimsoll Swing Bridge accounted for £400 000.

The Plimsoll Bridge

The problem
Early in its operational life the Plimsoll Bridge gave cause for concern. On occasions it jammed in the open-to-road-traffic position and could not be swung immediately on demand. This detracted from the efficient operation of the whole scheme, interfering with shipping

movements and with road traffic, the bridge being closed while the operators strove to free it. Short-term interruptions of this kind were unwelcome and annoying; they also raised the possibility that on some occasion the bridge might jam and remain jammed despite the best efforts of the operators and engineering staff. The implications of this latter situation were very grave indeed; the roots of the problem's severity lay in the geography of the situation, specifically in the configuration of the Avon channel and its large tidal range. For ships sailing from Avonmouth to the City Docks on the tide there is a point of no return. Once beyond this point, they must complete the journey to the Cumberland Basin and City Docks, for they cannot turn in the river channel, nor can they safely beach as the tide level falls. Once ships have reached the entrance to the Cumberland Basin the Plimsoll Bridge must open to allow them into the sanctuary of the Basin with its lock-controlled water level. If the Plimsoll Bridge were jammed against them, two or three ships, depending on their size, could be safely accommodated using the entrance lock and a beaching grid. If, however, a greater number of vessels were involved, the excess number would become grounded in the channel at low tide and might break their backs. This would result in considerable financial loss and might also, by blocking the channel, impound any ships that were at the time of the occurrence in the Cumberland Basin and City Docks. Clearly the jamming of the Bridge had to cease.

The nature and cause of the jamming
The jamming of the Bridge cannot be adequately explained without reference to its design and the mechanical procedures governing its operation.

The Plimsoll Bridge is a balanced cantilever centre bearing swing bridge (Figure 9.1). The main cross girder A, of box construction, rests on a centre bearing B, and from it are cantilevered twin box girder members C, whose width remains constant but whose depth decreases from the central area of the bridge to its ends. The upper surface is an orthotropic longitudinally stiffened plate D, which forms not only the bridge deck but also the upper flange of the box girders. The main centre foundation carries the centre bearing and a ring beam track of 12.2 m diameter E, which can be met by any of the four sets of balance rollers, F, as occasion demands. In a state of perfect balance, the bridge, when swinging free, rests only on the centre bearing and the balance rollers are clear of the ring beam track. The balance rollers serve to accommodate certain conditions including two that are climatically induced. Any action of the wind on the bridge superstructure or uneven snow or ice loading results in the balance rollers meeting the ring beam, so providing support and ensuring stability.

When the bridge is open to road traffic, it is fixed in the correct alignment and given support. The two ends of the main cross girder are

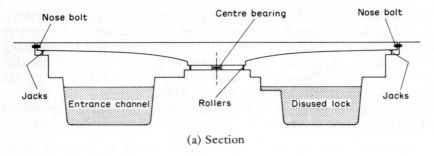

(a) Section

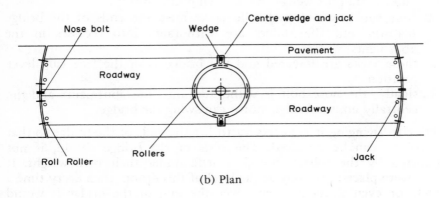

(b) Plan

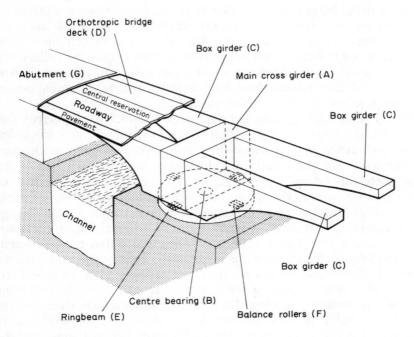

Figure 9.1   Plimsoll Bridge: sketch diagram of components (not to scale).

wedged to give, with the centre bearing, a three-point support system. Each end of the bridge is supported by four roller bearings which project from the concrete road abutments, G. Finally there are nose-locking bolts which are driven out of the abutments into a recess in the bridge to ensure its correct longitudinal alignment (Figure 9.1. Full details are in Vavasour, Wilson, Baldwin and Wolley, 1966a).

To free the bridge prior to swinging it so that shipping movements can take place, a clearly defined sequence of operations is followed:

1. the ends of the centre cross girder are raised by hydraulic jacks and the support wedges withdrawn hydraulically;
2. four synchronised hydraulic jacks raise the ends of the bridge 6.4 mm and the rollers are withdrawn into recesses in the abutments;
3. these jacks are lowered and the bridge is in the free cantilever position;
4. finally, the nose bolt is withdrawn into the abutments and the centrally housed bridge motor can swing the bridge.

Prior to swinging it is necessary to lift the ends of the bridge so that the rollers can be removed. The ends of the bridge would, if not supported by the rollers, droop a little under their own weight. If rollers were placed precisely at the level of this droop, then every time a vehicle or even a cyclist went over the end of the bridge it would oscillate a little, barging on the roller support. Apart from any strain on the structure, the noise would be unacceptable in an urban area. To overcome this effect, the ends of the bridge are pushed up a little against their own weight and supported at this height by rollers. To insert the rollers at this height, powerful jacks have to lift the ends of the bridge and then release them back onto the rollers. Jamming occurs when the jacks are unable to make this lift.

The end jacks initially installed were each of 348.7 kN capacity[1] and were interlocked in such a way that if the load on any jack exceeded that on any other jack by more than 10% its movement was checked until the loads became equal; in addition the jacks at each end of the bridge were linked in operation. In this way, the possibility of longitudinal or lateral tilting by the independent operation of jacks acting out of unison, with excessive resultant strains in the bridge superstructure, was avoided. Vavasour and Wilson writing in Vavasour, Wilson, Baldwin and Wolley (1966a, 1966b) wrote that the assessment of the required jacking forces was made in the light of the assessed dead and live loadings and of temperature deflections. They reported the inclusion of a reserve jacking force of 30% to allow for the stiffening effect of the bridge surfacing. They further observed that this reserve might be of value in view of the design allowance for temperature difference of 8.3°C between the top and bottom bridge flanges and the 11°C noticed at an early stage in the bridge's life.[2] They also note that it was necessary to increase the capacity of the jacks at the centre wedges from 557.9 kN to 1388.1 kN to allow the insertion of the centre wedges under all conditions, because transverse deflections due to temperature had been ignored in the original design. In the event, however, the continued jamming of the bridge once normal operating commenced demonstrated the inadequacy of the jacking system and, as no failure in the assessment of the dead or live loadings was apparent, a re-examination of the temperature differences that were leading to thermal deflections was necessary.

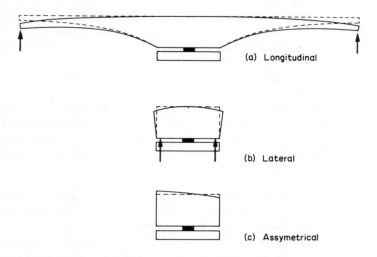

Figure 9.2   Simplified thermal distortions (scale exaggerated).

It seemed possible that three types of thermal deflection were occurring. First, a longitudinal deflection as in Figure 9.2a, resulting from a temperature difference between the top and bottom flanges of the bridge boxes. The effect, analogous to the bending of a heated bimetallic strip, would be to increase the forces needed to lift the ends of the bridge. Second, in response to the same temperature difference a lateral deflection could occur, as in Figure 9.2b. In this case, the force required from the centre wedge jacks would be increased. In both cases the size of the deflection and increase in jacking force required would be related to the magnitude of the temperature difference between the top and bottom bridge flanges. Lastly, the possibility of asymmetrical deflection (Figure 9.2c) had to be considered. This could arise as a result of temperature differences between the opposite faces of the bridge. Such asymmetries would create a situation where the end loads would no longer be evenly distributed between the four jacks.

The temperature investigation

Macroclimatic influences
In August, 1967, I undertook to provide the City Engineer, Surveyor and Planning Officer's Department of Bristol Corporation with a report (Bailey, 1968) on the temperatures experienced by the Plimsoll Bridge superstructure, with particular reference to the magnitude of the temperature differences developing in the structure on hot days. As a first step, the relationship between occurrences of jamming and the macroclimatic conditions was examined (Table 9.1). When, in the opinion of the bridge operator on duty, the jamming was caused by a mechanical or electrical malfunction the occurrence was not included in the table. Not infrequently, however, mechanical malfunctions may have arisen in response to the excessive calls made on the equipment to free the bridge when it was in a 'nearly-jammed' condition. Also, though the bridge might jam several times on the same day this has been logged as a single occurrence of jamming.

Study of the macroclimatic conditions at the times of jamming showed that jamming was probable with a diurnal air temperature range of 10°C accompanied by clear skies and wind speeds <20 kph. Absence of rain during the period further increased the probability of jamming. The following tentative conclusions were drawn:

1. no month could be considered entirely free of the possibility of jamming, though the period from March to October would encompass the majority of occurrences;
2. the climatic conditions under which the bridge might jam were by no means exceptional. Indeed they could be described as almost commonplace;
3. high values of air temperature were comparatively unimportant.

The empirical investigation
This general macroclimatic analysis formed the background against which the programme of microclimatological measurement was mounted. In this programme, detailed studies were made of the temperature distribution throughout the bridge superstructure. Measurements were made over a period of some months, generally at times when the climatic conditions approximated to those that resulted in jamming. A standard meteorological screen was maintained on site and the enclosed thermometers and thermohygrograph provided air temperature and humidity values. In addition, air temperatures and relative humidities were monitored within the box girders using thermohygrographs. Surface temperature measurements were made using copper-constantan thermocouples and surface contact resistance thermometers. Towards the end of the site measurements a period of intensive observation coincided most fortunately with a situation

TABLE 9.1

Distribution by months of the days on which jamming occurred, January 1966–May 1968

	Jan.	Feb.	March	April	May	June	July	Aug.	Sept.	Oct.	Nov.	Dec.
1966	1	0	0	4	2	0	2	2	0	0	0	0
1967	0	1	0	5	4	5	6	9	1	0	0	0
1968	0	2	7	0	4							

judged by the operators and site engineers to represent a 'critical' condition, in the sense that the bridge could just, but only just, be swung. The temperatures measured at that time were of particular interest as they gave a clear picture of the temperature differences between the top and bottom flanges of the bridge. The values cited in this paper represent conditions on this occasion (at c.1400 hours (G.M.T.)). At this time no significant lateral temperature differences were detectable in the structure.

Top and bottom flange temperatures
Although a simple structure in engineering terms, the surface and sub-surface variations in temperature presented a complex pattern from which to sample. Since at no time were significant temperature differences noted between the North and South bridge sections, attention was concentrated on the North section and, in the light of site experience, eleven sampling points were selected for surface temperature consideration (Figure 9.3), though in the case of points E, G and I temperatures were obtained by estimation rather than direct measurement. The general pattern was typical of results obtained on other occasions when observations were made.

The temperature of the top flange upper surfaces exceeded air temperature by $14° - 16°$C. This is in accordance with the simple microclimatological principle that during the period of incoming solar radiation, particularly when wind speeds are low, steep temperature gradients develop between the surface and the air above it. The explanation of the 2.0°C temperature difference between A, B and C with $B > A ≃ C$, almost certainly lies in the darker colour of the road deck, which increases its absorption of incident solar radiation.

The temperatures of the lower surfaces of the top flange will depend largely upon the balance between the supply of heat conducted down

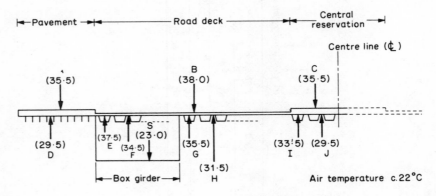

Figure 9.3   Sketch section to show measurement points and temperatures in °C, c.1400 hours 10th June, 1968.

from the surface and the removal of heat by convection and radiation. The variation in bridge deck composition together with variations in observed surface temperature would result in different values for the conductive heat flows reaching the lower surface of the top flange. It is, however, in the second term, the removal of heat by convection and radiation that the most probable explanation of the observed temperature differences lies. Points D, H and J outside the box girders and exposed to the free atmosphere registered temperatures of $29.5°$, $31.5°$ and $29.5°C$ respectively; F, inside the box girder where the circulation is limited, had a correspondingly higher temperature of $34.6°C$. There is only a very limited exchange of air between the free atmosphere and the interior of the box girders. This occurs as a response to the diurnal temperature cycle, a point made by van Neste in the discussion of Langhoff and Granzen (1973).

Also, convectional movements within the box girder are very limited. Recordings revealed that the diurnal air temperature cycle in the box immediately below the top flange lower surface lagged behind the upper surface maximum temperature by only 3 hours, the maximum occurring at 1500 hours. Air temperatures recorded immediately above the bottom flange top surface in the box revealed a lag of 7 hours, maximum temperature at this level being reached at 1900 hours.

The convective heat transfer is usually expressed in the following form:

Heat lost at surface by convection = $h(\Theta_s - \Theta_a)$

where h is the heat transfer coefficient in $W/m^2\,°C$

Θ_s is surface temperature in $°C$

Θ_a is air temperature in $°C$.

The value ascribed to h by Emerson (1973) for the exposed under surfaces of a bridge is $9W/m^2$ $°C$ and for the inside surface of a box section flange is $2W/m^2$ $°C$. The difference of more than a factor of 4 between the values is not surprising. Directly comparable published values are not available. Most of the work in this field has been based on industrial cooling processes and experimental results based on small plate areas c.1 m^2. Examples are cited by Geiger (1969) of variations of heat transfer coefficient values for heat loss from plant leaves in still air and high wind conditions in the ratio 1:30.

Points G and I were within trough girders in the free atmosphere, while E was within a trough girder and also within the box girder. These points could not be reached for direct measurement but in the light of the temperatures that were measured and bearing in mind the very much reduced values of the heat transfer coefficient that could be expected in such locations, estimated temperatures of 37.5, 35.5 and $33.5°C$ were proposed for E, G and I respectively. It was unfortunate that these values had of necessity to be estimated as they are representative of a significant area of the lower surface of the top flange.

The measured lower flange temperature at the 'critical' time was 23°C. It can be safely assumed that little temperature gradient will exist through the 9.5 mm sheet steel of this lower flange. The temperature gradient in such a case is related to the thermal conductivity of the material and the quantity of heat flowing in a steady state.

Q is heat flow in W/m^2

K the thermal conductivity W/m^2 °C — for steel 50W/m^2 °C

X is plate thickness in metres — here 9.5 x 10^{-3} m

For a temperature difference of 1°C to be maintained between the opposite faces of the plate, the necessary heat flow Q would be

$$Q = K \cdot \frac{Q}{x}, \quad \text{here } Q = \frac{-50}{9.5 \times 10^{-3}} = 5263 \text{ W/m}^2$$

There is no natural condition that I know of where such a value could be approached; even exposure of the steel plate to peak solar radiation values would give a receipt of less than 1000 W/m^2.

The temperature distribution revealed in the section investigated on the 'critical' day showed a maximum temperature difference between the upper and lower surfaces of 15°C. Experience on other hot days showed an absence of longitudinal temperature variations in the top flange. There were, however, longitudinal variations of a measureable magnitude in the lower flange and they showed a clear distribution pattern, with the temperature increasing progressively from centre to nose. On the 'critical' day, temperatures were 18°C at the bulkhead, adjacent to the main centre cross girder, increasing to 24°C at the nose. This increase from centre to nose appeared to be the result of two factors acting together. First, the increased opportunity for heat exchange in the air between the top and bottom flanges because of the reduced separation towards the nose; also the smaller separation increased the possibility of conductive exchange down the shorter webs and diaphragms of the boxes. Second, and probably more important, the central part of the bridge had a much higher thermal inertia by virtue of the concentration of mass there. Temperature responses around the central bulkheads were very slow; after a cool period of some duration, the temperature there would tend to increase slowly over a period of days. Thus, if a day of strong insolation succeeded a cool spell, the surface could attain high temperatures while the central area at the base would have temperatures more characteristic of the early cool spell. On the 'critical' day, with temperatures in the central area of 18°C and a deck temperature of 38°C, the maximum temperature difference was 20°C, well in excess of the design difference of 8.3°C. It seemed that a top-to-bottom temperature difference of

20°C would be sufficient by itself to cause jamming without the superimposition of lateral variations.

This carried with it the implication that the macroclimatic conditions necessary for jamming were unremarkable. It seemed strange that jamming was shown as occurring so infrequently in Table 9.1. A reappraisal of the macroclimatic records for the study period, in conjunction with the bridge log of shipping movements, provided the explanation for this anomaly. On some days when jamming was predictable on macroclimatic grounds, shipping movements calling for bridge operation had not occurred. On still others the tide times, which control shipping movements, necessitated bridge operations at times of the day and night when the solar radiation necessary for the differentials was absent or too weak.

The report prepared on the Plimsoll Bridge included estimates of the maximum temperature difference that could be expected to arise in the structure. The estimate for the maximum surface temperature was based on a study of meteorological records of maximum temperatures for the past 41 years, consideration of local site climate and the results of the empirical investigation on the site. The suggested value for maximum upper surface temperature was $55° - 60°C$, the range reflecting variations in the nature of the upper surface. The determination of the simultaneous lowest value of temperature in the structure was more difficult, though its location at the central bulkhead area was certain. In the light of experience at the site and paying due attention to the considerable thermal interior of the central zone a minimum value of 22°C was arrived at. This gave a maximum top-surface to bottom-surface temperature difference of $33-38°C$.

Lateral temperature differences
Figure 9.4 shows how lateral temperature differences might occur in response to elevation and azimuth of the sun. Figure 9.4a locates the places (K−R) for which temperatures were measured, the points lying on the same section line as Figure 9.3. At 1400 hours on 10th June 1968, none of the webs was in receipt of solar radiation, since the cantilevered footpaths shaded the outer faces of the box girders. With the exception of Q and R, all the temperatures were 24°C. However, the outside face of the East box recorded values varying from 27°C at the base to 25°C at the top. This variation was due to the retention of the greater solar radiation receipt at the bottom of the face earlier in the day.

With steel plate box girder faces the response to changes in environmental conditions is very rapid. An approximation to the rate of this response is obtained by considering the physical properties of the steel plates. The plates have a thickness of 9.5 mm, a density of c. 8000 kg/m³ and a specific heat of c. 460J/kg°C.

One square metre of this plate will have a thermal capacity of

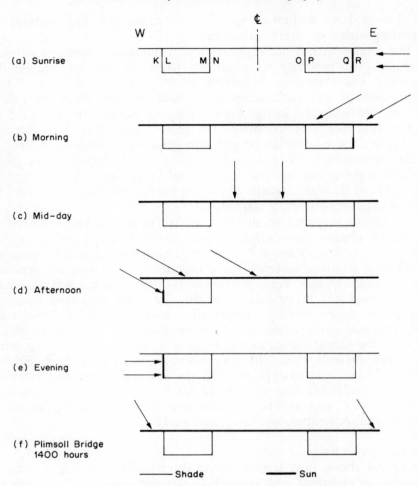

Figure 9.4   Sun and shade on the Plimsoll Bridge.

8000 × 460 × 9.5 × 10^{-3}, i.e. 34 960 J/m^3 °C. With a solar radiation receipt leading to an absorption of 400 W/m^2 the temperature of the plate would increase by 1°C in only 87.5 secs. This is an approximation but gives a clear indication of the order of response time one is dealing with. Differential exposure to solar radiation between different parts of the structure leads very rapidly to temperature differences between these parts. Although the intensity of the solar beam will be low for low solar elevations, it will nevertheless meet the vertical face at a comparatively high angle, so increasing its effectiveness. After a clear night during which the lightweight bridge deck will have reached a temperature well below air temperature, even such low angle solar receipt on a box girder face can result in large temperature differences. The basal area of the face is favoured in terms of solar radiation receipt because of the pavement overhang and temperature differences between the top and bottom of the face of 10°C were recorded. On one occasion, when the deck recorded 39.5°C, the side of the box girder varied in temperature from 18°C at the top to 42°C at the bottom, a difference of 24°C. Bearing in mind the possible effects of easterly and westerly winds in either accentuating or reducing temperature differences between the east and west faces, it is clear that the maximum differential between the faces could exceed 25°C.

Consider now the top-to-bottom differentials of temperature that can occur, together with the lateral differentials, and the following conclusions may be drawn. The top-to-bottom differential is itself sufficient to jam the bridge, as on the critical day. The occurrence of the substantial lateral temperature differences that have been shown to occur would exacerbate the situation. Even if these lateral differences were judged not to be capable of causing jamming by themselves when no top-to-bottom temperature differential existed, they would reduce the magnitude of the latter differential necessary to cause jamming.

Such lateral variations of temperature, certainly very important in the case of this swing bridge, receive little or no attention in the standard works and information on thermal loading in bridge design. It is interesting to consider why this should be the case.

Solution of the Plimsoll Bridge problem

Given the measured temperature differences on the Plimsoll Bridge and estimates of the maximum differentials that might be expected, modifications were made to the jacking system. The capacity of the centre jacks was raised from 1435 kN to 3487 kN, while that of the end jacks was increased from 348.7 kN to 797 kN. So far, this modification has provided a working solution to the problem.

Previous work relating to lateral temperature variations

Lack of communication probably explains much of the neglect of lateral temperature variations. For example, Geiger (1969) quotes work on the daily regime of temperature differences under the bark of a Sitka Spruce; as Figure 9.5 shows, at 1700 hours the difference between the North and South sides was 20°C. Perhaps more relevant, engineers in West Germany have for a long time recognised large temperature differences in lightweight steel bridges, partly because of the exigencies of the post-war situation in 1945. Many bridges had to be replaced, materials were scarce and there was a surplus of aeronautical designers able to bring sophisticated design concepts to bear on the problem. As early as 1958, Kirschmer noted the need to allow for a surface temperature range of +60°C to −20°C on lightweight bridges. Also in 1958, Radojkovic reported an experimental programme on a new road bridge across the River Sava at Belgrade,

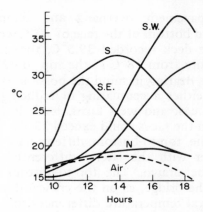

Figure 9.5   Daily temperature variation in the bark of the Sitka Spruce. (*Source*: Geiger, 1960, after N. Haarlov and B. Petersen.)

some of his results being shown in Figure 9.6. Deutsche Normen 1072 (1967a, 1967b) suggest that an overall temperature range of $10°C \pm 35°C$ should be allowed for, discuss differentials between parts of the structure and refer explicitly to lateral temperature variations. And though Lee (1971) includes a translation of Din 1072, he omits to note that current German practice for determining the movements of bearings and expansion joints extends the range $10°C \pm 35°C$ to $10°C \pm 45°C$ (Köster, 1968).

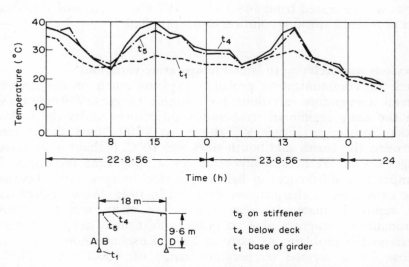

Figure 9.6   Variation of temperature within the structure. (*Source:* Radojkovic, 1958.)

The temperature design allowances for the 2 Donaubrücke Linz are detailed by Schimetta in Schimetta, Burgholzer and Garn (1973). In addition to allowance for a temperature difference between the upper and lower surfaces of 15°C in either direction we find direct reference to lateral temperature variation. In the case of this box girder bridge, a temperature gradient of ± 15°C normal to the bridge axis is considered in design. The magnitude of the design temperatures for the lateral difference is here the same as for that between top and bottom flanges, and is the same in kind and order as that measured in the Plimsoll Bridge.

Finally, work by Emerson (1972, 1973) in this country has dealt in some detail with the temperature distribution in bridges. Nevertheless, she does not deal with lateral temperature variations, though consideration of bending and lateral temperature differences is promised for the future.

When information is transferred, either between disciplines or between engineers in different countries, it is essential that the relevant context is fully understood. In this context, note that the Avonmouth Bridge, opened in 1974 to carry the M5 across the Avon, is designed for maximum and minimum mean temperatures of +36°C and −15°C respectively (for a definition of mean bridge temperature, see Emerson, 1973). This is a boxgirder bridge with a composite deck, for which the normal specification in B S. 116 Draft is a range of +40°C to −20°C. Departure from B.S. 116 Draft was decided upon on the basis of the bridge's estuarine position. The assumption that temperature extremes will be reduced in comparison with inland locations is difficult to support. Although maximum temperatures may be reduced by sea-breeze effects, minimum temperatures are likely to occur when winds are from the North or East and therefore devoid of local oceanic influences.

The possible significance of lateral temperature differences and expansion in bridge design
Although the final version of B.S. 116 may remedy the situation, lateral differences and expansion have not received the attention they merit. There are documented occurrences of some problems in bridge erection, as when the last section of the boxgirder bridge over the River Veveyse (Switzerland) had to be delayed until sunset. Lateral temperature differences of 20°C to 30°C due to a low-angle sun caused the unrestrained nose to deflect by about one metre (Langhoff and Granzen, 1973).

Emerson (1968) suggested a theoretical expansion allowance of 0.75 mm per metre for a steel box girder bridge with a steel deck. Expansion joints are provided to accommodate changes in length. In some twin boxgirder bridges the box girders slide across the support pillars on roller bearings as the length changes, as in Figure 9.7a. Roller

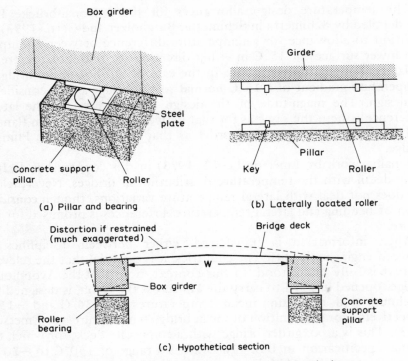

Figure 9.7   Lateral expansion of a bridge deck.

bearings so used are frequently designed to prevent lateral displacement by the incorporation of keys, as in Figure 9.7b. The width of the deck, W, between the rollers can change by as much as 10 mm as a result of temperature changes. This value is based on expansion allowances for bridges where the temperatures of a top and bottom flange are considered in the calculation. Where, as in Figure 9.7c a section of bridge deck only is involved, with no bottom flange, values so calculated will probably be exceeded. When the rollers prevent lateral movement, the deck must either be stressed in compression, or rotate. To avoid these undesirable effects the keys could be removed from the rollers on one side of the bridge, though it remains to be seen how effectively lateral movement would then be accommodated.

Factors influencing the development of lateral temperature differences
Two groups of factors influence the establishment of temperature differences between the walls of the boxes. The first group deals with solar radiation receipt and includes the following.

1. Latitude.
2. Sunshine duration and intensity.

3. Alignment of the bridge. In the case of a swing bridge the position is complicated because the alignment changes as the bridge is swung.

4. Topographic features (natural or man made) that will influence the pattern of sun and shade.

5. Geometry of structure, particularly the relationship of pavement overhang, to box girder depth.

6. Any lateral disparity in surface nature which will influence the absorption of incident solar radiation (one side may be darker because of a pollutant source upwind).

7. Depth of wall. The deeper the wall the less will heat-flow to cooler parts of the structure affect the effective temperature of the wall. The solar radiation disparity between the faces can cause large temperature differences between the face exposed to the sun and the other faces under clear sky conditions.

The second group of factors is made up of influences which, acting on the shaded surfaces, ensure that the differential is at a maximum.

1. Air movement such that a maximum cooling effect will occur at the shaded face and a minimum on the sunny face. This cooling can remove the heat conducted from the deck down the webs which would tend to raise their temperature above air temperature. In the case of a box girder bridge with a wind perpendicular to the shaded face and in the horizontal plane, other surfaces will be lee surfaces and will be subjected to less cooling. Schack (1965) quotes Reiher who observed that for a small plate the heat transfer coefficient due to convection increased sevenfold when the airflow was at right angles to the plate instead of parallel to it. In the case of large plates this effect will clearly be reduced because of divergence along the plate face but it can be expected to operate.

2. The possibility of precipitation receipt cooling only part of the structure is important. In the worst case, just the deck and shaded face could be wetted. This can commonly occur with summer showers of short duration. Wind-driven rain falling at an angle may well leave part of the structure completely dry. As a result of such precipitation patterns, one face can suffer direct cooling by contact with the rain and evaporation could reduce its temperature to the wet bulb temperature. This can occur while the sunny face is still in receipt of solar radiation. In the case of a hail or sleet storm it is possible to imagine, with part of the precipitation at $0°C$, the surface temperature falling below air temperature. The amount of water retained by the surface would depend on its nature and roughness. The significance of precipitation in the development of within structure temperature differentials is considered by Volke (1973) in the static analysis

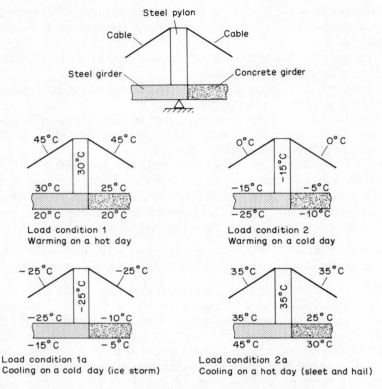

Figure 9.8   Hypothetical temperature distributions for a suspension bridge. (After Volke, 1973.)

of the Nordbrucke Mannheim-Ludwigshaven. Although he does not concern himself with lateral variation he adopts a dynamic approach to the thermal considerations. Figure 9.8 shows the differentials he suggests.

3. Lateral variations of temperature can also occur across a bridge deck by virtue of its camber and longitudinal inclination. Howell (1973) states that a difference of 3°C in hourly mean surface temperature at all times of day between surface temperatures measured at a point on the Wye Bridge and the Severn Bridge was thought to be due to differences in camber and longitudinal inclination. Heat flow preferentially to one web as a result of such variation could increase side-to-side differentials, but clearly only by a very small amount.

The design criteria

When design work on the Plimsoll Bridge commenced in the early 1960s, the relevant British standard was B.S. 153 (1954) Part 3A. This included a section on temperature differences in bridge superstructures. The standard suggested that allowance be made for forces resulting from superstructure temperature differences due to sun and shade of 8.3°C (15°F). Today it is clear that the B.S. 153 value is too low but when B.S. 153 came into being lightweight bridge decks and steel box girder bridges were not widely used. It was only later that it became clear that B.S. 153 could not be applied, unmodified, for thermal loadings in the new bridge forms. Among other conclusions, Emerson (1968) notes that 'the ranges of bridge temperatures quoted in current British standards are inadequate, in particular the minimum temperatures are not sufficiently low'. Her report suggests more generous allowance for the maximum mean bridge temperatures and the minimum mean bridge temperatures. Some Road Research Laboratory notes and leaflets of around this time suggested that in steel box section bridges large top-to-bottom temperature differences could occur. Such suggestions were based on, for example the Beachley Viaduct, but the configuration of this bridge is very different from that of the Plimsoll Bridge and the direct extrapolation of results from one structure to the other would be very questionable. Certainly a viaduct bridge has nothing resembling the central area of the Plimsoll Bridge with its high thermal inertia. The Plimsoll Bridge was very much a pioneering effort and as such had to do without the benefit of directly relevant previous experience. The Merrison report (D.O.E. 1972) and B S. 116/Draft (1972) contain, at the time of writing, the most recent suggestions for thermal loading in bridge design. The Merrison committee recommends, in the section on thermal loading, a maximum temperature differential of + 24°C in the case of a surfaced steel bridge. The text states that for the temperature differentials suggested 'they shall be assumed to be the difference in temperature between all components of the deck and the remainder of the structure'. B.S. 116/Draft uses the same data and specifies the same conditions. Even if this assessment had been available ten years earlier it would not have resulted in allowance for the lateral temperature differentials that caused such problems on the Plimsoll Bridge.

Postscript: Brunel's foresight

Although 'modern' bridge design literature mentions lateral variation little, if at all, we do find some interesting comment from a source separated from the Plimsoll Bridge by a large time gap but a small spatial one. Among Brunel's early letters (Brunel, 1829) concerning the Clifton Suspension Bridge he writes of remedying a design 'evil' that he had experienced in the case of the Menai Bridge. The problem he foresaw was that the suspension chains might be heated by direct sun on one side and simultaneously cooled by wind on the other. He postulated a temperature difference from this cause of 15°F (cf. B.S. 153). In this event, he foresaw that either the chains would twist or the shorter and colder links would bear an unequal portion of the load, the expanded (longer) links being relieved. To obviate this problem he proposed the provision of sheet iron plates on each side of the chains to shield them and prevent the occurrence of a lateral temperature differential.

Porter-Goff (1974) drew attention to this part of Brunel's thinking and calculated that the differential stress so caused would have been less than 0.161 kN for the 15°F temperature difference, suggesting that Brunel may on reflection have considered his proposed shields to be an unduly cautious provision. The significant thing is that Brunel foresaw the potential significance of this climatic environmental influence. If, eventually, he decided that it was insignificant it had at least been considered. This is preferable to situations where climatic effects are ignored, even though the design proves in practice that it can accommodate such effects anyway.

ACKNOWLEDGEMENTS

At the time the work on the Plimsoll Bridge was carried out, Mr. A. P. Cliffe and Mr. C. R. Chapman, then of the Highways Department of the City and County of Bristol, provided invaluable assistance and advice which the author gratefully acknowledges.

NOTES AND REFERENCES

[1] One Newton is the force which will give a mass of one kilogramme an acceleration of one metre per second squared ($1N = 1\ kgm/s^2$). It is approximately equivalent to 0.1 ton gross lifting capacity.

[2] Vavasour et al (1966a) quotes 15°C and 20°C. There were misprints which are corrected to 15°F and 20°F in Vavasour et al (1966b).

Bailey, J. (1968). 'Report on the temperature and temperature differences throughout the Plimsoll Bridge with special reference to hot days', unpublished report for City Engineer, Surveyor and Planning Officer's Department, Bristol Corporation.

B.S. 153 (1954). 'Steel Girder Bridges', Part 3A, British Standards Institution.

British Standards Committee 116 B 116/2 (1972). Draft Report, British Standards Institution.

Brunel Papers (1829), University of Bristol Archives. Letter Book, Vol. 1, 17—20. Clifton Bridge.

Department of the Environment (1973). Inquiry into the basis of design and method of erection os steel box girder bridges. Report of Committee, Appendix I, Parts I and II, H.M.S.O.

Deutsche Normen (1967a) DIN 1072, 'Strassen-und Wegbrücken. Lastannahmen', DK 624.21.042 : 625.745.1.

Deutsche Normen (1967b) DIN 1072 Beiblatt 'Strassen-und Wegbrücken. Lastannahmen. Erlauterungen'. DK 624.21.042 : 625.745.1.

Emerson, M. (1968). *Bridge Temperatures and Movements in the British Isles*, Road Research Laboratory Report LR.228.

Emerson, M. (1972). 'Temperature effects in bridges', *Highway Design and Construction*, 10—14.

Emerson. M. (1973). *The Calculation of the Distribution of Temperature in Bridges*, Transport and Road Research Laboratory, Report LR 561.

Geiger, R. (1969). *The Climate Near the Ground*, Harvard University Press.

Howell, H. (1973). *Temperature Spectra Recorded in Surfacings on Steel Bridge Decks*, Transport and Road Research Laboratory Report, LR 587.

Kirschmer, O. (1958). 'Neuere Erkenntnisse bei Brückenbelagern', *Der Stahlbau*, 27, 16—19.

Köster, W. (1968). *Expansion Joints in Bridges and Concrete Roads*, Maclaren and Sons.

Langhoff, H-J., and H. Granzen (1973). 'Fabrication of boxgirder bridges', paper presented at International Conference of Civil Engineers, published in *Steel Box Girder Bridges*, Telford.

Lee, D. (1971). *The Theory and Practice of Bearings and Expansion Joints for Bridges*, Cement and Concrete Association.

Porter-Goff, R. F. D. (1974). 'Brunel and the design of the Clifton Suspension Bridge', *Proc. Institute of Civil Engineers*, 56, 393—421.

Radojkovic, M. (1958). 'Die Neue Strassenbrücke über die Save in Belgrad', *Der Stahlbau*, 27, 70—78.

Schack, A. (1965). *Industrial Heat Transfer*, Chapman and Hall.

Schimetta, O., L. Burgholzer, and E. Garn (1973). 'Die 2 Donaubrücke Linz', *Die Stahlbau*, 42, 321—332.

Vavasour, P., J. S. Wilson, R. A. Baldwin, and C. W. Wolley (1966a). 'Cumberland Basin Bridges Scheme', *Proc. Institution of Civil Engineers*, 33, 261—312.

Vavasour, P., J. S. Wilson, R. A. Baldwin, and C. W. Wolley (1966b). 'Cumberland Basin Bridges Scheme', *Proc. Institution of Civil Engineers*, 33, 261—312.

Volke, E. (1973). 'Die Strombrücke in Zuge der Nordbrücke Mannheim-Ludwigshaven. Konstruction und Statik', *Der Stahlbau*, 42, 138—52.

Wilson, J. S. and R. A. Baldwin (1965). 'The Cumberland Basin Bridges Scheme, Part 1', *Civil Engineering and Public Works Review*, 60, 553—58.

Chapter 10

Models for the Estimation of Firnlines of Present and Pleistocene Glaciers

Henry Osmaston

'Glaciers are very sensitive climatic indicators, the indicator scale being given by the rising of the snowline.'
(Finsterwalder, 1952, p. 310)

Glaciologists have long sought to define and determine a snowline that would permit climatic comparisons between the same area at different times and between different areas at the same time, particularly for periods or places where instrumental climatic records are lacking; but although the concepts both of a fluctuating temporary local snowline, and of an annual (or longer) mean snowline, are easy to invoke, they are less easy to use in practice. In contrast, present or historical limits of glaciers are often known very precisely, while their Pleistocene limits are clearly marked by moraines, etc., but this evidence has often formed the basis of oversimplified and inaccurate climatic interpretations. Nevertheless, the purely physical equilibria which determine the extent of glaciers and the level of the snowline are much simpler than the biological equilibria which determine that other popular climatic indicator, the vegetation (and still more its fossil pollen remains), and therefore offer the hope of less equivocal conclusions.

To this end theoretical concepts have been invoked, such as the altitude at which the total annual snowfall on a fully exposed horizontal surface is just balanced by the ablation (Drygalski and Machatschek, 1942), but such conditions cannot be observed in nature and it is uncertain how the figure could be estimated; certainly not by merely averaging the results from the glaciers on all sides of a given mountain. Apparently more practical definitions such as the lower limit of permanent snowpatches (Ratzel, 1886) the level at which 50% of the ground is permanently snow-covered (Paschinger, 1912), or a 'smoothed' value for the lower limit of permanent snowpatches both on and off the glaciers (Flint, 1957), are tiresome to observe as they must be recorded every year just at the end of the variable ablation season, cannot be estimated for past glaciations, and are so affected by topography and aspect that comparisons between different areas may be invalid. The common term 'climatic snowline' is misleading; if the user is trying to imply something that is independent of the land surface, he is pursuing an illusion, for all snowlines (and all climates?) are the product of the interaction between relief and radiation, atmospheric circulation, etc.

Attention has therefore been concentrated on the firnline across glaciers (Hugi, 1830). Firn[1] (German, meaning 'of last year') is snow which persists from one year (or half-year in the tropics) to the next, and the firnline is the line that bounds the lower edge of all firnbanks and the accumulation zones of glaciers. Firnbanks occupy sites favourably situated for collecting drifting snow, being usually sheltered from the sun and wind but too small for the development of glaciers; in especially favourable sites on rugged, cloudy mountains, they may occur 450 m below the usual lower limit of the firnline on glaciers (Manley, 1949), but where the mountain slopes above the glaciers are steep and smooth, and the summer sunny, the lowest firnbanks may be well above the firnline on the glaciers.

The very existence of a glacier implies a minimum extent and degree of exposure for its surface, so that firnlines across glaciers are less variable than those at the foot of firnbanks; however, within any group of glaciers some differences in firnline will usually occur, owing to variations of aspect, exposure, slope, etc. Because of this, Drygalski and Machatschek concluded that the average altitude of the firnlines of a group of glaciers is not a valid measure of the regional climate, but it is unreasonable to deny the validity of a mean value just because some of the observations do not exactly conform to it. Nor, if one is comparing the climates of the same area at different times, is there any need to try to divorce the climate completely from the local topography which influences it.

Provided that the glaciers are grouped into fairly homogeneous regions, are numerous, and are well enough distributed to provide a statistically acceptable sample for each region, the mean of their firnlines will give a sensitive and useful measure of the regional climate in the framework of the regional topography. The sensitivity is indicated by the fact that a change in mean annual temperature of 1°C, which would need prolonged and careful recording to establish directly, would change the altitude of the firnline by about 150 m if all else remains constant.

In any year (or ablation season) the actual firnline does not form a neat contour across the glacier but is represented by irregular patches of firn which spread and coalesce with increasing altitude. Ahlmann (1948) suggests that one should take the lower limit of these patches, but the line where they occupy 50% of the surface is a better division between the accumulation and ablation zones. This annual firnline may be averaged both in place and time: the mean altitude of the irregular line across the glacier may be calculated; this in turn may be averaged over a period of years, or over a regional group of glaciers, or over both. Alternatively, the position of an actual sloping or irregular firnline across a single glacier or group of glaciers may be averaged over a period. It is important to make it clear what type of firnline is being discussed; in this paper, unless otherwise stated, the word refers to the mean altitude of the firnline across one or more glaciers, during a period of several years.

The annual firnlines of previous years can sometimes be located by digging pits in the surface of the glacier and observing the strata, remembering that earlier ones have been displaced downstream by the flow of the glacier. However, if a subsequent ablation season was more severe than an earlier one, the thin lower edge of the latter's firn will have been removed, so that the original firnline can only be estimated.

Surface observations and the digging of pits are the only direct methods of finding the firnline, but many indirect methods have been proposed, some of which can be used for glaciers that no longer exist.

Indirect methods: previous work

The indirect methods of firnline estimation form four distinct groups as listed below.

1. *Indirect meteorological*
   (a) Precipitation and temperature comparisons (Ahlmann, 1924, 1948; Manley, 1949)
   (b) Days of snow-cover comparisons (Manley, 1949)

2. *Morphological*
   (a) Glacier cross-section profile (Hess, 1904)
   (b) Upper end of moraines (Reid, 1907; Lichtenecker, 1937; Penck and Brückner, 1909)

3. *Top or bottom*
   (a) Top method, Glacierization[2] limit (Partsch, 1882; Enquist, 1916; Ahlmann, 1948)
   (b) Cirques (Seddon, 1957; Flint, 1957; Linton, 1959; Peterson and Robinson, 1969; Robinson et al, 1971)
   (c) Firnbanks (Manley, 1949)

4. *Proportional*
  (a) Mid-height (Höfer, 1879; Suter, 1940; Hastenrath, 1967)
  (b) Proportion of area (Brückner, 1886; Penck and Brückner, 1909)
  (c) Mean height of surface (Kurowski, 1891)
  (d) Area, ablation and mass balance[1] (Finsterwalder, 1952; Llibou-
       try, 1955; Mercer, 1961; Meier and Post, 1962; Østrem and
       Liestøl, 1964)

Indirect meteorological methods
Ahlmann has published a relationship between precipitation and mean summer temperature for glacierized[2] areas in Scandinavia at the altitude of the local glacierization limit (see below). This can then be used in reverse to deduce the glacierization limit in other areas of similar climate. Manley has used it thus to estimate past and present (hypothetical) glacierization limits in Britain. The results must be accepted with caution, however, as the similarity of the climate of different areas is always uncertain, and furthermore many of the figures were estimated by extrapolation from the meteorological records of lowland stations.

Manley also made estimates of the glacierization limit in Britain from records of the number of days on which snow lies on the ground, but this method is of limited application and can only give rough results.

Morphological methods
Hess observed that in the ablation zone of a glacier the surface cross-profile is convex, owing to the melting of the sides by long-wave radiation from the adjoining ground, whereas in the accumulation zone, where snowdrifts form at the sides of the glacier, the profile is concave. The change from one profile to the other is, however, dependent on the topography as well as on the firnline, so that the method can give only a rough indication of the latter. The technique would be difficult to apply to glaciers flowing from an icecap and is of no use for past glaciations.

Except when large rockfalls have occurred, surface moraines can only be exposed, and lateral moraines be formed, in the ablation zone, so that they give a value for the minimum altitude of the firnline. However, if the surface moraine was originally formed high up the glacier, the overburden of snow which has accumulated on it will not be melted till some time after it has passed below the firnline; similarly, if the valley sides are steep, lateral moraines may only be formed some way below the firnline. There is therefore an unpredictable difference between the highest limit of moraines and the actual firnline, but the occurrence of moraines does provide a useful check on values calculated by other methods, and is useful with the lateral moraines of former glaciations.

Top or bottom methods

The earliest of these methods was the 'top' method used by Simony and Partsch to determine the glacierization limit. This is the altitude which divides the peaks bearing glaciers from those which do not, and is usually about 100 m above the firnline. The method has been further developed by Enquist and Ahlmann to plot isoglacihypses, lines that represent the contours of a theoretical surface; all peaks that project above this surface carry glaciers. To be successful, there should be plenty of peaks just above and just below the glacierization limit throughout the area; the technique has proved very useful in areas such as Switzerland and Norway, but is inapplicable on isolated mountains.

On small independent cirque glaciers, so small that the ice hardly flows, the firnline lies only just above the foot of the glacier, which is the lip of the cirque. Where such glaciers, or their cirques, are common they may be used to give a very reliable estimate of the present or former firnline, though in some areas, such as the East African mountains, they are curiously scarce. Unfortunately, the method has often been misused by the inclusion of cirques at the heads of former valley glaciers, the altitudes of which are determined more by topography and rocks than by the firnline. Sometimes too, uncertainty arises because the cirques have been occupied and excavated during more than one glaciation.

Small firnbanks in protected sites are limiting cases of the same phenomenon; if they were larger and higher they would develop into cirques. Manley used small firnbanks in areas too low for the existence of actual glaciers, to estimate the theoretical glacierization limit, but it is difficult to be sure just how much below it they may lie.

Proportional

This group of methods all start from the evident proposition that the firnline must lie somewhere between the upper and lower ends of a steady-state[1] glacier. The simplest approximation is that used by Höfer, who took the mean of the altitudes of the top and bottom. However, on piedmont glaciers the greater part lies in the spreading foot, and a firnline placed half way between top and bottom would imply an impossibly large ablation zone. With plateau glaciers, the situation is reversed.

An improvement to the method, taking area into account, is usually attributed to Brückner, but there seems to be some misapprehension about this. Brückner individually, and with Penck, studied the moraines and other relics of the Pleistocene glaciations in the Alps and observed the altitude which marked the morphological division of each glacier into collecting basin and tongue; this they erroneously equated with the firnline, ignoring the fact that local topography is of great importance in determining the shape of a glacier. They then went on to show that this line divided the surface area of the glaciers in the ratio of about

2—3 parts above to 1 part below, though sometimes the ratio was as little as 1.5:1. They themselves do not seem to have used this method very much for deducing firnlines, except sometimes as a check on other methods, but it became popularly known as 'Brückner's method of deducing the firnline' and as such was subjected both to misuse and to misinformed criticism, although Drygalski and Machatschek pointed out its morphological basis in their admirable treatise on the snowline (1942). The impressive array of divergent figures which Charlesworth (1957) quotes to show the unreliability of this method and ratio do not all bear investigation. For example, he quotes Visser (1928) as saying that the glaciers of the upper Indus show a ratio of 5:1; in the original paper this is given as 0.5:1 and appears to have been based merely on an observation of the transient snowline[1] at a single visit in 1926. Again, he quotes Reid (1907) for an opposite extreme ratio of 1:3 on Mt. Hood and Mt. Adams in North America, but the original paper shows that this was based on the assumption that the firnline lay half way between the altitude of the bergschrund and that at which moraines first appeared; from the accompanying map it can be calculated that if the firnline lay at the upper limit of the moraines, the ratio would instead be 1:1, a much more reasonable figure. This is a good example of what has been common practice in the literature on firnlines: to obtain one estimate by an indirect method and based on an unverified assumption, and then to use it to criticise other estimates.

Meier and Post (1962) used detailed observations on the South Cascade Glacier to show that in a steady state it would have a mean accumulation area ratio (A.A.R.)[1] of 0.58:1 (A.A.:whole), i.e. a Brückner ratio of 1.4:1. However, an aerial survey of the actual firn edges[1] of several hundred glaciers along the Pacific coast of North America near the end of the ablation season in 1961 indicated annual A.A.R.'s from 0.04 to 0.68, so in that year ablation must have exceeded accumulation on many of them.

Hitherto the discussion has been in terms of the firnline, because on temperate glaciers this coincides with the equilibrium line[1], where the mass balance is zero. On cold glaciers, however, where snow is melted from the surface but refrozen lower on or in the glacier, the firnline will be at a slightly higher altitude. Some of the methods just described, e.g. the highest appearance of moraines, are relevant to the firnline, while others, e.g. proportional methods, are relevant to either line, using appropriate proportions. Those to be described now, however, really concern the equilibrium line, since they are based on considerations of mass balance, but on non-Polar mountain glaciers the difference is usually small, and for convenience the term 'firnline' will continue to be used.

The major improvement in the proportional type of approach was introduced by Kurowski who saw that, rather than considering either height or area alone, they should be combined to give a weighted mean altitude for the whole surface of the glacier, which he equated with the firnline. In support of this he gave figures to show that both precipitation and ablation rates were linearly related to altitude, that their difference was therefore also linearly related to altitude, and that therefore the total net accumulation above the firnline calculated by his method would be exactly balanced by the total net ablation below it. Kurowski's method is merely a particular case of the general rule that the total mass balance[1] on a steady-state glacier must be zero:

Let T be the altitude of the upper end (top) of the glacier;
   B be the altitude of the lower end (bottom) of the glacier;
   F be the altitude of the firnline;
   a be the mean altitude of successive contour strips of the glacier;
   s_a be the areas of successive contour strips of the glacier;
   n_a be the net balance rates on successive contour strips of the glacier (negative below the firnline);
   p be a constant;

then

$$\sum_{a=B}^{T} (n_a s_a) = 0 \qquad \ldots \text{Mass balance equation}$$

but: $n_a = p(a - F)$ ... Kurowski's assumption

substituting:

$$\sum_{a=B}^{T} (pas_a - pFs_a) = 0$$

therefore:

$$\sum_{a=B}^{T} (as_a) = \sum_{a=B}^{T} (Fs_a)$$

therefore:

$$\frac{\sum_{a=B}^{T} (as_a)}{\sum_{a=B}^{T} s_a} = F \qquad \ldots \text{Kurowski's formula} \qquad (1)$$

Direct observations of mass balance on various glaciers have been published (e.g. Ahlmann, 1948; Renaud, 1952; Meier and Post, 1962; Østrem and Liestøl, 1964; Nye 1965a). For individual years, on individual glaciers, the curves of mass balance against altitude often show irregularities which may be recurrent features due to local relief, but usually the smoothed mean form over several years is either roughly rectilinear, or curved due to large increases in ablation below the firnline and sometimes also to reduced precipitation at high altitudes.

The application of these curves to other glaciers or to the same glacier at different extents is complicated by the fact that they must be related not to altitudes above sea level but to the as yet unknown firnline. Only when the function is linear can a very simple solution like that of Kurowski be used, though Finsterwalder (1952) has given a manual method for use with parabolic functions. A more usual method, especially for irregular curves plotted from direct observations rather than theoretical functions, is to juggle with curves of total mass balance and try to balance the positive and negative areas beneath them (Østrem and Liestøl, 1964); or to do the same with the curves of gross precipitation and ablation (Lliboutry, 1955), though these are less often known.

Renaud (1952) made observations on the Gorner glacier (Switzerland) which showed that the mass balance was nearly linearly related to altitude. Mercer (1961) applied a series of factors, derived from these observations with slight modifications, to the area/height distributions of North American glaciers on which he had observed the temporary firnline on air photos taken near the end of the ablation season, making in some cases an estimated addition to allow for further ablation. However, he found that on apparently stable glaciers he had to multiply the total ablation so obtained by a factor of about 6 to make it balance the total accumulation, which suggests that his estimates of the altitude of their firnlines were still too low, or that their net budgets that year were exceptionally positive. Meier and Post (1962) give mass balance altitude graphs for ten North American glaciers; four graphs are straight, two are gently curved, and four are more complex shapes, but, except for the straightest one which is the mean for three years of observations, the remainder all refer to only a single year.

Two problems arise with all the area methods. The first is that the calculations should be based on the glacier surface but, in the case of glaciers which have changed much in thickness or even completely melted, the difficulties and errors involved in trying to estimate the ice surface at some previous time may be much greater than those arising from using the present ice or ground surface and applying a correction to the firnline by adding the estimated former additional thickness of ice at that altitude. This is certainly so for valley glaciers where the thickness is small in relation to the altitude range, but not for a thick ice sheet.

The second problem is whether to take the area of the actual upper part of the glacier, or the area of the whole of its collecting basin, including bare slopes; the former is preferable (and is essential when actual accumulation data are to be applied) but for past glaciers it may be difficult.

A further apparent restriction is the assumption of all the height and area methods that the glacier is in a steady state and thus in equilibrium with the current climate. There is an inevitable lag in the response of a glacier, in thickness and extent, to a change of climate which has resulted in a change of mass balance. Nye (1965a) has shown that this lag depends on such factors as the length and velocity of the glacier, and may amount to 180° of phase for oscillations with periods of up to 100 years; observations have shown that even neighbouring glaciers may be in opposing states of retreat or advance (or exceptionally surge) due to differences in their internal dynamics. The assumption, apparently implicit later, that sets of correlated terminal moraines were formed simultaneously by a group of steady state glaciers in equilibrium with some particular climate, may be too simple, but moraine data do have the advantage over an instantaneous glacier survey that they record the maximum response of every glacier to a particular climatic oscillation, irrespective of variations in lag. Perfect equilibrium is therefore a theoretical ideal; individual variability must be met by taking groups of glaciers together, while the response lag can be looked for in the results and remembered in their interpretation.

Comparisons of proportional methods: some simple models
Despite the frequent criticisms that have been made of the simpler proportional methods of firnline estimation, no detailed assessment has been made of their accuracy and relative merits, using firnline data obtained by direct observations. This is clearly a matter of considerable importance for both remote areas and past glaciations, when knowledge of mass balance rates is lacking and more elaborate and precise methods therefore cannot be used.

The observations mentioned above show that most curves relating mass balance to altitude lie between two limiting cases; the simple linear one; and a curve which, as a simplification, can be represented by two straight segments, that below the firnline having twice the gradient of that above. For instance the Blue Glacier, Washington (LaChapelle 1965) falls nicely within these limits with a ratio of 1:1.3, while the South Cascade Glacier, Washington (Meier & Tangbourne, 1965) lies just outside with a ratio of about 1:2.1. The firnline of a glacier can therefore be estimated from these two cases with a high probability that it lies between them, and thus they may be used as criteria for assessing other simpler approximations. The actual value of the gradient (the 'energy of glacierization' of Schumskiy (1946) and 'activity index' of Meier (1962)) is irrelevant, since this affects primarily the discharge and thickness at the firnline, and only very slightly the extent of the glacier.

Figure 10.1 represents six model glaciers seen in plan view with shapes chosen to cover all the main types. Model A is a parallel sided valley glacier, the simplest shape to deal with, while B is typical of many actual valley glaciers; C and D are respectively piedmont and plateau glaciers of moderate degree, while E and F are more extreme cases. A conical icecap would be equivalent to a large number of type C

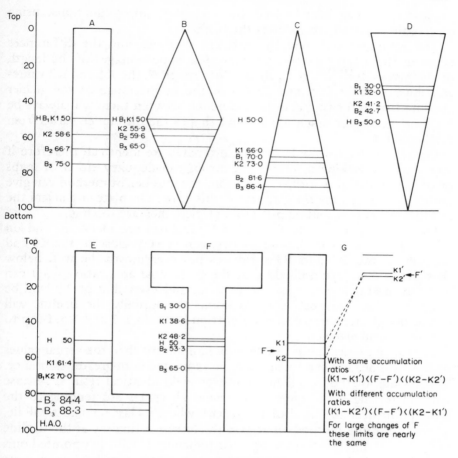

Figure 10.1   Model glaciers.

glaciers, and the firnline would lie at the same level. Each glacier stretches over 100 units altitude range, and on it are marked the altitudes of the firnlines calculated by different methods:

(i) the mid-height method, Höfer's, which places the firnline at 50 in all cases, is indicated by H;

(ii) the proportional area method, Brückner's, used with three different ratios: B1 (1:1), B2 (2:1), B3 (3:1);

(iii) the mean area method, Kurowski's, which gives the correct firnline if mass balance/altitude is linear, and therefore provides one of the limiting criteria: K1;

(iv) the other limiting case, K2, given by substituting K = 2 in the formula

$$\sum_{a=F}^{T} [s_a(a-F)] - K \cdot \sum_{a=F}^{B} [s_a(F-a)] = 0 \tag{2}$$

Equation (2) has been solved by successive approximations, using repeatedly adjusted estimates of the firnline.

The estimates obtained by different methods and the differences between them can therefore be expressed as percentages of the length of the glacier for each given shape. With shape A, the K1 and K2 values will always lie at 50% and 58.6% of the height range of the glacier measured from the top, and the difference between them will always be 8.6% of the height range. With other shapes the difference varies from 5.9% to 9.6%.

On valley glaciers the H and K1 estimates are identical; therefore if area data are lacking or uncertain, through inadequacy either of maps or of the traces of a former glaciation, the mid-height method can give quite good estimates on glaciers of this type. On plateau glaciers the results are too low, and on piedmont glaciers they are too high.

On valley glaciers the B1 and K1 estimates are identical, and on others the B1 estimate lies either between or very close to the K1 and K2 values; the B2 and B3 estimates however mostly lie well below these. It is therefore unlikely that the traditional area ratio of 3:1 can give any useful estimate of the firnline, and even that of 2:1 will be much too low in most cases. It seems that usually the firnline will divide the glacier surface in a proportion between 1:1 and 1.5:1 (up to 2:1 on plateau glaciers).

A change of firnline is usually more important than the actual values of the firnline, and can fortunately be estimated with greater assurance. The various methods will not however yield identical results, because with increasing shrinkage of the glacier all values are tending to the same point near the head of the glacier where its last remnants will lie. Therefore, those methods that give the lowest estimates of the firnline will indicate the greatest changes. As Callendar (1950) has pointed out, Höfer's and Brückner's methods can be used to infer firnline changes when only the lower part of a glacier is surveyed; a retreat of unit altitude or area represents a rise in the firnline of about half this amount. Pal'gov (1962) found the following linear relation (correlation coefficient 0.96) on the Centralny Tuzuksu Glacier

$$P = 29.4F - 106945, \text{ i.e. } P = 29.4\Delta F \text{ where } \Delta F = F - 3637$$

where P is the annual loss from the snout in m^2, and F is the altitude of the annual firnline in m, but it should be noted that this describes a rate of retreat for a given rise of firnline, *not* the total retreat to a new steady-state position. Moreover it should be noted that Nye (1965b) found a very poor correlation between the annual variations in length and ablation at the termini of two glaciers, and, though he suggested that there was more consistency over periods of a decade, his method of inferring the mass balance history from the terminus record is not relevant to the scanty data of past glaciations.

A method such as Höfer's, which takes no account of the shape of the glacier, will give misleading results if the shape changes much: at maximum retreat a glacier may be little more than an ice plateau, in mid-expansion more of a valley glacier and at full extent it may be a piedmont glacier. Brückner's method, which takes some account of the area of the glacier, will be better, but still not as good as those methods which use the precise altitudinal distribution of the ice. Thus the Kurowski (K1) and (K2) estimates always provide the probable limits for the firnline if the form of the mass balance curve has remained the same, which observation suggests to be usually the case for moderate fluctuation (Meier, 1962); i.e. where K1 and K1', K2 and K2' are estimates of real firnlines F and F'

$$(K1 - K1') < (F - F') < (K2 - K2')$$

Hence, on a valley glacier which has retreated by 20% of its height range, the firnline has probably risen by 10—12% of the original height range of the glacier, an uncertainty of only 20 m in a rise of 100 m on a 1000 m glacier, which is likely to be less than errors in some of the glacier measurements.

If we are concerned with a larger retreat, say by 80%, due to a major change in climate, as between a glacial maximum and the present day, we cannot, *without further evidence*, rely on any constancy of the mass balance curve, and the limits are given by

$$(K1 - K2') < (F - F') < (K2 - K1')$$

representing an uncertainty of about 100 m in a 400—500 m rise.

The application of statistical methods to groups of glaciers
To be reliable, climatic inferences must clearly be based on the mean and standard error of the estimated firnline changes of several glaciers, but we can use simple statistics rather more subtly than this in the actual determination of the best estimate of their firnlines. If we can group the glaciers into climatically homogeneous regions, then we can postulate that, within the regions, deviations of the individual firnlines (or our estimates of them) are due to irrelevant and perhaps random variations in local relief and aspect, and that the best estimate of the regional firnline is one which minimises these deviations. To this end we can adopt more flexible approaches than those described above and, instead of using rather arbitrary constants in our equation, we can select those which fit the data best. Thus, from Höfer's approach we can develop a General Height method; from Brückner's, a General Area method; and, from my own modification of the mass balance, a General Area-Height-Mass-balance method.

These three techniques are described below, with brief examples of their application to Kilimanjaro (19 340 ft. or 5996 m) and the Ruwenzori Range (16 763 ft. or 5109 m)[3]; both of these carry small glaciers now, and, in common with other high mountains in East Africa, have extensive traces of former glaciation. Besides erosional features, there are moraines, some very large and extending down to 2000 m, which are very clearly identifiable on air photographs. These features can be differentiated by appearances, altitude and stratigraphy and grouped into series which show excellent correlations both between valleys on each mountain and between mountains. Apart from the traces of earlier glaciation there are particularly complete terminal moraines dating from a glacial maximum 15—20,000 years B.P. (designated the Mahoma stage on the Ruwenzori and the Main Glaciation stage on Kilimanjaro); there are also small, probably nineteenth-century, terminal moraines not far below the present glacier termini (designated the Recent stage on Kilimanjaro) (Livingstone, 1962; Osmaston, 1965, 1967, 1972; Downie, 1964). Data for these two distinct stages provide good material for testing methods of firnline estimation.[3]

The general height method
As shown above, Höfer's mid-height method can give accurate results on valley glaciers; it has the advantage of simplicity and of being usable in the absence of area data. Often, however, a better estimate of the firnline might be given by taking some other fraction or 'Höfer coefficient' of the height range. A more generalized form of this method has therefore been developed, which allows the coefficient (H) to be determined by the data themselves, rather than being chosen arbitrarily in advance, the relationship being:

$$F = B + H(T - B) \qquad\qquad \dots (3)$$

where usually $0.6 > H > 0.4$.

If a graph is prepared for plotting the altitude of the top of each glacier against the altitude of the bottom end, it can be divided into different sectors as shown in Figure 10.2. The diagonal line through the origin covers all points where the altitudes of the top and bottom of the glacier are the same, i.e. those glaciers of negligible size that are hardly more than firnbanks; since they can only occur at the firnline, they must all be concentrated at a single point F at the altitude of the firnline. All other larger glaciers occupy the sectors above the diagonal.

If from point F a line (x) is drawn vertically upwards, all glaciers represented by points to the right (in sector A) have their bottoms above the firnline; they can therefore only comprise hanging glaciers, the lower ends of which terminate over steep cliffs and are therefore determined by topography and not climate. If from point F a line (y) is drawn horizontally to the left, all glaciers lying below this line (in sector B) have their tops below the firnline. Therefore they comprise either glaciers reconstituted from the fallen debris of a hanging glacier

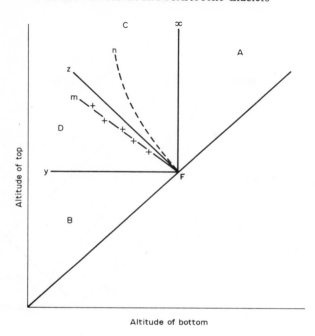

Figure 10.2   Basic general height graph.

above them, or, during a period of rising firnlines, they may be relics, just gradually melting away. The remaining sectors C and D therefore comprise all normal glaciers in approximate steady states. Those that lie exactly along the line (z) are those on which the firnline lies exactly at their mid-heights. Those in sector C have their firnlines below their mid-heights and are therefore either of piedmont type or have a non-linear net accumulation graph; those in sector D are of plateau type.

   If glaciers of different sizes from a homogeneous region are plotted on such a graph, they should ideally lie along a line, e.g. (m), that intersects the diagonal and thus indicates the firnline, the slope of the line being the Höfer coefficient. Such a line need not be straight: a curve that is concave upwards (n), suggests that the longer glaciers are tending towards the piedmont type, or that ablation is particularly severe on the lower glacier snouts.

   Figure 10.3 shows the practical application of this method to the 75 glaciers of the Mahoma stage in the Ruwenzori mountains, as inferred from their moraines. The glaciers have been divided into three large regional groups, consisting of (A) the eastern and central; (B) the southwestern and northern; and (C) the western parts of the range, and it is clear that the glaciers of each region occupy mutually exclusive parts of the graph. Within each region, individual glaciers indicate

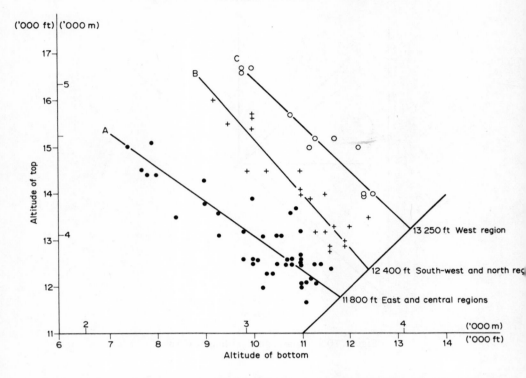

Figure 10.3   Firnlines of the Mahoma stage glaciers, Ruwenzori, by the graphical height method.

firnlines over a range of about 300 m altitude, but the mean firnline indicated by the best hand-fitted line can be determined with an uncertainty of only about 30 m, compared with differences of 200–500 m between the mean values for the three regions. The slope of each best-fit line is different, only one being at 45° to the axes, indicating regional differences of glacier type or mass balance curve. Consequently, in two of the regions the use of the original Höfer method would have resulted in a loss of accuracy.

The other advantages of this General Height method are first that the statistics of each glacier are clearly displayed in relation to the others, so that any discordance can easily be seen. This may lead to a revision of ideas on the correlation of different moraines, to a re-arrangement of the glaciers into more homogeneous groups, or to the detection of some interesting cause. The second advantage is that in locating the firnline extra weight can be given to the small glaciers which lie near the diagonal, and which, because they are small, are more precise indicators of the firnline than are big glaciers. Thus the method shares the advantage of the cirque method in making use of these small glaciers, but incorporates information from the larger glaciers too. The third advantage is that where data are scanty they may be supplemented by plotting firnbanks on the same graph, and the altitudes of the upper ends of the lateral moraines may also be marked on the diagonal. All these features can then be used together to estimate the firnline.

After using the graphical approach to do the preliminary examination and sorting, it may be more convenient, when data are numerous, to do the final calculation of the firnline numerically rather than graphically. Equation (3) was fitted to the data for each of the three regions (a convenient factor to weight the smaller glaciers more heavily being the integral part of $(T - B)^{-0.5}$). The results indicate values for the coefficient H of (A) 0.55, (B) 0.46 and (C) 0.50 with standard deviations from the regression of only 1.2% to 3.2%, and the values given for the firnline are 11 690 ft (3570 m), 12 420 ft (3790 m) and 13 280 ft (4050 m).

The general area method
Taking Brückner's ideas as the starting point, the percentage area/height distributions of several neighbouring glaciers of various sizes can be plotted on the same graph; they will have a pattern like that in Figure 10.4, with the lines close together near the middle of the

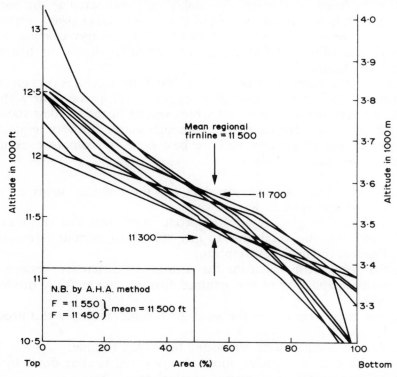

Figure 10.4   General area graph for Rwimi valley glaciers, Mahoma stage, Ruwenzori.

diagram. If all the glaciers were of exactly the same type, with similar climate and topography, their firnlines would all be identical and would divide the area of each in the same proportions, say 60% from the top; therefore when plotted like this all the curves would intersect at the point where the altitude of their common firnline crosses the 60% line. In practice, small differences are inevitable, but the region where the lines lie closest together will be a good indication of the firnline. Thus Figure 10.4 suggests that, in the Rwimi Valley group of glaciers during the Mahoma Glaciation, the firnline lay at about 11 600 ft (3540 m) at 55% of the area, and this agrees with estimates made by other methods.

The general area—height—mass balance method
Kurowski's particular case of this method can be improved by a more generalized statistical approach, testing other likely simple functions of mass balance against altitude, to see which fits the data best. When dealing with past glaciations, the accuracy of the data will seldom justify fine distinctions: it is difficult to be certain of the exact extent of the upper parts of the glacier; few of the world's mountains are mapped with contours more precise than 30 m intervals; the ground surface may have been modified by subsequent erosion; the correction for the thickness of the ice is probably only estimated to the nearest 30 m; and it is not usually a case of studying small changes on a single glacier, for which accuracy is important, but of larger changes in the mean firnline of several glaciers, all of which differ slightly in their mass balance functions.

The simplest range of mass balance functions to test is that given by substituting different values of K in equation (2) as was done with the model glaciers and selecting that which results in the smallest standard error of the mean. The calculations, though simple, are very tedious for a large number of glaciers, and are best done by computer using an iterative programme as follows.

1. Supply area and altitude data for the contour strips of each glacier, and value of K.
2. For the first glacier, sum the products of areas and altitudes and divide by the total area to give the mean altitude (Kurowski's firnline, the initial assumption).
3. For each strip calculate the arithmetic difference between its altitude and that of the assumed firnline, and multiply this by its area.
4. For each strip below the assumed firnline, multiply this product by minus K.
5. Sum all the products, above and below the firnline.
6. If the sum is negative, move the assumed firnline down by one height interval, or vice versa; recalculate.
7. When the sum changes sign, the present and last estimated values

of the firnline must straddle its true value, which can then be found by interpolation, or by the use of finer height intervals.

8. Repeat for the other glaciers.

Then (a) plot the firnline altitudes on a map and delineate homogeneous regions; and (b) calculate mean and standard error for each region. Repeat for another value of K.

TABLE 10.1

Mean regional firnlines, Lake Mahoma stage, Ruwenzori, by the area—height—accumulation method (altitudes in feet ± twice standard error)

Region (No. of glaciers)	K = 1	K = 2	Rounded estimate	Ice	Final estimate
A. East (39)	11 710 ± 80	11 530 ± 80	11 600	200	11 800 (3610 m)
B. { South-west / Central / North } (25)	12 600 ± 130	12 380 ± 180	12 600	200	12 800 (3980 m)
C. West (9)	13 400 ± 150	13 130 ± 170	13 300	200	13 500 (4120 m)
D. Far West (2) (Mugule)	12 240 ± 540	12 030 ± 500	12 100	200	12 300 (3750 m)

Note: The grouping of Figure 10.3 has been modified by the transfer of the four central glaciers from A to B, and by separating the far western group D from C.

The results yielded by this method for the Lake Mahoma stage are given in Table 10.1. The standard errors show that the differences between the firnlines of adjoining regions are very significant, but that there is not much to choose between the fit of the K1 and K2 estimates. Since the General Height method had already indicated firnlines between these two estimates, no further values of K were tested, the K1 value being accepted for regions B and C where its standard error was slightly the lesser, and the mean of the K1 and K2 values for regions A and D; a mean ice thickness correction of 200 ft (60 m) was inferred from valley cross-sections yielding final regional estimates of 11 900 ft (3630 m) to 13 600 ft (4150 m).

Estimates were obtained similarly for the 42 small present day glaciers, using data derived from a combination of maps, air-photos and ground-checks. They fall into well defined and consistent regional groups near the centre of the range with mean firnlines ranging between 14 750 ft (4500 m) and 15 550 ft. (4740 m), having standard errors of 10—70 ft (3—20 m).

A straightforward comparison between the firnlines of the Mahoma stage and the present day indicates, therefore, a difference of 1950—2850 ft (590—870 m). Most of the Mahoma glaciers, however, have completely melted and there has been such great recession of the remainder that a crude comparison which takes no account of the horizontal displacements of the firnline values concerned must be inadequate.

These results may be contrasted with a comparison of the Recent and Main Glaciations on Mount Kilimanjaro (Downie, 1964; Osmaston, 1965), when the same glaciers flowed down the steep volcanic cone of Kibo, and the relative retreats and displacements were less. Groups of glacier tongues flowed from common sectors of the ice-cap, so although there were clearly large differences between sectors, no statistical precision could be estimated for the sector firnline; and hence no statistical criterion is available for comparing K values. Table 10.2 gives the results for two sectors, and shows that though there are differences of up to 500 ft (150 m) between the K1 and K2 values of each firnline, the indicated *changes* of firnline only differ by 20—30 ft (5—10 m) assuming constancy of K. This confirms the similar conclusion drawn previously from the simple models. Such considerable differences between the K1 and K2 firnline values would probably be associated with significant differences in precision on a mountain where individual glaciers could be distinguished, thus providing grounds for choice between them.

TABLE 10.2
Regional firnlines of the main and recent glaciations, Kilimanjaro

	$K = 1$	Difference	$K = 2$	Difference
Kibo S.W.				
Main glacier	14 710	2500 ft. (762 m)	14 200	2530 ft. (771 m)
Recent glacier	17 210		16 730	
Kibo N.W.				
Main glacier	14 590	2960 ft. (903 m)	14 230	2980 ft. (910 m)
Recent glacier	17 550		17 210	

Note: these figures are unadjusted for ice thickness.

Firnline surface models

The methods described above provide good estimates of the mean firnline for a group of glaciers, but treat the divergences of individual glaciers as being due to irrelevant and minor differences in local relief, aspect, etc. If the group is fairly compact and homogeneous this assumption may be satisfactory, but, in the case of the Ruwenzori

Mountains, inspection of Figure 10.3 shows that the glaciers in fact form a continuous distribution, and that there are not discrete jumps in firnline between the somewhat arbitrary contiguous regions. This accords with the results obtained by earlier workers when mapping glacierization limits in Europe, and by the more recent mapping of corrie altitudes in Tasmania (Peterson and Robinson, 1969) and Scotland (Linton, 1959; Robinson *et al*, 1971), and of annual equilibrium line altitudes in North America (Meier and Post, 1962). Thus a more realistic concept is that of a *firnline surface*, of more or less complex shape, intersecting with the land surface of the mountain range; wherever the line of intersection crosses a valley, it follows the firnline of the local glacier, but on intervening ridges it has no real meaning. This surface has no existence except in the context of a particular mountain range: accumulation is determined by the oro-graphic precipitation and if the range is so dissected that for example, half the snow is rapidly shed from steep ridges into the valleys, the accumulation on the glacier surface will be doubled and the firnline will be lower than on a smooth ice cap.

Unfortunately, one is here faced with a dilemma. The methods just described, for determining the best Höfer or Brückner constants or the best accumulation function to use, depend on grouping the glaciers, thereby obtaining group means of high precision; whereas for deter-mining a best-fit surface it is preferable to use estimates for individual glaciers to provide as many points as possible to define the surface, even if the observations are somewhat clustered (Robinson, 1972). Thus in principle one might wish to calculate the best individual relation to use for each glacier, such that the resultant firnlines conform to a surface with minimum squared deviations. However, this approach is not possible with the information available, since the estimated firnline for each glacier can be made to fit perfectly *any* surface which intersects the glacier, provided no consistency of relation is demanded for neighbouring glaciers.

The first step therefore is to use the graphical General Height method for preliminary checking and sorting of the data, followed by demarcation of homogeneous regional groups on both map and graph, taking into account firnline altitude, glacier type and aspect. For each group, the best fit constant for equation (4) — or for equation (3) if area data are not available — is obtained by the iterative process described previously; with this the firnlines of individual glaciers can be recalculated and replotted on the map, after correcting for ice thickness if necessary; and finally a firnline surface can be fitted to these altitude points. If desired, the smaller glaciers can be given special weighting at each stage of the operation.

This surface is one for which a conventional least squares fit is fully appropriate, but the choice between fitting a surface by hand or by computer depends on the variability of the data points and the degree of generalisation required. If a high degree of generalisation is desired for numerous and very variable data, a computer is preferable, though the interpretation of such a surface needs caution; but if the data are consistent it may be easier and quite adequate to fit a surface by hand, and this is essential if the data indicate a rather complex surface which one desires to represent, particularly if additional information is to be used, such as the restriction that unglacierized peaks should not project more than 100 m above the surface. In fact firnline data do seem both to be remarkably consistent, and, if they are sufficiently numerous and well distributed, to show complex surface shapes which are beyond the normal capacity of a computer, but are closely related to the regional relief of the land surface (e.g. Meier and Post, 1962; cf. Unwin, 1968). The best compromise may be to use a computer initially if the number of points warrants it, and to improve the fit subsequently by hand, guided by a plot of the residuals. Unwin (1970) has shown that for 50 points a reduction of at least 30% in the sum of squared deviations is necessary to indicate a significant statistical improvement, and the fit of both the computer and hand-fitted surfaces should be assessed in this light. The use of extraneous information may however decrease the apparent fit of the hand-fitted surface, and improvements which conform better to the relief may be insignificant statistically but important theoretically.

Figures 10.5 and 10.6 show examples of this approach applied to the Ruwenzori Mountains. Figure 10.5 shows a hand-fitted firnline surface for the 42 present glaciers (based on 1955 air photography and field observations), grouped into 8 regions; the points are too clustered to justify a more elaborate fitting procedure. Figure 10.7 shows computed and hand-modified firnline surfaces fitted to data for the 75 Mahoma Stage glaciers. Table 10.3 shows the effectiveness of successive stages of firnline modelling in terms of the reduction of the sums of squares and of the standard deviation.

TABLE 10.3
Comparison of firnline models

Model	Sum of squared deviations (ft^2)	% Reduction in S.S.D. with respect to Model 1	Standard deviation (ft.)
1. Population mean of 79 glaciers	43×10^6	—	740
2. 4 group means	5×10^6	88	250
3. Computer-fitted linear plus quadratic surface	10×10^6	77	360
4. Hand-fitted surface	1.2×10^6	97	120

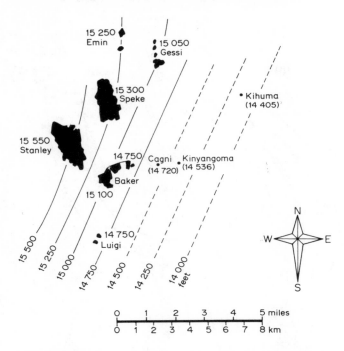

15 550 indicates mean firnline altitude of a group of glaciers in feet
(14 720) indicates summit altitude of an unglacierized peak in feet

Figure 10.5   The present glaciers of the Ruwenzori and their mean regional isofirnlines.

Inspection of the data points shows that the surface consists of a fairly simple hump, elongated NNE—SSW, for which a quadratic surface should be a suitable model. In fact, a best-fit linear and quadratic surface expressed by

$$\text{Altitude} = 1.14 + 0.0515\,E + 0.0573\,N - 0.116\,E^2 + 0.0931\,EN - 0.0271\,N^2$$

where E = map grid Eastings in 100 km
      N = map grid Northings in 100 km

provides a 77% explanation of the altitudinal variation. This level of explanation would be regarded as very satisfactory in most trend surface problems, and indeed the programme rejected attempts to introduce higher order variables because their contributions did not reach a critical level of significance.

However, inspection shows that there is still a cluster of mutually supporting discrepancies in the central east region, and that elsewhere there are lesser but still clear consistencies in the discrepancy between

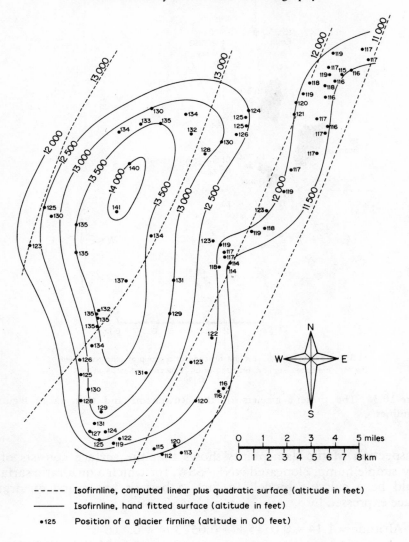

Figure 10.6   Firnline surfaces of the Mahoma stage, Ruwenzori.

data points and the surface. Moreover, the sum of squares and the standard deviation are greater even than those obtained by the simple regional grouping of the glaciers. The hand-fitted surface represents an attempt to accommodate these residuals, and, by slightly bending the whole hump, to provide a better fit while yet maintaining smooth curves for the isofirnlines. The effect of this is striking, as the sum of squares is reduced to only 1.2% of the total deviations, and the standard deviation of the data points from this surface is only 120 ft. The form of this surface is clearly related to the regional relief and the

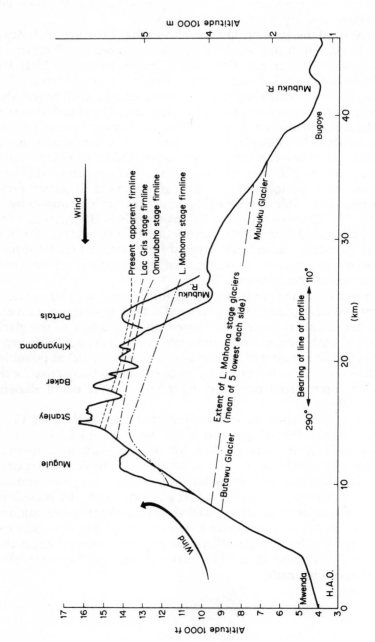

Figure 10.7   Profile of the Ruwenzori showing firnlines.

high precision of its fit in relation to the difference between the altitude of surfaces representing different periods of glacierization gives one confidence in using it for such comparisons.

Comparison of the firnline surfaces shows that their major slopes are so similar in direction and gradient (unusually steep at 60 m/km: the steepest found by Meier and Post was 13 m/km in the St. Elias Mts.) that the dominant wind direction must have been similar too at both times; thus theories which associate climatic change with major shifts of the wind systems are unsupported in this case. The simplest measure of the climatic difference between the surfaces is given by their difference in altitude as displayed in Figure 10.7, which shows that the *vertical* difference between them ranges from 450 m to 600 m. As the local lapse rate is 1°C per 150 m, a crude temperature difference between the two periods of 3°−4°C is indicated if other factors remained the same. This is reasonably in accord with estimates by this method for Mt. Kenya (5°C) and Kilimanjaro (6°) (Osmaston, 1965), and with pollen evidence on Mt. Kenya (5−9°C) (Coetzee, 1967); the differences probably reflect the large differences in precipitation on these three mountains, and movements of the firnline in relation to the zone of maximum precipitation.

The Mahoma surface itself has an altitude range of 750 m and the present surface a range of 250 m (over a shorter horizontal distance), so it is clear that a casual comparison based on only a few of the glaciers of each time, with firnlines not vertically coincident, could be grossly misleading, and it is essential to use as complete a model as possible of each firnline surface, constructed by a consistent and objective method such as that summarized here and described in more detail elsewhere (Osmaston, 1965).

In conclusion it must be emphasised that this method of firnline estimation depends first on accurate observations of the limits of actual glaciers, or of former ones marked by reliably correlated moraines; second, on the application of an empirical physical relationship between altitude, area and mass balance, using a range of constants compatible with observations on actual glaciers; third, the selection of the most probable of these from statistical considerations of minimum variance. The result is an estimate based on sound physical principles, but dependent partly on probabilistic assumptions about the sources of variation. In the absence of further information, it is the most reliable estimate that can be made.

NOTES AND REFERENCES

[1] These terms are used in accordance with the definitions in Meier (1962) as modified by I.A.S.H. (1968); in particular:

Mass balance (formerly often called mass budget) is the algebraic sum of the accumulation and ablation during a year (or other stated period), either at a point (in units of water equivalent depth), or integrated over part or all of the glacier area (in units of w.e. volume).

Steady state describes a hypothetical condition in which a glacier is neither advancing nor retreating, and the total mass balance is zero.

[2] The distinction between *glacierization* and *glaciation* (and between their related forms) has been thoroughly discussed in the *Journal of Glaciology*, vol. 2, Nos. 16, 17 and 18, and in the British Geomorphological Research Group *Occasional Paper*, No. 3; a final editoral note in the former asks all contributors to maintain the distinction carefully.

Glacierized = covered (partly or wholly) with glaciers.

Glaciated = sculptured (by deposition or erosion) by glaciers, which may or may not still exist, e.g. *despite long weathering since deglacierization, the glaciated and unglaciated parts of the range are clearly distinguishable.*

Sometimes *glaciated* can serve in both senses together without confusion, but the use of *deglaciated* in any sense is slipshod.

[3] The observations on East African mountains are presented in Imperial units (feet), since the excellent photogrammetric maps (by the Directorate of Overseas Surveys) were contoured on this basis. Metric equivalents are given for the more important figures.

[4] I am very grateful to Alex Chalmers for help with the computing, and to John Nye for much good advice.

Ahlmann, H. W. (1924). 'Le niveau de glaciation comme fonction de l'accumulation d'humidité sous forme solide', *Geografiska Annaler*, 6, 223–72.

Ahlmann, H. W. (1948). 'Glaciological research on the N. Atlantic coasts', *Royal Geographical Society*, Research Series 1.

Brückner, E. (1886). 'Die vergletscherung des Salsachgebietes', *Geografische Abhandlungen*, 1, 1–183.

Callendar, G. S. (1950). 'Note on the relation between the height of the snowline and the dimensions of a glacier', *J. Glaciology*, 1, 459–61.

Charlesworth, J. K. (1957). *The Quaternary Era, with special reference to its glaciation*, 2 vols, Arnold.

Coetzee, J. A. (1967). 'Pollen analytical studies in East and Southern Africa', *Palaeoecology of Africa*, 3, 1–146.

Downie, C. (1964). 'Glaciations of Mount Kilimanjaro, Northeast Tanganyika', *Bull. Geological Society of America*, 75, 1–16.

Drygalski, E. von and F. Machatschek (1942). 'Gletscherkunde', in *Enzyklopädie der Erdkunde*, Deutich.

Enquist, F. (1916). 'Der einfluss des Windes auf die Verteilung der Gletscher', *Bulletin of the Geological Institution of the University of Uppsala*, 14.

Finsterwalder, R. (1952). 'Photogrammetry and glacier research with special reference to glacier retreat in the eastern Alps', *J. Glaciology*, 2, 306–15.

Flint, R. F. (1957). *Glacial and Pleistocene Geology*, Wiley.

Haefeli, R. (1962). 'The ablation gradient and the retreat of a glacier tongue', International Association of Scientific Hydrology, Commission of Snow and Ice, Pub. No. 58, *Variations of the Regime of Existing Glaciers*, 49–59.

Hastenrath, S. L. (1967). 'Observations on the snowline in the Peruvian Andes', *J. Glaciology*, 6, 541–50.

Hess, H. (1904). *Die Gletscher*, Braunschweig.

Höfer, H. (1879). 'Gletscher und Eiszeit studien', *Sitzungsberichte der Akademie der Wissenschaften in Wien, Mathematische-naturwissenschaftliche Klasse*, 79.

Hugi, G. J. (1830). *Naturhistorische Alpenreise*, Solothurn.

I.A.S.H. (1968). 'Mass-balance terms', *J. Glaciology*, 8, 3—7.

Kurowski, L. (1891). 'Die Höhe der Schneegrenze', *Geografische Abhandlungen*, 5, 119—60.

LaChapelle, E. (1965). 'The mass budget of Blue Glacier, Washington', *J. Glaciology*, 5, 609—23.

Lichtenecker, N. (1937). 'Die rezente und diluvale Schneegrenzein den Östalpen', *Verhandlungen 3 Internationalen Quartärkonferenz*.

Linton, D. L. (1959). 'Morphological contrasts of Eastern and Western Scotland', in Miller, R., and J. W. Watson (Eds.), *Geographical Essays in Memory of A. G. Ogilvie*, Nelson, 16—45.

Livingstone, D. A. (1962). 'Age of deglaciation in the Ruwenzori range', *Nature*, 194, 859—60.

Lliboutry, L. (1955). 'Finsterwalder's and Ahlmann's rules', *J. Glaciology*, 2, 510—11.

Manley, G. (1949). 'The snowline in Britain', *Geografiska Annaler*, 31, 179—93.

Meier, M. F. (1962). 'Proposed definitions for glacier mass budget terms', *J. Glaciology*, 4, 252—61.

Meier, M. F. and A. Post (1962). 'Recent variations in mass net budgets of glaciers in Western North America', International Association of Scientific Hydrology, Commission of Snow and Ice, Pub. No. 58, *Variations of the Regime of Existing Glaciers*, 63—77.

Meier, M. F. and Tangbourne, W. V. (1965). 'Net budget and flow of South Cascade Glacier, Washington', *J. Glaciology*, 5, 547—66.

Mercer, J. H. (1961). 'The estimation of the regimen and former firn limit of a glacier', *J. Glaciology*, 3, 1053—62.

Nye, J. F. (1965a). 'The frequency response of glaciers', *J. Glaciology*, 5, 567—87.

Nye, J. F. (1965b). 'A numerical method of inferring the budget history of a glacier from its advance and retreat', *J. Glaciology*, 5, 589—607.

Osmaston, H. A. (1965). *The Past and Present Climate and Vegetation of Ruwenzori and its Neighbourhood*, unpublished D.Phil. thesis, University of Oxford.

Osmaston, H. A. (1968). 'The method of successive approximation in glaciology', British Geomorphological Research Group, Occasional Paper No. 6, 87—90.

Osmaston, H. A. (1967). 'The sequence of glaciations in the Ruwenzori', *Palaeoecology of Africa*, 2, 26—28.

Osmaston, H. A. (1972). *Guide to the Ruwenzori*, Mountain Club of Uganda.

Østrem, G. and O. Liestøl (1964). 'Norway: field work', *Glaciological Society Bulletin*, 15, 4—7.

Pal'gov, N. N. (1962). 'The relation between glacier retreat and the position of the firnline with special reference to the Zentralny Tuyuksu Glacier', International Association of Scientific Hydrology, Commission of Snow and Ice, Pub. No. 58, *Variations of the Regime of Existing Glaciers*, 40—48.

Partsch, J. (1882). *Die Gletscher der Vorzeit in den Karpathen und den Mittel-gebirgen Deutschlands*, Breslau.

Paschinger, V. (1912). 'Die Schneegrenze in verschiedenen Klimaten', *Petermanns Mitteilungen*, Erganzungsh, 173.

Penck, A. and E. Brückner (1909). *Die Alpen in Eiszeitalter*, Leipzig.

Peterson, J. A. and G. Robinson (1969). 'Trend-surface mapping of cirque floor levels', *Nature*, **222**, 75—76.

Ratzel, F. (1886). *Zur Kritik der naturlichen Schneegrenze*, Leopoldina.

Reid, H. F. (1907). 'Studies of the glaciers of Mt. Hood and Mt. Adams', *Zeitschr. f. Gletscherkunde*, **1**, 113—32.

Renaud, A. (1952). 'On the surface movement and ablation of the Gorner Glacier (Switzerland)', *J. Glaciology*, **2**, 54—57.

Robinson, G. (1972). 'Trials on trends through clusters of cirques', *Area*, **4**, 104—13.

Robinson, G., J. A. Peterson and P. M. Anderson (1971). 'Trend-surface analysis of corrie altitudes in Scotland', *Scottish Geographical Magazine*, **87**, 142—46.

Schumskiy, P. A. (1946). 'Energiya oledeneniya i zhizn'lednikov', *Ogiz. Gosudarstvennoye Izdatel'stvo Geograficheskoy Literatury*, Moscow.

Seddon, B. (1957). 'Late-glacial cwm glaciers in Wales', *Journal of Glaciology*, **3**, 94—99.

Suter, K. (1940). 'Le glaciation quaternaire de l'Appenin central', *Révue de Géographie Alpine*, fasc. 4.

Unwin, D. J. (1968). 'Some complications underlying trend surface analysis', *British Geomorphological Research Group Occasional Paper* No. 6, 9—18.

Unwin, D. J. (1970). 'Percentage RSS in trend-surface analysis', *Area*, **1**, 25—28.

Visser, P. C. (1928). 'Von den Gletschern am obersten Indus', *Zeitschrift f. Gletscherkunde*, **16**, 169—229.

PART IV

Soils and Biogeography

Chapter 11

Landscape Periodicity and Soil Development

Leonard Curtis

This essay seeks to discuss evidence of the effects of geomorphic processes of erosion and deposition found in soil profiles. Soil can be defined as any unconsolidated mineral or organic layer thicker than 10 cm occurring at the earth's surface. Surface layers that do not meet these requirements are designated as rock-land, water, ice or snow.

If a vertical section is cut down through the soil several layers or horizons are exposed for which a system of nomenclature is used. This places horizons under the headings O, A, B, C and sometimes D, (U.S.D.A. Soil Survey Staff, 1951). The whole of the soil profile is significant to the agriculturalist; the surface (A) horizon because it is the seat of biological activity and the principal source of nutrients; the subsoil (B) horizon because it affects drainage, soil moisture retention, aeration and root development. Both A and B horizons are important in respect of their influence on soil temperatures. The underlying parent material (C horizon) is mainly significant because it may contain weatherable minerals yielding nutrients and its texture may affect permeability. Deeper parts of the regolith (D horizon) are generally of less importance to plant growth and are not always described. The organic (O) horizon overlying the solum is not always present.

In contrast, the engineer normally defines soil as 'the unconsolidated sediments and deposits of solid particles derived from the disintegration of rock' (Jumikis, 1962). In fact, the engineer is mainly interested in what the agriculturalist or pedologist would term the C and D horizons.

The recognition of soils as organised natural bodies is generally accredited to Dokuchaiev (Basinski, 1959). In his early classic work on soils in Russia, Dokuchaiev put forward the view that soils were the products of complex interactions of climate, parent material (regolith type), topography, plants and animals. The resultant soil characteristics were also dependent upon the time during which these factors operated on a particular landscape. Thus Dokuchaiev was very conscious of the geographical and |environmental relationships of particular soil types; some kinds of soil were found in given geographical situations (sites) over and over again. Eventually his ideas reached America (Coffey, 1912a and b) and Western Europe (Glinka, 1914) and soil units were subsequently mapped on the basis of the soil profile and the characteristics of the A, B and C horizons. Later, several workers (Cline, 1949; Jenny, 1958; Simonson, 1962; Johnson, 1963) found it necessary to consider the three-dimensional characteristics of basic soil entities comprising segments of the rind of the earth, and Knox (1965) proposed the soil-landscape unit as a natural soil category. The boundaries of such units are defined as the points where the lateral rate of change in soil properties is at a local maximum.

The early work in Russia (Basinski, 1959), America (Thorp and Smith, 1949) and Europe (Kubiena, 1953) formed the basis for the later classificatory schemes used in various national surveys. The '7th Approximation' system of soil classification (U.S.D.A. 1960) is now widely adopted for surveys in temperate regions, and the work of D'Hoore (1965) has formed the basis of much work in the humid tropics. These classificatory schemes vary in detail, but the general hierarchical system consists of Soil Order, Soil Sub-Order, Great Soil Group, Soil Series, Soil Type (U.S.D.A. Soil Survey Staff, 1951).

In most of the early studies the soil horizons were regarded as being essentially the products of pedological processes acting upon a stable landscape and regolith. It was recognised that relief affected soil formation through its effects on soil movement, water transfer and receipt of solar radiation. Where profiles occurred in a repeated manner, and were geographically associated with relief features, they were termed a soil catena. The term soil catena was first proposed by Milne (1936) for a geographically linked group of soils in East Africa. These changed character along a traverse in accordance with conditions of drainage, differential transport of eroded material and the leaching, translocation and redeposition of mobile chemical constituents. However, the processes operating to create these relationships between soil and landscape were generally considered to be continuous and gradual in their operation as the landscape evolved, e.g. soil creep and the leaching action of percolating water.

The K-cycle concept of soil development

Thus general relationships between soil profiles and the elements of the landscape were understood at an early stage. As more detailed studies were carried out, however, it became clear that soil development and erosion have often been periodic rather than continuous in many parts of the world. In many soil landscapes it is possible to distinguish a number of cycles of soil development, each of which comprises alternating phases of instability and stability. Butler (1959) has accordingly suggested that there is a case for developing a framework of soil studies on the basis of landscape periodicity. In the unstable phase, erosion of soils from one area and burial of soils elsewhere takes place. A considerable diversity of geomorphic processes and events may take place within a single unstable phase, e.g. mass movement, slope washing and loess deposition. The areas of soil erosion and deposition are likely to be scattered and patchy in a landscape depending on such variables as slope, aspect, exposure, surface cover and character of soil material. In some cycles, areas of erosion and deposition may spread from points of initiation to involve the whole of the soil landscape. More often, however, relict areas will temporarily escape erosion and will persist as landscape elements in which soil development is continuous for a considerable period (Figure 11.1).

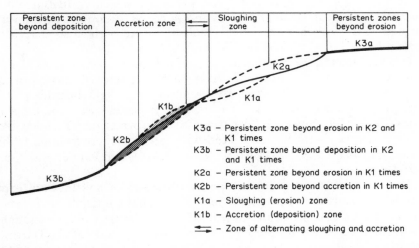

Figure 11.1   Schematic representation of K_1, K_2 and K_3 ground surfaces on a hillslope illustrating the relationships of the sloughing and accretion zones. (Developed from Butler, 1959.)

In the stable phase there is a period of plant colonisation and pedogenesis, with a relative pause in active erosion and deposition. Butler has used the term 'K-cycle' to indicate the time unit in which each combination of both unstable (u) and stable (s) phases occurs. Thus a number of K-cycles can sometimes be identified extending back from the present, e.g. K1(s), K1(u); K2(s), K2(u); K3 (s),K3(u), etc.

The evidence for such K-cycles is found within the soil profile in the form of buried soils and lithological discontinuities, including the presence of 'stone lines' (Ruhe, 1959). 'Stone-lines' are thin patches or layers of stones within the soil profile which appear as bands or lines in the cut section. Stone lines vary considerably in thickness, stone size and persistence (Parizek and Woodruffe, 1957). In some instances, complete soil profiles are buried beneath eroded material and the former organic surface (A) horizon is preserved. Elsewhere, however, the buried soil itself becomes eroded before being covered by material from higher points in the landscape. In such cases, discontinuities in the profile may only be detected by analyses of particle size, pollen content or mineral assemblages.

Processes affecting British soils and associated K-cycles

The events responsible for K-cycle phenomena in British soils are varied. The climatic and geomorphological episodes of the Quaternary period resulted in widespread instability of the soil surfaces. In particular, major amendments of soil profiles have been made by glacial and periglacial processes. Peltier (1950) has outlined the geographical cycle in periglacial regions and the processes which contribute to the formation of periglacial landforms and deposits. Examples of the varied surface and soil characteristics resulting from periglacial activity in Britain have been reviewed by Fitzpatrick (1956a, 1958).

It is evident that redistribution of surface soil materials took place on a large scale at the close of the Quaternary era. Removal of fine textured soil materials from the summit areas left behind a stony regolith exposed to subaerial erosion and, in some cases, these became block fields (felsenmeere). The processes of formation of screes, block fields and tors, typically associated with periglacial environments, have been described by Ball (1966), Williams (1968), and Palmer and Neilsen (1962).

The materials moved downslope by processes of solifluction formed extensive head deposits which are often characterised by layers of different textures. Some of these solifluction layers lie close enough to the surface to be within present soil profiles, e.g. some of the Dartmoor granitic head deposits described by Waters (1961, 1964). Layered head deposits are readily seen in cliff exposures, and soils in coastal situations can be readily inspected. The complex layerings associated with these solifluction deposits have been described by Stephens (1966) and by Dylik (1966) for sites in North Devon. Some examples of twentieth-century debris flows in north-east Ireland are given by Prior et al (1970), in which mantles of till debris some 50–100 cm in thickness were deposited. These processes of solifluction and mass movement frequently operate where the soil and regolith are saturated with water. In the periglacial episodes the impermeable layers formed by perma-frost contributed towards surface saturation. In addition, freeze-thaw processes led to the formation of indurated B/C horizons in many soils which reduced downward percolation of water (Fitzpatrick, 1956b). Internal soil conditions were reinforced by external climatic conditions, and aspect of slope appears to have been important in respect of periglacial and modern examples of mass movement phenomena. Gregory (1965) has described the orientation of fossil mass movement phenomena in the Esk drainage basin, Yorkshire and shown that a north-easterly aspect is the most common. Curtis (1971) noted the directions of landslides on Exmoor following the 1952 storm: North — 37, South — 3, East — 20, West — 2. Mean moisture contents in the period 1963—1969 for Exmoor soils on north and east facing slopes were approximately 79% compared with 59% on south and west facing slopes. The author has, therefore, suggested that the many slides on north and east facing slopes can be attributed to differences in pore water pressure. These are due to the larger moisture contents of north and east facing slopes leading to rapid saturation following storms, and to the presence of impermeable pan layers which occur on north facing slopes more extensively than on south facing slopes.

Perhaps the most extensive process affecting British soils and leading to lithological discontinuities has been wind erosion and deposition. In the periglacial period, considerable areas received additions of loessial materials and these have a marked influence on soil properties. The Chalk heath soils were recognised by Perrin (1956) as providing an example of a loess veneer altering the soil character. Findlay (1965) has carried out mineralogical analysis of deep soils on the Carboniferous limestones of Mendip, which shows that the silty topsoil includes minerals not present in the underlying rock. Curtis (1974) has observed that soils on the margins of the uplands of Exmoor are often characterised by Ea horizons, with more than 90% of particles in the range of 2—125 microns. These particle sizes are characteristic of many aeolian sediments; also it may be noted that the heavy mineral composition differs from that of the underlying rock deposits.

It should be borne in mind, however, that Man has been a potent agent in promoting periodicity in landscape phenomena. Dimbleby (1952) first drew attention to the possible role of man in relation to complex polycyclic profiles occurring in the Silpho and Broxa areas of the North York Moors. These areas were first recognised by their characteristic polygonal patterning of the type normally associated with ice wedge polygons. Sections through these soils displayed filled-in ice wedges containing Cheviot erratics but, more importantly, above the wedge three solifluction layers were discovered. The boundary between the lower and middle solifluction layers was marked by burnt stones and charcoal on what appeared to be an old forested surface. It can be postulated, therefore, that destruction of the forest led to instability of the surface and hence erosion and deposition leading to solifluction layers. Further work by Dimbleby (1962) showed that in about one third of a number of profiles examined by soil pollen analysis, there were older levels buried beneath later deposits. The buried levels were generally within 45 cm of the surface and were dominantly at depths of about 23 cm. They occurred in what are now designated as Ea, B and C horizons and were sometimes not easily distinguished by eye but were detected by pollen analysis.

Dimbleby (1952, 1954, 1955, 1962) has also shown that many

upland heaths of Britain formerly supported deciduous forest. Similar changes from deciduous forest to heathland are reported for Dartmoor (Simmons, 1964), South Wales and Exmoor (Crampton, 1963, 1966, 1968). The clearance of forest by early man appears to have been the initiating factor for the development of heathland. As a result, the former brown forest soils were subjected to more intensive leaching and an acid mor type of humus developed. These changes led to the development of many of the existing upland podzol soils.

Many of the buried levels encountered by Dimbleby appeared to be related to the end of the Atlantic period and beginning of the Sub-Boreal, coincident with the Neolithic period. Thus some K-cycle phenomena can be related to this period of Neolithic clearance of some areas of upland vegetation. Dimbleby stresses, however, that the impact of man may have come earlier because there is evidence of the use of fire by Mesolithic man to drive his game and to open up the landscape for hunting. If these fires got out of control periodically, the soil surfaces would be much more vulnerable to subaerial erosion and deposition with resultant layering within the soil profiles.

Sloping soils can be expected to be those first affected by such erosion and it is interesting to note that the classification of slope soils in Britain has been the subject of controversy. Various terms have been used to describe them, including crypto-podzols, truncated podzols, brown podzolic soils, strongly leached brown earths and sols bruns acides (Robinson, 1949; Crompton, 1960; Mackney and Burnham, 1964). The term 'truncated podzol' was used by Robinson for soils in which high sesquioxide ratios were found close to the surface. He suggested that these soils were those in which, following deforestation, erosion had removed the A horizon leaving the sesquioxide-rich B horizon exposed near the surface. Thus, in terms of K-cycle phenomena, one would expect to find the buried soil counterpart of these slope soils at lower elevations.

The destruction of natural woodland was a piecemeal process extending over several centuries. In the Romano-British period, it was partly due to extension of settlement and farming down into the vales from the uplands. Later, however, especially in the mediaeval period through to the early nineteenth century, it was dominantly due to the desire to extend the capabilities of lowland settlements and, especially in the earlier period, to provide fuel for mineral smelting, e.g. lead and iron production. For example, the monastic holdings in Lancashire and Yorkshire developed vaccaries (cattle breeding stations) in the thirteenth and fourteenth centuries. Although most cattle stations had a streamside location, some were sited on valley slopes and on the moorland edge where they doubtless played a part in modifying the vegetation cover. In the sixteenth century, a rising population and a quickening of economic activity brought new farms in appreciable numbers. Whereas Leland (c. 1540) noted that 'Weredale is wel woodid', by 1652 a survey showed 'no timber . . . in Weardale and no coppice or underwood near Wearhead'. The impact of man on the vegetation covering valley slopes was evidently considerable and probably triggered off local patches of erosion and deposition.

In the nineteenth and twentieth centuries burning of the heather moors (swaling) has become common practice and has further depleted vegetation cover. Many upland soils have lost the protective litter layers and interception of rainfall by heather has been reduced. As a result, many moorland areas are in a very unstable state at the present time. For example, on Levisham Moor (North York Moors), repeated burning has resulted in surface erosion on areas where the heather burn was so severe that regeneration has been slow or has been prevented. Quadrat studies in 1965 showed that, in some places after burning, 72% of the surface consisted of bare soil with only 6.5% live Calluna remaining. Following rainstorms, the channels on such burned areas carry a load consisting of bleached sand grains from Ea horizons and peat granules from O horizons. In sites where the flow of water is temporarily checked, deposition occurs. The sand, being of higher specific gravity, settles out separately from the organic matter fragments. These channel deposits show laminations made up of bleached sand alternating with thinner laminations of organic matter. The sand layers are normally 1–2 cm in thickness, whereas organic layers may be measured in millimetres (Plate 11.1a shows this K0u stage).

On nearby heath-covered moorland showing no contemporary evidence of instability, there are peaty gleyed podzols in which, beneath a peaty loam approximately 7.5 cm in thickness, there is an albic Ea horizon composed of laminated sand and organic matter. These laminations clearly resemble the depositional layers occurring in contemporary channels of the eroding parts of the moor. Thus the soil profiles (Plate 11.1b) provide evidence of an earlier K-cycle in which instability affected parts of the moor which now seem stable, i.e. evidence of an earlier K1u phase.

Many of the heads of the valleys in moorland areas consist of ill-drained, shallow hollows, in which the first rivulets caused by overland flow are formed. It is in these valley head sites that buried profiles commonly occur. On the North York Moors (Figure 11.2), mature soil profiles consisting of peaty gleyed podzols, humus-iron podzols and peaty gleys have been buried beneath about 1 metre of eroded material. The detail of the deposited layers varies somewhat from one valley head (griff) to another but there is a general similarity in the pattern (Figure 11.3). The general horizon sequence (Plates 11.2a, 11.2b) is as follows:

Horizon 1 Thin root mat or peat layer.
Horizon 2 Yellowish brown loamy sand/sandy clay loam containing gravel layers (subangular and angular stones up to 3–4 cm diameter).

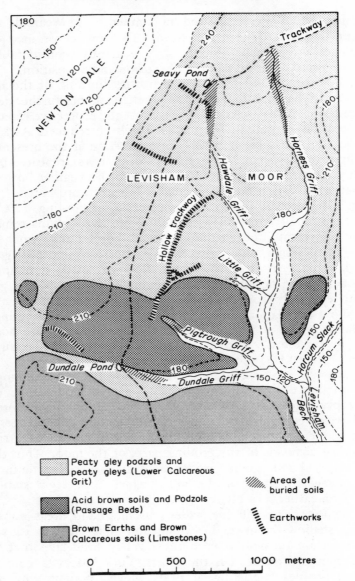

Figure 11.2   The distribution of buried soils on Levisham Moor, North York Moors.

Horizon 3   Laminated layers of sand and organic matter (similar to layers occurring in contemporary eroding channels as described above).
Horizon 4   Buried topsoil (organic O layer or A layer).

The deposits vary in thickness between the four griffs and from point to point within each one (Table 11.1).

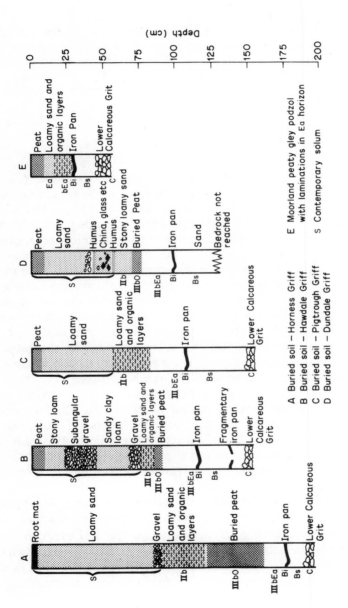

Figure 11.3   Generalised sections of buried soils in griffs and on moorland in the Levisham Moor area, North York Moors.

TABLE 11.1

Variations in the depth of buried soils, North York Moors

Site	Depth (cm) to buried topsoil (Horizon 4)	Maximum thickness (cm) of Yellow Brown Sandy layer (Horizon 2)	Maximum thickness (cm) of laminated sand and organic matter (Horizon 3)	Depth of gully incision at head of griff (metres)
Horness Griff	115—26	82	33	2.00
Hawdale Griff	115—38	115	8	1.42
Pigtrough Griff	102—51	46	56	1.83
Dundale Griff	61—56	61	10	1.52

Interpretation of these profiles suggests that in the Late Glacial period periglacial activity created extensive new surfaces without soil differentiation on them (K2u). In the succeeding stable phase (K2s) soil development created a varied soil landscape including acid brown earths, gleys and podzols. At the later stages of soil development, peaty gleyed podzols, humus-iron podzols and peaty gleys were dominant. A proportion of the K2s groundsurface was then eroded and buried in an unstable phase occurring in the late nineteenth century on Levisham Moor (elsewhere on the North York Moors mediaeval clearances may have led to phases of instability). Mainly stable ground surfaces were established following the K1u phase and acid brown earths under 10 cm of peaty loam were developed on the K1s deposits. At the present time, small amounts of localised erosion are giving rise to laminations in channel deposits and these can be ascribed to a K0u phase.

The occurrence of buried soils at the heads of valleys accords well with evidence of overload flow on upland heaths on Mendip, Somerset (Stagg, 1973). Waterlogging of the surface layers of soil above impermeable horizons (e.g. Bi of peaty gleyed podzols) leads to overland flow following storms. Where the surface vegetation is broken or reduced by firing or overgrazing, such areas are prone to erosion and material is redeposited on lower slopes.

The valley side slopes of such areas often display evidence of layering indicating surface erosion, together with evidence of slipping. An example of horizons occurring on steep (30°) slopes in Pigtrough Griff illustrates the complex pattern of buried horizons which occurs where land slipping takes place (Figure 11.4). The increased lamination in the slipped zone suggests that this portion of the slope became waterlogged more frequently than the upper slope.

The occurrence of buried soils is frequently accompanied by the formation of stone lines, and soil profiles showing evidence of stone or gravel commonly occur in upland soils of Britain. Three profiles in upland soils of Wales were described by Ball (1963) and further

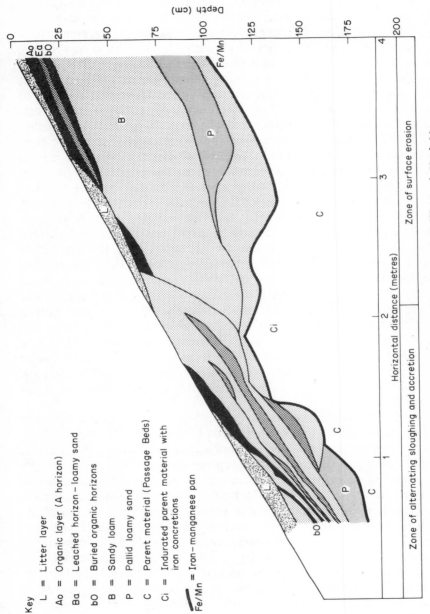

Key

L = Litter layer

Ao = Organic layer (A horizon)

Ea = Leached horizon – loamy sand

bO = Buried organic horizons

B = Sandy loam

P = Pallid loamy sand

C = Parent material (Passage Beds)

Ci = Indurated parent material with
     iron concretions

Fe/Mn = Iron–manganese pan

Figure 11.4 Section through valley-side soils, Pigtrough Griff, North York Moors. Buried soil horizons occur on the lower part of the slope indicating alternating sloughing and accreting conditions.

examination of these profiles (Ball, 1967) showed that, in some instances, there was a fairly closely packed layer of stones (in Ruhe's terminology 'stone lines') forming a conspicuous concentration approximately parallel to the ground surface. The long axes of individual stones were parallel to the general slope of the stone pavement as a whole. Stone layers in peaty gleyed podzols (Ashen Series) on Mendip, Somerset, normally occur at the base of the Ea horizon (Curtis, 1974). The weight of stones present at varying depths was determined in four profiles. The results showed a maximum concentration at a depth of 15 cm, the stone content then decreasing to a depth of 40 cm. Similarly, measurements showed that the maximum stone size within the soil profile occurs at the top of the stone layer. Stone size then decreases to a depth of 30 cm, below which it increases again as bedrock is approached. The orientation of stones as observed by stone fabric analyses indicates that long axes are mainly oriented downslope. Buried stone layers within Exmoor soils are relatively common (Curtis, 1971). At the heads of Exmoor valleys, peat bogs have developed where flush water (lateral seepage) has maintained surface wetness. These flush bogs are often over 2 metres deep (Green, 1955) and stony horizons within them provide evidence of localised erosion and deposition. Sections exposed at Great Vintcombe, Prayway Head and Exe Head show stone layers consisting of subangular fragments of sandstone and slate overlain by approximately 45 cm of peat (Plate 11.3). The stone layers represent an unstable phase of erosion and deposition followed by a stable phase of peat accumulation. The cause of the unstable phase is difficult to ascertain. It may have been due to human action such as turf cutting or agistment of animals (MacDermot, 1911, 1973), or to major flood conditions such as those of 1769 (Chanter, 1907).

The recognition of lithological discontinuities and buried horizons has led to the adoption of a special horizon terminology (Avery, 1973). Roman numerals are prefixed to horizon designations, to indicate distinct lithological discontinuities representing vertical variations in parent material as evidenced by changes in particle size distribution, stone content or mineralogy. Horizons comprising the uppermost lithological layer are not numbered in profile descriptions, the number I being understood. Horizons in succeeding depositional layers are numbered II, III, etc., consecutively with depth. Pedogenic horizons that have evidently been buried by deposition of fresh material with little subsequent modification are indicated by the prefix b (buried). The buried horizon may be contained in similar material (e.g. b Ah) or by dissimilar material (e.g. II b Ah), indicating a lithological discontinuity.

The effects of buried horizons on subsequent pedogenic processes have been little studied. Where buried horizons are composed of organic matter, they may give rise to distinctly different microbial populations.

In these circumstances, precipitation of elements translocated in solution, or by the process of cheluviation, may take place at the discontinuity. Bloomfield (1953, 1955) has studied the mechanism of reprecipitation of the translocated oxides of iron and aluminium. He suggested that microbial action may be largely responsible for reprecipitation and this view was supported by Crawford (1956). There may, therefore, be a case for the re-examination of humus-iron podzols, to determine whether humus B horizons are entirely pedogenic or whether some are b Ah or II b Ah horizons which have triggered off iron precipitation.

Where mineral particles are buried, the effects on pedogenesis will largely depend on the particle size at the discontinuity. Coarse materials, such as stone layers, frequently promote lateral throughflow. Evidence of this can be seen in many upland soils, e.g. in podzolised soils and brown earths on the Mendip Hills (Weyman, 1971).

Particles of medium or coarse sand may provide better conditions for oxidation and thereby promote precipitation. Discontinuities in particle size composition can, therefore, lead to zones of iron or aluminium concentration. Bloomfield (1953, 1955) has shown that sorption of ferrous iron on ferric oxide nucleii can produce surfaces capable of sorbing more material. Thus a II B horizon which is sandy and contains iron coated particles may be an effective precipitation agent, leading to further iron deposition.

Where buried horizons are composed of fine textured material, they may resemble the textural B horizons characteristic of the process of lessivage (Duchaufour, 1965). If the buried layer is of low porosity and high bulk density, it may act as an impedance to soil drainage. In these circumstances, the phenomenon of gleying may be associated with buried horizons. Gleying is essentially a process of reduction and in the case of iron the ferrous state of iron becomes mobile, usually together with manganese and some other trace elements. The gleying process may lead to translocation of iron and other elements by a process of lateral water movement. In such cases, the occurrence and geographical pattern of distribution of elements may often be affected by the pattern of buried discontinuities which affect gleying and water movement.

Conclusion

The extent to which periodic phenomena have affected profile development in the world soil groups has yet to be explored. Studies in Australia (Walker, 1962; Jessup, 1960), New Zealand (Dalrymple, 1958), Africa (Williams, 1968) and America (Jackson, 1965; Thorp, 1965) indicate the widespread occurrence of buried soils. In many cases buried horizons give rise to characteristic features, e.g. the 'gumbotil' clay layers buried beneath Wisconsian till in the United States (Kay,

1916). Such features lead one to question whether profile features such as subsoil columnar structures in solonetzic soils of arid regions, or the ashy-grey Ea horizons of podzols, are entirely the product of vertical leaching as traditionally believed. Perhaps the columnar structures represent buried polygonally cracked surfaces and the bleached horizons of podzols are related to periglacial erosion and deposition in many instances. The triggering of erosional and depositional phases by human impact on the landscape is evident in many countries. Perhaps it is best displayed in arid regions where successive pastoral and irrigation civilisations have induced instability of the soil surface over wide areas. Indeed, in these regions traditional soil classification categories are difficult to apply. Soil mapping is often best carried out on the basis of geomorphic units which reflect the erosional and depositional land-scapes (Western, 1972) and which closely correspond to soil profile characteristics. It seems likely, therefore, that soil classification will require progressive modification to take into account the changes wrought by pedogenic processes resulting from the action of periodic phenomena at the ground surface.

REFERENCES

Avery, B. W. (1973). Soil classification in the Soil Survey of England and Wales, *J. Soil Science,* 24, 324—38.

Ball, D. F. (1963). *Soils and Land Use of the District around Bangor and Beaumaris,* Memoir, Soil Survey of Great Britain, H.M.S.O.

Ball D. F. (1966). 'Late glacial scree in Wales', *Biuletyn Peryglacjalny,* 15, 151—63.

Ball, D. F. (1967). 'Stone pavements in soils of Caernarvonshire, North Wales', *J. Soil Science,* 18, 103—108.

Basinki, J. J. (1959). 'The Russian approach to soil classification and its recent development', *J. Soil Science,* 10, 14—26.

Bloomfield, C. (1953). 'A study of podzolisation. Part I: the mobilisation of iron and aluminium by Scots pine needles. Part II: the mobilization of iron and aluminium by the leaves and bark of "*Agathis australis*" (Kauri)', *J. Soil Science* 4, 5—23.

Bloomfield, C. (1955). 'A study of podzolisation. Part VI: the immobilisation of iron and aluminium', *J. Soil Science,* 6, 284—92.

Butler, B. E. (1959). *Periodic Phenomena in Landscape as a Basis for Soil Studies,* Soil publication, Commonwealth Scientific and Industrial Research Organisation, Australia, 14.

Chanter, J. F. (1907). *A History of the Parishes of Lynton and Countisbury,* James G. Commin, Exeter.

Cline, M. G. (1949). 'Basic principles of soil classification', *Soil Science,* 67, 81—91.

Coffey, G. N. (1912a). 'The development of soil survey work in the United States. with a brief reference to foreign countries', *Proc. American Society of Agronomists,* 3, 115—29.

Coffey, G. N, (1912b). 'A study of the soils of the United States', *Bull. Bureau of Soils*, **85**, U.S. Department of Agriculture.

Crampton, C. B. (1963). 'The development and morphology of iron pan podzols in Mid and South Wales', *J. Soil Science*, **14**, 282–302.

Crampton, C. B. (1966). 'Analysis of pollen in soils on the peaks of South Wales', *Scottish Geographical Magazine*, **82**, 46–52.

Crampton, C. B. (1968). 'Changes in hill vegetation revealed by selected British soils', *Scottish Geographical Magazine*, **84**, 179–84.

Crawford, D. V. (1956). 'Microbiological aspects of podzolisation', *Trans. 6th Int. Cong. Soil Sci.*, (c), 197–202.

Crompton, E. (1960). 'The significance of the weathering/leaching ratio in the differentiation of major soil groups, with particular reference to some very strongly leached brown earths on the hills of Britain', *Trans. 7th Int. Congr. Soil Sci.*, V., 406–12.

Curtis, L. F (1965). 'Soil erosion on Levisham Moor, North York Moors', *Institute of British Geographers Symposium Occasional Publ.*, *No. 2*, British Geomorphological Research Group, 19–21.

Curtis, L. F. (1971). *Soils of Exmoor Forest*, Special Survey No. 5, Soil Survey of Great Britain.

Curtis, L. F. (1974). *A Study of the Soils of Exmoor Forest*, unpublished Ph.D. thesis, University of Bristol.

Dalrymple, J. B. (1958). 'The application of soil micromorphology to fossil soils and other deposits from archaeological sites', *J. Soil Science*, **9**, 199–209.

D'Hoore, J. L. (1965). *Soils Map of Africa*, Centre de Commission de Cooperation Technique en Afrique, Lagos.

Dimbleby, G. W. (1952). 'The historical status of moorland in north-east Yorkshire', *New Phytologist*, **51**, 349–54.

Dimbleby, G. W. (1954). 'The origin of heathland podzols and their conversion by afforestation', *Report 8th International Botanical Congress*, 13, 74–80.

Dimbleby, G. W. (1955). 'The ecological study of buried soils', *Advancement of Science*, **12**, 11–16.

Dimbleby, G. W. (1962). *The Development of British Heathlands and their Soils*. Oxford Forestry Memoirs 23.

Duchaufour, P. (1965). *Précis de Pédologie*, Masson.

Dylik, J. (1966). 'In the Exeter Symposium: Discussion', (eds. D. L. Linton and R. S. Waters), *Biuletyn Peryglacjalny*, **15**, 133–149.

Findlay, D. C. (1965). '*The Soils of the Mendip District of Somerset*, Mem. Soil Survey of England and Wales.

Fitzpatrick, E. A. (1956a). 'Progress report on the observations of periglacial phenomena in the British Isles', *Biuletyn Peryglacjalny*, 4, 99–115.

Fitzpatrick, E. A. (1956b). 'An indurated soil horizon formed by permafrost, *J. Soil Science*, 7, 248–54.

Fitzpatrick, E. A. (1958). 'Periglacial geomorphology of Scotland', *Scottish Geographical Magazine*, 74, 28–36.

Glinka, K. D. (1914). *Treatise on Soil Science*, 4th Edition, Translated by A. Gourevitch, Israel Programme for Science Translations Ltd., 1963.

Green, G. W. (1955) 'North Exmoor floods, August 1952', *Bulletin Geological Survey of Great Britain*, 7, 68–84.

Gregory, K. J. (1965). 'Aspect and landforms in North East Yorkshire', *Biuletyn Peryglacjalny* 15, 115–120.

Jackson, M. L. (1965). 'Clay transformation in soil genesis during the Quaternary', *Soil Sci.* **99**, 15–22.

Jenny, H. (1958). 'The role of the plant factor in the pedogenic functions', *Ecology*, **39**, 5–16.

Jessup, R. W. (1960). 'Identification and significance of buried soils of Quaternary age in south-east Australia', *J. Soil Science*, **11**, 197–205.

Johnson, W. M. (1963). 'The pedon and the polypedon', *Proc. American Soil Science Society*, **27**, 212–15.

Jumikis, A. R. (1962). *Soil Mechanics*, Van Nostrand.

Kay, G. F. (1916). 'Gumbotil, a new name in Pleistocene geology', *Science*, N.S. **44**, 637–38.

Knox, E. G. (1965). 'Soil individuals and soil classification', *Proc. American Soil Science Society*, **29**, 79–84.

Kubiena, W. L. (1953). *The Soils of Europe*, Murby.

MacDermot, E. T. (1911). *The History of the Forest of Exmoor*, The Wessex Press.

Mackney, D. and G. P. Burnham (1964). 'A preliminary study of some slope soils in Wales', *J. Soil Science*, **15**, 319–30.

Milne, G. (1936). 'A soil reconnaissance journey through parts of Tanganyika Territory', published in 1947 in *J. Ecology*, **35**, 192–265.

Palmer, J. and R. A. Neilson (1962). 'The origin of granite tors on Dartmoor, Devonshire', *Proc. Yorkshire Geological Society*, **33**, 315–40.

Parizek, E. J. and J. F. Woodruffe (1957). 'Description and origin of stone layers in soils of the South Eastern States', *J. Geology*, **65**, 24–34.

Peltier, L. C. (1950). 'The geographic cycle in periglacial regions as it is related to climatic geomorphology', *Annals. Association of American Geographers*, **40**, 214–36.

Perrin, R. M. S. (1956). 'The nature of "Chalk Heath" soils', *Nature*, **178**, 31–32.

Prior, D. B., N. Stephens, and G. R. Douglas (1970). 'Some examples of modern debris flows in north-east Ireland', *Zeitschrift für Geomorphologie*, **14**, 275–88.

Robinson, G. W. (1949). *Soils: their origin, constitution and classification*, Thos. Murby.

Ruhe, R. V. (1959). 'Stone lines in soils', *Soil Science*, **87**, 223–31.

Simmons, I. G. (1964). 'An ecological history of Dartmoor', in Simmons, I. G. (Ed.), *Dartmoor Essays*, Devon Association for the Advancement of Science, 191–215.

Simonson, R. W. (1962). 'Soil classification in the United States', *Science* (N.Y.), **137**, 1027–34.

Stagg, M. (1973). *Storm Runoff in a Small Catchment in the Mendip Hills*, unpublished M.Sc. thesis, University of Bristol.

Stephens, N. (1966). 'Some Pleistocene deposits in North Devon', *Biul. Peryglac.* **15**, 103–14.

Thorp, J. and G. D. Smith (1949). 'Higher categories of soil classification: order, sub-order and great soil groups', *Soil Science*, **67**, 117–26.

Thorp, J. (1965). 'The nature of the pedological record in the Quaternary', *Soil Science*, **99**, 1–8.

U.S.D.A. Soil Survey Staff (1951). *Soil Survey Manual*, U.S. Department of Agriculture Handbook 18.

U.S.D.A. Soil Survey Staff (1960). *Soil Classification (7th Approximation)*, (supp. 1964 and 1967), U.S. Department of Agriculture.

Plate 11.1a
Surface erosion of organic (O) and leached loamy sand (Ea) horizons on Levisham Moor,
North York Moors. Pallid layers are bleached (Ea) sandy layers. Penknife handle is
approximately 9 cm.

Plate 11.1b
Podzolised soil on Levisham Moor.
Note laminations of sandy loam
and organic matter at a depth of
approximately 15 cm. Card shows
depths at 5 cm intervals.

— Horizon 1

— Horizon 2.

— Horizon 3.

— Horizon 4

— Iron pan

Plate 11.2a
Buried soil (peaty gleyed podzol) in Horness Griff, Levisham Moor.
Penknife handle (9 cm) gives the scale.

— Horizon 1

— Horizon 2

— Horizon 3
— Horizon 4

— Iron pan

Plate 11.2b
Buried soil (peaty gleyed podzol) in Pigtrough Griff, Levisham Moor.

Plate 11.3
Buried stone layer in peaty loam, Great Vintcombe, Exmoor. The exposed
half of the auger handle is 25 cm long.

Walker, P. H. (1962). 'Soil layers on hillslopes, Nowra, Australia', *J. Soil Science*, 13, 167—77.

Waters, R. S. (1961). 'Involutions and ice-wedges in Devon', *Nature*, 189, 389—90.

Waters, R. S. (1964). 'The Pleistocene legacy to the geomorphology of Dartmoor', in Simmons, I. G. (ed.), *Dartmoor Essays*, Devon Association for the Advancement of Science, 73—96.

Western, S. (1972). 'The classification of Arid Zone Soils, I and II', *J. Soil Science*, 23, 266—78, 279—97.

Weymann, D. R. (1971). 'Surface and sub-surface runoff in a small basin', unpub. Ph.D. thesis, University of Bristol.

Williams, M. A. J. (1968). 'A dune catena on the clay plains of West Central Gezira, Republic of the Sudan', *J. Soil Science*, 19, 367—78.

Williams, R. B. G. (1968). 'Some estimates of periglacial erosion in Southern and Eastern England', *Biuletyn Peryglacjalny*, 17, 311—35.

Chapter 12

A Review of Methodological Advances in Pollen Analysis

Keith Crabtree

The technique of pollen analysis has been widely used by archaeologists, biologists, geographers and geologists since the inception of the method by von Post in 1916. In Britain, after initial work by Erdtman (1928), Godwin developed the technique along the lines suggested by von Post, that is as a tool for stratigraphic work and as a record of the British flora. Increasingly, the objective of many palynological studies has become palaeoecological, especially since radio-carbon dating has largely replaced the stratigraphic significance of pollen spectra. To use pollen assemblages as indicators of former plant communities many of the basic assumptions of the method of pollen analysis have come under detailed scrutiny and research over the past twenty years.

At the outset it should be stressed that pollen and spores are but one type of evidence in palaeoecological work. The sediments containing the pollen usually also contain algal remnants; macroscopic plant remains (seeds, twigs, leaves, etc.); invertebrate remains (shells, elytra); and vertebrate remains (bones). The form of the sediment and its chemistry may also give indications of the environmental conditions at the time of its deposition (Mackereth, 1966; Pennington, 1970; Pennington and Lishman, 1971). Total analysis of the sediment is desirable to enable the fullest possible understanding of the palaeoecology of the site.

In this essay some of the work aimed at giving greater objectivity to pollen studies of the Quaternary period will be reviewed. The various aspects will be considered under a series of headings:

1. Pollen recognition and identification.
2. Pollen transfer from source to site of accumulation.
3. Site conditions and their effect on pollen assemblages.
4. Pollen assemblages and the vegetation from which they have been derived.

5. Sampling problems.
6. Data presentation and analysis.

Pollen recognition and identification

When pollen analysis was primarily used as a stratigraphic tool, only the main tree pollen types were identified and recorded. As interest in palaeoecological interpretation increased, attempts were made to recognise all pollen and spore types found in sediments down to species level. The chief research laboratories concerned with pollen analysis built up large reference slide collections (Andrew, 1970), and from these monographs on single families or complete keys for the identification of pollen and spore types have been produced. The keys of Faegri and Iversen (1964) and of Erdtman, Praglowski and Nilsson (1963) based on the N.P.C. (number, position and character of the aperture) system have enabled a more rigorous approach to describing and identifying the pollen of north-west Europe. A number of pollen types are only described to family or genus level in the standard keys and for sub-division one has to consult specialist studies. Many of these have been based on 'good' specimens of fresh or herbarium material and often rely upon the morphology and size differences in the fine sculpturing of the pollen grain wall, features which are often distorted or corroded in fossil specimens, especially after the chemical treatment given during slide preparation. Size-frequency diagrams for *Isoetes* and for *Lotus* and pore frequencies for *Plantago* are given by Birks (1973), while detailed single family studies such as those of the Caryophyllaceae and Rosaceae by Anderson (1961), of the Saxifragaceae by Ferguson and Webb (1970) and of the Compositae by Stix (1960) have enabled the recognition of pollen grains down to species level in otherwise difficult families. Some separations within the Cyperaceae and Gramineae families have been possible by the use of phase-contrast microscopy (Faegri and Iversen, 1964).

The electron microscope, and especially the scanning electron microscope, has been used more in determining the ultra-structure of the pollen grain wall during taxonomic studies than for pollen identification, (Martin, 1969). However, Pilcher (1968) records some applications of the scanning electron microscope in pollen studies and there are several studies of pollen morphology within families which include its use. Sivak (1973) uses the scanning electron microscope in separating 12 species of recent *Tsuga* by their pollen, while Gillett, Bassett and Crompton (1973) likewise are able to distinguish North American *Trifolium* pollen down to species level. In both cases fresh pollen is used. In the case of fossil grains surface corrosion may reduce the value of electron microscopy in routine identifications, though it has been successfully used on *Erica* seeds by Huckerby, Marchant and Oldfield (1972).

Pollen transfer

The pollen and spores encountered by pollen analysts have normally been transported to the accumulating site either by wind or by water. It has often been assumed that wind transport is dominant in most depositional sites but recent work has demonstrated the significant contribution of water transport and water disturbance in lake bed (limnic) deposits.

Early workers in pollen analysis wrote vaguely of 'the pollen rain' and only a very simple model for the transfer of pollen was envisaged, giving an homogeneous mix of pollen in local air currents and the subsequent deposition of this mix either in rain, or by settling out from the air, all within a 'short' distance of its point of release. Tauber (1965) applied the data on the air transport of small particles derived from air pollution and insecticide aerosol dissemination studies, to make a re-evaluation of the actual mode of transfer of pollen grains from the vegetation to the lake or bog sites. He demonstrated how particles the size of pollen grains might behave under different weather conditions. For small lakes or bogs within forested areas, Tauber concluded that transfer above the canopy plays only a partial role and that the greater part of the pollen is derived from air flow within the trunk space. In this context, it is relevant to note the date of flowering of the trees and shrubs. *Corylus, Alnus, Populus, Ulmus* and some *Salix* flower before leafing; *Fagus, Quercus, Betula, Fraxinus* and *Acer* flower as the leaves open, while *Tilia* flowers after the leaves are fully open. Wind speeds within the trunk space tend to decrease with leafing and hence one might expect the early flowering trees to have their pollen dispersed further than that of the late flowering trees. Tauber (1965) suggested that the relative contributions of pollen from above-canopy transfer, high level transport (washed down in the rain) and trunkspace transfer might vary from ratios of 1:1:8 for a small lake or bog within a forested area to perhaps 7:2:1 for a very large lake or bog. From this one infers that the size and openness of the collecting site are of considerable significance in trying to account for the source area of the pollen. This may be illustrated diagrammatically as in Figure 12.1. Furthermore, over time the collecting basin might become smaller with normal infilling and so the relative contributions of the pollen sources might change.

In the same paper, Tauber (1965) gives evidence for the differential filtration of pollen by trunks and branches. Depending upon the wind speed and the density of the branches, trunks or stems, the larger, heavier pollen types are likely to be differentially filtered out of the air flow and the proportions of the pollen types reaching the accumulating site will differ substantially from those within the woodland. Tauber raises doubts about the validity of results obtained from some of the methods used by palynologists to trap air-borne pollen grains on slides within an air flow in woodland. As denser shrub and herb communities

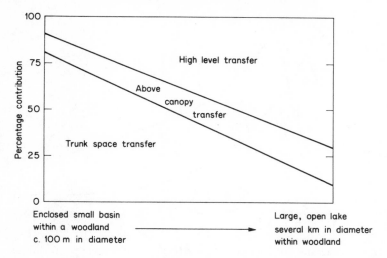

Figure 12.1   Diagram to show the changing contribution of pollen as size of lake basin increases, using the terms and figures of Tauber (1965).

commonly occur at the woodland margin and around small lakes the effect of filtration may be marked. Filtration rates may also vary over time with changing shrub density and thus real changes in the pollen component being supplied from the woodlands may be masked.

In 1967 Tauber backed up largely theoretical ideas with an empirical study of pollen transport in a forest in Denmark using a specially designed sampler mounted on a raft floating on a small lake. One immediate result of the study was the realisation that up to 50% of the pollen collected was 're-floated'. It had been deposited on leaves, stems and twigs during the flowering season and then re-distributed during the later summer and autumn. A large part of this component was associated with rain drops. Tauber in the same paper records figures for pollen impacted onto twigs, contrasting the high numbers on the rough bark of willow (*Salix cinerea*) with much lower numbers on the smooth bark of birch.

Various authors have noted the markedly exponential nature of dispersion of pollen from a single source. Potter and Rowley (1960) report the work of Federova (1956) on cereal pollen. At the edge of a rye plot, 1360 cereal pollen grains per cm^2 were found while at 300 metres from the edge the value fell to 3 per cm^2. Turner (1964) found that the influence of a pine stand was noticeable in pollen assemblages only within a distance of about 300 metres. Similarly, undergraduate project work in Bristol University Geography Department has shown that the decline in pine pollen is most marked over the first 340 metres from the margin of a plantation.

The distance-decay curve for pollen deposition will vary for each species and with different meteorological conditions. For pollen

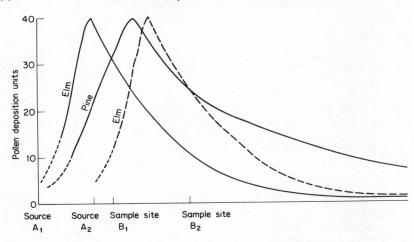

Figure 12.2   Diagram to illustrate the effects of distance from source when considering two pollen types of different buoyancy in the air.

N.B. Assume a steady drift of air from left to right and an elm and pine elevated point source (e.g. one tree of each kind) at A_1. Then a pine : elm pollen ratio at sample point B_1 would be 1:1 and at twice the distance from the source (B_2) the ratio would be 2.25:1. To obtain a ratio of 1:1 at B_2 the elm tree would have to be located at A_2 or there would have to be an increase in the number of trees at source A_1 by a factor of 2.25.

deposition from an elevated point source, Tauber (1965) produced a theoretical curve which was used by Oldfield (1970) in a discussion on the problems of changes over time of pollen source areas. The same relationship is used as a basis for Figure 12.2, which shows the possible curves for pollen deposition for pine and elm derived from an elevated point source (a single tree) at Site A_1. A steady constant drift of air is assumed, resulting in maximum pollen deposition being slightly downwind of the source. Relative pollen productivities between the two trees are ignored. Elm pollen is heavier and less easily transported than pine pollen. One sees that at distance B_1 from source A_1 the ratio of pine to elm pollen is 1:1 while at twice the distance, at B_2 the ratio is roughly 2.25:1. The same relative proportions at B_2 could be obtained by moving the one elm tree source to A_2 or by increasing the number of elm trees at A_1 to 2.25. From the previous paragraph it will be realised that these effects will be most marked within a few tens or hundreds of metres from a point source; at about one kilometre the effect may be negligible.

The effects of water transport of pollen upon pollen assemblages has recently been examined by a number of workers. The phenomenon of concentration of easily floatable pine pollen on the windward shores of lakes had been noted by Hopkins (1950). The transport of pollen from aquatic plants was recognised, but the full role of the transport of pollen by water was not appreciated until studies of marine deposition had demonstrated the transport of terrestrial pollen into the oceans by rivers (Muller, 1959). Peck (1973) reviews relevant literature and describes studies from a small catchment basin on the North York Moors. She found significant differences in pollen numbers and percentages caught in traps above the surface of a small reservoir compared with those found in the surface sediments of the lake. Peck concluded that stream-borne pollen was contributing very significantly to the lake sediment and that this in turn was derived by rainwash and by direct deposition onto the land surface and then transport to the stream by overland-flow or by through-flow. The actual figures showed that the air traps above the lake accounted for only 4—10% of the total pollen influx. In addition, the composition of the stream-borne component was distinctly different, including large numbers of Pteridophyte spores and Ericaceae pollen which were only poorly represented in the air traps. Crowder and Cuddy (1973) in Ontario investigated river water samples on a regular basis. Again it was concluded that a large proportion of the pollen was transported from the soil surface into the rivers. They also found marked differences between the spectra found in moss polsters, those found in the river water and in the lake sediments.

Studies such as these lead to the conclusion that comparisons of spectra from different depositional environments must take into account the modes of transport to that environment. Further, that changes in pollen spectra in a single deposit may be related to changes in transport media; for example, the change from lake mud to raised bog peat commonly found in British deposits represents a change of transport media from air plus water to air alone.

Site conditions

A standard assumption of many pollen assemblage assessments is that sequential accumulation of the 'pollen rain' has occurred and that once it has been deposited no further changes occur. This assumption has been shown to be false in a number of environments.

Differential destruction of pollen occurs and some of the more delicate pollen grains are rapidly lost, except in conditions ideal for preservation. Havinga (1967) studied the preservation of pollen in soils and litter, looking particularly at biological and chemical erosion. He published a table of susceptibility to oxidation, showing that *Polypodium*, *Pinus*, *Myrica* and *Tilia* are some of the least susceptible grains while *Salix*, *Acer*, *Fraxinus*, *Fagus*, *Quercus* and *Populus* are some of the most susceptible. Cushing (1967) looked at sub-fossil pollen, noting the form, type and degree of preservation on a six-point scale. In Minnesota lake sediments degraded pollen grains were dominant in algal copropel, and corroded pollen grains predominated in moss peat. Since the ease and level of determination varies with different states of preservation, deposits where rapid changes in the former sedimentary environment have occurred may have to be viewed very carefully. Pollen types such as *Tilia, Pinus* and *Alnus,* which can be easily recognised even when partly eroded, may be over-represented in the counts while *Quercus, Populus* and Cyperaceae may be under-represented.

Unless the pH is less than 5.5, pollen is rapidly lost in soils, leaving only the most resistent grains (usually *Polypodium* spores). In acid soils there is often good preservation, though interpretation has to take into account down-profile movement of pollen (Dimbleby, 1962).

Any physical movement of pollen after deposition will tend to alter the value of a deposit for the interpretation of past conditions. In peats it is generally assumed that downward transfer of pollen is minimal and as animal activity in wet peats is low, mixing of peats by natural means is unlikely. In lake sediments there is evidence for disturbance. Fluctuating lake levels result in the reworking of marginal sediments. The presence of two distinct pollen populations, one more eroded and crumpled than the other, may indicate inclusion of reworked pollen in a deposit.

Work by Davis (1968) has shown that the characteristic build-up of thermal stratification in small temperate lakes in summer, followed by the sudden and often relatively violent overturning of the waters in autumn as stratification breaks down, leads to disturbance of the surface sediments and some differential movement of pollen. One effect of this sediment mixing may be the apparently fairly uniform rate of deposition in a single year at stations within any one of the lakes studied by Davis. Variations, however, did occur from year to year and between the lakes. The sediment traps indicated a pollen deposition rate 2 to 4 times greater than that determined from surface sediment cores under ten metres of water. Berglund (1973) using similar methods but a smaller, shallower and non-stratified lake also obtained much higher apparent depositional rates in the sediment traps compared with the sediment cores. His values were 10 to 20 times greater in the traps. He confirms the view of Davis (1968) that 'the process of redeposition may be largely responsible for the uniformity and consistency of pollen content that has made lake sediments such favourable material for palaeoecological study'.

Davis, R. B. (1967) considered the effect of bottom fauna on the pollen in sediments. In New England, datum points are provided by the records of first lumbering and agriculture (c. 1800); the decline in agriculture (c. 1900); the decline in *Castanea* due to fungal attack (c. 1930); and the dated local fires. Observation of the cores showed signs of faunal burrows down to 10 cm and with a local sedimentation rate of about 2 mm per year, Davis suggested that about 50 years accumulation was likely to be disturbed. Charcoal fragments from the dated fires gave an indication of this mixing in that, instead of forming a clear marker horizon at the depth calculated as equivalent to the date of the fire, the charcoal was diffused both upwards and downwards, with the peak concentration just below the depth expected. The author produced a simple mathematical model to indicate what the effects of mixing were likely to be on the pollen sequences. These are that the minor oscillations of pollen curves are smoothed out; heights of peaks in the curves are reduced; small amounts of pollen from very much earlier dates may be included; peaks or troughs of curves are shifted downwards in the profile; and finally, that the current mixing horizons are likely to be fairly homogenous in pollen spectra. This last point may tend to reduce the value of lake sediment surface pollen spectra as representing the pollen rain reaching the sediment today.

Pollen assemblages and vegetation
The lack of a clearly identifiable source area for the pollen accumulating at a site, and changes in source areas plus the varying relative pollen productivities of plants depending upon species and upon individual plant age, vigour, habitat or ecotype, mean that the relationship between pollen spectra and the vegetation from which they have been derived is rather speculative. Many researchers have tried to match contemporary pollen spectra with contemporary vegetation and then, by applying the doctrine of uniformity, have tried to match sub-fossil pollen spectra with present-day vegetation. As already indicated, some of the data sources for contemporary pollen spectra and for sub-fossil pollen spectra many not be strictly comparable. Figure 12.2 showed how similar spectra may be produced by a different combination of species. The approach also assumes that similar flowering characteristics and similar habitat associations occurred in past time. In the case of 'semi-natural' vegetation there can patently be no analogies with older vegetation communities. Janssen (1970) cites numerous examples of communities which appear to have evolved during the later part of the post-glacial period.

The differential pollen productivity of various species means that pollen percentages cannot be equated with plant percentages. Faegri and Iversen (1964) review attempts to apply some factor to the percentage values to try to relate them to plant numbers. Davis and Goodlett (1960) related basal area percentage of trees in Vermont to percentage pollen representation in recent mud samples. Trees were divided into groups which were considered over-represented (*Quercus, Pinus, Betula* and *Alnus*), proportionately represented (*Fagus, Tsuga, Ulmus, Picea, Fraxinus* and *Ostrya*) and those which were under-represented (*Acer, Thuja, Abies, Populus, Larix* and *Tilia*). Davis (1963) developed these data to obtain R values as correction factors:

$$R_s = \frac{\text{Species s pollen percentage}}{\text{Species s vegetation percentage}}$$

Application of R values led Davis (1963) to doubt the general agreement (based on pollen percentages) that there was a pine forest period in early post-glacial New England. However, using absolute pollen data in 1967, M. B. Davis revised her views. Janssen (1967) calculated R values for a number of forest stands in Minnesota using surface mud samples. He showed how the same taxon in three different forests produced three different R values and concluded that the R value for a given taxon depended upon its abundance in a particular community and its vegetational environment.

Andersen (1967) studied a very local scale by taking humus polsters in a mixed deciduous forest. He showed that the pollen spectra were strongly related to the tree composition within 30 metres of the sampling point and from his data he produced a series of pollen representation rates for local deciduous trees. In a more detailed study (Andersen, 1970) he confirmed his earlier results and again presented a table of correction factors for pollen spectra in a closed woodland, noting that their application to more open sites (e.g. lakes or bogs) may be limited. He applied his correction factors to a pollen sequence from the Eldrup Forest covering the last 6000 years and showed the much greater significance of *Tilia* and *Fagus* in the vegetation than the uncorrected pollen record would suggest.

Birks (1973) used a qualitative approach to try to characterise a range of modern vegetation types by contemporary pollen spectra. He collected a number of moss polsters from 'plots of uniform floristic composition and structure of at least 25 square metres' in various parts of north-west Britain. He hoped to find pollen and spore types of indicator species for each community to provide taxa of narrow ecological or sociological range. In general terms, the major vegetation components could be characterised: the montane summit vegetation had high Cyperaceae pollen and consistent *Lycopodium* spore values; sub-alpine tall herb communities had high Gramineae and consistent *Rumex acetosa*, *Ranunculus acris* type and *Thalictrum* pollen plus a representation of a number of the other herbs found in the local vegetation. In neither case could further sub-division be achieved on the basis of pollen alone. In woodlands Birks did find significant correlation coefficients between local pollen percentages in surface samples and the canopy cover for both *Betula pubescens* and *Corylus avellana*. He was able to suggest that pollen alone could be used to separate the tall herb dominated birch woodlands from the bilberry dominated birch woodlands.

A number of the problems associated with relative pollen percentage counts may be overcome by the use of absolute pollen data. Von Post in 1916 had recognised that changes in pollen percentages were not necessarily proportional to changes in plant community composition, and indeed an increased pollen percentage of one species may occur despite a decrease in the number of that species, if there is a simultaneous decrease in number of a high pollen producing species.

Hesselman (1919) suggested that measurements of pollen per unit weight or volume of sediment might be compared, but von Post noted the fluctuating rate of sediment accumulation and the effect this would have on absolute data. Though several authors had used the relative abundance of pollen at different depths to indicate changes in the rate of peat accumulation, it is only recently that methods using absolute pollen counts have become widely used and recommended. It was Davis and Deevey (1964) and again Davis (M. B. Davis, 1967) who used a series of radiocarbon dates to calculate sedimentation rates and then prepared pollen slides quantitatively so as to express pollen data in terms of pollen grain inputs per cm^2 per year. This led to the reinterpretation of the late-glacial vegetational changes in North America. Subsequently, Pennington and Bonny (1970), using a similar method in the English Lake District, demonstrated that the classical percentage approach gave a false impression of a warming of climate coincident with the birch pollen rise in the late-glacial, while the absolute method showed that the warming and consequent increase in overall pollen production occurred earlier. This conclusion was supported by work by Coope (1970) on Coleoptera remains which showed that the beetles indicated the warmest part of the late-glacial oscillation to have occurred prior to the vegetation response as indicated by the spread of tree-birches.

There are now several different methods of sample preparation for obtaining absolute pollen counts, methods which are reviewed by Peck (1974). One way is to add a known quantity of exotic pollen at the beginning of the preparation (Matthews, 1969); another is by sampling a known proportion of the total population, taking a known weight (Jorgensen, 1967) or volume (Davis, 1965) of the sample. Peck notes that count reproducability will depend on sediment type, since homogeneity of the sediment is a key factor in all preparations. There may be quite considerable losses during preparation, e.g. about 15% in the Davis technique. Furthermore, losses vary with sediment type. In view of this, an apparent change of the order of 20–25% across a stratigraphic boundary may be of little significance. Bonny (1972) determined some of the confidence limits for a method of absolute counting and compared percentage and absolute counts for selected taxa from the Blelham Bog profile. She records that the variations in influx from 150 to 3000 grains per cm^2 per year are much greater than those attributable to experimental error. Work in the Bristol University Geography Department suggests that losses of the order 14 to 20% are to be expected with preparations made from lake muds using an exotic *Lycopodium* spore as an addition at the beginning of the preparation. The major advantage of all absolute pollen counts is that the sedimentation rate for each pollen type will vary independently with changes in the rates for other pollen types, whereas percentage changes are interdependent.

Some of the recent pollen rain studies have considered the absolute pollen influx. Ritchie and Lichti-Federovich (1967) used Hirst auto-matic volumetric spore traps at Churchill, Manitoba and a number of open petri dish samplers in various Arctic, sub-Arctic and northern coniferous forest margin sites in Canada. They demonstrated the existence of long-distance transport of pollen to Churchill, over distances of 1000–2000 km, and also the arrival of pollen of species occurring locally but actually derived from plants flowering consider-ably further south, and hence earlier, than at Churchill. The data they presented in quantitative terms showed a rapid decline in total pollen inputs of 11 570 grains per cm^2 per year in forest to less than 70 grains per cm^2 per year in sedge-moss tundra. In high- and mid-Arctic sites over 50% of the pollen was 'exotic', i.e. it had been transported at least 1500 km. The forest and forest tundra showed little significant difference in pollen composition though in absolute terms the forest showed higher values. Davis, Brubaker and Webb (1973) investigated inputs into Michigan lakes which contained a firm datum. They illustrate spatial variation of influx reaching the sediment in relation to basin size and shape, and the nature of the vegetation. In two small basins studied they found differences of the order of three between the number of pollen grains accumulating per cm^2 per year in shallow water (less than 5 m) compared with deeper parts of the lake (greater than 10 m). The authors gave pollen influx values for the five major forest regions of the area, varying from 11 100 grains per cm^2 annually in the beech-maple and ash-elm regions to 38 000 in the pine region. Pennington (1973) reviews absolute pollen influx data for lake sediments. She prefers the term pollen deposition rates to influx as she finds evidence for a considerable loss of pollen from large lakes with rapid through-puts of water during summer melt in regions or times of large snow or ice accumulation. She also finds evidence that some small upland basins accumulate reworked pollen from soils or peats during times of soil instability. Pennington concludes that lake basin morphometry considerably affects pollen deposition rates and that some inferences based on absolute pollen accumulation rates may be misleading unless account is taken of the basin morphometry. Two contrasting lakes in Scotland lying close to each other had deposition rates differing by a factor of seven during the later part of the post-glacial period.

Sampling problems
Pollen analysis is based on a sampling procedure which in itself introduces opportunities for uncertainties. Woodhead and Hodgson (1935) made a study of sampling errors from peat preparations. They looked at errors in preparing and counting ten slides from the same peat sample; ten slides from separate preparations of the same peat sample, and ten slides from the same horizon of peat but taken from up to 20 metres apart. Their data show good agreements with low standard

deviations. In 1948, Faegri and Ottestad used eight sub-samples from a disc of deposit and found no significant differences between sub-samples, though they note that differences of up to 10% between percentages of certain species do not necessarily signify that the true percentages are different. Work by undergraduates in the Bristol Geography Department using samples from a disc of lake mud, supports these conclusions (as might be expected from the work on modern pollen sedimentation in lakes reported on pages 272—73).

The preparation technique of boiling with potassium hydroxide solution to remove humic acids; oxidising with saturated sodium chlorate solution, glacial acetic acid and a few drops of concentrated sulphuric acid to remove lignin; and then acetolysing with glacial acetic acid and a few drops of concentrated sulphuric acid to remove cellulose, is assumed to have no differential influence on the pollen spectra. Work on absolute data has shown that losses of 15—20% are frequent during preparation and if sieving is included losses may be considerably larger. One Bristol student project determined the pollen content after each stage in the preparation technique using both fresh and sub-fossil pollen samples. Certain grains were found in about the same proportion after each step (*Alnus, Ulmus, Corylus* and *Osmunda*), while others showed a proportional decrease (*Betula* and *Filipendula*) or increase (*Lycopodium clavatum*). *Quercus* appeared to decrease after boiling in potassium hydroxide solution. Excess oxidation did not seem to have any significant effect on relative proportions. A subsidiary problem demonstrated by student project work has been the need for care when sub-sampling with a pipette from a suspension of pollen. Very narrow aperture pipettes cause differential uptake, and with any pipette it is only by taking sub-samples from a fixed depth within the suspension immediately after shaking that reproducible results are obtained.

The actual sub-sample on the slide may also introduce error into the work. Barklay (1934) was concerned with the pollen sum required and used a coefficient of reliability between paired counts to show that a count of about 200 grains gave a 0.9 correlation. This has again been confirmed by work at Bristol. Unless complete slides are counted any differential distribution of pollen on the slide may bias the counts made. The differential flotation of small grains to the margins of cover-slips has been noted (Jorgensen, 1967), though at Bristol we have found no significant difference between counts made at the edge of cover-slips compared with the centre, nor between counts made on part of a slide compared with a whole slide.

Data presentation
The standard form of portrayal of pollen data has been the pollen diagram and this has normally been sub-divided according to some standard scheme in order to facilitate discussion, comparison and

description of pollen sequences. Godwin (1956) gives a basis for the division of English pollen diagrams based upon changes in pollen percentages. Recently, although relating pollen zones tentatively to the basic scheme, most workers have used local zonation schemes so as not to imply correlations with other sites more exact than is warranted. Birks (1973) defines a pollen zone as a 'body of sediment with a consistent and homogeneous fossil pollen and spore content that is distinguished from adjacent sediment bodies by differences in kind and frequencies of its contained fossil pollen grains and spores'. The biostratigraphic unit is an assemblage zone and as such receives its name from one or more of its characteristic fossils (American Commission on Stratigraphic Nomenclature, 1961). Assemblage zone boundaries are normally identified by visual inspection, but Birks (1973) used Chi-square tests between all vertical contiguous pairs of samples in five sites from the Isle of Skye in order to verify the visual boundaries. High Chi-square values correspond to heterogeneity between adjacent vertical levels and these coincided well with the visual boundaries, though some distinct heterogeneity also existed within some of the zones.

Computerised numerical techniques have been applied to pollen data by Gordon and Birks (1972). They used an agglomerative (constrained single-link analysis) and two divisive (constrained divisive analysis using information content, and constrained divisive analysis using sum of squares deviation) procedures. Strong similarities existed between the visual and the computerised zonation schemes, though the numerical methods did consistently identify further zones which had not been originally recognised or had been discarded on visual inspection. Birks (1974) also applied principal components analysis and a multi-dimensional scaling technique to Flandrian diagrams. All five methods showed good internal consistency though only the principal components analysis picked out the elm pollen decline as a zone boundary indicator. Birks sees promise in the methods as a means for identifying and delimiting pollen assemblages solely on their contained fossils, eliminating bias on the part of the investigator.

Gordon and Birks (1974) also used computerised numerical methods to compare pollen diagrams. Comparison of assemblage zones suggested that some might be of regional significance while others were only of local significance. Comparison of individual levels between sequences removes the chance of possible error in defining the original zones. The authors suggest that the methods provide a new way of examining the data and that they are useful aids to the pollen analyst faced with the problem of handling and comparing large masses of data. They provide a means of detecting similarities between profiles and also aid in the delimitation of regional pollen zones.

Conclusion

The geographer involved in palaeoecological work must be inter-disciplinary in approach. The great wealth of data available for his study and appraisal makes multivariate and computer techniques for handling the data increasingly necessary. The data are as yet relatively crude and this essay has tried to indicate some of the attempts which have been made to improve them. Rigorous quantitative studies on the present-day processes and factors which affect organisms during their transfer from the living environment to their ultimate preservation in the sediments has been a major concern of pollen analysts and of other palaeontologists over the last two decades. Figure 12.3 indicates some of the steps and processes relevant in pollen analysis when trying to relate the final pollen spectra on the microscope slide to the former vegetation and hence the former environmental conditions. In-creasingly, stimulus has been provided by studies into other floral

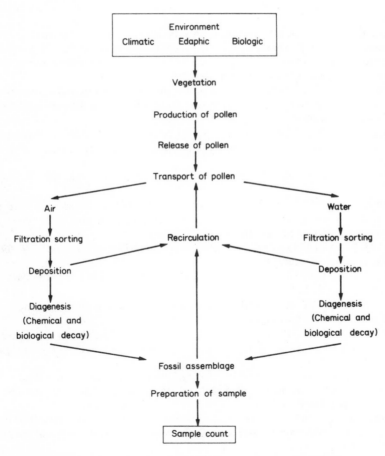

Figure 12.3   The process of relating pollen spectra to environmental conditions.

remains, faunal remains, and the chemistry of sediments. From all the evidence, a much clearer and more detailed picture of environmental conditions in past time is revealed plus evidence for the evolution of new environments in terms of populations, soil conditions, climates and ecosystems. As exploitation of the earth of necessity increases our need for knowledge as to the effects of that exploitation, the palaeoecologist with his knowledge of changes in past time and their causes should be able to contribute in a predictive role.

REFERENCES

American Commission on Stratigraphic Nomenclature (1961). 'Code of stratigraphic nomenclature', *Bull. American Association of Petroleum Geologists*, **45**, 645—55.

Andersen, S. Th. (1961). 'Vegetation and its environment in Denmark in the early Weichselian glacial', *Danmarks Geologiske Undersøgelse* Ser. II, 75, 1—175.

Andersen, S. Th. (1967). 'Tree pollen rain in a mixed deciduous forest in South Jutland', *Review of Palaeobotany and Palynology*, 3, 267—75.

Andersen, S. Th. (1970). 'The relative pollen productivity and pollen representation of north European trees, and correction factors for tree pollen spectra', *Danmarks Geologiske Undersøgelse* Ser. II, 96, 1—99.

Andrew, R. (1970). 'The Cambridge pollen reference collection', in Walker, D. and R. G. West (Eds.), *Studies in the Vegetational History of the British Isles*, C.U.P., 225—31.

Barklay, F. A. (1934). 'The statistical theory of pollen analysis', *Ecology* **15**, 283—89.

Berglund, B. E. (1973). 'Pollen dispersal and deposition in an area of southeastern Sweden — some preliminary results', in Birks, H. J. B. and R. G. West (Eds.), *Quaternary Plant Ecology*, Blackwell, 117—29.

Birks, H. J. B. (1973). *Past and Present Vegetation of the Isle of Skye — a palaeoecological study*, C.U.P.

Birks, H. J. B. (1974). 'Numerical zonation of Flandrian pollen data', *New Phytologist*, 73, 351—58.

Bonny, A. P. (1972). 'A method for determining absolute pollen frequencies in lake sediments', *New Phytologist*, 71 , 393—405.

Coope, G. R. (1970). 'Climatic interpretations of Late-Weichselian Coleoptera from the British Isles', *Révue de Géographie Physique et de Géologie Dynamique*, **XII**, 149—55.

Crowder, A. A. and D. G. Cuddy (1973). 'Pollen in a small river basin: Wilton Creek Ontario', in Birks, H. J. B. and R. G. West (Eds.), *Quaternary Plant Ecology*, Blackwell, 61—77.

Cushing, E. J. (1967). 'Evidence for differential pollen preservation in Late-Quaternary sediments in Minnesota', *Review of Palaeobotany and Palynology*, 4, 87—101.

Davis, M. B. (1963). 'On the theory of pollen analysis', *American J. Science*, **261**, 897—912.

Davis, M. B. (1965). 'A method for the determination of absolute pollen frequency', in Kummel, B. and D. Raup (Eds.), *Handbook of Palaeontological Techniques*, Freeman, 674—86.

Davis, M. B. (1967). 'Pollen accumulation rates at Rogers Lake, Connecticut, during Late and Post-glacial time', *Review of Palaeobotany and Palynology*, 2, 219—30.

Davis, M. B. (1968). 'Pollen grains in lake sediments: redeposition caused by seasonal water circulation', *Science* (N.Y.), 162, 796—99.

Davis, M. B. and E. S. Deevey (1964). 'Pollen accumulation rates: estimates from Late-glacial sediment of Rogers Lake', *Science* (N.Y.), 145, 1293—95.

Davis, M. B. and J. C. Goodlett (1960). 'Comparison of the present vegetation with pollen spectra in surface samples from Brownington Pond, Vermont', *Ecology*, 41, 346—57.

Davis, M. B., L. B. Brubaker and T. Webb, (1973). 'Calibration of absolute pollen influx', in Birks, H. J. B. and R. G. West (Eds.), *Quaternary Plant Ecology*, Blackwell, 9—28.

Davis, R. B. (1967). 'Pollen studies of near surface sediments in Maine Lakes', in Cushing E. J. and H. E. Wright Jnr. (Eds.), *Quaternary Palaeoecology*, Yale University Press, 143—73.

Dimbleby, G. W. (1962). 'The development of British heathlands and their soils', *Oxford Forestry Memoir*, 23.

Erdtman, G. (1928). 'Studies in the post-arctic history of the forests of north-west Europe. 1. Investigation in the British Isles', *Geoliska Foreningens i Stockholm Forhandlingar*, 50, 123—92.

Erdtman, G., J. Praglowski and S. Nilsson (1963). *An Introduction to a Scandinavian Pollen Flora*, Vol. II, Almqvist and Wiksell.

Faegri, K. and J. Iversen (1964). *Textbook of Pollen Analysis*, Blackwell.

Faegri, K. and P. Ottestad (1948). 'Statistical problems in pollen analysis', *Universitet i Bergen arbok Naturvitenskapelig rekke* 3.

Federova, R. V. (1956). 'Dissemination of cereal pollen by air', *Akademiya Nauk. S.S.S.R. Doklady*, 897—98, (in Russian).

Ferguson, I. K. and D. A. Webb, (1970). 'Pollen morphology in the genus *Saxifraga* and its taxonomic significance', *Botanical Journal of the Linnean Society.*, 63, 295—311.

Gillett, J. M., I. J. Bassett and C. W. Crompton (1973). 'Pollen morphology and its relationship to the taxonomy of North American *Trifolium* species', *Pollen Spores*, XV, 91—108.

Godwin, H. (1956). *History of the British Flora*, C.U.P.

Gordon, A. D. and H. J. B. Birks (1972). 'Numerical methods in Quaternary palaeoecology. 1. Zonation of pollen diagrams', *New Phytologist*, 71, 961—79.

Gordon, A. D. and H. J. B. Birks (1974). 'Numerical methods in Quaternary palaeoecology, 2. Comparison of pollen diagrams', *New Phytologist*, 73, 221—49.

Havinga, A. J. (1967). 'Palynology and pollen preservation', *Review of Palaeobotany and Palynology*, 2, 81—98.

Hesselman, H. (1919). 'Lattagelser över skogsträd pollens spridningsförmågau', *Meddel. fr. statens skogförsöksanstalt*, 16, 27 ff.

Hopkins, J. S. (1950). 'Differential flotation and deposition of coniferous and deciduous tree pollen', *Ecology*, 31, 633—41.

Huckerby, E., R. Marchant and F. Oldfield (1972). 'Identification of fossil seeds of *Erica* and *Calluna* by scanning electron microscopy', *New Phytologist*, 71, 387—92.

Janssen, C. R. (1967). 'A comparison between the recent regional pollen rain and the sub-recent vegetation in 4 major vegetation types in Minnesota, U.S.A.', *Review of Palaeobotany and Palynology*, 2, 331—42.

Janssen, C. R. (1970). 'Problems in the recognition of plant communities in pollen diagrams', *Vegetatio*, 20, 187—98.

Jorgensen, S. (1967). 'A method of absolute pollen counting', *New Phytologist*, 66, 489—93.

Mackereth, F. J. H. (1966). 'Some chemical observations in post-glacial lake sediments', *Philosophical Transactions of the Royal Society*, B 250, 165—213.

Martin, P. S. (1969). 'Pollen analysis and the scanning electron microscope', *Proceedings of the Second American Symposium IIT*, Research Institute of Chicago, U.S.A., 89—102.

Matthews, J. (1969). 'The assessment of a method for the determination of absolute pollen frequencies', *New Phytologist*, 68, 161—66.

Muller, J. (1959). 'Palynology of recent Orinoco delta and shelf sediments', *Micropalaeontology*, 5, 1—32.

Oldfield, F. (1970). 'Some aspects of scale and complexity in pollen analytically based palaeoecology', *Pollen Spores*, XII, 163—71.

Peck, R. M. (1973). 'Pollen budget studies in a small Yorkshire catchment', in Birks, H. J. B. and R. G. West (Eds.), *Quaternary Plant Ecology*, Blackwell, 43—60.

Peck, R. M. (1974). 'A comparison of four absolute pollen preparation techniques', *New Phytologist*, 73, 567—87.

Pennington, W. (1970). 'Vegetation history in north west of England, a regional synthesis', in Walker, D. and R. G. West (Eds.), *Studies in the Vegetational History of the British Isles*, C.U.P., 41—79.

Pennington, W. (1973). 'Absolute pollen frequencies in sediments of lakes of different morphometry', Birks, H. J. B. and R. G. West (Eds.), *Quaternary Plant Ecology*, Blackwell, 79—104.

Pennington, W. and A. P. Bonny (1970). 'Absolute pollen diagram from the British late-glacial', *Nature*, London, 226, 871—73.

Pennington, W. and J. P. Lishman (1971). 'Iodine in lake sediments in northern England and Scotland', *Biological Reviews*, 46, 279—313.

Pilcher, J. C. (1968). 'Some applications of the scanning electron microscope to the study of modern and fossil pollen', *Ulster J. of Archaeology*, 31, 87—91.

von Post, L. (1916). 'Om skogstädpollen i sydsvenska torfmosslagerföldjer', *Geologiska Föreningens i Stockholm Förhandlingar*, 38, 384—94.

Potter, L. D. and J. Rowley (1960). 'Pollen rain and vegetation, San Augustin Plains, New Mexico', *Botanical Gazette*, 122, 1—25.

Ritchie, J. C. and S. Lichti-Federovich (1967). 'Pollen dispersal phenomena in arctic and sub-arctic Canada', *Review of Palaeobotany and Palynology*, 3, 255-66.

Sivak, J. (1973). ''Observations nouvelles sur les grains de pollen de *Tsuga*', *Pollen Spores*, XV 397—457.

Stix, E. (1960). 'Pollen morphologische Untersuchungen an Compositen', *Grana Palynologica*, 2, 41—114.

Tauber, H. (1965). 'Differential pollen dispersion and the interpretation of pollen diagrams', *Danmarks Geologiske Undersøgelse*, Ser. II, 89, 1—69.

Tauber, H. (1967). 'Investigations of the mode of pollen transfer in forested areas', *Review of Palaeobotany and Palynology*, 3, 277—86.

Turner, J. (1964). 'Surface sample analysis from Ayrshire, Scotland', *Pollen Spores*, 6, 583—92.

Woodhead, N. and L. M. Hodgson, (1935). 'A preliminary study of some Snowdonian peats', *New Phytologist,* 34, 263—82.

Reference was also made in the text to undergraduate project work. This was carried out by the following students: P. J. Dunkley, W. M. Greenwood, C. A. Headley, A. E. Mitham, E. Snook and B. Tomlinson.

PART V

Political Processes in Human Geography

Chapter 13

Values and Political Geography

Michael Morgan

Political geography has arguably the longest pedigree of all branches of geography, tracing its descent from Hippocrates and Aristotle, through Bodin and Montesquieu to the work of Ratzel and Mackinder. In the early decades of this century the conscious links between geography and statecraft were probably stronger than they had ever been. Bowman's *New World* and Mackinder's *Democratic Ideals and Reality*, in their different ways, represent high points of confidence. Both were written in the shadow of the treaty of Versailles. Mackinder's warning of the need for politics to overcome the logic of geography if a fragile peace were to be preserved and historic forces contained came a decade or so before Bowman charted some of the dimensions of the problems of the new post-war political realities. With the rise of Geopolitics in Germany under the aegis of Haushofer, the explicit use of geographical arguments to justify political action brought the whole subject into disfavour, and it is only recently that signs of a renewed interest in the relationship between geography and politics have appeared.

Lack of interest in political geography

There are several other reasons for the recent neglect of the subject. A major factor is the lack of a strong conceptual or theoretical framework, without which the very breadth of the field, the enormous number of themes presented by the real world, dissipates effort. Individual studies lack reference points and the possibility of creative oppositions centred on basic philosophical or methodological positions is at best remote. Important work in areas that ought to be of concern to political geography, especially in sociology and political science, can only marginally be incorporated when political geography exists in such a formless state.

Another reason is that the positivist tradition is strongly, if unconsciously held. Many have believed that by the process of observation and classification of data and testing, phenomena can, if properly approached, be made to yield laws governing social and political phenomena and ultimately create the power to predict the future course of events. Yet, believing this, the gap between promise and performance is patently so vast in the field of political geography that most workers have tended to direct their attention to other areas where the prospect for limited success seems greater. Possibly the most important reason for the neglect of political geography stems from a belief, challenged in this essay, that a value-free discipline is both possible and desirable. Leave the politics to the political scientists, the argument goes, leave the questions of value to the metaphysicians, the task of political geography is to provide a body of empirical information and evidence, independently of either value judgement or political position. Opinion must be rejected in the pursuit of truth. The weakness of this position is exposed by Vickers (1968): 'Facts are relevant only by reference to some judgement of value, and judgements of value are meaningful only in regard to some configuration of fact.' Vickers uses the term 'appreciative system' to describe the fusion of the 'reality system' and the 'value system' because in ordinary usage 'appreciation' implies a combined judgement of value and fact. 'The culture in which each one of us grows up is normative in three dimensions – in discrimination ('this is a that'), in evaluation ('this should be thus'), and in action ('in these circumstances this should be done')'. It is this normative process that is the appreciative system, and its effectiveness is measured by the fact that 'in a societal context the individual, who at birth is virtually sealed to information, within twenty years possesses a set of readinesses for action appropriate to most varied situations and possesses a variety of interests and commitments if not without conflict at least without allowing them completely to frustrate each other.'

Belief in the value-free approach implies that one does not at any point explicitly criticise the goals, the values and the consensus-building procedures of any society, though some of the most fundamental and obdurate problems of evolving society concern the nature of the goals that have to be set in the future; and at the very lowest level, the notion of a goal implies an evaluative appraisal. The conventional view of the 'objective' school is that the rejection of a value-free approach would mean that the social sciences would be divided into as many ideologies as there are sets of personal values. Many might feel, however, that this particular prospect is less disturbing than that posed by the un-challenged continuation of many of the present technological and institutional processes. What in any case could prevent a situation of intellectual anarchy would be appropriate conceptual frameworks, and were these to be available in political geography it would allow the subject to accept revivifying transfusions from other disciplines. Naturally, all of the conceptual frameworks that offer themselves have different characteristics that reflect the particular appreciative systems of their exponents. We now consider some of the possible frameworks of which the political geographer ought at least to be aware, dealing first with examples of what MacKenzie (1967) calls 'overarching theory', attempts to build comprehensive, all-embracing systems of explanation that can accommodate most of our social and political experience.

Conceptual frameworks — 'overarching theories'

Possibly the two most influential contributions to social and political theory in the past two generations have been made by David Easton (1967) and by Talcott Parsons (1956, 1959, 1960, 1963). Each has written authoritative but in places obscure works containing dense passages that seem unintelligible without reference to the overall pattern, and each is massively and almost exclusively orientated to theory with almost no empirical material. One necessarily relies on the work of close collaborators to provide an exegesis. It would be absurd to attempt even the sketchiest outline of their respective contributions in an essay of this length, but a comment on parts that are particularly relevant to political geography may be helpful.

Easton

The Easton model of the political system draws on work in economics on 'exchange' models: those who are in political power are treated as producers and their followers as consumers; votes are analogous to money, and the legislative performance of the executive branch is treated as output. The bare outlines of the model are represented in Figure 13.1 and it should be evident that there are many elements in the processes and relationships within the model that come within the interest of a broadly-based political geography. The input takes the form of four types of demands. The authorities make allocations between competing demands and continue to do so as long as they receive support. Supporting attitudes may be classed as (a) support for the concept of a political community, (b) support for the regime, (the two attitudes not necessarily co-varying positively), and (c) support for the authorities. Lack of support for the authorities may centre on their failure as gatekeepers in the area of demand articulation. An overload in this area can lead to a breakdown in the system. The more sophisticated societies develop systems of political differentiation and the prolifer- ation of organised groups increases the ability of the system to handle overload. 'Rising expectations' in a less flexible or less complex political system, combined with gateways that remain too small for the demand, can lead to the output of the system falling well short of the demand and a revolutionary situation is then more probable. The essence of the Easton model is that it regards the political system as open and

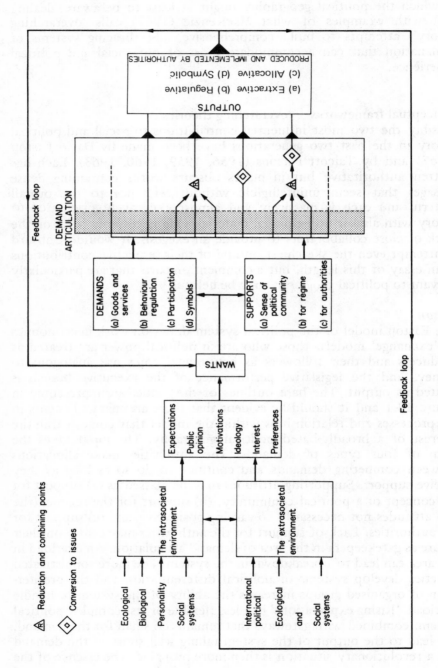

Figure 13.1   A dynamic response model of a political system. (After Easton.)

adaptive. Change and stability are affected by feedback mechanisms. The more sensitive they are the more rapid and perhaps subtle the response.

It must be admitted that the performance of systems analysis in the social sciences as a whole has fallen somewhat short of its early promise. It has proved very difficult to make it operational. Establishing the precise nature and relationship of the links between different parts of a system has always presented formidable problems in practice. Some progress has been made in this direction, particularly since the pioneering work by Deutsch (1964) who used transaction-flow analysis in his studies of possible ways of measuring the strengths of links within and between communities as indicators of their level of integration, or their capacity to develop integration in the future (see, for example, Soja (1968)). Yet there is a sense in which transaction-flow analysis, despite its quantitative basis, is too blunt a tool in that the phenomena it studies are themselves the result of complex interactions within the system. The actual transactions may conceal as much as they reveal.

Concern with the problems of the inner city and with the access of the poorest to community resources has drawn attention to the role of the 'gate keepers' in local and national agencies of government who, to a degree, control access to these resources, and who, though individually not very powerful, may as a group play an important role in the system as a whole. The 'gatekeeping' role links closely with the Easton model in the area of demand articulation. Morgan and Kirkpatrick (1972) have brought together a number of studies showing the relevance and value of the systems approach in the whole area of urban political analysis, and the total weight of evidence from all sources suggests that for political geographers the systems approach is one that still offers some promise at a variety of levels.

Parsons

Parsons is the leading exponent of the structural-functionalist approach. A function in this sense means 'an activity performed by a structure which maintains a system of which it is a part' (Jones, 1967). The essence of functionalism is the system-maintaining activity and the functional approach allows widely differing societies to be analysed because it emphasises their basic functional characteristics which in turn, it is argued, are reflected in deep-seated relatively permanent structural characteristics. A social system has four functional prerequisites for existence and for maintaining a state of approximate equilibrium. First, it must maintain its own continuity. This role of Pattern Maintenance, the Latency function, is performed in most Western societies by the family and the household, which support new members of the society and pass on the cultural norms. Second, society must Adapt to changing conditions both in the physical and the human environment. The main Adaptive subsystem is the economy, reinforced by distinctive and often separate scientific and technological sub-systems as a society becomes more sophisticated materially. Third, society must Integrate its different elements and it does this mainly within its cultural subsystem through education, art, religion, philosophy, etc. Fourth, it must, through the polity, or more narrowly the government, aim at Goal Attainment. It is the responsibility of government to steer the community towards community-set goals. Obviously none of these subsystems exists independently of the others; each of the subsystems involves the entire community whose members appear simultaneously in each subsystem in a variety of roles, and who are linked with each other by complex relationships. The relationships between the subsystems are made explicit by transactions of various kinds. The paradigm, Figure 13.2, happens to be of great value in drawing attention to relationships that are, or arguably should be, of interest in political geography. The A—G axis relates to questions about the extent to which goals and strategies of government are affected by the nature of the economy and vice versa. This axis relates to the limits on government action imposed by the extent of natural resources and also to the nature of resource mobilisation procedures. The I—G axis embraces questions about how collective group interests, overt and latent, limit the strategies and influence the decisions of governments and their agencies. The L—G interactions come within the general field of legitimation and relate to the regularities of individual and

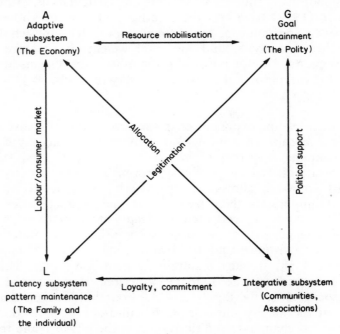

Figure 13.2   The Parsonian paradigm of societal interchange.

government behaviour in the field of elections, taxation, legislation and so on.

The basic paradigm has received curiously little attention from geographers. In the political science field, contributions by Lipset and Rokkan (1967), and Rokkan (1970) deserve wider circulation because they promise a valuable methodological insight. They are concerned to build a conceptual model of the dynamics of the nation-building process — one that will identify and relate in a meaningful sequence the stages in the evolution of a nation-state. The process of nation building historically involves each of the functional subsystems reacting with each other, and depending on which particular subsystem is of interest, the remaining three subsystems are seen in terms of the one selected. Lipset and Rokkan concentrate on the I quadrant, the integrative subsystem, the one concerned with ideological matters, with communities rather than individuals. This is an appropriate one in the circumstances because in all cases the nation-building process has been activated and maintained by a variety of internal oppositions many of which have ultimately strong ideological or cultural bases. The Lipset-Rokkan model is a simple three-stage one (Figure 13.3). In stage one the interaction and tension take the form of thrusts from the centre towards the periphery. The effect of these thrusts is generally to increase resistance and to raise powerful issues of cultural identity in the periphery, for example, where the centre pursues policies of religion

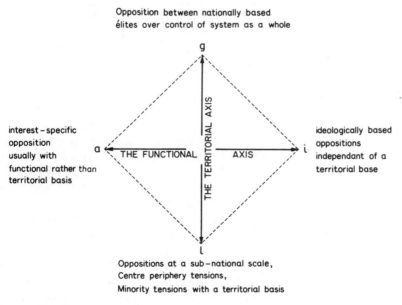

Figure 13.3   An interpretation of the internal structure of the I quadrant. (After Lipset and Rokkan, 1967.)

or language which antagonise or threaten the periphery. In the paradigm this is represented by an intensification of strain between the GL and GI subsystems. It often happens that the GA strains are also increased at this stage, for example where the thrusts from the centre are fiscal or economic in character, and where an ethnic or cultural minority in the periphery may argue that its local resources are either being neglected or are being exploited for the benefit of others. In stage two localised oppositions to the influence and policies of the centre produce a variety of defensive alliances across the entire periphery. At this stage, the L—I interactions are high and in some cases consolidation of interests pit one territorially-based group against another. At this stage, a determined strategy from the centre could successfully pursue a policy of divide and rule, at least for a while. In stage three, however, alliances formed in the I subsystem will develop the strength to enable them to enter the G subsystem, to achieve representation of their interests in the polity as a whole, and thereby gain some measure of control, not only over the allocation of national resources (GA interchanges intensify) but also over flows of legitimation (L—G interchanges) leading perhaps to franchise reforms (e.g. the recent electoral reforms in Northern Ireland).

In this evolving process there are always strains and tensions, conflicting relationships both resolved and unresolved between all or most of the subsystems. At any time the locus of the relationships between any two subsystems can be placed within the model by the notion of transforming it into some spatial coordinates along an axis linking the two subsystems. At the present time the transformation has to be intuitive and qualitative but in due course it may be possible to evolve a more quantitative approach. The A—I axis on the whole represents a 'functional dimension', oppositions here relating to functional oppositions, for examples workers-v-employers, landlords-v-tenants in the A quadrant, Protestants-v-Jews for example in the I quadrant. If it were a case of oppositions between Jewish employers and Protestant workers the locus of that particular relationship would be near the middle of the A—I axis. The G—L axis, on the other hand, represents a territorial dimension, which may or may not be reinforced by functional oppositions. The G—L axis reflects the centre periphery relationship. A situation where there is a very strong centre and a weak periphery (e.g. France after the Revolution) would be represented by a point near the G end of the G—L axis. As the periphery becomes mobilised, as distinctive and remote areas become politically active and effective in their relationship with the centre, the locus of the opposition moves towards the L end of the G—L axis. Areal oppositions usually have either an ideological or an economic basis, so it is often the case that territorial oppositions are located on one side or the other of the G—L axis. All oppositions in fact can be located with respect to these two axes. Clearly the territorial dimension is of particular interest in political geography and the use of this paradigm would do a great deal to provide a framework to draw together some of the studies of political modernisation that have been undertaken, e.g. Gould (1969), and Weinstein (1966), and to indicate new ways of looking at familiar relationships.

The Lipset—Rokkan model is also interesting in that within a functionalist framework it deals specifically with conflict and change, suggesting that the Parsonian framework need not be associated wholly with consensus rather than conflict, nor with equilibrium rather than change, as some of its critics have charged.

Marx

The most distinguished of the socio-political theorists is of course Marx, whose work has until recently been largely ignored by geographers and especially by political geographers. Harvey's *Social Justice and the City* is a notable and welcome exception, and makes quite specific the links between social processes and spatial form in the city. The pertinence of a Marxist analysis is discussed at length in relation to our interpretation of contemporary urban problems. 'The only method capable of uniting disciplines in such a fashion that they can grapple with issues such as urbanisation, economic development and the environment, is that founded in a properly constituted version of dialectical materialism as it operates within a structured totality in the sense that Marx conceived it' (Harvey, 1973, p. 302). It remains for a single full-scale dialectical analysis by a geographer to be undertaken, but the ground has already been prepared by Harvey. Marx of course has been regarded, not wholly accurately, as the principal proponent of the conflict model of society, and Parsons as the leader of the consensus school. Certainly, to Marx, society was not pre-eminently a smoothly functioning system of order. Its dominant characteristic is continuous change, not only change of its elements but of its very structural form. Conflicts are not random; they are a systematic product of the structure of society. On this basis, there is no order except in the inevitability of change, or, in Marx's words, 'without conflict, no progress'. For Marx the key to understanding structure and conflict in any society at any period lay in the mode of production. Everything else — for example, values, institutions and systems of belief — arises basically from the mode of production. Structural change is effected as one class acquires power at the expense of another and the mode of production changes. Further change may be prevented for a period but only by coercion, and conflict and tension are endemic, relieved only by violent upheaval at intervals when one class succeeds in overthrowing another.

Dahrendorf

Dahrendorf (1959, 1964, 1967) occupies a middle position in the consensus—conflict spectrum, critical of both Parsons and Marx. He criticises Parsons because his system cannot account for change, and Marx for limiting the resolution of class conflict to violent upheaval. Both these models imply an essentially static view of social structures. Both Parsons and Marx 'freeze the flow of the historical process in the idea of the system'. Dahrendorf also rejects what he calls the 'philosophical elements of Marx's theory of class', the Marxist metaphysics. 'Propositions such as that capitalist society is the last class society of history . . . can be disputed and denied but they cannot be refuted with the tools of science.' Marx's theory of class Dahrendorf describes as 'a theory of structural change by revolutions based on conflicts between antagonistic interest groups'. The genuinely liberal society is one that creates institutions to reflect and rationally regulate conflict, rather than abolish it at source and impose a consensus: 'The rationality of the liberal attitude to conflict comes ultimately from the fact that it alone does justice to the creativity of social antagonisms as motive forces of change.' Dahrendorf proposed a non-Marxist model based on the following propositions:

1. every society is subject at every moment to change, social change is ubiquitous;
2. every society experiences at every moment social conflict, social conflict is ubiquitous;
3. every element in society contributes to its change;
4. every society rests on the constraint of some of its members by others.

This framework of conflict theory will allow the social scientist to 'derive social conflicts from structural arrangements and thus show these conflicts to be systematically generated'. It will allow us to answer such questions as: How do conflicting groups arise from the structure of society? what forms can the conflict amongst such groups assume and how does the conflict effect a change in the social structure? Recently, the concept of structural violence has been gaining ground in some quarters. It has been pointed out that if one adds up the number of man years lost in the developing countries through high and preventable levels of malnutrition, infant mortality and disease since 1945, these far exceed those losses from death and injury during violent conflicts and rebellions during the same period. Overt conflict has claimed fewer victims than the more diffuse and insidious impact of structural violence, caused by the failure of institutions. Radicals see structural violence as a time-bomb with a long fuse, primed with education and exposure to the media, awaiting only the spark of ideology to turn it into open rebellion. This reflects a view put forward by the nineteenth-century historian and revolutionary, Alexander Herzen, and quoted by G. Piel (1964), who wrote, 'In order to develop it is necessary that things should be much better for some and much worse for others, then those who are better off can develop at the expense of the others'. This situation, called by Piel 'coercive deprivation' is effectively structural violence in contemporary terms: 'So long as the educated minority, living off all previous generations, hardly guessed why life was so easy to live, so long as the majority working day and night did not quite realise why they received none of the fruits of their labour, both parties could believe this to be the natural order of things. People often take prejudice or habit for truth and, in that case, feel no discomfort, but if they once realise their truth is nonsense the game is up. From then onwards it is only by force that a man can be compelled to do what he considers to be absurd.'

Conceptual frameworks and partial models

Apart from the grand theorists, there are, as there have always been, many analysts of the contemporary situation who are concerned either with identifying causes of present discontents or with drawing attention to the need for change in particular directions to avoid what are regarded as otherwise inevitable and undesirable consequences of present trends. In the nature of things these writings proliferate. Yet some are clearly very influential. In a complex situation some analyses strike one as intuitively reasonable, and they can serve as a point of reference, a touchstone of personal relevance, they can draw together disparate strands or help to put a hard outline around once formless concepts. Many of the contributions are partial, more intuitive with weaker conceptual or methodological supports, but are none-the-less approaches that repay attention if not loyalty, in that to a degree they may help us broaden, modify or at least re-evaluate our academic interests and goals. The selection of such material that follows is a personal one and represents some of the viewpoints and ideas that merit discussion, at least when considering the sort of directions in which work in political geography might move. In no sense is the selection designed to point in any particular direction, if anything serving to encourage the belief that there is as yet no orthodoxy.

Illich

Of all the analysts of the contemporary condition, Illich (1971a, 1971b, 1973, 1974) is possibly the most readable, the most radical and arguably the one whose ideas most invite a constructive response from geographers. In *Deschooling Society* Illich argues that rich countries are developing an educational system they can barely afford and which can never be afforded by the poor countries. Schooling serves to perpetuate and control a meritocratic hierarchy which, whether in advanced or developing countries, reinforces the assumptions of an acquisitive and growth-oriented society. The changes in education over the century are paralleled by changes in other institutions, all of which have shifted from the left to the right of the institutional spectrum. The effect of this shift has been that over time nearly all institutions have developed effects contrary to their original purposes, passing over some critical watershed from the point where they are still benign, self-limiting and 'convivial' to the point where they are self-enlarging and 'manipulative'. This theme of institutional shift is central to all of Illich's writing and his arguments, always couched in brilliant aphoristic style, regularly come to rest on the need for a shift from the manipulative to the convivial end of the institutional spectrum: 'Fundamental social change must begin with a change of consciousness about institutions.'

The politics of the future must be primarily concerned not with allocating and maximising the means of production but with the 'design criteria for tools' that will allow a more convivial society. He lists six different ways in which our present tools frustrate this aim. 'Overgrowth' leads to biological degradation of the environment and brings the possibility of severe ecological damage. Overgrowth also creates 'radical monopoly', i.e. monopoly of a product by a firm but also of a service or an activity by an institution. Thus, 'motorised vehicles create new distances which they alone can shrink. They create them for all but they can shrink them only for a few. Wherever the transportation industry has accelerated passengers beyond a certain critical speed, it has become a social excavator which boosts a few people far above the pit it digs for society.' So too schools monopolise learning by institutionalising it as a commodity, education.

Linked with radical monopoly is 'over-programming', a growing dependence on specialist expertise acquired by expensive training, and this creates 'knowledge capitalists' and a competitive market in educational commodities. This structure is maintained by professional restrictions and controls which in turn stultify self-help of all kinds. 'Overprogramming' brings 'polarisation', the growing sense of helplessness and deprivation of the individual in a world dominated by large scale institutions, and a widening of the gulf between those who control power in society and the rest.

All this generates a pace of change and obsolescence that deprives people of the 'right to tradition'. The sixth feature is 'frustration', arising from the conflict between what people value and what they actually experience. Examples of this are education systems that create drop-outs, welfare systems that create poverty, medical systems that create illness, and transport systems that reduce equity and restrict personal mobility and increase time scarcity. Illich's arguments lead in the direction of new institutions, smaller in scale, of a size where they tend to be self-limiting, and a reversal of many of the processes of the past two hundred years. For the developing countries, the need is not to attempt the impossible task of trying to recreate the same social and economic processes that have so signally failed the advanced countries, but rather to work towards institutional change that never crosses the critical watershed that separates the benign from the malignant. 'To expand life beyond the radius of tradition and yet not hook in on accelerating diffusion, is a goal which any poor nation could achieve within a few years. But it is an achievement that will be reserved to those who reject industrial development guided by the ideology of indefinite energy growth.'

Galbraith

In a number of provocative and original books K. L. Galbraith has progressively evolved a model of the characteristics of the American society and economy, which while by no means commanding universal endorsement has contributed significantly to current thinking about the goals to which the system is, or should be, leading, and which in some senses echoes Illich's analysis. In *Economics and the Public Purpose* (1974), Galbraith argues that the present mixed economy in the United States is divided into two very different sub-systems. The Planning system is the sector of the economy dominated by the 1000 top firms and in this sector corporate planning dominates the industrial structure, controls increasingly the behaviour of its customers and manipulates the government. The Market system on the other hand is made up in the United States of some twelve million marked-orientated entre-preneurs who supply about half of the output of the private sector. Members of the market system are individually vulnerable and in times of crisis it is they who suffer, while the large corporations can survive, even prosper, because of their very large resources. The large corpor-ations develop aims which are often contrary to those wished for by the community as a whole. The ends of the planning system are not those of society, rather are society's ends perverted into those of the planning system. This perversion is effected subtly by the advertising profession and the educational system, and is made easier by the collection of 'convenient social virtues' which the individual is encouraged to embrace as unquestioned beliefs, such as the 'work ethic' and 'competition'.

Vickers

Vickers' (1968) analysis of the present condition again has some familiar dimensions: 'Our present state,' he writes, 'is the last stage in free fall, the fall from the agricultural to the industrial epoch, from a natural into a man made world and so into an increasingly political world, a world so unpredictable that it demands to be regulated nationally and internationally by political decisions of increasing scope ... the world as an ecological niche is filling up as never before and brings demands for political innovation and cultural change, both threatening ...' and it seems obvious that the changes required will be far greater than spontaneous adjustment will allow. 'The mere existence of policy making attests to the will to impose on the flux of events some form other than that which the interplay of forces would give it.'

The knowledge and power that has been gained over the past two hundred years has had the paradoxical result of increasing our ability to predict and control whilst making the world as a whole increasingly unpredictable and uncontrollable. This arises in Vickers' view because we have used technologies to alter the course of events so that the outer worlds began to change in form and complexity at a rate far faster than the power of our control systems. 'None the less in the face of incontrovertible evidence to the contrary, the belief still persists that increased power to alter the environment brings increased control over it.' This belief is a manifest delusion. The present situation shows the effect on societies of knowing a great deal about energy and matter but very little about information and even less about meaning. Whether information really informs and, if so, what meaning it conveys, depends on how the participants in the information process are organised within the network in which it is used and how their organisation develops by participation in the network.

Vickers is concerned with the problems of exercising control over complex societies in a situation of conflicting value systems and of 'multi-valued choice', and suggests that 'appreciation' is a form of behaviour that merits study in its own right. In other words, that much more attention needs to be paid to the nature of the 'appreciative system', to the mechanism whereby 'multi-valued choice' is made. This in turn involves a greater research effort in the psycho-social sciences.

Skinner
B. F. Skinner is possibly the leading behavioural psychologist and in *Beyond Freedom and Dignity* (1973) he argues the case for scientific control of human behaviour in order to achieve a betterment of the general social and physical environment. Major world social problems such as disease, famine, over-population and war can only successfully be tackled by a conscious application of a 'technology of behaviour'. 'We could solve our problems quickly enough if we could adjust the growth of the world's population as precisely as we adjust the course of a space ship, or improve agriculture and industry with some of the confidence with which we accelerate high-energy particles, or move towards a peaceful world with something like the steady progress with which physics has approached absolute zero (even though both presumably remain out of reach).' The interrelationships between environment and behaviour remain obscure. 'We can see what organisms do to the world around them, as they take from it what they need and ward off its dangers, but it is much harder to see what the world does to them.' It is now possible to argue that we must take into account what the environment does to an organism not only before but after it responds; behaviour is shaped and maintained by its consequences. Behaviour which operates on the environment, altering it to produce consequences, is called 'operant' behaviour and Skinner believes that a

technology of operant behaviour which is already well advanced may be the answer to some of the more vexing social and economic problems. Once appropriate goals have been set (leaving aside the difficult problem of who actually defines the goals) appropriate techniques could be devised to reinforce and reward behaviour that leads to the desired goals. By these means, with less loss of freedom or dignity than at present, the purposes of society could be harnessed to achieve common goals.

N. Chomsky (1975) discusses the problem of relationships between government and society and provides a very powerful critique of Skinner's approach.

Moore

In *Reflections on the Causes of Human Misery*, J. Barrington Moore Jnr. begins with the fact that the lot of mankind as a whole has not noticeably improved and argues that the reasons for this are as they have always been, hunger, disease, war and economic and social repression and restrictions on intellectual freedom. In common sense terms, political action should be directed to improving the lot of mankind, yet any study of the sources of our present condition makes it abundantly clear that the obstacles to improvement are far more subtle, complex and difficult than most strategies allow, from whatever ideological position they are put forward. Political conflict, the source of so much misery, directly or indirectly has two origins. First, there is the logic of a complex organised system made up of distinct sub-systems that must compete in order to survive. This logic is based not on an instinctual biological drive but on competitiveness and insecurity, and is both a cause and an effect of power drives found amongst élites everywhere. It operates at various levels, within a state and between states, though in an international context the regulatory mechanisms are more amorphous and less easily enforced. The second souce of conflict is 'principled', built into the very dynamism of a society in time. As generations succeed each other, there inevitably arises conflict between those who wish to preserve the established order and those who wish to change it, knowing that even the most established orders were themselves relatively recent creations. Moore has little regard for the 'sanguinary chic' of the intellectual and academic élites who call for insurrection from the sheltered and secure groves of Academe, because they have failed to appreciate the strength and obstinacy of the social groups that stand in the way of reducing misery. He is also sceptical about the regeneration that can emerge from schemes to de-industrialise the advanced countries, again because of the unimaginably vast institutional shifts that such goals would demand. The role of the academic as Moore sees it is not to preach revolution but to 'use his skills to draw up a balance sheet involving the likely obstacles and costs in human suffering entailed in any proposal for reform'. To do this successfully we need to know far more than we do at present about the nature of society. 'The men of action and conviction have failed enough of late to warrant reversing a famous apophthegm of Marx — philosophers have tried to change the world, now is the time to understand it.'

Lessons and directions for political geography

From this limited selection of some recent writings about the present condition and future prospects of society, it will be apparent that certain underlying motifs occur in various forms. The notion of a system with normative regularities of some kind or another is at least implicit in all. The notion of stress within the system, of basic difficulties in the way the system adjusts to stress, the notion of conflict at various levels, and the need for institutional changes to minimise the areas of stress, most of these are present in all the writings cited.

Sociologists have maintained a long and on the whole constructive debate over which paradigm is most appropriate to the study of society and social problems, the order (consensus) model or the conflict model. Broadly, the order models are system-based models, analysing structural regularities and the within-system processes that maintain a balance in the system as a whole with or without changes in the system's characteristics. Conflict models concentrate on the struggle between groups in society holding opposing goals and values. Stability in the contemporary situation would be seen from this perspective as only the temporary result of the coercion of one group by another. The conflict model invites a questioning of the legitimacy of existing practices and values, the order model tends to accept these as standards of normality and yardsticks by which the regulatory mechanisms are determined.

The intensity of the debate within sociology has diminished because it has been seen in so many cases to consist of the demolition of straw men. None of the exponents of the original models has ever claimed that any actual society has ever been one wholly of consensus and stability, or wholly of change and conflict. Order theories contain a great deal of conflict, and conflict theories a great deal of order. 'Our real task,' writes R. W. Williams Jnr. (1966), 'is to build workable models that depict social systems in which both conflict and consensus are continuous processes in differentiated structures ... actual societies are held together by consensus, by interdependence, by sociability and by coercion, this has always been the case and there is no reason to expect it to be otherwise in the future.'

If political geographers are stimulated to contribute more actively to the analysis of contemporary social and political processes, it seems desirable that they should do so without rekindling the dead embers of past controversies in other disciplines. That is not of course to argue that a consensus is likely as to what paradigm is appropriate, since it is apparent that there is no general agreement on what is an appropriate paradigm to the understanding and analysis of society, nor on what constitutes an appropriate methodology. Where a subject is at the beginning of another stage of development, as political geography is at the present time, it often happens that the scattered contributions cover so broad a field, or are so idiosyncratic in character that the total seems frequently to be less than the sum of the parts. This points to the advantage of working within a broad conceptual framework and it has been partly the purpose of this essay to suggest several such frameworks that seem to be worth investigating in greater depth. It follows that in our selection of themes and choice of methodology none of us should press our point of view to the extreme where it makes a dialogue impossible, or deprives us of a critical appraisal of our work from the academic community at large. On the other hand, perhaps we could be more adventurous in the range of themes we judge it appropriate or prudent to investigate. At this stage, it seems inevitable that any contribution in the area of political geography is likely to be a fairly modest one with strictly limited objectives. What is important is that such contributions should not be inhibited unnecessarily as a result of a desire to work in a value-free context. It matters not that the work should be value-free, but that the values should as far as possible be explicitly stated.

REFERENCES

Applebaum, R. P. (1970). *Theories of Social Change*, Markham Publishing Co.

Barrington Moore, J. (Jnr.) (1974). *Reflections on the Causes of Human Misery*, Allen Lane.

Chomsky, N. (1975). *For Reasons of State*, Fontana.

Dahrendorf, R. (1959). *Class and Class Conflict in Industrial Society*, Stanford U.P.

Dahrendorf, R. (1964). 'Towards a theory of social conflict', reprinted in A. and E. Etzioni (Eds.), *Social Change*, Basic Books.

Dahrendorf, R. (1967). 'Out of Utopia – towards a reorientation of sociological analysis', in Demereth, N. J. and R. A. Peterson (Eds.), *System Change and Conflict*, Free Press, Collier-Macmillan, 465–80.

Deutsch, K. W. (1964). 'Communication theory and political integration and transaction flows as indicators of political cohesion', in Jacob, P. E. and J. V. Toscano (Eds.), *The Integration of Political Communities*, Lippincott, 49–97.

Easton, D. (1967). *A Systems Analysis of Political Life*, Wiley.

Easton, D. (1957). 'An approach to the analysis of political systems', *World Politics*, April 1957, 383–400.

Galbraith, K. (1974). *Economics and the Public Purpose*, Deutsch.

Gould, P. (1969). 'Tanzania 1920–63, the spatial impress of the modernisation process', *World Politics*, 22, 149–170.

Harvey, D. (1973). *Social Justice and the City*, Arnold.

Illich, I. (1971a). *Deschooling Society*, Calder and Boyars.

Illich, I. (1971b). *Celebration of Awareness*, Calder and Boyars.

Illich, I. (1973). *Tools for Conviviality*, Calder and Boyars.

Illich, I. (1974). *Energy and Equity*, Calder and Boyars.

Jones, R. E. (1967). *The Functional Analysis of Politics*, Routledge.

Lipset, S. M. and S. Rokkan (1967). *Party Systems and Voter Alignments — Cross National Perspectives*, Free Press. (International yearbook of political behaviour research, No. 7). See especially 'Cleavage structures, party systems and voter alignments', by S. M. Lipset and S. Rokkan, 1—64.

Mackenzie, W. J. M. (1967). *Politics and Social Science*, Pelican Books.

Morgan, D. R. and S. A. Kirkpatrick (1972). *Urban Political Analysis — a Systems Approach*, Collier-Macmillan.

Parsons, T. (1959). 'General theory in sociology', in Merton, R. K. *et al* (Eds.), *Sociology Today*, Basic Books, 36—78.

Parsons, T. (1960). 'Pattern variables revisited', *American Sociological Review*, 25, 467—483.

Parsons, T. (1963). 'On the concept of political power', *Proc. American Philosophical Society*, 107, 232—62.

Parsons, T. and N. J. Smelser (1956). *Economy and Society*, Routledge and Kegan Paul.

Piel, G. (1964). 'For the living generation', in Goldsmith, M. and A. Mackay, *The Science of Science*, Scientific Book Club, 56—70.

Rokkan, S. (1970). *Citizens, Elections, Parties*. Oslo U. Press. (especially Chapter 3, 'Nation-building, cleavage formation and the structuring of mass politics').

Skinner, B. F. (1973). *Beyond Freedom and Dignity*, Penguin Books. (First published U.S.A. 1971).

Soja, E. W. (1968). 'Communications and territorial integration in East Africa, an introduction to transaction flow analysis', *The East Lakes Geographer*, 4, 35—57. Reprinted in Kasperson, R. and J. Minghi, *The Structure of Political Geography*, University of London Press, 1970.

Vickers, G. (1968). *Value Systems and Social Process*, Pelican Books, 1970.

Weinstein, B. (1966). *Gabon — Nation-Building on the Ogoué*, M.I.T. Press.

Williams, R. W. (Jnr.) (1966). 'Some further comments on a chronic controversy'. A comment on J. Horton, 'Order and conflict theories of social problems as competing ideologies', *American Journal of Sociology*, LXXXI, 701—721.

Chapter 14

The Reformation of Local Government in England

Michael Chisholm

Thorough reform of local government has been an episodic affair. The groundwork for the modern system was laid with the passage of Acts in 1834 and 1835, concerned respectively with the Poor Law and municipal corporations. At that time, a tripartite system operated, consisting of counties, hundreds and parishes, with the boroughs in a special and privileged position. Thereafter, various *ad hoc* bodies were established to provide specific services or facilities, e.g. sanitation and highways, while some powers were transferred upwards through the local government hierarchy. By the 1880s, the situation cried out for reform, an objective that was first achieved for the counties by an Act in 1888, followed six years later by another to rationalise the lower-tier authorities within the provincial counties (Lipman, 1949), and by the establishment of London's metropolitan boroughs in 1899.

The system established in 1894 survived with only minor modifications until 1974, except for the creation of the Greater London Council which became fully functional in 1965 (Lipman, 1949; Stanyer, 1967; Royal Commission, 1969; Redcliffe-Maud and Wood, 1974). The 1972 Local Government Act applied to both England and Wales, with full effect as from 1st April 1974. Ulster experienced a separate reorganisation in 1973, while the picture was completed when the new Scottish councils, elected in 1974, took over in 1975. Between 1894 and the early 1970s, the number of authorities in England and Wales initially increased to a maximum around 1921 but the more recent tendency has been in the opposite direction (Table 14.1), consummated in 1974 by the drop from about 1400 to only 455 authorities. Furthermore, whereas there were formerly four types of authority other than the counties, each class with its own powers, now the counties are divided only into districts, all of which are of equal status (though districts in the Metropolitan and non-Metropolitan counties within England differ

TABLE 14.1

The number of authorities in England and Wales, 1888–1974

Year	County Councils	County Boroughs	Municipal Boroughs	Urban Districts	Rural Districts	London Metropolitan Boroughs and the City of London	Total	Parishes
1888	61	61	—	—	—	—	—	—
1901	62	67	249	805	664	29	1876	14 900
1911	62	75	250	812	657	29	1885	14 614
1921	62	82	274	798	663	29	1908	14 483
1931	62	83	285	780	645	29	1884	14 209
1945	62	83	309	572	476	29	1531	11 100
1951	62	83	309	572	477	29	1532	11 175
1961	62	83	317	564	474	29	1529	10 890
1971	58	83	259	522	468	33	1423	—
1974	53	←—— 369 ——→				33	455	—

Note: the Greater London Council became fully established in 1965.

Sources: Stanyer (1967), p. 106.

Department of the Environment and Welsh Office (1971).

L.G.B.C. (1972).

Local Government Act 1972, H.M.S.O.

in their powers, and there are also differences between English and Welsh districts).

Given the infrequency of radical reform, it seems likely that the present system will last for many decades substantially in its present form, though the Local Government Boundary Commission for England (L.G.B.C.) has been established as a permanent part of the system, charged to make a periodic thorough review of boundaries as well as to ensure that smaller but urgent changes are effected.

Discussion of local government organisation ought simultaneously to take account of various pairs of considerations

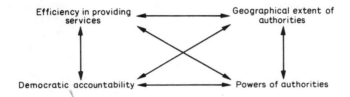

At the time of writing, it is impossible to make a reasoned assessment of how 'successful' the new system will be, partly because no criteria of success have been adumbrated or have emerged as generally agreed in public discussion, and partly because it will take the new system several years to settle down. Nevertheless, there are several topics on which it is presently valid to comment, being enduring features of the new system and relevant to its success. Two in particular deserve comment, namely the place of the city-region concept, and the extent to which the new system has tended to equalise the resources of local authorities, both in absolute and *per caput* terms. However, before proceeding to these two issues, something must be said about the 1972 Act.

The 1972 Local Government Act
In the initial reorganisation, London and its constituent boroughs were left undisturbed. Thus, although London is henceforth subject to boundary review by the L.G.B.C., we may justifiably leave the Greater London Council aside and concentrate on the application of the Act to the rest of England, where the previous system, based on Counties, County Boroughs, Municipal Boroughs, Urban Districts and Rural Districts has been replaced by two forms of two-tier system. Six Metropolitan Counties have been established, based on the conurbations of Birmingham, Merseyside, Manchester, Leeds—Bradford, Sheffield—Doncaster and Tyneside: each of these counties is divided into a limited number of powerful districts. Elsewhere in England, 39 counties exist which also comprise second-tier districts, but these districts have fewer powers than their Metropolitan counterparts (see Table 14.2). In both the Metropolitan and non-Metropolitan counties,

TABLE 14.2
*Summary of the main functions of the new authorities in England
(London excluded)*

County Councils (outside the Metropolitan counties) and Metropolitan District Councils	All County Councils	All District Councils
Education	Housing (reserve powers)	Housing
Youth employment	Town development	Town development
Personal social services	(concurrent powers)	(concurrent powers)
Libraries	Planning — strategic, plus concurrent powers on development control, etc.	Planning — local, plus concurrent powers on development control, etc.
	Transport — main responsibility	Transport — some concurrent powers
	Animal diseases	Environmental health other than animal diseases
	Police	
	Fire	

Source: Department of the Environment (1972).

the parishes have been retained as the lowest tier and in suitable cases some new parishes have been created, but this has been done mainly outside the conurbations.

Initially, two features of the new system must be noted. First, the Metropolitan counties have been created with boundaries limited to the urbanised areas, as interpreted in a fairly restrictive manner. Indeed, especially in Cheshire, substantial commuter suburbs have been excluded from the adjacent Metropolitan counties, and provision has certainly not been made for these new Metropolitan counties to control the rural areas that surround them. In the second place, the pre-existing county system has been retained to a considerable degree, many counties remaining intact or being modified only in small measure. Others have been formed by amalgamation:

New County	Comprising old counties
Cambridgeshire	Cambridgeshire and Isle of Ely Huntingdon and Peterborough
Cumbria	Cumberland, Westmorland, Furness area of Lancashire
Hereford and Worcester	Herefordshire, Worcestershire
Leicestershire	Leicestershire, Rutland
Lincolnshire	Holland, Kesteven, Lindsey
North Yorkshire	North Riding, West Riding
Suffolk	East Suffolk, West Suffolk

In addition, the counties of Avon, Cleveland and Humberside are entirely new creations, carved out of their neighbours.

At the county level, therefore, the changes have been comparatively modest, the most important innovation probably being the administrative recognition of the six conurbations. However, within the counties the reorganisation has been much more drastic; 953 authorities have been replaced by 296 new districts (L.G.B.C., 1972). 22 other authorities have also disappeared, having been split between Metropolitan and non-Metropolitan counties.

Whereas the extent of the counties and also of the districts within the Metropolitan counties was laid down in the Act, the task of making proposals for the districts in the non-Metropolitan counties of England was left for the L.G.B.C., who recommended the formation of the 296 that now grace the map. For this task, the Commission was given fairly comprehensive guidelines. The preferred population was in the range of 75 000 to 100 000 and only in very exceptional circumstances were new districts to have a population of less than 40 000. Regard was to be had for local wishes, the effectiveness of local government, etc. The building blocks were to be whole old districts; only exceptionally should an old district be divided. Finally, the identity of large towns was to be maintained, i.e. towns of about 100 000 population and upwards were not to be divided for re-allocation, nor were they to be extended at this juncture. (The new county of Cleveland is the one major exception to this rule, consisting mainly of a dismembered Teesside C.B.)

What happened to city regions?

Since the publication in 1933 of Christaller's *Central Places in Southern Germany*, the concept of the functional city region has been dear to the hearts of geographers and had entered into general circulation. Furthermore, the concept seems to provide a rational basis on which to organise the provision of local services and hence the best starting point for local government reform. Thus, it is not surprising that the 1969 Royal Commission received much evidence in support of the city region approach. The majority report started from the premise that greater efficiency required the new authorities to lie in the range of 0.25 million to 1.0 million inhabitants. In applying this principle, they were much influenced by the city region concept, using commuting patterns as the main criterion of urban influence. The practical expression of these principles was the proposal to establish 58 unitary (i.e. all-purpose) authorities covering all England except London and three other metropolitan regions centred on Birmingham, Merseyside and Manchester. In contrast to the all-purpose authorities proposed for most of the country, the metropolitan authorities were to have a second tier of 20 districts. These proposals were not acceptable to Senior, who wrote a trenchant minority report (Royal Commission, 1969, vol. 2) championing the city region as the starting point for reform. He was willing to accept a much wider range in population size as a price worth paying to achieve areas that more nearly reflected the functional pattern of town and country than did the majority report recommendations. He advocated 35 regions covering all England outside London, 4 of these regions to be all-purpose authorities (Cambridge, Leicester, Lincoln and Peterborough), the remainder to be sub-divided into 143 second-tier districts. In drawing the boundaries for both tiers, Senior did not feel obliged to amalgamate whole districts, drawing entirely new boundaries where he felt this was appropriate.

The Labour Administration of the day broadly accepted the majority proposals of the 1969 Royal Commission early in 1970 (Secretary of State for Local Government and Regional Planning, 1970), but the Conservatives were elected to office later that year and made entirely new proposals (Secretary of State for the Environment, 1971) which formed the basis of the reform actually implemented. The city region concept is barely evident in this second White Paper. Therefore, we may ask what in practice has actually happened to city regions in the new set-up?

By definition, the major conurbations have been separated from their surrounding rural areas, in a manner similar to that proposed by the 1969 Royal Commission (but their recommendations applied to only three). The question therefore only has relevance lower down the urban hierarchy. Table 14.3 summarises the changes in the non-Metropolitan counties introduced by the 1972 Act, identifying towns that have been amalgamated with rural areas, new towns created by the union of two existing urban areas, and towns that have been left intact in their previous boundaries. For the purpose of this exercise, a town has been taken as a County Borough, Municipal Borough or Urban District, while rural areas are equated with Rural Districts. These defunct administrative units have many defects for this purpose but provide the only geographical units that can be realisically used.

The general pattern displayed by Table 14.3, foreshadowed in the 1971 White Paper, is striking. Virtually all towns below 60 000 have been amalgamated with adjacent rural areas, whereas above that size very few have been so treated. This pattern becomes even more distinct when the following points are noted. The five towns created by amalgamation and with a population below 70 000 are all special cases; to obtain a balanced pattern within the respective counties, these small towns had to be left on their own, e.g. Weymouth and Portland in Dorset. Above 70 000, 'new' towns created by amalgamation vary in character from the sprawling development of Ellesmere Port, through the union of two separate towns as in the case of Barrow-in-Furness/Dalton-in-Furness and Cannock/Rugeley, to the recognition of a continuously built-up urban area, as in the union of Cheltenham and Charlton Kings.

Among the towns left untouched by amalgamation, special cases

TABLE 14.3

Town and country in the non-Metropolitan counties, in terms of 1971 population totals

Population range[1]	Towns[2] amalgamated			Towns[2] not amalgamated	
	With rural[3] areas[4]	With other towns[2,5,6]			
		Free-standing	Continuously built-up	Free-standing	Continuously built-up
0— 10 000	178				
10 001— 20 000	111				
20 001— 30 000	62				
30 001— 40 000	30				1
40 001— 50 000	24		1	3	—
50 001— 60 000	20	1	—	1	—
60 001— 70 000	6	—	3	1	—
70 001— 80 000	7	5	3	8	2
80 001— 90 000	—	—	1	2	2
90 001—100 000	2	3	2	6	—
100 001—125 000		3	1	5	3
125 001—150 000			1	2	1
150 001—175 000				4	1
175 001—200 000				—	1
over 200 001				8	
Total	440	12	12	40	11

[1] Population figures are for the new districts, except in the case of towns amalgamated with rural areas; in the latter case, the population is for the town alone. The county of Cleveland has been omitted.

[2] A town is taken as being a former County Borough, Municipal Borough or Urban District. Excluded are two Urban Districts (Lakes in Cumbria and Thurrock in Essex) that have been split in the process of forming new districts.

[3] Rural areas are taken as being former Rural Districts.

[4] In some cases, two towns have been united with a rural area, e.g. Bedford M.B. and Kempston U.D.; in such cases, both towns have been separately included in this tabulation.

[5] In some cases, a small rural area has been added, usually a few parishes to 'tidy up' the situation resulting from the division of districts, e.g. Slough and Corby.

[6] Excludes the special case of Newport M.B., Ryde M.B. and Cowes U.D. in the Isle of Wight.

Source: L.G.B.C. (1972), supplemented.

again account for all those below 70 000 in population; some are New Towns with further significant growth expected in the near future, as at Stevenage; others were difficult cases that could not be amalgamated with other areas without violating one or more of the constraints under which the exercise was carried out, e.g. Christchurch and Hereford.

Above 70 000, the unamalgamated towns are for the most part clearly identifiable as 'large', surrounded by a rural area of greater or lesser extent — Gloucester, Lincoln, Cambridge, York and Stoke-on-Trent, for example, with Bristol by far the largest at 425 000 inhabitants.

Thus, in general terms, existing towns above 70 000 have been kept intact as districts, separated from the surrounding rural areas; in addition, some 'new' ones have been created by amalgamation. Altogether, therefore, the size-band 60—70 000 forms something of a threshold, below which town and country have been united and above which they have been kept apart. While it would be wrong to imply that for towns below 60—70 000 the new system represents the full implementation of the city-region concept, the new local government pattern is nevertheless a major step in that direction. King's Lynn makes a natural focal point for the district of West Norfolk, as does Malvern for much of Malvern Hills. On the other hand, the natural hinterlands of both Maidstone and Chester are truncated on the westward side, and East Lindsey has been separated from its local town, Boston. Yet, at the time reorganisation was going through there was very little evidence, in terms of public protest, petitions, etc., to suggest that at this lower end of the urban hierarchy the amalgamation of town and country was anything but fully acceptable in almost all cases.

An important clue to what has happened in the reorganisation of local government is provided by the work of Hall and his associates (1973). They identified 100 Standard Metropolitan Labour Areas in England and Wales, using a careful definition designed to embody the concept of functional interdependence and using 1961 commuting data. The smallest S.M.L.A. so recognised was centred on Stafford and had a 1961 population of 66 000, a figure which is in the threshold range identified above. Now Hall and his associates were examining the *containment* of urban growth and hence the pressures exerted by the expansion of the larger towns, i.e. the S.M.L.A.'s they identified. The process of urban expansion implies the conversion of rural land to housing and urban uses, creating pressures that rural dwellers regard as a serious threat. Perhaps equally important is the fact that for towns over 60—70 000 population the urban hinterlands are in fact rather fuzzy when multiple criteria are used — journey to work, shopping habits, social patterns, etc. This point was admitted by Senior:

'Regional centres vary considerably in strength. Where a comparatively weak one has neighbours of similar calibre, the claim of its region to form a separate planning unit is hardly in doubt; but where such a region adjoins one with a much stronger centre, it forms part of that stronger centre's hinterland for the more specialised end of the spectrum of regional activities.' (Senior, Royal Commission, 1969, vol. 2, para. 220.)

In sum, therefore, the city-region concept, or something approximating to it, has emerged at the lower end of the urban hierarchy, i.e.

below about 60—70 000 urban population. At this scale, it would appear that the populace at large can and does recognise a community of interest. Towns of greater size than this have been retained as districts and in this sense remain separated from their adjacent or surrounding rural areas. However, since the counties have important administrative powers over these larger towns, which was not always previously the case, it is clear that a major step has been taken to unite town and country even though the city-region concept has not been applied. At the county level, especially as between Metropolitan and non-Metropolitan counties, the new system gives administrative expression to the different interests of town and country.

A move to greater equality?

Referring specifically to the conflict of interests between town and country, as the former sought to extend their boundaries at the expense of the latter, Redcliffe-Maud and Wood (1974, p. 3) describe the pre-reform situation as one in which 'A cold war between authorities . . . continued to develop until it could be checked only by the creation of a new structure of local government'. Two approaches to this kind of conflict may be adopted, or some compromise between them. The conflicts of interest may be institutionalised and made overt — as was manifestly the case previously in many instances and as has been provided for in the creation of Metropolitan counties — or they may be 'internalised' by the enlargement of authorities, especially on the city region principle, in which case the interests of the rural minority would usually be over-ridden by those of the urban majority. As we have already seen, the reform actually implemented was a compromise, with the two opposing principles applied in varying degree according to geographical scale. The fact remains that the interests of one district will not necessarily coincide with the interests of its neighbours; a degree of conflict, though hopefully not at the level of a 'cold war', will remain an integral feature of local government. Therefore, it is of more than passing interest to enquire how far the reform has in fact produced a situation in which the local government units are more nearly equal in resources and political standing. In the next few paragraphs, we will briefly examine some issues that bear on this question, with reference to non-Metropolitan districts in England, leading to a more extended discussion of the change in *per caput* resources as measured by rateable values.

The first and most evident equalisation lies in the creation within each county of a single class of second tier districts to replace the four that previously existed. Only where Metropolitan and non-Metropolitan counties and districts are contiguous is there any difference in the range of powers exercised on either side of a boundary. Perhaps the single most important facet of this change relates to the previous section and the city region concept. Previously, the towns, and especially the larger ones, were not only expanding in geographical extent but they also exercised a wider range of powers than the neighbouring Rural Districts; the latter constantly felt under threat from the ambitions of the towns for territorial aggrandisement. Though the reality of urban expansion is unchanged, the political consequences attending boundary adjustments or the maintenance of the *status quo* should now be much less explosive an issue.

At the same time, there has been a very substantial reduction in the length of boundaries separating districts, because of the smaller number of districts. Though it would clearly be wrong to suggest that overt, institutionalised conflicts of interest will be directly proportional to the number of authorities or the total boundary length, a reduction in the latter must have some bearing on the probabilities of a conflict either persisting or developing. To provide some indication of the effects of reform on boundary length, two exercises have been undertaken. The total area of non-Metropolitan England amounts to 122 000 km^2 giving an average area of 128 km^2 for the 953 old districts and 412 for the reduced number of new districts. Making the improbable assumptions that all districts were the same size and shaped as regular hexagons, it is a straightforward task to calculate the perimeter length for the old and new situation: the total length of district boundaries can be estimated as having been reduced by 44%. This is a very approximate estimate since it ignores the effects of the coast, the fact that prior to reform some districts were split into non-contiguous parts and also omits consideration of any net smoothing of boundaries that may have occurred by the elimination of some very oddly-shaped districts. To see whether the above approximation is reasonable, the landward boundaries for the South West Region (counties of Avon, Cornwall, Devon, Dorset, Gloucestershire, Somerset and Wiltshire) were measured from maps at a scale of 1:100 000. For this exercise, the boundary of the Region with contiguous Regions was treated as if it were a coast and was also omitted from the exercise. For this Region, the actual reduction in length of boundary was 49%.[1] On the basis of these two pieces of evidence, it appears that for the country as a whole the total boundary length for the new districts is approximately one-half of the previous length.

As we have already seen, the reform process eliminated the very large number of minute local authorities but left the larger ones untouched. By definition, therefore, there has been a reduction in the range of absolute sizes of the districts. A convenient measure of this change is provided by the following figures (Table 14.4) for the total population (1971 census, thousands) before and after reform:

The dramatic reduction in the coefficient of variation indicates that, in terms of population size, the new districts are much less widely dispersed about the mean value than formerly. With this greater equalisation in absolute terms, has there been an equivalent equalisation in resources per head of population?

TABLE 14.4
Districts in non-metropolitan counties, 1971

	953 old districts	296 new districts
Mean population ('000)	27.7	90.3
Standard deviation	36.1	43.8
Coefficient of variation	130	49

The finance of local government is an extremely complex matter, compounded mainly of the rate income levied on property and grants from the Exchequer. The formula under which the latter are calculated is now so intricate that apparently few people fully understand it; in 1974, therefore, the government promised a thorough review of the system. Thus, in terms of *income* the position is both fluid and much affected by central government decisions, as exemplified by the shifting of Exchequer funds away from the rural to urban areas in 1974, an event that gave rise to widespread protest. Consequently, the most useful single measure of local *resources* is the rateable value of property. The first report of the Local Government Boundary Commission (L.G.B.C., 1972) allows an examination of the effects of reform upon the rateable value *per caput*, for the year 1971. Where an old district has been divided among two or more new districts, an estimate was necessary of the allocation of rateable values among the constituent parts. The local authorities concerned were asked to make these estimates; in some cases the allocation was done directly in proportion to the population but in general an attempt was made to take account of the actual geographical distribution of the rate stock. Thus, while the *per caput* rateable values for the 953 old districts are reliable, there is an element of uncertainty concerning the equivalent 1971 figures for the new districts. This uncertainty is small, not only because a genuine attempt was generally made to produce accurate estimates for the split districts, but also because only 75 old districts were in fact divided (22 between Metropolitan and non-Metropolitan counties and 53 within the latter). Altogether, therefore, there is no reason to doubt the veracity of the picture which emerges, shown in Table 14.5.

TABLE 14.5
Districts in non-metropolitan counties, 1971

	953 old districts	296 new districts
Mean rateable value *per caput* (£)	40.9	44.0
Standard deviation	12.3	11.5
Coefficient of variation	30.1	26.1

The first point to note about these figures is the relatively small reduction in the coefficient of variation, indicating only a modest move toward greater equality of *per caput* resources. In the second place, the mean *per caput* rateable value has increased by about 10%. The reason for this increase lies in the fact that unweighted values have been used to calculate the mean values and standard deviations. These bald summary figures are not very illuminating as to what has actually occurred in the process of reform, beyond indicating a very limited move to greater equality in resources per person. To explore the matter further, Table 14.6 has been compiled, showing rateable values per head for various sizes of the old local authorities, distinguishing rural areas and towns.

TABLE 14.6
Rateable values, £ per caput 1971, for the 953 old districts before reform

Population ('000)	Rural areas[2]			Towns[1]		
	£/hd	S.D.	N	£/hd	S.D.	N
0 — 10.0	31.0	10.4	65	40.6	10.6	190
10.1— 20.0	32.6	7.0	140	42.6	11.7	132
20.1— 30.0	35.0	6.0	78	43.9	11.8	74
30.1— 40.0	40.4	10.5	50	48.2	13.4	44
40.1— 50.0	42.6	11.2	21	47.6	12.2	34
50.1— 60.0	42.0	8.7	10	51.0	12.8	27
60.1— 70.0	43.1	9.1	9	55.3	13.2	13
70.1— 80.0	49.1	13.8	8	54.1	16.3	18
80.1— 90.0				56.0	21.3	6
90.1—100.0	63.4	—	1	48.3	6.9	6
100.1—125.0				52.1	12.5	9
125.1—150.0				52.6	7.5	3
150.1—175.0				64.8	8.9	5
175.1—200.0				52.3	—	1
200.1 and over				49.3	7.6	9

[1] See note 2, Table 14.3.
[2] See note 3, Table 14.3.

For the rural areas, there is an unmistakeable tendency for *per caput* rateable values to increase with the absolute size of population. A similar pattern exists for towns up to the size range 80—90 000, whereafter there appears to be no distinct trend. Furthermore, below 80 000 population, towns consistently have larger resources per person than do rural areas of equivalent population total. Thus, within the size-range of authorities that have been amalgamated to form the new districts, two processes tending to equalisation of relative resources have been operative. The difference in rateable values per person in urban and rural areas means that amalgamation of these two types of authority will give values that lie nearer the average for all authorities. In the second place, the union of very small and poor districts with larger and wealthier ones will have the same effect.

The fact that these two processes have resulted in such a small equalisation of relative rate resources undoubtedly reflects the operation of a further factor. Since the districts represent the new unit of *local* government, amalgamation of neighbouring authorities has done nothing to average out the wider regional variations in incomes and resources generally. If one area is either poor or rich in relation to its absolute population, so too are its neighbours, i.e. there is a high level of spatial autocorrelation. This is a matter that I have not been able to pursue any further as yet, but without doubt this has been the dominant factor limiting the equalisation of resources per head.

Conclusion
In this essay, I have been able to examine only two facets of local government reform in any depth. Both of these facets reveal imperfections in the system that has now been established but also indicate that real progress has indeed been made. While it remains for future historians to assess whether the reform has been a success, the evidence presented in this essay tends to confirm the essentially optimistic view taken by Lord Redcliffe-Maud and Wood (1974) as a result of their wider-ranging survey of reformed local government. At the same time, there is clearly a large field for important research by geographers and other social scientists on the operation of the new system.

NOTES AND REFERENCES

[1] I am indebted to Miss Valerie Beekes, Department of Geography, University of Bristol, for making these measurements.

Christaller, W. (1933 and 1966). *Central Places in Southern Germany*, first published in German and translated into English by C. W. Baskin, Prentice-Hall.
Department of the Environment (1972). *Local Government Act*, Circular 121/72, H.M.S.O.
Department of the Environment and Welsh Office (1971). *Rates and Rateable Values in England and Wales 1971–72*, H.M.S.O.
Hall, P. *et al* (1973). *The Containment of Urban England*, Allen and Unwin.
Lipman, V. D. (1949). *Local Government Areas, 1834–1945*, Blackwell.
Local Government Boundary Commission (1972). *Report No. 1*, Cmnd. 5148, H.M.S.O.
Lord Redcliffe-Maud and B. Wood (1974). *English Local Government Reformed*, Oxford University Press.

Royal Commission (1969). *Royal Commission on Local Government in England, 1966—1969*, 3 vols., Cmnd. 4040, H.M.S.O.

Secretary of State for the Environment (1971). *Local Government in England : government proposals for reorganisation*, Cmnd. 4584, H.M.S.O.

Secretary of State for Local Government and Regional Planning (1970). *Reform of Local Government in England*, Cmnd. 4276, H.M.S.O.

Stanyer, J. (1967). *County Government in England and Wales*, Routledge and Kegan Paul.

Chapter 15

The Effect of Local Government Reform on Access to Public Services: A Case Study from Denmark

Barry Garner[1]

Although minor adjustments in the boundaries of local government areas occur from time to time, for example by annexation, the basic pattern of local government areas is normally stable during long periods of time. Major changes in the size and number of administrative units can only be brought about by the reform of local government on a national basis. Such a national reform was implemented in Denmark on 1st April 1970. The spatial aspects of the reform of the Danish kommunes forms the basis of a current research project at the Geographical Institute at Aarhus University. In this paper, some preliminary results from the first stage of this project are presented. Attention is focussed on the effect of the centralisation of local government services on the individual's access to services provided from local government offices. Emphasis is thus placed on the relationship between the provision of services in the public sector and individual spatial behaviour, rather than on the spatial organisation of local government itself. The discussion is set in the context of time-space constraints on the behaviour of the individual.

The individual's environment structure
Every individual or household is surrounded by what Hägerstrand (1970) calls an *environment structure*. The environment structure is a pattern of resources, services and activities that are unevenly distributed in space and time, and which are necessary for the satisfaction of needs and wants. The composition of the environment structure varies,

often quite considerably, from place to place. At the macro scale, differences exist between urban and rural areas and, for example, between core regions and peripheries. At the micro scale, variations exist between individuals, depending upon the location of the home-base with respect to the way resources and activities are distributed locally (Harvey, 1973).

The role played by government in moulding the individual's environment structure is increasingly important. Urban and regional planning and national location policies in general have been instrumental in bringing about differences in the composition of environment structures from place to place. Increasingly, planning and other legislation is being used as a way of smoothing out the spatial distribution of resources and activities in an attempt to reduce inequalities in living conditions and quality of life at the regional and local scale. The welfare of the individual is to an increasing extent intimately related to the level of resources, activities and services provided by government (Teitz, 1968).

At the local scale, the environment structure is the basic spatial framework within which individual patterns of day-to-day behaviour unfold. The way in which the elements making up the environment structure — both public and private — are used and exploited differs from person to person. In part, this is related to individual differences in needs, wants, and values; it is also related to the way in which the individual perceives the opportunities available to him in space. At the local scale, then, the environment structure is relative to the individual. Its composition is to a large extent conditioned by the amount and quality of information the individual possesses, the economic resources at his disposal, and his psychological make-up. The way in which one attempts to explain individual spatial behaviour within this framework depends primarily on whether the emphasis is placed on the individual himself or on the nature of his environment structure.

Preferences and choice

Attempts to explain patterns of spatial behaviour in terms of the way in which the individual views the world about him have been made in the so-called behavioural approach to human activities (Cox and Golledge, 1969). Following Horton and Reynolds (1971), two sub-spaces in the environment structure can be recognised for any given individual. The first of these is his *action space.* This is defined as the collection of locations, resources and activities about which the individual has information together with the subjective utility or preference he associates with these. The second is the individual's *activity space* — the subset of all locations, activities and resources with which the individual has direct contact as the result of his day-to-day activities over a period of time.

Differences in an individual's action and activity spaces on the one hand, and between these and the environment structure on the other, are explained largely in terms of cognitive images. These images are thought of as comprising the interface between the individual and his environment, and it is in terms of the images that behaviour can be understood (Downs, 1970). How well the images are structured depends on the individual's exposure to information, his ability to assimilate it and the way he uses it. The process of acquiring information is viewed in terms of a search and learning process in space. The images of reality the individual builds up in this way enable him to attach different levels of subjective utility or preference to the objects in the action space. The particular set of activities which go to make up the individual's daily activity space are assumed to be those for which the individual's preferences are highest. Individuals can express preferences without necessarily being able to act upon them — as is often the case, for example, with regard to housing. However, in the context of the individual's day-to-day activity, the emphasis on images and preferences assumes that a reasonable level of choice exists between the various opportunities in the action space (Garner, 1968). How much choice exists for a given individual depends on many different factors. From the individual's standpoint, choice is partly a function of economic resources since these relate, for example, to mobility levels. The level of choice increases the larger the space over which the individual can move to carry out his day-to-day activity pattern. However, the most severe restrictions to individual choice are those inherent in the physical composition and spatial organisation of the environment structure itself.

Acquiring information about where services — both public and private — can be obtained in space takes time. Lack of information about where to go, especially for public services, can result in considerable waste of time and alteration of the daily time budget. In fact, of all the restrictions to individual choice and behaviour patterns the manifold relationships between time and space are perhaps the most important. In the behavioural approach, the role of time is to a large extent neglected and one often gets the impression that behaviour takes place in a timeless environment. Neglect of the ways in which time acts as a constraint on choice and movement makes much of the work couched in behavioural terms in no small degree non-behavioural.

Constraints in time and space

It is the central role given to the relationships between time and space, and to constraints on the spatial behaviour of the individual, which makes the recent work of Hägerstrand so interesting and valuable (Hägerstrand, 1970a, 1970b). It is interesting because it adds a new dimension for the development of theory; valuable because it is potentially rich in practical application. Since the details of Hägerstrand's time—space model of society have now been thoroughly summarised in English by Pred (1973), it is not necessary to do more than emphasise some of the main points here.

That part of the environment structure which a person can reach within a single day and yet still return to the home-base for the night can be thought of as the individual's daily environment space. This has a theoretical and determinable outer boundary, the location of which depends on the individual's capability for movement. Locations and the activities at them which occur within the daily environment space can be called stations; the movements linking them together and time spent at a particular station can be called paths. The daily environment space can be represented diagrammatically in the time—space dimensions as prisms, the walls of which represent its outer boundary (Figure 15.1). Although the time—space walls of the daily prism will vary from day to day depending on the activities the individual engages in, and hence the stations he stops at (Figure 15.2), all behaviour during the day must take place within its walls. It is impossible for him to move outside the prism and he cannot backtrack within it since time is an irretrievable resource. Every stay at a station for a particular purpose causes the range of the prism to shrink in proportion to the length of stay there.

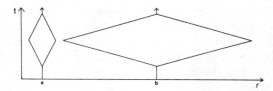

Figure 15.1   Cross-section of an individual's daily prism. r indicates distance and t time. a and b are home-bases which cannot be left before a certain time in the morning and which must be returned to some time later in the day. The shape of the prism is determined by the level of mobility. Behaviour can only take place within the prism. (After Hägerstrand, 1970a.)

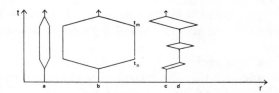

Figure 15.2   The range of the daily prism shrinks in proportion to the length of stay at a station. $t_n - t_m$ can be thought of as time spent at work. Individual a has less choice in place of work than individual b, because of his lower level of mobility. When the individual's place of work is close to the home-base, c, the daily prism can be decomposed into sub-prisms. (After Hägerstrand, 1970a.)

The daily prism is thus a way of conceptualising the physical dimensions of the action space in which individual behaviour can take place.

The activities (stations) with which the individual has direct contact in the course of his daily activity are located somewhere within the daily prism. Although it is recognised that individuals differ in information and that preferences enter into behaviour patterns, these are not considered by Hägerstrand to be the most important factors affecting the activity space. Rather he stresses the fact that the individual's freedom of access to stations, his ability for movement between them, and hence his level of choice, are often limited by various kinds of constraints. Individuals normally have only limited capacity to overcome these. Certain constraints are imposed by physiological and physical necessity; others are derived from private and public decisions; still others are imposed by behavioural norms. Most of the various kinds of constraints which mould the individual's activity space fall into one of the following three categories: capability constraints; coupling constraints; and authority constraints.

Capability constraints limit the activities of the individual through his own biological make-up and the tools, including transport, at his command. It is not necessary here to go into the effects of this type of constraint in detail although it is important to note that to a large extent they determine the size of the daily prisms and the extent of the individual's action space.

Coupling constraints largely govern the paths through the daily prism. They define 'where, when, and for how long the individual has to join other individuals, tools, and materials in order to produce, consume, and transact'. A grouping of paths of several individuals at a particular station can be called an activity bundle, for example workers and machines at a factory, salesmen and customers in shops, doctors and patients in a surgery. The important point about activity bundles is that they follow predetermined timetables which act as powerful constraints on the individual's freedom of choice in participating in activities. In highly packed situations, the individual's daily programme can be thrown drastically out of kilter by seemingly small adjustments in the way events are scheduled in time. When an activity or service can only be obtained from a single location and when, as is the case with most local government services, the individual is forced to travel to that place and opening hours are restricted, coupling constraints often become acute. This is particularly true when the facility or service in question is asymmetrically located with respect to the individual's usual daily activity space. The severity of the problem of course depends on the frequency with which local government services are demanded by a given individual. In aggregate terms, however, poorly located facilities will intensify coupling constraints and increase problems of access to the services provided at them.

Authority constraints exist in a variety of different forms. They can be thought of as giving rise to *domains* in the organisation of space. A domain is defined as a space—time entity within which activities are under the control of a person, group, or organisation. In time—space terms, domains appear as cylinders the insides of which are either not accessible at all to certain individuals (non-members of a club for example), or are only accessible upon payment of a fee or by invitation, and so on. Domains are related to each other hierarchically. Superior domains can determine or alter the spatial extent of subordinate domains and can remove or impose restrictions on the access of individuals to them.

The division of space for administrative purposes is one of the important ways in which authority constraints arise. Local government areas and administrative areas in general constitute a particularly important kind of domain in spatial organisation. Their boundaries act as very real and powerful barriers to individual behaviour. This is because individuals normally only have access to public facilities and services that are provided within the domain to which they have been spatially assigned. In this sense, the individual goes where he is told to go to acquire many kinds of services provided in the public sector. As we have seen, this may often require a substantial alteration to daily time budgets and result in increased coupling constraints. Strategies designed to ensure a 'liveable' day-to-day existence for the individual and 'to provide substance to that portion of each individual's environment which lies outside the realm of income acquisition' (Pred, 1973, p. 37) must be found. An important part of any strategy to this end must be the greater recognition and awareness of the individual's capacity constraints, the lessening of coupling constraints, and the reduction of authority constraints explicit in existing spatial arrangements and organisation.

The Danish kommune reform

Major reforms of local government provide a golden opportunity for reducing at least some of the coupling and authority constraints in spatial organisation since domains are usually extensively redefined and the spatial distribution of certain public facilities altered as a result. This was most certainly the case with the reform of the Danish kommune structure in 1970, which simplified the structure of local government and drastically reduced the number of local government areas — from 1384 to 277 (Table 15.1).

The structure of local government which existed prior to 1970 was, for the most part, a legacy of the period 1837—41. The basic features

TABLE 15.1

Population size of urban and rural districts 1960 and primary kommunes 1970, excluding Copenhagen

Population size ('000)	1960				1970	
	U.D.	R.D.	Total	% of total	No.	%. of total
Under 1	—	468	468	34	—	—
1— 2	11	539	550	41	1	—
2— 3	9	173	182	13	2	1
3— 6	17	84	101	7	65	23
6— 10	12	14	26	2	97	35
10— 15	9	10	19	1	40	14
15— 20	8	2	10	1	24	9
20— 40	13	6	19	1	25	9
40— 60	2	1	3	—	13	5
60—100	1	3	4	—	5	2
over 100	2	—	2	—	5	2
Total	84	1300	1384	100	277	100

Source: Betænkning nr. 420 (1966).

of the pattern of local government areas had remained almost intact since then. Voluntary amalgamation of areas had taken place from time to time, but it was not until after 1960 that this process began substantially to alter the basic pattern. For example, in the period 1962—66, 118 new local government areas were created from 398 former ones. By this time, discussions about the reform of the structure of local government were well under way.

Three kinds of administrative area (kommune) then existed: urban districts (købstadskommuner), rural districts (sognekommuner), and counties (amtskommuner). Excluding Copenhagen, 84 towns formed the basis for the urban districts; parishes the basis for the 1300 rural districts. These two kinds of authority were responsible for providing public facilities, for example schools and libraries, and for the administration of a growing complexity of government services at the local level. The 22 counties, which comprised the rural districts, provided higher level services such as hospitals, and co-ordinated various other activities at the regional scale, for example road building. By the mid-fifties, it was becoming increasingly apparent that this system was no longer adequate.

The rural districts — by far the most numerous — were in particular increasingly incapable of providing the level of service demanded by the population and required by the law. They were too small; 75% had a population of under 2000 in 1960 (Table 15.1), and many of them were suffering a decline in population as migration to urban centres, especially the Copenhagen region, gathered momentum. For most of them the costs of providing a satisfactory level of public service was becoming prohibitive without substantial financial help from the national purse. This in turn necessitated the maintenance of a cumbersome and costly administrative machinery at the national level for the redistribution of taxes between kommunes. Moreover, the national government itself was forced to an increasing extent to assume direct responsibility for the financing and administration of a wide range of activities at the kommune level. Locally elected councils were finding it almost impossible to keep up with the flood of new legislation, particularly that relating to social services, which increasingly required specialist knowledge to administer. The net result was a rapidly declining level and quality of services provided by the rural districts.

These problems were to a greater or lesser extent also typical of the urban districts, especially the smaller ones. Generally speaking, however, the problems were less acute in the towns since, with their larger population, they were in a better position to finance the provision of facilities and services. Also, many of them had the resources to appoint full-time administrative personnel. Thus a noticeable imbalance was being created in the provision of public services as between rural and urban areas. The main problems of the urban districts, however, resulted from the spread of the built-up area into the adjoining rural districts. While the growth of 'suburban' population created special problems for the rural districts, the urban districts were required to maintain a high level of investment in the core of the urban area, often despite a declining tax-base accompanying suburbanisation. The problems of a fragmented administrative framework, albeit at a local scale, made it increasingly difficult to solve problems within the urban area as a whole, and made planning virtually impossible.

It was against this background that a Government Commission was set up in 1958 to investigate the reform of local government. The Commission's job was twofold: first to work out a framework for new legislation for the structure of local government itself and second to consider the possibilities of creating a more suitable division of the country into administrative areas. It is interesting to note that questions relating to the spatial structure of local government were of secondary importance. The Commission reported in 1966 (Betænkning nr. 420, 1966). In short, three main recommendations were made. The first of these was that the existing structure of local government should be simplified and replaced by a two-tier hierarchy, in which the basic administrative unit was to be the primary kommune, which was to replace the existing urban and rural districts. In turn, primary kommunes were to be grouped into secondary kommunes — the so-called counties.

The other two recommendations concerned the way in which the new primary kommunes were to be established. The first related to their size; they were to be substantially larger in area and population than hitherto. Normally, they were not to be smaller than 5—6000 inhabitants. Recent studies of the new primary kommune budgets suggest that this threshold was far too low, since the *per caput* cost of providing public services appears to increase markedly in kommunes smaller than 10—15 000 inhabitants. Table 15.1 shows that over half of the newly created primary kommunes were smaller than this threshold immediately after the reform in 1970.

The second recommendation was founded upon the principle of 'one town — one kommune'. The new kommunes were to be based on the pattern of towns and, wherever possible, boundaries were to be drawn so that the town and its hinterland were included in the same kommune. In the interests of rationalisation and economies of scale in the public sector as a whole, the provision of local government services was to be centralised at the new administrative centre within each kommune. One of the basic ideas behind the reform of local government was, then, the reduction of spatial inequalities in the level and quality of public facility provision and local government services. Since the latter were to be centralised at the new kommune centres, the location of these centres with respect to the distribution of population and new kommune boundaries is important, particularly from the viewpoint of access. It can be argued that the level of service is not entirely independent of the ease with which it can be obtained.

The delimitation of local government areas in such a way as to minimise distance and maximise access to the new administrative centres is in essence a 'location—allocation' problem (Massam, 1972). However, since in the Danish case certain towns were selected as the centres of the new kommunes at the outset, the problem was considerably simplified in that attention need only be focussed on the problem of drawing boundaries, a task that is usually undertaken by a Boundary Commission. However, this was not the case in Denmark. Instead, the rural districts were left to sort out the problem themselves. The creation of the new primary kommunes, and hence their delimitation, was to be achieved by amalgamation of the rural districts on a voluntary basis. In the case of disagreements between the districts, the government reserved the right to allocate them to a particular kommune by decree. This happened in very few instances. As a result, the new primary kommunes are in many cases far from optimal as regards the individual's access to local government offices, which in a large number of cases are located asymmetrically within the local government area, e.g. Ringkøbing (Figure 15.3).

Changes in access to a local government office
To shed some light on the extent to which access to local government offices has been changed as a result of the creation of the new

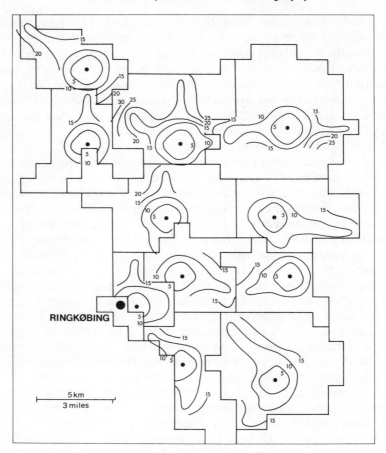

Figure 15.3   Travel times in minutes for one-way journeys to former rural district offices, the locations of which are shown by the small filled circles. Travel times are for journeys by bus, including time needed to walk to a bus stop, and for journeys on foot where it is possible to walk directly to an office in under ten minutes. The location of the new local government office in Ringkøbing is shown by the large filled circle.

kommune structure, the situation in Ringkøbing Kommune, in western Jutland, has been studied (Alsted, 1974). The new kommune comprises the previous urban district of Ringkøbing, which is the new administrative centre, plus 11 former rural districts (Figure 15.3). In 1970, the kommune had a population of 15 186, 6629 residing in the town of Ringkøbing itself. The results of the research presented here are those based on access to the new local government office by public transport. We have chosen these data because they illustrate the effects of coupling constraints and because they show the way mobility is limited by capacity constraints. The extent to which public transport is actually used in visiting the local government office has not yet been determined. Consequently, the picture presented is to some degree hypothetical. However, it can be thought of as representing the situation for the most disadvantaged section of the population in the kommune.

Information shown on the maps and in the tables has been obtained using the following procedures and rules. The kommune is covered by a grid of 1 km squares and the population measured as the number of households per square. Households in the former urban district of Ringkøbing are omitted from the calculations because for them there has been no change in access to the local government office. In the former rural districts, only those squares whose centres are within a maximum distance of 2 km from the former kommune offices and/or 1 km from a bus route are included in the calculations. 79% of the total number of households in the former rural districts is located in these squares; 21% of the rural population is consequently omitted from the study. It is assumed that people will walk to the kommune office if it is within 2 km, otherwise they take the bus. The time taken to walk to the office is set at 5 minutes within a radius of 1 km and 10 minutes within a radius of 2 km of the office. The time taken to walk to the bus route is set at 5 minutes for households living in the squares through which the bus route passes; otherwise, the time taken to walk to the bus stop is set at 10 minutes. It is assumed that the bus will stop anywhere along the route upon request — a situation that is quite normal in the rural areas of Denmark. The time for a transaction at the present local government office and at the former rural district offices is set at 15 minutes. Officials in Ringkøbing kommune estimate this to be the normal length for a consultation. For a visit to the new local government office in Ringkøbing, it is 10 minutes' walk from the bus station to the office, and 10 minutes back again. Consequently, the minimum time needed after arriving in Ringkøbing in order to do business at the present office is 35 minutes. The present office is open in the periods 9.30—12.30 and 13.30—15.30.

The patterns of travel times to the former rural district offices and to Ringkøbing are shown on Figures 15.3 and 15.4 respectively. The differences between the two maps need little comment. The effects of centralisation are obvious and as expected. Suffice it to remark that the maximum time needed to travel to the former rural district offices was 20—25 minutes; today it is 70—75 minutes. The differences in travel times before and after centralisation of local government services are shown in Table 15.2. Before the reform, 52.0% of the population could reach the kommune office within 5 minutes. In the new kommune, just under 50.0% of the population need 30 minutes or more. If every household were to make one visit to the local government office in Ringkøbing, the aggregate increase in travel time would be 718 'household hours'. Since the figures in Table 15.2 are for single

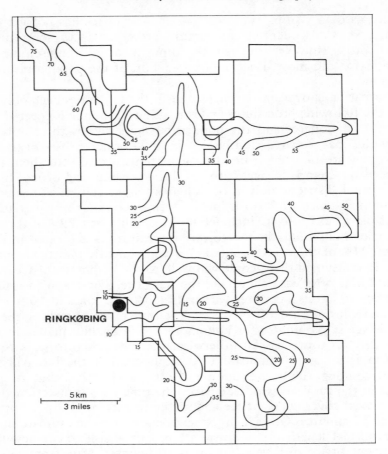

Figure 15.4   Travel times in minutes for one-way journeys to the new local government office in Ringkøbing. Travel times are for journeys by bus, including time needed to walk to a bus stop and from the bus station in Ringkøbing to the office, and for journeys on foot where it is possible to walk directly to the new office in under ten minutes.

journeys, the total increase in time needed for travelling – 1436 'household hours' – is equivalent to the time one man spends working 40 hours a week for 36 weeks.

The effect of coupling constraints becomes apparent as soon as the time required for a consultation at the local government office is included. Spatial variations in the total time needed to visit local government offices are shown in Figures 15.5 and 15.6. On these maps, the average total times per household in each of the former rural districts are shown for visits to acquire local government services before and after the reform. Figure 15.5 shows the pattern when a visit must

TABLE 15.2

Distribution of households by travel times in minutes before and after the kommune reform, for a one-way journey

Travel time in minutes	Before			After		
	No. of house-holds	Travel time x house-holds	%	No. of house-holds	Travel time x house-holds	%
5	1174	5870	52	190	950	8
10	623	6230	28	213	2130	9
15	414	6210	18	214	3210	9
20	33	660	1.5	286	5720	13
25	15	375	0.5	244	6100	11
30	4	120	—	529	15870	24
35	—	—	—	76	2660	3
40	—	—	—	167	6680	7
45	—	—	—	39	1755	2
50	—	—	—	101	5050	4
55	—	—	—	51	2805	2
60	—	—	—	93	5580	4
65	—	—	—	43	2795	2
70	—	—	—	10	700	2
75	—	—	—	7	525	
Total	2263	19465	100	2263	62530	100

Source: Alsted (1974).

be made during the morning. For a morning trip, the journey must start and end at the home-base between 8.00 and 13.00 hours. The figures are for the shortest possible round-trip during this period. As can be expected, the total time per visit to the local government office is considerably greater after the reform. Sdr. Lem in the southeast corner of the kommune is the only exception. For households in Vedersø and Torsted it is not possible to visit the Ringkøbing offices. The most interesting feature revealed on the map is, however, the considerable time which must be spent waiting in Ringkøbing before there is a bus home. This is especially the case for people living in the northwestern part of the kommune. Of course this time is not necessarily wasted since the opportunity exists for shopping in the town. The corresponding pattern for an afternoon trip is shown in Figure 15.6. An afternoon trip must start and end at the home-base between 12.00 and 17.00 hours. The figures are again for the shortest possible round-trip during this period. Total trip times are clearly shorter in the afternoon than in the mornings. Moreover, waiting times are also considerably shorter in the afternoons. In addition, however, the time required for a

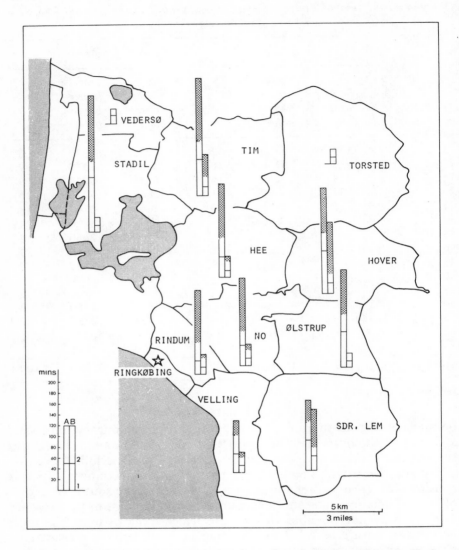

Figure 15.5   Average total round-trip times in minutes per household for a morning visit to local government offices before and after the kommune reform. The lower parts of the columns (1) show total travel time (round-trip); the upper parts (2) show visit time and waiting time between connections (the shaded portion). The column to the left is for a visit to the new kommune office in Ringkøbing; the column to the right for a visit to the former rural district offices. The stippled areas are water bodies.

Figure 15.6   Average total round-trip times in minutes per household for an afternoon visit to local government offices before and after the kommune reform. See the caption for Figure 15.5 for explanation of the bar-graphs.

trip in the afternoon appears to increase with distance from Ringkøbing.

Table 15.3 shows the distribution of households by total trip times before and after the kommune reform for visits in the morning and afternoon respectively. Under the old system, 56.0% of households could visit the rural district offices in less than half an hour for a morning trip and 52.0% of households could make the visit in the same

TABLE 15.3

Distribution of households by total round-trip times before and after the kommune reform

	Morning trips				Afternoon trips			
Minutes	Before	%	After	%	Before	%	After	%
0— 30	1218	56	—	—	1812	52	—	—
31— 60	338	15	—	—	356	15	—	—
61— 90	—	—	61	3	75	3	723	31
91—120	15	1	248	12	538	23	941	40
121—150	367	17	574	28	27	1	413	17
151—180	79	4	625	30	98	4	230	10
181—210	90	4	251	12	30	2	59	2
211+	68	3	307	15	—	—	—	—
Total	2175	100	2066	100	2348	100	236.	100

Source: Alsted (1974).

time in the afternoon. In the new kommune, over half of the households need at least 2½ hours to visit the Ringkøbing office in the morning and no one can make the trip in less than an hour. For afternoon trips, 31.0% of households must use 1—1½ hours while over 70.0% require 1—2 hours.

Finally, Table 15.4 shows the average time in minutes per household

TABLE 15.4

Average time in minutes for shortest possible round-trip to local government offices before and after the kommune reform, by rural districts

			Difference	
Rural district	Before	After	Minutes	%
Vedersø	54	149	95	175
Stadil	49	129	80	163
Tim	50	110	60	120
Torsted	87	181	94	108
Hee	38	78	40	105
Hover	119	178	59	50
Ølstrup	35	149	114	326
No	31	111	80	258
Sdr. Lem	89	102	13	14
Velling	61	89	28	46
Rindum	29	85	56	193
All districts	58	124	66	114

Source: Alsted (1974).

for the shortest possible round-trip to the offices before and after the reform, by former rural districts. The average increase in time varies from 13 minutes in Sdr. Lem to 114 minutes in Ølstrup. In almost all districts the time needed to acquire local government services has increased by over 100.0%.

Figures 15.5 and 15.6 are a good illustration of the effects of coupling constraints. If time is at a premium, then clearly an afternoon trip is best. But to make the trip during the afternoon may require substantial alteration to the daily time-budget. On the other hand, a morning trip may fit more easily into the daily routine, but the total time needed for the trip is considerably greater. The rigidity of timetables and the low frequency of bus services may act as powerful forces shaping the day-to-day behaviour of individuals in the area.

The extent to which this is the case depends in large part on what we can think of as the trip-flexibility — that is the number of opportunities for making the trip within a given time period. For visits to the Ringkøbing office the time period is determined by the opening hours. To avoid a long wait before the office opens at 9.30, the earliest the individual should arrive at the bus station is 9.20, and the latest time of arrival is 15.05 because 25 minutes is needed to walk to the office and obtain a consultation before the office closes. Calculations show that 40.0% of households have two possibilities of making the trip within this period; 9.0% have more than three possibilities. However, 20.0% of the households have no choice — there is for them only one possibility of making the trip. The areas in which this is the case are shown in Figure 15.7. The figures at the foot of the columns indicate the percentage of households in this no-choice situation before and after the reform. In Vedersø and Torsted, the number of households with no choice has increased significantly. It is interesting to note that the lack of trip-flexibility is notably concentrated in the northern periphery and in Ølsted at the eastern edge of the new kommune.

Given the existing situation, especially in the peripheral areas, there are perhaps three strategies for improving access to local government services given the fact that the establishment of sub-offices is ruled out by the new legislation on the structure of local government outside the four largest urban areas in the country. First, by improving the level of public transport services in the area. In view of the problems of maintaining the existing level of services, this would only be possible with massive government assistance. Such assistance is not likely to be forthcoming. Second, by introducing mobile facilities. These are already well developed for library services and it would not seem difficult to extend this practice in providing other forms of public service. Third, by allowing individuals access to facilities and services provided in adjoining kommunes whenever these are closer. Such arrangements already exist between kommunes for primary and secondary schools and there is no reason why they should not be extended to other activities of the public sector.

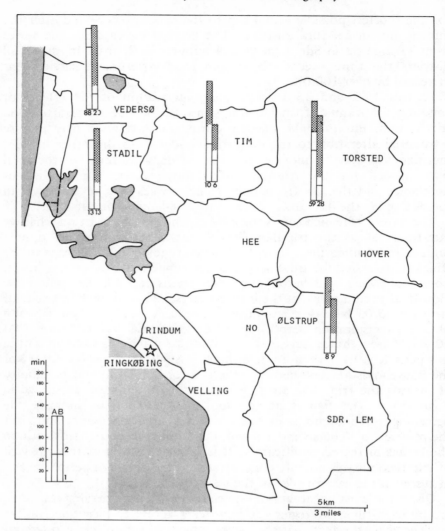

Figure 15.7   Average total round-trip times in minutes per household for a visit to
local government offices before and after the kommune reform for households with
only one possibility a day of making a visit. The figures show the percentage of
households in the former rural districts in this situation. See the caption for
Figure 15.5 for explanation of the bar-graphs.

Comment

The centralisation of local government services in the new kommune
has resulted in longer travel times and often longer waiting times —
particularly for households living in the peripheral part of the study
area. This is to be expected. However, the problems of the peripheral
areas in the new primary kommunes could certainly have been reduced

had more attention been given to the delimitation of the new kommune boundaries. Because this was not the case, the kommune reform appears to have increased authority constraints and coupling constraints instead of reducing them.

Two further comments are in order. First, we have only looked here at one aspect of the centralisation of local government services — the time—space costs to the individual. But there are also benefits, since centralisation of local government services has certainly improved the level and quality of services provided by local government. The study of the benefits to the individual resulting from centralisation is more complex, and our results are not yet available. Secondly, the problem of access to local government services has not been set within the context of the actual patterns of spatial behaviour — the individuals' activity spaces. How serious the problem of access to local government services really is depends not only on the frequency with which different people demand them but particularly on the degree to which Ringkøbing is part of the activity space for the surrounding population. Studies of actual behavioural patterns and activity spaces in the kommune will enable this problem to be seen in proper perspective.

NOTES AND REFERENCES

[1] I am indebted to Henrik Alsted for undertaking the calculations and drawing the maps used in the empirical part of this paper.

Alsted, H. J. M. (1974). *En Undersøgelse af Virkningen for Individet af Central-iseringer Indenfor den Offentlige Sektor — Belyst ved Kommunalreformen i 1970*, Geographical Institute, Aarhus University.

Betaenkning nr. 420. (1966). *Kommuner og kommunestyre*, Copenhagen.

Cox, K. R. and R. G. Golledge (1969). *Behavioural Problems in Geography*, Studies in Geography, 17, Northwestern University.

Downs, R. (1970). 'Geographic space perception', in Board, C. *et al* (Eds.), *Progress in Geography*, Vol. 2, Arnold, 65—108.

Garner, B. J. (1968). 'The analysis of qualitative data in urban geography: The example of shop quality', *Techniques in Urban Geography*, Institute of British Geographers, 16—30.

Harvey, D. (1973). *Social Justice and the City*, Arnold.

Horton, F. E. and D. R. Reynolds (1971). 'Effects of urban structure on individual behaviour', *Economic Geography*, 47, 36—48.

Hägerstrand, T. (1970a). 'Tidsanvandning och omgivningsstruktur', *Statens Offentliga utredningar*, 14, 4.1—4.146.

Hägerstrand, T. (1970b). 'What about people in regional science?', *Papers of the Regional Science Association*, 24, 7—21.

Massam, B. H. (1972). *The Spatial Structure of Administrative Systems*, Resource Paper No. 12, Association of American Geographers.

Pred, A. (1973). 'Urbanisation, domestic planning problems and Swedish geographic research', in Board, C. *et al* (Eds.), *Progress in Geography*, Vol. 5, Arnold, 1—76.

Teitz, M. (1968). 'Toward a theory of public facility location', *Papers of the Regional Science Association*, **21**, 35—51.

Chapter 16

Regional Road Investment Planning for Developing Countries: An Indonesian Application

Patrick O'Sullivan[1]

In many countries the inadequacy of transport facilities is one of the major bottlenecks to economic growth and national integration. The high cost of transport makes it difficult to introduce social infra-structure such as educational and medical services. The dissemination of new agricultural methods and the linkage of agriculture to the rest of the economy through the market are hampered by the absence of efficient transport facilities. This contributes to the continued low productivity of agriculture and consequently to the low income of the bulk of the population, which, in turn, limits the potential growth of manufacturing. This problem is recognised by governments and international lending agencies and much capital investment is directed to the improvement of transport. There is every indication that for agrarian economies the pay-off from road transport investment is greater than that from other modes; therefore, in this essay attention will be confined to road planning.

Approaches to transport planning
Three approaches to transport planning in developing countries may be identified. At one extreme, the attempt may be made to relate the transport decision process to a model of the whole economy, as in the case of the work by Kresge and Roberts (1971). Their Columbia model attempts to identify and trace the feedbacks between the economic system and the transport sector, calculating the benefits from transport investment in terms of increase in the gross national product. This

approach requires many data and involves heroic simplifying assumptions. A simpler approach, therefore, is that adopted by Kuhn and Lea (1969) for Dahomey. They focussed attention on the transport sector, ignoring the macro-economic analysis of the whole economy, partly to reduce the cost (time and data) of the exercise, but also partly because of doubts about the accuracy of macro-economic simulation procedures. The Dahomey model attempts to optimise the transport sector of the whole country, accepting extrapolated projections of commodity supplies and demands in various regions and making some allowance for planned industrial expansion. However, the third and most common approach currently used in planning transport in developing countries is the evaluation of independent projects. This reduces the task to manageable proportions but neglects the interdependencies between projects.

The purpose of the work reported here is to devise a practical method for transport investment programming at the provincial or regional scale, where 'practicality' is defined largely in terms of data requirements. The aim has been to overcome some of the inadequacies of the approaches mentioned above — the disregard for interdependency of conventional project analysis and the complexity and dubious applicability of macroeconomic models in developing countries at present.

The most suitable strategy for investment programming varies from situation to situation. In some cases the purpose may be to ascertain where and when to build what facilities during a certain period of time for which there is a given annual budget. Investment programming should then determine which links in a network are to be built and the standard to which they should be constructed. In other instances, the transport planner may be given the estimated potential development and demand for transport without a budgetary constraint, in which case he has also to determine how much money should be allocated annually to finance construction and maintenance work. In this essay, the former situation is considered to apply. The steps involved in the decision process can then be specified as follows:

1. estimation of the future demand for transport, both for goods and passengers;
2. designation of a set of possible links in the transport network from which to select those to be built in each budgeting period;
3. specification of a set of road standards relevant for given traffic volumes, which may be applied to the construction of road links;
4. estimation of the construction costs (at different road standards) for each tentative road link to be evaluated in the programming process;
5. estimation of vehicle operating costs for each type of vehicle that may travel on each link;

6. determination of the budget that will be available in each budgetary period for construction works;
7. development of a decision procedure for selecting what, where and when to build from among the given set of feasible links;
8. actual selection of a specific investment programme.

These steps constitute the outline of this study. The method applied to the problem is a region-wide optimisation of road transport by means of a branch-and-bound, mixed-integer programming algorithm. The two basic inputs to this model — estimates of commodity flows and transport costs — are generated using surplus-deficit and vehicle cost models. The surplus-deficit model, together with population estimates, generates the traffic flow requirements between nodes of the transport system. The vehicle cost model provides estimates of vehicle operating costs. Using these inputs and the budget as a constraint, the programming model determines the network that can be financed by the available budget which, at the same time, minimises total vehicle operating costs throughout the system.

The study area: south Sulawesi (formerly Celebes), Indonesia

The procedure was applied to road planning in south Sulawesi, a province of the Republic of Indonesia. The province has an area of 77 600 km^2 and occupies the oblong south-western peninsula of Sulawesi Island. This appendage is roughly 400 kilometres from north to south, 200 kilometres wide at its broadest in the north and about 100 kilometres wide for most of its length. The north of the peninsula consists of an extension of the Greater Central Sulawesi Range with many peaks rising to over 2000 metres above sea level. The southern part of the peninsula consists of another mountain range, with a maximum altitude of 2871 metres, characterised by a north-south grain which hinders communication between the east and west coasts. The two highland blocks are separated by a middle plain, at its narrowest on the west coast near Parepare and widening to the east. Elsewhere, the narrow coastal plain widens in Luwu and Mamudju. Intense tropical rainfall and consequent flooding and mass-movement of unstable slopes provide additional physical inhibitions to cross country movement in the region.

The population of the province rose from 4 492 000 in 1961 to 5 093 000 in 1971, giving an annual growth rate of about 1%. The mean density is 57 persons per km^2, which is above the national average of 51 but considerably lower than the 300—700 per km^2 of Java, Madura and Bali. The heaviest concentration is along the south coast, where densities reach over 100, declining northwards to 15 in the northernmost kabupaten. The two largest cities are Makasar and Parepare (respectively 434 809 and 72 646 in 1971). The other centres of population are the kabupaten capitals, all of which exceed 10 000 persons. 70% of the population is engaged in agriculture. The province's principal domestic trade is in rice, while foreign exports are fish, forest and livestock products: exports of nickel ore have risen in value of late but nickel's influence on the economy of the province is not great since the mining operation employs few people and the ore is not processed locally. 5% of the population is employed in manufacturing, in cement, paper and textile plants located in or near Makasar.

The principal harbours for inter-island and international trade are Makasar and Parepare. For inter-island traffic there are five harbours with facilities for small sailing vessels where larger vessels must stand offshore and transfer cargo by lighter. The province's coastal traffic is between kabupaten where road transport is costly or impossible, e.g. to and from Mamudju and between Palepo and Kadjoe. Given the size of

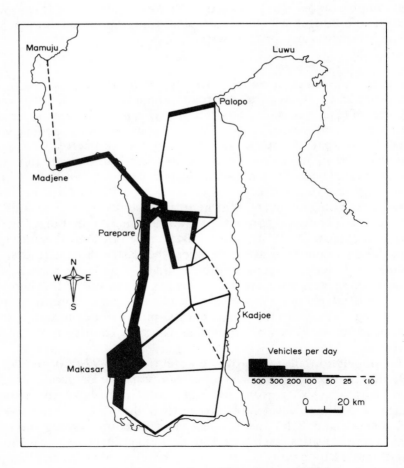

Figure 16.1   Daily traffic volumes, 1968.

the peninsula, it seems likely that if all existing roads were in good condition, sea transport could not compete in terms of cost and time.

The existing road network reflects the physique and disposition of land uses in the province. The main crops depend on the availability of irrigation water and, therefore, intensive agriculture and associated settlement is found only on the littoral, the middle plains and in river valleys. Roads traverse and connect these areas. The network also reflects the market system, radiating from the ports of Makasar and Parepare to local centres which function as collectors of local produce and distributors of imported goods. The road system is in very bad condition. Of the 2188 kilometres under the jurisdiction of the provincial Public Works Department, 1561 kilometres were gravel roads, mostly in bad condition, and 585 kilometres were bituminous roads, of which 175 kilometres were of low standard. Lack of finance, the war of independence and the Darul Islam rebellion from the mid-1950s to 1963 have all contributed to this situation. In the late 1960s, the government, realising the relationship between a declining economy and degraded roads, began to renew the most important links but, because of the dearth of finance and the large number of roads, little could be done. The results of a traffic count taken in 1968 are shown in Figure 16.1. The major traffic flows occur between and around Makasar and Parepare but the low volume on many links does not necessarily imply a low latent demand. Most roads were in bad condition at the time; indeed, 500 metres of the road from Madjene to Mamuju had been wiped out by a landslide.

Forecasting the demand for transport

The demand for transport stems largely from the need to obtain other goods and services, reflecting the place utility which makes the movement of goods and people necessary. Thus, any attempt to estimate the future demand for transport must be based on the future geographical disposition of resources, population and economic activities. Projections of land use and economic activity provide the basis for forecasting the demand for transport by freight shippers and passengers. Transport planning in Sulawesi will most sensibly be linked to the improvement of and addition to existing facilities, rather than to the provision of other modes of transport. This reduces the forecasting of transport demand to the analysis of traffic-generating factors and their distribution, relegating analysis of modal choice to a minor role.

To estimate the demand for transport it is necessary to define the areal units between which traffic is deemed to flow — the kabupaten, in this case, being the units for which demographic and economic data were available. Within these units, locations had to be chosen to serve as origins and destinations, so that the traffic on each road of the network could be specified. The dominant market centre of each kabupaten, usually the administrative capital, was chosen to represent the focus of traffic for the area.

As a basis for forecasting consumption, the population of each kabupaten had to be projected. Because of the dearth of data, a simple extrapolation was the only recourse available, based on the kabupaten populations for 1961 and 1971. Assuming these rates of change to be stationary, target year populations were calculated at a compound growth rate. A linear relationship was not assumed as the implied constant absolute annual change was judged unreasonable. It was considered that any ratio apportionment method, which assumed a fixed relationship between national and regional population, was also unsuitable as the actual 1961—71 provincial rate of 1% was at variance with the national figure of 2.5%.

In a predominantly agrarian, undeveloped economy, the demand for freight transport can be determined, with some justification, by means of a 'surplus-deficit' model involving the following five steps:

1. estimation of kabupaten production of major commodities;
2. estimation of kabupaten consumption of major commodities;
3. determination of kabupaten marketable surpluses or deficits for various goods;
4. allocation of the surpluses to the deficit areas;
5. estimation of the whole region's surpluses for export and import of items in short supply.

The most difficult task is then forecasting levels of production and consumption.

Taking consumption first, growth rates of *per caput* consumption were applied to current consumption, the product being multiplied by estimates of target year populations. Theoretically, the rate of growth of *per caput* consumption represents the growth rate of *per caput* income and the income elasticity of demand for food. However, the only data available were F.A.O. (1971) estimates of growth rates of consumption per head for the whole of Indonesia, so it was necessary to assume that the national estimates applied to south Sulawesi.

To forecast agricultural output, it is necessary to predict crop areas and yields. Given the poor data base in Sulawesi it was not appropriate to extrapolate values for these. There was, however, a land use plan for the province. In 1968 the Ministry of Agriculture carried out a land-use survey in each kabupaten and produced two maps: one showing the current position and the other the recommended land use pattern for both a short-run and long-run agricultural development programme. The latter map was compiled after detailed investigations of soil, topography, climate and the potential for expanding cultivation and irrigation facilities. This plan provided rates of expansion and conversion for land under various crops. Rates of yield increase were based on the realised increases between 1965 and 1970, which were assumed to persist through the planning period. Production of various crops in the target year was calculated as the product of area and yield, with due allowance for field and milling losses.

The only manufacturing plants in the region, producing cement and paper, were assumed to expand to their full capacities by 1973, as intended in the Five-Year Plan, with provincial consumption increasing in line with population and any surplus being exported to other islands via Makasar. Export of other items was assumed to grow at the current provincial rate. The province imports motor, household and industrial fuel, and manufactured goods. For lack of sufficient data, but based on the experience of other developing countries, consumption was assumed to grow at the same rate as the populations of the kabupaten. Motor fuel consumption was assumed to grow at 10% *per annum* (the expected growth rate of motor vehicle numbers in the province). The cement industry was assumed to double its consumption of fuel by the end of 1973 and then remain constant with the assumed achievement of full capacity by the industry. The growth rate of consumption by other manufacturing was assumed to be 5% per annum, in accordance with the Five-Year Plan.

The planning period for which these projections were made was 45 years commencing in 1974, the year in which Indonesia's second Five-Year Development Plan commenced. However, since the base data were for 1968, the projection period actually used was 50 years (1968—2018). Area cultivated, yield, population, imports and exports for 2018 were used to estimate production and consumption of various goods by kabupaten, and the differences yielded surpluses or deficits to be used as inputs for the estimation of traffic volume.

Assumptions for the model
The objective of the study was to establish a road investment programme which would encompass rehabilitation, upgrading and new construction. To estimate the cost of road works, it was necessary to specify standards in terms of surface type and width for various traffic volumes. With the evidence of an international comparison of standards by de Weille and Angeles (1967), gravel surfaces were deemed appropriate for up to 100 vehicles per day, seal coat for 100—1000 and asphalt concrete for over 1000 vehicles per day. Suitable widths are: a pavement of 3.5 metres for up to 100 vehicles per day, 6 metres for 100—2000 vehicles and 7 metres for over 2000 vehicles.

Estimates of rehabilitation costs for individual roads in the province were available (KAMPSAX, 1969).

The only technical data with which to estimate new construction costs were 1:250 000 official maps with 500 metre contour intervals. Local conditions were indicated qualitatively by differentiating flat, rolling and mountainous terrain. Average per kilometre cost of the wearing surface, road base, foundation, earthworks, bridge building and right-of-way were calculated and summed for each terrain category and applied to each possible new link in the network. Upgrading costs per kilometre were calculated as the differences in construction costs or cost of additional requirements between two classes of road, assuming the initial state to be in good repair, or, failing this, including rehabilitation costs.

The budgetary assumptions of the study were that a constant annual construction budget would be available for rehabilitation, upgrading and new construction and that maintenance costs would be allocated separately. The actual sum assumed, 1100 million rupiahs per annum, was based on the first five-year development budget (1969–73). Any increase in government expenditure, therefore, would only arise from increased maintenance work resulting from construction.

The fundamental concern of the whole exercise is the trade-off between investment in fixed roadway facilities and vehicle operating costs. Therefore, it was necessary to evaluate the cost and performance of different classes of vehicle operating over roads of specified physical characteristics.

The network was specified as pairs of directed arcs between nodes. The output of later stages of the analysis gives flows over these arcs in tonnages of commodities. A procedure was devised to convert these to movements of vehicles of specified classes and load factors. The speed of vehicles of a given class and payload was found in terms of top speed, grade, alignment, surface conditions, traffic volume and capacity of each link. Speed and the characteristics of the link were then translated into fuel consumption, tyre wear, oil consumption, maintenance, drivers' time and depreciation costs per link.

The investment programming model
The strategic setting for the work reported here is a three-stage road investment programme in which an annual construction schedule for five years is based on a five-year network plan, which, in turn, is dependent upon a 25-year construction plan. The works which should most advantageously be undertaken at each stage can be determined by the application of dynamic programming (Roberts, 1971).

The long term, 25-year network, is selected from among a set of all feasible links in the network which have been designated using engineering and economic judgement. For South Sulawesi these are shown in Figure 16.2. The configuration of the 25-year network chosen is based on estimated demand for transport 20 years after construction (the customary lifetime of a road), which is 45 years from the base year. Its form and extent is constrained by the available budget within the 25-year planning period and is determined as if all new and improved links were constructed in the 25th year using the accumu-lated, undiscounted budget during the 25-year period. Potential traffic

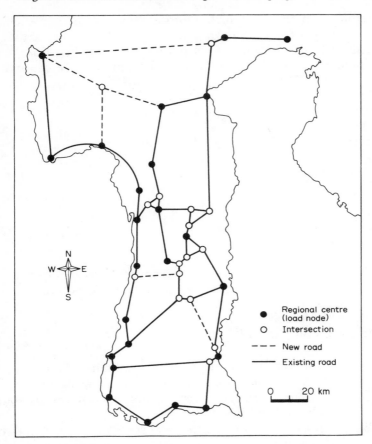

Figure 16.2   Initial network configuration.

in the 45th year is estimated on the basis of projections of production and consumption, imports and exports.

(a) 45th-year traffic on all possible links is initially approximated by applying a compound growth rate to base year traffic count data. A traffic volume is assigned to prospective new links in accordance with the level of economic activity at the nodes it connects. Based on these first approximations, the standards of various links are specified according to the classification of standards by volume. With these data, the transport cost for each commodity on each link can be estimated. A minimum path algorithm can then be used to determine the cost of transporting one unit of a commodity between each pair of nodes in the network.

(b) Based on estimates of 45th-year surpluses and deficits of each commodity in each kabupaten, the optimal flow of commodities on each link of the tentative network can be found with a linear programming formulation which allocates flows to links in such a way as to minimise total vehicle operating costs while satisfying a predetermined distribution of surpluses and deficits. For M nodes (subscripted i, j) and K commodities (subscripted k) we can write this as:

$$\text{MINIMISE } Z = \sum_{k=1}^{K} \sum_{i=1}^{M} \sum_{j=1}^{M} X_{ijk} C_{ijk} \tag{1}$$

subject to:

$$\sum_{i=1}^{M} X_{ijk} = D_{jk} \tag{2}$$

$$\sum_{j=1}^{M} X_{ijk} = S_{ik} \tag{3}$$

$$X_{ijk} \geqslant 0 \tag{4}$$

where X_{ijk} = the flow of commodity k from area i to area j
$\quad C_{ijk}$ = the minimum transport cost between i and j for commodity k
$\quad D_{jk}$ = the deficit of k in j
$\quad S_{ik}$ = the surplus of k in i.

Having obtained the distribution of commodity flows, the next operation is to route them through the network using the previously determined minimum cost paths; total flows on each link are found by summing over all commodities.

(c) Based on these total flows the road standard for each link can be revised and unit transport costs for each commodity on each link can be recalculated.

(d) From the tentative network with standards established in step (c), the links which should be constructed within the 25-year period can be chosen. The objective is to determine the links that should be built to serve the potential traffic in the 45th year in such a way that the total vehicle operating costs in that year will be minimised. This is subject to the constraint that total construction cost must not exceed the accumulated budget for the 25-year period. This simple objective was taken, as it presents us with a tractable problem, given the available means of solution, despite the fact that it does not guarantee a global minimum over the entire planning horizon. The problem can be written as a mixed-integer, linear programme as follows:

$$\text{MINIMISE } Y = \sum_{k=1}^{K} \sum_{i=1}^{M} \sum_{j=1}^{M} X'_{ijk} C'_{ijk} + \sum_{k=1}^{K} \sum_{i=1}^{M} \sum_{j=1}^{M} X''_{ijk} C''_{ijk}$$

$$- \sum_{k=1}^{K} \sum_{i=1}^{M} \sum_{j=1}^{M} A_{ijk} d_{ij} \tag{5}$$

subject to

$$\sum_{k=1}^{K} X'_{ijk} + \sum_{k=1}^{K} X''_{ijk} - \sum_{k=1}^{K} X'_{jik} - \sum_{k=1}^{K} X''_{jik} = D_{jk} - S_{jk}$$

(for j = 1, 2, ... M, k = 1, 2, ... K)   (6)

$$\sum_{k=1}^{K} X'_{ijk} + \sum_{k=1}^{K} X'_{jik} \leqslant U'_{ij}, \quad (ij \in N)$$ (7)

$$\sum_{k=1}^{K} X''_{ijk} + \sum_{k=1}^{K} X''_{jik} \leqslant U''_{ij} d_{ij}, \quad (ij \in R)$$ (8)

$$\sum_{ij} d_{ij} P_{ij} \leqslant B$$ (9)

$$d_{ij} = 0 \text{ or } 1$$ (10)

$$X'_{ijk} + X''_{ijk} = X_{ijk} \geqslant 0.$$ (11)

Where the unfamiliar variables and parameters are:

X'_{ijk} = the flow of commodity k from i to j if the road is not improved
X''_{ijk} = the additional flow of k if ij is improved, above its initial capacity
C'_{ijk} = the unit transport cost of k on ij before improvement
C''_{ijk} = the unit transport cost of k on ij after improvement
A_{ij} = a constant equal to the difference in transport cost on ij before and after improvement for a traffic volume equal to the capacity of the unimproved road
U'_{ij} = the upper capacity on ij for both directions before improvement
U''_{ij} = the additional capacity of ij due to improvement
d_{ij} = the decision variable corresponding to the construction work on link ij, d_{ij} = 1 if ij is constructed or improved, otherwise d_{ij} = 0.
N = all the existing links
R = all road links that need construction work (rehabilitation, upgrading or new construction)
P_{ij} = the construction cost of link ij.
B = the allocated budget.

Thus, the constraints have the following interpretations:
Equation (6) requires that for each commodity the sum of shipments into a node plus the surplus at the node should equal the amount of shipments from that node plus the deficit at that node.
Inequality (7) requires that if the road is not improved, then the total flow in both directions on the link should not exceed the upper capacity limit of the unimproved road.
Inequality (8) requires that if the road is improved the additional traffic should not exceed the additional capacity.
(9) is the budgetary constraint, (10) constrains the decision variable to unity or zero and (11) requires that there should be no negative flows on any link.

(e) Road standards for the 25th-year links are redesignated based on the flows calculated in step (d) and unit transport costs for each commodity on each link are recalculated.

(f) Using these new unit costs from step (e), steps (d) and (e) are repeated until there is no change in the selected network or in the value of the objective function – in which case we have the best 25th-year network.

The fifth-year network is chosen from this 25th-year network, based on the demand for transport in the 25th year. Projections of production, consumption and population distribution in the 25th year can be used to estimate surpluses and deficits and trade flows can be derived. Knowing the flows, the standard of each link can be established and the programming formulation can be applied to choose the 5th year links within the constraint of the accumulated 5-year budget.

The links that should be built during the 5-year period must obviously be elements of the 5th-year network. The sequence of construction is established by working back from the 5th year. The 4th-year network is selected, based on the accumulated budget for the first four years and on estimates of the distribution of supplies and demands for commodities. Those works on the 5th-year network that disappear from the 4th-year network represent the construction programme during the 5th year. In the same manner it is possible to establish those works which should be undertaken during the 4th, 3rd, 2nd and 1st years.

Utility of the model

It must be clear that the determination of the 5th-year and annual construction schedule involves merely the repetition of the method used for the 25-year network; therefore, only the results of the 25-year exercise are presented here.

The computational capacity available for solving the problem was somewhat limited and it was necessary to reduce the extent of the network to which the procedure was applied. The quality of one major route in the system, currently of high standard, was predetermined and several peripheral routes, deemed essential politically, were assumed to be built to the minimum standard and excluded from the decision calculus. The costs for these links were ascertained and subtracted from the total budget. The reduced set of links is shown in Figure 16.3, with the major predetermined route included, as it was in the evaluation of the network.

The outcome of the programme in terms of a 25th-year road network is shown in Figure 16.4. Fifteen of the twenty links submitted to the procedure for appraisal were upgraded at a total cost of 7552 m. rupiah, which left 72 m. rupiah of the budget unassigned. This solution

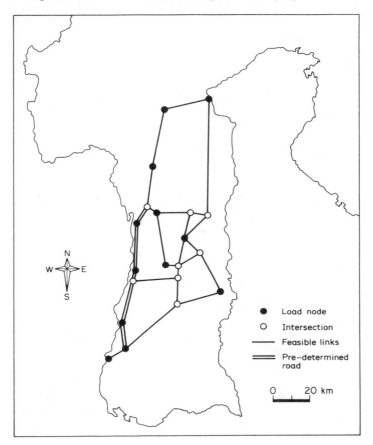

Figure 16.3   The reduced network.

reflects the dispersion of agricultural production and population which was assumed for Sulawesi at the turn of the century, giving rise to a radial structure of improved roads focussing on the ports of Makasar and Parepare. The generally broad level of improvements is a result of the generous budget assumed. The intricate pattern of improvements in the central belt of the network reflects the intricacy of the densely settled central plain.

An important question on this kind of procedure concerns the sensitivity of the solution to the inputs used. For example, within what range could unit vehicle operating costs be varied without affecting the solution? Sensitivity analysis indicated that the unit transport cost could vary over a range about equal to the average magnitude of actual transport cost without significantly changing the results. This suggests that refinement of estimates of vehicle operating costs is not a critical task. The solution was, however, found to be sensitive to slight changes

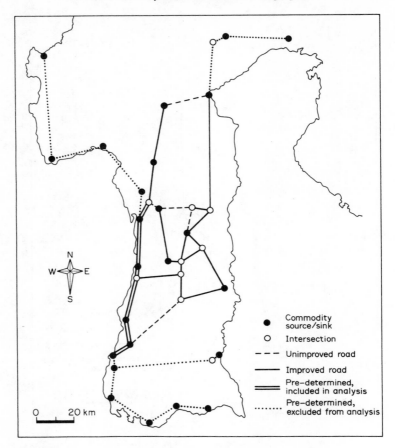

Figure 16.4   The twenty-fifth year road network.

in the estimates of surpluses and deficits indicating that effort should be concentrated here in order to improve performance and validity.

The method might be construed by many as a heavy-handed means of producing fairly obvious results. However, we can claim the merits of explicit reasoning and calculations which make the procedure amenable to improvement, simplification, and generalisation. In addition, despite the immediate computational problems faced in this study, the programming method used is not, in fact, excessive in its capacity requirements and can readily tackle much larger problems than the one posed here.

NOTES AND REFERENCES

[1] The hard work and imagination involved in this study must be credited to Yusuf Ahmed, Sujono and Derek Wilson.

De Weille, J. and H. Angeles (1967). 'A review of road project appraisal reports 1960–1966', *IBRD Economics Department Working Papers No. 5*, Washington, D.C.

F.A.O. (1971). *Agricultural Commodity Projections 1970–80*. Vol. II, United Nations, LV–LVI.

KAMPSAX (1969). *Indonesia, 1968–70 Highway Services, Summary Report*, for the government of Indonesia, United Nations Development Programme, Djakarta.

Kresge, D. T. and P. O. Roberts (1971). *Systems Analysis and Simulation Models*, Vol. II of *Techniques of Transport Planning* (ed. J. R. Meyer), Brookings Institution.

Kuhn, T. E. and N. D. Lea (1969). 'Engineering-economic systems and analysis for transport planning in Dahomey, West Africa', *Highway Research Record*, **285**, 33–46.

Roberts, P. O. (1971). 'Selecting and staging additions to a transport network' in Meyer, J. R. (Ed.), *Techniques of Transport Planning*, Vol. I, Brooking Institution, 251–75.

Chapter 17

Class Structure in a Capitalist Society and the Theory of Residential Differentiation

David Harvey

The theory of residential differentiation is desperately in need of revision. Sociological explanations of residential differentiation (see the review by Timms, 1971) have never progressed much beyond elaborations on the rather simplistic theme that similar people like to, or just do, live close to each other. The *seeming* complexity of sociological accounts derives from the difficulty of defining 'similar' and the difficulty of showing whether people are similar because they live close to each other or live close to each other because they are similar. The explanations constructed out of neo-classical economic theory are no less simplistic in that they rely upon consumer sovereignty and utility maximising behaviour on the part of individuals which, when expressed in the market context, produces residential differentiation. Complexity in this case arises because it is not easy to give concrete meaning to the utility concept and because it is possible to envisage a wide variety of conditions under which individuals might express their market choices.

Most thoughtful commentators on the matter have concluded that the problem lies in specifying the *necessary* relationships between social structure in general and residential differentiation in particular. For example, Hawley and Duncan (1957, p. 342) remark that:

> 'one searches in vain for a statement explaining why residential areas would differ from one another or be internally homogeneous. The elaborate discussion of social trends accompanying urbanization is nowhere shown to be relevant to this problem.'

Most attempts to integrate social theory and the theory of residential differentiation have produced, in fact:

> 'not a single integrated theory, connecting residential differentiation with societal development, but, rather, two quite distinct theories

which are accidentally articulated to the extent that they happen to share the same operational methods.'

The problem here lies in part in the realm of methodology. Plainly, it is inappropriate to speak of residential differentiation causing or being caused by changes in the total social structure, while a functionalist language, although somewhat more appropriate, is so dominated by the notion of harmonious equilibrium that it cannot deal with the complex dynamics and evolutionary character of a capitalist society. Yet most analysts have been trapped into the use of an inappropriate causal or functionalist language when they have dared to venture beyond statistical descriptions. All of this has produced an enormous amount of material on a variety of facets of the residential differentiation process, but no clue is provided as to how this material might be integrated into general social theory.

The Marxian method, however, founded in the philosophy of internal relations (Ollman, 1971), is fashioned precisely to provide a coherent methodology for relating parts to wholes and wholes to parts. Indeed, the central conception in Marx's version of the dialectic was to view things relationally in order that the integrity of the relationship between the whole and the part should always be maintained. Consequently, Marx criticized the categories of bourgeois social science on the grounds that they are abstractly fashioned without reference to the 'relations which link these abstractions to the totality' (Ollman, 1973, p. 495). Marx's abstractions are of a different kind for they focus on such things as social relations. Relatively simple structures might be isolated from the whole for purposes of analysis, but:

'What is decisive is whether this process of isolation is a means towards understanding the whole and whether it is integrated within the context it presupposes and requires, or whether the abstract knowledge of an isolated fragment retains its "autonomy" and becomes an end in itself' (Lukacs, 1968, p. 8).

The theory of residential differentiation has never been subjected to an analysis from a Marxian standpoint and it is predictable, therefore, that the 'theory' consists of an incoherent mass of 'autonomous' bits and pieces of information, arrived at by means of studies each conceived of as an end in itself and each conceived in terms of relationships specified in a causal, functional or empiricist language (with all the limitations that each of these imposes). And it is predictable that attempts to integrate this material into some general social theory would meet with little or no success. In this essay I shall therefore attempt an outline of the relation between residential differentiation and social structure. Such an investigation is bound to be preliminary and sketchy at this stage. But I shall hope to show where the key relations lie and thereby indicate where we have to look for a revision of the theory of residential differentiation that will make sense.

We will begin with an analysis of the forces creating class structure in advanced capitalist society.

Class and class structure

Theories of class and class structure abound. Marx and Weber laid the basis and a host of contemporary interpreters have added insights, glosses, reinterpretations and, it must be added, mystifications. Rather than attempt a synthesis of this work, I shall sketch in a theory of class which derives primarily from a reading of Marx and secondarily from adapting materials from Giddens (1973) and Poulantzas (1973).

A central tenet of Marx's historical and materialist method is that a concept such as 'class' can take on a meaning only in relation to the historical context in which it is to be applied. 'Class' has a contingent meaning depending upon whether we are considering feudal, capitalist or socialist modes of production. Class theory is not, therefore, a matter of identifying a fixed set of categories which are supposed to apply for all times and places. The relational view of class which Marx espouses focuses our attention on the forces of 'class structuration' (as Giddens, 1973, calls them) which shape actual class configurations. In the context of the capitalist mode of production, however, 'class' has a more specific meaning which relates to the basic social relationships pertaining in capitalist society. The forces of class structuration under capitalism are identical to those contained in the dynamics of capitalism; hence arises a necessary relation between the evolution of capitalist societies and the evolution of social configurations.

Marx argues that the basic social relationship within capitalism is a power relation between capital and labour. This power relation is expressed directly through a market mode of economic integration. Thus the proportion of national product set aside to 'wages' and 'profits' (which includes rents and interest) is determined by the outcome of a class struggle between the representatives of labour (now usually the unions) and capital (usually the employers). Marx also argues that the power relation between the two great classes in society can be understood only in terms of the particular historical conditions achieved with the emergence of the capitalist order. Thus labour power has to assume a commodity character which means that it can be 'freely' bought and sold in the market and that the labourer has legal rights over the disposition of his or her labour. Ownership and control over the means of production gives capital its power over labour since the labourer has to work in order to live and the employer holds control over the means of work. A relatively stable power relation between capital and labour requires for its maintenance a wide variety of institutional, legal, coercive and ideological supports, most of which are either provided or managed through state institutions.

The power relation between capital and labour may be regarded as the *primary* force of class structuration in capitalist society. However, this force does not necessarily generate a dichotomous class structure. The two-class model which Marx presents in Volume 1 of *Capital* is an assumed relation through which he seeks to lay bare the exploitative character of capitalist production – it is not meant as a description of an actual class structure (Marx, 1967 edition, Vol. 1, 44, 167–70 and 508–10; Vol. 2, 421). Marx also distinguishes between the roles of capital and labour and the personifications of those roles – the capitalist, although functioning as a mere personification of capital much of the time is still a human being. The concepts of 'class' and 'class role' function in *Capital* are analytic constructs. Yet Marx often used the dichotomous model of class structure as if it had an empirical content and in his more programmatic writings he insists that socialism will be achieved only through a class struggle that pits the capitalist class against the proletariat.

The reason for this stance is not hard to find. Marx attributed the exploitative character of capitalist society to the capital-labour relation and he also traced the innumerable manifestations of alienation back to this one fundamental source. These negative aspects of capitalist society could be transcended in Marx's view only by transcending the power relation which permitted the domination of labour by capital. The analytic constructs of *Capital* consequently become normative (ought to be) constructs in his programmatic writings. And if actual class struggle crystallised around the capital-labour relation, then both the analytic and normative constructs would come to take on an empirical validity as descriptions of actual social configurations.

But social configurations could crystallise along quite different lines in an actual situation. In *The Eighteenth Brumaire of Louis Bonaparte*, for example, Marx analyses conflict in the France of 1848–51 in terms of the 'class interests' of lumpenproletariat, industrial proletariat, petite bourgeoisie, industrialists, financiers, a landed aristocracy and a peasantry. In using this more complex model of a social configuration, Marx was plainly not saying that France was not capitalist at that time. He was suggesting, rather, that capitalism had evolved at that particular time and in that particular place to a stage in which 'class interests' (often of a myopic and non-revolutionary sort) could and did crystallise around forces other than the fundamental power relation between capital and labour.

It is convenient to designate these forces as 'secondary forces of class structuration' and to divide them into two groups. The first I shall call 'residual' for they stem either from some historically prior mode of production, or from the geographical contact between a dominant and subordinate mode of production. In the early years of capitalism residuals from the feudal order – a landed aristocracy and a peasantry, for example – were very important. Moreover there is evidence that these residual features can be very persistent and last for centuries after the initial penetration of capitalist social relationships. The geographical expansion of capitalism into a global system has also created residuals. The patterns of dominance and subservience associated with colonialism and neo-colonialism are products of an intersection between the forces of class structuration in a dominant capitalist society and forms of social differentiation in subordinate 'traditional' societies. Residual elements may disappear with time or be so transformed that they become almost unrecognisable. But they can also persist. And insofar as transformed residuals become incorporated into the social structure of advanced capitalist societies, they help to explain the existence of 'transitional classes'. Landlordism, preserved in a capitalist form, or a group subjected to neo-colonial domination and transformed into a relatively permanent 'underclass' (Blacks, Puerto Ricans and Chicanos in the United States, for example) are the kinds of features in a social configuration that have to be explained in terms of the residual forces of class structuration.

The other forces of class structuration derive from the dynamics of capitalist society. These 'derivative forces', as we shall designate them, arise because of the necessities generated by the need to preserve the processes of capital accumulation through technological innovation and shifts in social organisation, consumption, and the like. We can identify five such forces (following Giddens, 1973) and we will consider them briefly in turn.

The division of labour and specialization of function
The expansion of production requires improvements in labour productivity and in the forms of industrial organisation, communication, exchange and distribution. These improvements usually mean an increasing division of labour and specialisation of function. As the technical and organisational basis of society changes, so there must be concomitant shifts in social relationships which create the potential for social differentiation. The distinction between manual and intellectual work, for example, may be reflected in the social distinction between blue-collar and white-collar workers. At the same time the growing complexity of economic organization may require the emergence of specialised financial intermediaries in the economy (banking and other financial institutions) which may be reflected in distinctions between financiers and industrialists within the capitalist class as a whole. The division of labour and specialisation of function may fragment the proletariat and the capitalist class into distinctive strata. Social conflict may take place between strata and thus replace class struggle in the Marxian sense as the guiding principle for social differentiation.

Consumption classes or distributive groupings
The progress of capitalist accumulation may be inhibited by the lack of an effective demand for its material products. If we leave aside the

growth of demand inherent in demographic growth and tapping export markets, effective demand depends upon the creation of an internal market to absorb the increasing quantities of material product. Marx (1973 edition, 401–23) argues that the creation of new modes of consumption and of new social wants and needs is essential to the survival of capitalism — otherwise capital accumulation faces an impenetrable barrier of fixed demand which means overproduction and crisis. Malthus (1951 edition, 398–413), in first proposing a version of the Keynesian theory of effective demand, had argued that the existence of a class of 'conspicuous consumers' (primarily the landed aristocracy in his time) was a necessity if sufficient effective demand were to be sustained to permit the accumulation of capital. Malthus's perspective is an interesting one. Not only does he suggest that specific mechanisms have to be employed to stimulate consumption, but that certain consumption classes have to exist to ensure sustained consumption. If this is the case, then social differentiation arises in the sphere of consumption. Distinctive 'consumption classes' or 'distributive groupings' are therefore bound to emerge in the course of capitalist history (Giddens, 1973, 108–10). Since it is empirically observable that 'life-style' and consumption habits vary across different strata in the population and since this is an important differentiating feature in modern society, we may conclude that the emergence of distinctive consumption classes is inherent in the dynamics of capitalist society. Social differentiation can be structured, therefore, according to distribution and consumption criteria (Marx 1973 ed., 402).

Authority relations
The non-market institutions in society must be so ordered that they sustain the power relation between capital and labour and serve to organise production, circulation and distribution. Marx (1967 edition, Vol. I, 330–33) argues, for example, that cooperative activity in production requires a 'directing authority' and that as capitalist production becomes more elaborate, so a specialised group of workers — administrators, managers, foremen, and the like — must assume an authority role in the direction of production. For the economy as a whole these 'management' functions largely lie in the sphere of state activity — understood as the collective amalgam of legal, administrative, bureaucratic, military and political functions (Miliband, 1969). Within this sphere, and within the corporate enterprise, authority relations are the basis for social relationships. In general, the structure of authority relations is coherent with the necessities imposed by the dynamics of accumulation within a social system organised along capitalist lines. But the authority relations *appear* independent of the relation between capital and labour and indeed are, to a certain degree, autonomous in their functioning. The structure of authority relations can, therefore, provide a basis for social differentiation within

the population. Marx (1969 ed., 573) thus writes about the significance of 'the constantly growing number of the middle classes [who] stand between the workman on the one hand and the capitalist and landlord on the other'.

Class consciousness and ideology

Marx argues that a class will become an observable aggregate of individuals only when that aggregate buries all the differences within it and becomes conscious of its class identity in the struggle between capital and labour. Since capitalism has evolved and survived, then presumably it has in part done so by an active intervention in those processes whereby 'class consciousness' in the Marxian sense is created. There is, as it were, a struggle for the 'mind' of labour between, on the one hand, a political class consciousness directed towards the transcendence of the capital-labour relation and, on the other hand, states of 'social awareness' which allow of social differentiations consistent with the accumulation of capital and the perpetuation of the capital-labour relation. The struggle for the mind of labour is a political and ideological struggle. Marx considered that, in general, the ruling ideas in society are ever the ideas of the ruling class. Mass literacy and mass education have the effect of exposing the masses to a dominant 'bourgeois' ideology which seeks to produce states of consciousness consistent with the perpetuation of the capitalist order. Mass culture, or what Marcuse (1968) calls 'affirmative culture' has the function of de-politicising the masses rather than enlightening them as to the real source of alienation in society.

Certain parallel processes can be observed in the political sphere. The survival of capitalism necessitates an increasing state interventionism which, far from being neutral, actively sustains the power relation of capital over labour. In a given instance the state may throw its weight to the side of labour in order to restore some kind of balance between profits and wages, but state intervention is never geared to the transcendence of the capital-labour relation. Yet the state *appears* to be neutral. In part this appearance is real, for state institutions frequently arbitrate between factions of the ruling class (between financiers and industrialists, for example) and between strata in the working population. The separation between the economic and political-administrative spheres which typically arises under capitalism, also permits the state to appear as a neutral party in economic conflict. At the same time the prospects for legal and political equality held out in the political sphere tend to divert attention from the inevitable subordination of labour to capital in the market place. This separation between 'economy' and 'polity' has been, as Giddens (1973, 202–7) points out, a fundamental mediating influence on the production of class consciousness and social awareness in capitalist society. It typically feeds 'trade union consciousness' on the part of labour and a distinctive kind of 'middle class awareness' on the part of intermediate groups in the authority structure which focuses on civil and political liberties to the exclusion of questions of economic control.

Political and ideological struggles, and the manipulation of both, have great significance for understanding the states of consciousness of various strata within the population. Only in terms of such consciousness can we explain how and why a particular problem (say, unemployment) will elicit as a response conflict between capital and labour rather than conflict within labour. The second type of conflict might be between, say, the regularly employed and a largely unemployed 'underclass' which may also be a racial or ethnic minority. The first kind of conflict poses a threat to the capitalist order, whereas the latter kind of conflict does not. It is obviously in the interest of capitalism to transform conflict of the first sort into conflict of the latter variety. Consequently, bourgeois ideology and politics typically seek to forge a consciousness favourable to the perpetuation of the capitalist order and actively seek out ways to draw social distinctions along lines other than that between capital and labour.

Mobility chances
The accelerating pace of change in the organisation of production, exchange, communication and consumption, necessitates considerable adaptability in the population. Individuals must be prepared to alter their skills, geographical locations, consumption habits, and the like. This means that mobility chances must always be present within the population. Yet a completely 'open' society as far as mobility is concerned would undoubtedly create considerable instability. In order to give social stability to a society in which social change is necessary, some systematic way has to be found for organising mobility chances. This entails the structuring of mobility chances in certain important ways.

In capitalist society, mobility is organised so that most movement takes place between one stratum within the division of labour to another (from, say, the manual to the white-collar category). The mechanisms for achieving this 'controlled' kind of mobility appear to lie in part in the differential distribution (both socially and geographically) of opportunities to acquire what Giddens (1973, 103) calls 'market capacity' — that bundle of skills and attributes which permits individuals to market their labour power within certain occupational categories or to operate in certain functional roles. Restrictions and barriers to mobility chances give rise to social differentiations. Insofar as professional groups, for example, have better access to the acquisition of market capacity for their children, a professional 'class' may become self-perpetuating. Once intergenerational mobility is limited, social distinctions become relatively fixed features in the social landscape and provide the possibility for the crystallization of social differentiation within the population as a whole.

The argument so far suggests that we can identify three kinds of forces making for social differentiation within the population:

1. a primary force arising out of the power relation between capital and labour;
2. a variety of secondary forces arising out of the contradictory and evolutionary character of capitalism which encourage social differentiation along lines defined by (a) the division of labour and specialisation of function, (b) consumption patterns and 'life style', (c) authority relations, (d) manipulated projections of ideological and political consciousness and (e) barriers to mobility chances; and
3. residual forces reflecting the social relations established in a preceding or geographically separate but subordinate mode of production.

In general we can see a perpetual struggle amongst these forces between those which create class configurations antagonistic to the perpetuation of the capitalist order and those which create social differentiations favourable to the replication of capitalist society.

Residential differentiation and the social order

The accumulation of capital on a progressively increasing scale has set in motion a distinctive and rapidly accelerating urbanization process. The distinctive features of this process need not delay us here (see Harvey, 1973; Castells, 1972; Lefebvre, 1970; 1972). For the purpose at hand it is sufficient to note the progressive concentration of the population in large urban centres. There has been a parallel fragment-ation of social structure as the primary, residual and derivative forces of social differentiation have interacted over a century or more. Let us now locate these processes of progressive concentration and social fragmentation in the built environment we call the city, and fashion some basic hypotheses to connect residential differentiation with social structure. Four hypotheses can be stated:

1. residential differentiation is to be interpreted in terms of the reproduction of the social relations within capitalist society;
2. residential areas ('neighbourhoods', 'communities') provide distinctive milieus for social interaction from which individuals to a considerable degree derive their values, expectations, con-sumption habits, market capacities and states of consciousness;
3. the fragmentation of large concentrations of population into

distinctive communities serves to fragment 'class consciousness' in the Marxian sense and thereby frustrates the transformation from capitalism to socialism through class struggle; but

4. patterns of residential differentiation reflect and incorporate many of the contradictions in capitalist society; the processes creating and sustaining them are consequently the locus of instability and contradiction.

These hypotheses, when fleshed out and if proven, provide a necessary link between residential differentiation and the social order. In the short space of this chapter, I can only sketch in a very general argument in support of them.

Residential differentiation in the capitalist city means differential access to the scarce resources required to acquire 'market capacity' (Giddens, 1973; Harvey, 1973, Chapter 2). For example, differential access to educational opportunity — understood in broad terms as those experiences derived from family, geographical neighbourhood and community, classroom and the mass media — facilitates the inter-generational transference of market capacity and typically leads to the restriction of mobility chances. Opportunities may be so structured that a white collar labour force is 'reproduced' in a white collar neighbourhood, a blue-collar labour force is 'reproduced' in a blue collar neighbourhood, and so on. The community is the place of reproduction in which labour power suitable for the place of production is reproduced. This is a tendency only, of course, and there are many forces modifying or even offsetting it. And the relationships are by no means simple. Market capacity, defined in terms of the ability to undertake certain kinds of functions within the division of labour, comprises a whole set of attitudes, values and expectations as well as distinctive skills. The relationship between function and the acquisition of market capacity can sometimes be quite tight — thus miners are for the most part reproduced in mining communities. But in other cases the relationship may be much looser — a white collar grouping, for example, comprises a wide range of occupational categories but it is still differentiable, both socially and spatially, from other groupings.

Residential groupings which reproduce labour power to meet the needs of an existing division of labour may also form a distinctive grouping from the standpoint of consumption. Such a coalescence gives residential differentiation a much more homogeneous character. One thread of necessity as opposed to contingency in this relationship lies in the consumption of education which unifies a 'consumption class' with a grouping based in the division of labour. This thread is too slender to hang a proof on (although in the United States the connections between residential differentiation and the quality of education are very strong and a constant source of conflict and social tension). The full story rests on showing how attitudes generated out of the work experience imply certain parallel attitudes in the consumption sphere. To trace this connection is difficult, but it appears reasonable to suppose that the quality of the work experience and the attitudes necessary to perform that work under specific social conditions must be reflected, somehow or other, by attitudes and behaviours in the place of residence.

The relationships between values, consciousness, ideology and life experiences are crucial — and they are the most profoundly difficult to unravel. From the standpoint of the creation of residential differentiation, it is plain that individuals do make choices and do express preferences. To sustain the argument, therefore, I have to show that the preferences and value systems, and perhaps even the choices themselves, are produced by forces external to the individual's will. The idea of an autonomously and spontaneously arising consumer sovereignty as the explanation of residential differentiation could be fairly easily disposed of (even though it is the prevalent myth that underlies conventional theories of residential differentiation). But it is more difficult to know what exactly to put in its place. And it is far too glib to attribute everything to the blandishments of the 'ad-men', however, important they may be.

If we ask, however, where peoples' values come from and what is it that creates them then it is plain that the community provides a social milieu out of which distinctive value systems, aspirations and expectations may be drawn. The neighbourhood is, as it were, the primary source of socialisation experiences (Newson and Newson, 1970). Insofar as residential differentiation produces distinctive communities we can expect a disaggregation of this process. Working class neighbourhoods, for example, typically 'produce' individuals with values conducive to being in the working class and these values, deeply embedded as they are in the cognitive, linguistic and moral codes of the community, become an integral part of the conceptual equipment which individuals use to deal with the world (Giglioli, 1972). The stability of such neighbourhoods and of the value systems that characterize the people in them have been remarkable considering the dynamics of change in most capitalist cities. The reproduction of such value systems facilitates the reproduction of consumption classes as well as groupings with respect to the division of labour while it also functions to restrict mobility chances. Values and attitudes to education, for example, vary greatly and affect the consumption of education — one of the main means for obtaining mobility chances (Robson, 1969). The homogenisation of life experiences which this restriction produces reinforces the tendency for relatively permanent social groupings to emerge within a relatively permanent structure of residential differentiation. Once this is translated into a social awareness that has the neighbourhood or community as the focus and once this form of social awareness becomes the basis for political action, then 'community consciousness' replaces 'class consciousness' (of the Marxian sort) as the springboard for action and the locus of social conflict.

Once such groupings form it is relatively easy to understand how they may be perpetuated. But we also have to understand the history of such groupings because contemporary social differentiations have been arrived at by successive transformations and fragmentations of preceding social configurations. The reciprocity exhibited in working class neighbourhoods is to a large degree a defensive device constructed out of the transformation under capitalism of a well-tried and ancient mode of economic integration (Harvey, 1973, Chapter 6). In the United States immigrant waves at particular periods in the evolution of the capitalist division of labour gave a strong ethnic flavour to certain occupational categories as well as to certain residual neighbourhoods; both persist to the present day. The continued domination of blacks following the transformation of slavery, and the more modern neo-colonial domination of Puerto Ricans and Chicanos has produced the ghetto as a 'Third World Colony' in the heart of the American city, and it is broadly true that the 'underclass' in American society is identified with neo-colonial repression based in racism (Blaut, 1973). The historical roots of social and residential differentiation are important. But then so also are the processes of social transformation that produce new social groupings within a social configuration.

Consider, for example, the emergence of a distinctive 'middle class', literate and skilled in mental labour, possessed of the dominant bourgeois ideology that McPherson (1962) felicitously calls 'possessive individualism', attached as a consequence to certain distinctive modes of consumption, imbued with a political view that focuses on civil and political liberties and instilled with the notion that economic advancement is solely a matter of individual ability, dedication and personal ambition (as if everyone could become a successful doctor, lawyer, manager, and the like, if they only tried hard enough). The emergence of such a middle class over the past century or so has become etched into the city by the creation of distinctive middle class neighbourhoods with distinctive opportunities to acquire market capacity. In more recent times affluent workers and white collar employees have been encouraged to copy the middle class life style. And in the American city this process has been associated since the 1930s in particular with a strong suburbanisation process. How do we explain the way in which the emergence of such social groupings relates to the process of residential differentiation?

The answer to this question depends in part upon an understanding of the processes whereby residential differentiation is produced by the organisation of forces external to the individual or even to the collective will of the particular social grouping. These processes stretch back over a relatively long time period and it is probably the case that

residential differentiation in the contemporary sense was well established in most major cities in both the United States and Britain by
1850. In certain basic respects the processes have not changed however,
for we still have to turn to the examination of the activities of
speculator-developers, speculator-landlords and real estate brokers,
backed by the power of financial and governmental institutions for an
explanation of how the built environment and residential neighbourhoods are actually produced. I have attempted a full description of this
process in the American city elsewhere (Harvey, 1974) and so I shall
merely offer a summary of it here.

Financial and governmental institutions are hierarchically ordered by
authority relations broadly consistent with the support of the capitalist
order. They function to coordinate 'national needs' (understood in
terms of the reproduction of capitalist society and the accumulation of
capital) with local activities and decisions — in this manner, micro- and
macro-aspects of housing market behaviour are coordinated. These
institutions regulate the dynamic of the urbanisation process (usually in
the interest of accumulation and economic crisis management) and also
wield their influence in such a way that certain broad patterns in
residential differentiation are produced. The creation of distinctive
housing sub-markets (largely through the mortgage market) improves
the efficiency with which institutions can manage the urbanisation
process. But at the same time it limits the ability of individuals to make
choices. Further, it creates a structure which individuals can potentially
choose from, but which individuals cannot influence the production of.

If residential differentiation is in large degree produced, then
individuals have to adapt their preferences. The market mechanism
curtails the range of choice (with the poorest having no choice since
they can take up only what is left over after more affluent groups have
chosen). The shaping of preferences of more affluent groups poses a
more serious problem. The 'ad-man' plays an important role and
considerations of status and prestige are likewise important. Consider,
also, a white collar worker forced to suburbanise (by a process I have
elsewhere dubbed 'blow out' — Harvey, 1973, Chapter 5) because of
deteriorating conditions in the inner city; the preference in this case
may be a somewhat shallow post-hoc rationalisation of a 'choice' that
really was no choice. Dissatisfaction within such a group can easily
surface. For example, a suburbanite angered by the prospect of gasoline
shortages and recollecting the 'convenience' of inner city living,
complains that 'we have all been had' because in order 'to mould into
the lifestyle dictated by builders, developers and county planners, I
have no choice but to provide my family with two automobiles' — one
to get to work and the other to operate a household (Baltimore Sun,
11th February, 1974). The consumption values attached to suburban
living are plainly not open to choice once the location decision is made
and that decision may itself not be the outcome of a real choice.

Indeed, a strong argument can be made that suburbanisation is a creation of the capitalist mode of production in very specific ways. First, suburbanisation is actively produced because it sustains an effective demand for products and thereby facilitates the accumulation of capital. Second, the changing division of labour in capitalist society has created a distinctive group of white collar workers who, largely by virtue of their literacy and their work conditions, are imbued with the ideology of competitive and possessive individualism, all of which appears uniquely appropriate for the production of a mode of consumption which we typically dub 'suburban'. It is intriguing to note that since the 1930s the United States has experienced the most sustained rate of economic growth (capital accumulation), the greatest growth in the white collar sector and the most rapid rate of suburbanisation of all the advanced capitalist nations. These phenomena are not unconnected.

We can, thus, interpret the 'preference' for suburban living as a created myth, arising out of possessive individualism, nurtured by the 'ad-man' and forced by the logic of capitalist accumulation. But like all such myths, once established it takes on a certain autonomy out of which strong contradictions may emerge. The American suburb, formed as an economic and social response to problems internal to capitalist accumulation, now forms an entrenched barrier to social and economic change. The political power of the suburbs is used conservatively, to defend the life style and the privileges and to exclude unwanted growth. In the process a deep irrationality emerges in the geography of the capitalist production system (residential and job opportunities may become spatially separated from each other, for example). The exclusion of further growth creates a further problem for if a 'no-growth' movement gathers momentum, then how can effective demand and capital accumulation be sustained? A phenomenon created to sustain the capitalist order can in the long run work to exacerbate its internal tensions.

This conclusion can possibly be extended to all aspects of social and residential differentiation. The social differentiations reproduced within the capitalist order are so structured as to facilitate the reproduction of the social relations of capitalism. As a result 'community consciousness' rather than 'class consciousness' in the Marxian sense is dominant in the capitalist city. In this fashion the danger of an emergent class consciousness in the large concentrations of population to be found in urban areas has been averted by the fragmentation of class consciousness through residential differentiation. But 'community consciousness' with all of its parochialisms, once created, becomes deeply embedded and it becomes just as difficult to piece it together in a configuration appropriate to the national interest (as perceived from the standpoint of capital accumulation) as it is to transform into a class consciousness antagonistic to the perpetuation of the capitalist order. In order, therefore, to maintain its own dynamic, capitalism is forced to disrupt and destroy what it initially created as part of its own strategy for self-preservation. Communities have to be disrupted by speculative activity, growth must occur, and whole residential neighbourhoods transformed to meet the needs of capital accumulation (Harvey, 1975). Herein lie both the contradictions and the potentials for social transformation in the urbanisation sphere at this stage in our history.

Residential differentiation is produced, in its broad lineaments at least by forces emanating from the capitalist production process and it is not to be construed as the product of the autonomously and spontaneously arising preferences of people. Yet people are constantly searching to express themselves and to realise their potentialities in their day-to-day life-experiences in the work place, in the community, and in the home. Much of the micro-variation in the urban fabric testifies to these ever present impulses. But there is a scale of action at which the individual loses control of the social conditions of existence in the face of forces mobilised through the capitalist production process (in the community this means the congeries of interests represented by speculators, developers, financial institutions, big government, and the like). It is at this boundary that individuals come to sense their own helplessness in the face of forces that do not appear amenable, under given institutions, even to collective political mechanisms of control. As we cross this boundary we move from a situation in which individuals can express their individuality and relate in human terms to each other, to one in which individuals have no choice but to conform and in which social relations between people become replaced by market relations between things.

Residential differentiation at this latter scale plays a vital role in the perpetuation and reproduction of the alienating social relationships of capitalist society. Yet in the process of seeking stratagems for self-perpetuation, the forces of capitalist accumulation create value systems, consumption habits, states of awareness and political conscious-ness and even whole built environments, which, with the passage of time inhibit the expansion of the capitalist order. The permanently revolutionary character of capitalist society perpetually tears down the barriers it has erected to protect itself. The constant re-shaping of urban environments and of the structures of residential differentiation are testimony to this never-ending process. Instead, therefore, of regarding residential differentiation as the passive product of a preference system based in social relationships, we have to see it as an integral mediating influence in the processes whereby class relationships and social differentiations are produced and sustained. It is clear, even at this preliminary stage in the analysis, that the theory of residential differentiation has much to offer as well as to gain from a thorough-going integration with general social theory.

REFERENCES

Blaut, J. M. (1974). 'The ghetto as an internal neo-colony', *Antipode*, 6, 1, 37—41.

Castells, M. (1972). *La Question Urbaine*, Maspero.

Gappert, G. and H. Rose (Eds.), *Annual Reviews of Urban Affairs*, 9, Sage.

Giddens, A. (1973). *The Class Structure of the Advanced Societies*, Hutchinson.

Giglioli, P. (Ed.) (1972). *Language and Social Context*, Penguin Books.

Harvey, D. (1973). *Social Justice and the City*, Edward Arnold.

Harvey, D. (1974). 'Class-monopoly rent, finance capital and the urban revolution', *Regional Studies*, 8, 3.

Harvey, D. (1975). 'The political economy of urbanization in advanced capitalist societies — the case of the United States', in *The Political Economy of Cities*, Annual Review of Urban Affairs, 9, Sage.

Hawley, A. H. and O. D. Duncan (1957). 'Social area analysis', *Land Economics*, 33, 340—51.

Lefebvre, H. (1970). *La Revolution Urbaine*, Gallimard.

Lefebvre, H. (1972). *Le Droit à la Ville*, Editions Anthropos.

Lukacs, G. (1968 edition). *History and Class Consciousness*, Merlin.

McPherson, C. B. (1962). *The Political Theory of Possessive Individualism*, Oxford University Press.

Malthus, T. (1951 edition). *The Principles of Political Economy*, A. M. Kelley. New York.

Marcuse, H. (1968). *Negations: Essays in Critical Theory*, Beacon Press.

Marx, K. (1963 edition). *The Eighteenth Brumaire of Louis Bonaparte*, International Publishers.

Marx, K. (1967 edition). *Capital*, International Publishers.

Marx, K. (1969 edition). *Theories of Surplus Value*, part 2, Lawrence and Wishart.

Marx, K. (1973 edition). *The Grundrisse*, Pelican Books.

Miliband, R. (1969). *The State in Capitalist Society*, Weidenfeld and Nicholson.

Newson, E. and J. (1970). *Four Years Old in an Urban Community*, Pelican Books.

Ollman, B. (1971). *Alienation: Marx's Conception of Man in Capitalist Society*, Cambridge University Press.

Ollman, B. (1973). 'Marxism and political science: a prologomenon to a debate on Marx's method', *Politics and Society*, 3, 491—510.

Poulantzas, N. (1973). *Political Power and Social Classes*, New Left Books.

Robson, B. (1969). *Urban Analysis: a Study in City Structure*, Cambridge University Press.

Timms, D. (1971). *The Urban Mosaic: Towards a Theory of Residential Segregation*, Cambridge University Press.

PART VI

Temporal Processes in
Human Geography

Chapter 18

Simple Epidemics in Human Populations: Some Geographical Aspects of the Hamer-Soper Diffusion Models

Peter Haggett

Introduction

In 1906, the English epidemiologist, Sir William Hamer, described a simple mathematical model of the way in which epidemics diffuse through a human population. In the succeeding seventy-odd years, Hamer's model has been greatly enriched and extended by a succession of distinguished epidemiologists and mathematicians. Its original deterministic form has been replaced by more realistic stochastic assumptions and its structure has been enlarged to accommodate complex multi-stage diseases like malaria. But despite the gains made this class of models remains geographically somewhat naive, i.e. the models are dominantly aspatial or introduce space only in a simple and limited way.

Actual observation of epidemics shows them to have a complex and intricate geographical pattern. For example, studies of the origin and spread of the 1832, 1849, and 1866 cholera epidemics in the United States led Pyle (1969) to recognise two distinct spatial processes, a linear spread following the inland waterways and a hierarchical spread from large cities to small. Gilg (1973) studied the spread of the 1970—71 fowl-pest epizootic in England and Wales, finding a 'threshold wave' rather than a 'multiple-innovation centre' diffusion pattern. Studies of multiple epidemics of measles in South-west England conducted at Bristol University (Haggett, 1972; Cliff, Haggett, Ord, Bassett and Davies, 1975) show a swash-and-backwash cycle of outbreak and retreat around the endemic pacemaker centres of Bristol and Plymouth.

So far, the study of epidemics as a large-scale spread phenomenon (as distinct from the small-scale clinical problem) has proceeded along rather separate lines — abstract model building on the one hand, empirical case studies on the other. In this essay we look at ways in which some progress can be made towards twining the two strands into hybrid spatial models. Ideally, such hybrids should retain something of the mathematical rigour and generality of the one while catching some of the geographical detail of the other.

The Hamer—Soper models

In this first section we introduce some basic definitions and define the Hamer—Soper model in its simplest form.

Definitions: epidemics, systems, and models

By *epidemic* we refer to a phenomenon that invades a population and spreads through it at particular times, in contrast to one which is always present (*endemic*) in a population. Although contagious diseases are used here to illustrate epidemic processes it is worth noting that the original use of the term is entirely general (epidemic means literally, 'close upon the people'). Much of what we discuss here is also appropriate to other diffusion processes, such as the spread of rumours or technical innovations. Dietz (1967) provides a review of epidemic theory in both the traditional disease meaning and in these wider fields.

A set of components relevant to an epidemic together with the links between them form an epidemic *system*. For example, we should expect the system describing an influenza outbreak to include components describing the density of a population, its age and sex structure and its geographical distribution within any area affected. A *model* of any such system is a simplified version designed to illustrate its essential properties in an economical and efficient manner. We would expect the model to duplicate or 'mimic' the behaviour of the system.

Models of any epidemic system may vary greatly. Simple and uncomplicated situations may be described entirely in qualitative terms, or be contained wholly within the mind of a given investigator. More complex situations will demand that the initial conditions, assumptions, and structure be stated more formally, usually in a mathematical form.

Let us assume we have a population under attack by an infection. How can we describe this by a model? One approach would be to set down all the facts we can possibly find out about the situation and attempt to incorporate these into a model. Unfortunately, this procedure is likely to give rise to a very congested situation with too many variables to be adequately handled, even by today's large-scale computers. A more feasible approach is to begin with the simplest kind of statement we can make. From this very elementary model we can go on to add in complexities, one at a time, as we become more confident of our infant model.

Structure of the Hamer—Soper models
One such simple model was proposed at the beginning of the century by Hamer (1906), subsequently modified by Soper (1929) and greatly refined by modern workers like Bailey (1957) and Bartlett (1956). These models, which we shall term the Hamer—Soper models, assume a *population* (P) which is split into three distinct components. First, the *susceptibles* (S) who are at risk from an infection; second, the *infectives* (I) who have the disease and are liable to pass it on through contact with the susceptibles; and third, the *recovereds* (R) who have already been exposed to the infection and have recovered or who are immune to it from some other cause (e.g. vaccination). Note that in this simple case we ignore the possibility of carriers, individuals who appear to have recovered but can still pass on the disease. We also assume that infection gives eventual immunity and ignore the presence of non-human vectors of disease transmission. The Hamer—Soper models are not likely to be of help in modelling diseases like malaria, but may serve to throw light on much simpler contagious diseases like measles. Indeed, measles, because of its simplicity and its high rate of incidence, has tended to be the classic test disease for epidemic model building.

The three basic versions of the Hamer—Soper model are shown in Figure 18.1.

Model I. If we assume our population is subject to some process of homogenous mixing then the number of new infections will be a function of SI and the infectiousness of the disease, measured by an infection rate β. Changes occurring over time are given by two basic differential equations:

$$\left.\begin{aligned}\frac{dS}{dt} &= -\beta SI\\[2mm]\frac{dI}{dt} &= +\beta SI\end{aligned}\right\} \tag{1}$$

For computation purposes, we can replace these equations with simple step-by-step difference equations in which each interval of time (t) is a small period such as one week, viz.

$$\left.\begin{aligned}S_{t+1} &= S_t - \beta S_t I_t\\[2mm]I_{t+1} &= I_t + \beta S_t I_t\end{aligned}\right\} \tag{2}$$

Figure 18.2a shows a graph of the number of susceptibles falling and of infectives rising in characteristic logistic curves. These logistic curves

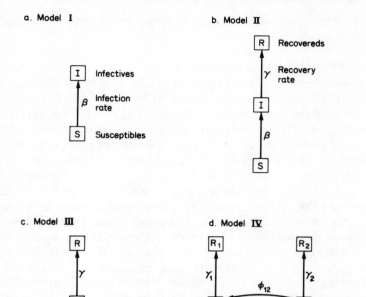

Figure 18.1 Structure of the four basic Hamer—Soper models.

have been widely reported in studies of cultural innovations in human populations.

Model II. Clearly our first model describes a situation in which an epidemic terminates only when all the population is infected. But most observed epidemics burn themselves out after only some proportion of the population is infected. Model II takes into account the removal rate or recovery rate of infected persons, given by γ (see Figure 18.1b). To incorporate this extension equations (1) and (2) must be modified as follows:

$$
\left.
\begin{aligned}
\frac{dS}{dt} &= -\beta SI \\[2mm]
\frac{dI}{dt} &= \beta SI - \gamma I \\[2mm]
\frac{dR}{dt} &= \gamma I
\end{aligned}
\right\}
\tag{3}
$$

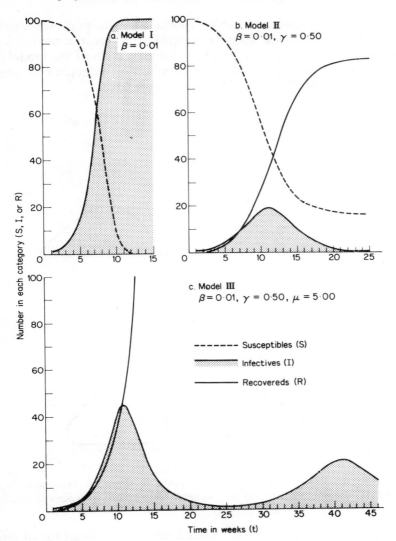

Figure 18.2   Graphs of the characteristic paths of Models, I, II and III with parameters β, γ, μ set at the values shown.

$$\left. \begin{array}{l} S_{t+1} = S_t - \beta S_t I_t \\ I_{t+1} = I_t + \beta S_t I_t - \gamma I_t \\ R_{t+1} = R_t + \gamma I_t \end{array} \right\} \qquad (4)$$

Figure 18.2b shows a graph of the values of S, I, and R varying over time. Note the characteristic bell-shaped curve of infections and the fact that not all susceptibles are infected. Clearly Model II describes certain occasional epidemics which follow a simple single-wave pattern and in which the disease must be reintroduced into the population to start another and separate wave. This 'closed' version of the model has a characteristic trajectory when the number of infectives is plotted against the number of susceptibles as in Figure 18.3.

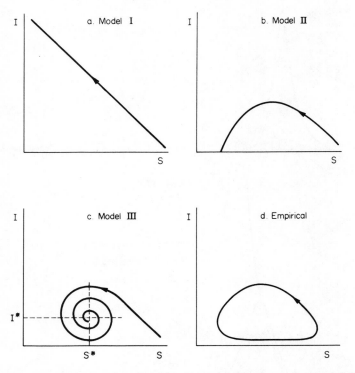

Figure 18.3   General pattern of epidemic paths in terms of susceptibles (S) and infectives (I) for Models I, II and III compared to the paths of recurrent outbreaks.

Model III. Can we extend this closed model to account for situations where the epidemic does not die out? For example, measles is a childhood disease that does not die out in a country the size of the United Kingdom but flares up in major epidemics approximately every two years. Figure 18.4 shows the remarkably regular pattern of the 33 major measles epidemics that have occurred in Denmark over the period 1868–1968. Clearly, we need to modify our model to attempt to replicate this regular wavelike form.

One candidate for the missing ingredient in the closed model is the influx of susceptibles, mainly due to births within the country. The simplest way to convert our closed model to an 'open epidemic' model is to introduce a birth parameter (μ) so as to give μdt new susceptibles in time dt. The first equation in our differential equations (1) must now

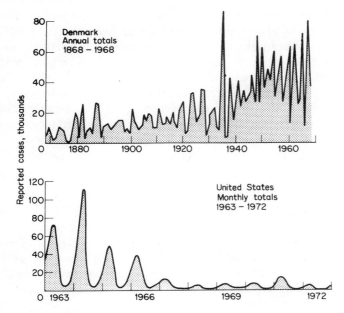

Figure 18.4　　Recurrent epidemic waves. Annual data for measles cases in Denmark over a hundred-year period. Monthly data for measles cases in the United States for a ten-year period: note the declining amplitude of epidemic waves due to vaccination campaigns begun in the late 1960s. (*Source:* Denmark, Udgivet af Sundhedsstyrelsen, 1972; United States Public Health Service, 1972.)

be rewritten:

$$\frac{dS}{dt} = -\beta SI + \mu \tag{5}$$

and our difference equation (2) similarly amended:

$$S_{t+1} = S_t - \beta S_t I_t + \mu \tag{6}$$

The impact of this additional parameter on the typical performance of the model is shown in Figure 18.2c. Note also the characteristic spiral form of the epidemic path (Figure 18.3c). If we follow this around it finally arrives at an equilibrium point (S^*, I^*) given by the equations

$$\left. \begin{array}{l} S^* = \gamma/\beta \\[2mm] I^* = \mu/\gamma \end{array} \right\} \tag{7}$$

The trajectories for the three components, S, I, and R show the characteristic trait of recurrent epidemic waves. While this is roughly in accord with the observed pattern of recurrent epidemics of diseases like measles, these show no tendency to die out (see Figure 18.3d), whereas in our model the amplitude of the waves decreases until an endemic equilibrium state is reached. Actual records show much variability in the length of the wave period whereas our simple model predicts waves with a constant period. Later workers have been able to modify the model in important ways to overcome these drawbacks through (a) introducing chance or stochastic elements into the model, and (b) introducing seasonal variations in the infectivity parameter (β) to give seasonal peaking. These developments are not pursued further in this essay.

Spatial extensions of the model

The simple models described so far are essentially aspatial: all flows between S, I, and R occur within a single population. Geographical detail can be built into the model's structure in a number of ways, not all of which have yet been explored. Here we review two lines of inquiry: (a) interactions between separate populations, and (b) epidemics as diffusion waves.

Interactions between separate 'island' populations

As a first step, let us assume our infected population is split into two components (P_1 and P_2) occupying two geographically separate 'islands'. If there is no contact at all between the two populations, equations (3) may be solved independently for each. More realistically, there will be some interaction between the two populations which can be built into the model by defining specific migration rates. Figure 18.1d is an extension of Figure 18.1c and shows Model IV which includes the migration rates of susceptibles (θ) and infectives (ϕ) between the two islands. Movements of recovereds are ignored since the model assumes they do not affect the course of the epidemic.

Equations (3) and (5) can now be extended for the first island:

$$\left.\begin{aligned}
\frac{dS_1}{dt} &= -(\beta_1 I_1 + \beta_2 I_2)S_1 + \mu + \theta(S_2 - S_1) \\
\frac{dI_1}{dt} &= (\beta_1 I_1 + \beta_2 I_2)S_2 - \gamma I_1 + \phi(I_2 - I_1)
\end{aligned}\right\} \tag{8}$$

(Bailey, 1957, p. 141). A similar pair of equations describes the distribution of the epidemic over time for S_2 and I_2 in the second island. Recent mathematical work has allowed extension of the stochastic version of the 'open' epidemic model to a series of islands. Although in principle there is no limit to the number of islands that could be included in the model, the fast growth in the number of island pairs to be considered tends to lead to computational intractability in practice.

Geographers have shown particular interest in modelling the spatial interaction between populations. The studies started with Ravenstein's work in the 1880s on migration flows and were extended in a series of 'gravity' type models from the 1920s onward. The heuristic form of these models has been replaced by an improved theoretical framework by Wilson (1970). The standard form of the model is as follows:

$$F_{ij} = A_i O_i B_j D_j e^{-\alpha d_{ij}} \qquad (9)$$

Where F_{ij} is the flow interaction or interaction between the ith and jth locations, o_i is the total population to be transferred from the ith origin, D_j the total population to be transferred to the jth destination, and d_{ij} is the distance between the ith and jth location. A_i, B_j and α are parameters, functions of the distance (d_{ij}), the Lagrangean multipliers and an overall budget constraint on the amount of transport costs.

Although such models have not been used extensively in epidemic studies, they are clearly of potential importance. The migration parameters θ and ϕ in equations (8) will themselves vary over space in a way analogous to F_{ij} in equation (9). We should expect both to be very high in situations where two island populations (or urban populations) were large and near each other; conversely, we should expect both to be low where the two island populations are simultaneously very small and remote from each other.

Epidemics as diffusion waves
The concept of an epidemic wave moving outwards from a single source or several sources (mononuclear or polynuclear) has formed the central idea in the last twenty years of diffusion research in geography. The early Swedish work of Hägerstrand in the 1950s, the subsequent development of Monte Carlo simulation models, and the extension to forecasting is now well established.

Diffusion as an isotropic process: Let us assume that our susceptible population S is evenly distributed over an area and that infectives I are freshly introduced at a single point. If we assume that the probability of contact is inversely related to geographic distance, then members of the susceptible population near to the introduction point will be infected early in an epidemic. Conversely, members of the susceptible population remote from the introduction point will be infected late in the epidemic. Thus the epidemic will take the form of a circle expanding outwards from the original focus of infection.

We can build this concept of an epidemic as a diffusion wave by changing the birth rate, μ, in equation (5) from a constant to a time-dependent variable. If we assume the infection spreads at a constant radial velocity in each time period, then:

$$\mu_{t+1} = \pi(2t + 1) \qquad (10)$$

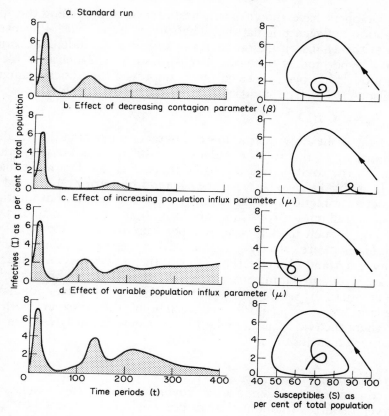

Figure 18.5   The impact of changing parameters on the path of a Model III epidemic. The standard run has values of $\beta = 0.0075$, $\gamma = 0.50$, and $\mu = 0.02$. (*Source*: Long, 1974.)

At each time period a new ring of susceptibles at the edge of the circle is added to the population. Figure 18.5c shows the effect of introducing this incrementing 'birth rate' into the Hamer–Soper model. When compared to constant values of μ (see Figure 18.5a) the two main effects are (i) to decrease the wavelength of the infection cycles and (ii) to increase their amplitude.

In practice, we would expect the geographical distribution of S not to be uniform. Let us assume that our susceptible population is distributed as a bivariate normal distribution and that our infection begins at a location somewhere on its slopes. As the epidemic spreads, the values of μ will at first increase rapidly with t but fall later on as the main distribution of S has been encompassed and the distant waves of the epidemic are extending into remote areas with progressively lower densities of susceptibles. As Figure 18.5d shows, the impact on the trajectory of I in the Hamer–Soper model is complex.

Directional vectors in the diffusion process: the essentially random nature of contacts in the diffusion of infection from a single source suggests that the phenomenon may be described as a simple Gaussian diffusion model. Let us assume an instantaneous point source for an epidemic diffusing in two dimensions. For a source of strength Q at origin (0, 0) the intensity is denoted by $R(u, v, t)$, where u, v are the co-ordinates of a point in space and t is the time of spread of the epidemic. The degree of spread is indicated by the standard deviation (δ) in the two spatial dimensions (σ_v, σ_u). If we assume an isotropic situation where diffusion is equally likely in all directions from the origin, then $\sigma_u = \sigma_v$.

More usually it is assumed that diffusion takes place independently in the two co-ordinate directions and that there is an additional vector Z operating in the u direction. Given these assumptions, then:

$$R(u, v, t) = \frac{Q(2\pi)^{-3/2}}{\sigma_u \sigma_v} \exp\left\{ -\left[\frac{(u - zt)^2}{2\sigma_u{}^2} + \frac{v^2}{2\sigma_v{}^2} \right] \right\} \tag{11}$$

(Gustafson and Kortanek, 1972, p. 31). This expression gives a so-called 'Gaussian puff kernel' which may assume various spatial forms depending on the relative strengths of the parameters. Figure 18.6 illustrates a representative spread process, where $\sigma_u = 2$, $\sigma_v = 1$, and $Z = 1$.

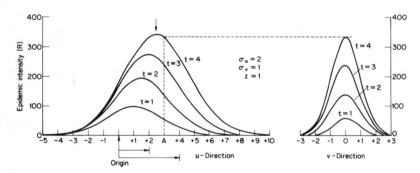

Figure 18.6   Cross section through a Gaussian diffusion spread process.

Equation (11) is one of a series developed in three dimensions by Sutton, Pasquill and other meteorologists for the study of atmospheric diffusion in general and pollution distribution in particular. They are of some interest in the study of disease diffusion if appropriate analogies can be found for the Z vector, normally identified with mean wind speed in the meteorological case. (There are of course cases of epidemics and epizootics where wind may play a critical part; see Tinline's 1973 study of the 1967 foot-and-mouth epizootic in England and Wales.) Linking back to equation (9) may give some clue to the direction in which research may lie. For any area, the direction of maximum interaction (max F_{ij}) may be the demographic equivalent of the dominant 'downwind' direction. Where there are several strong interaction forces, a vector resolution may be needed to determine a single direction.

The velocity of epidemic spread: Bailey (1957, pp. 143—45) has extended consideration of epidemics starting from a single focus and expanding radially to derive the limiting value for the velocity of propagation. But just how fast do diseases move through populations? A classic example, the spread of the Black Death in western Europe between the autumn of 1347 and the spring of 1351, suggests an average speed of travel of the wave-front of about 16 km per week. This average conceals a range of velocities in different parts of the continent, varying from as low as 4 km to as high as 28 km per week. In practice, direct measurement of the velocity of epidemic spread in human populations is likely to be made difficult by the complexity of local demographic factors (e.g. density, age structure, etc.).

Velocity of propagation may also be measured indirectly in terms of the duration of an epidemic. Epidemics that are short-lived may, *ceteris paribus*, be expected to move faster through a population than those which are long-lived. Some findings by Black (1966) on the spread of measles in island populations are shown in Table 18.1. This plots the duration of an epidemic (in months) against the expected spacing of the susceptible population (in km) for seven islands with roughly similar populations. Since small outbreaks were often stopped artificially by local quarantine arrangements, only epidemics involving 100 or more notified cases were used in calculating extinction times. Expected spacing (D_E) is calculated in the following manner:

$$D_E = \frac{1}{2\sqrt{S/A}} \tag{12}$$

where S is the size of the susceptible population and A is the area of the island in km^2. The 'susceptible population' is defined by Black as the annual number of births less infant mortality, effectively the number of children reaching their first birthday.

Despite the limited size of his sample, Black's results show a marked inverse relation between epidemic duration and population spacing. Epidemics appear to be much shorter on the high-density islands than on the low-density: the average relationship shown by the linear regression line suggests that with zero spacing (i.e. maximum crowding) an epidemic would burn itself out in about four months in populations of this size range.

An alternative approach to velocity of propagation is through the concentration of cases over time. An epidemic which moves swiftly through a population might be expected to be sharply peaked, many

TABLE 18.1

Epidemic characteristics for seven island communities

	Area (km²)	Population ('000)	Annual susceptibles input[1]	Density of susceptibles per km²	Expected spacing of susceptibles (km)[2]	Average length of major measles epidemics (months)[3]	Cases of measles reported (%)[4]
New Hebrides	14 800	52	1910	0.129	1.392	11½	9
Tonga	699	57	2040	2.919	293	5	28
New Caledonia	19 000	68	2600	0.137	1.351	9	9
French Polynesia	4000	75	2690	0.673	0.602	6	27
British Solomon Islands	29 800	110	4060	0.136	1.355	8½	6
Western Samoa	2840	118	4440	1.563	0.399	7	9
Iceland	103 000	160	4490	0.044	2.395	20	45

[1] Births less infant mortality for 1956.

[2] See equation (12).

[3] Average duration of major measles epidemics (100 cases or more) over 1949–64.

[4] Total number of reported cases divided by the total input of susceptible children during the period of study.

Source: epidemic data from Black (1966), pp. 208–209.

TABLE 18.2

Population spacing and epidemic peaking in an English county[1]

Mean characteristics	Urban districts	Rural districts	Difference (t-test)
Population spacing	0.671	2.401	10.108[3]
Coefficient of variability:			
All weeks	380	307	1.764
Weeks with 1 or more cases	158	142	2.464[2]
Percentage of cases in upper half of	87.5	84.1	1.850
weeks with 1 or more cases			

[1] Notified measles cases for 17 urban and 10 rural districts of Cornwall. Weeks: 1966(40) to 1970(52) inclusive.

[2] Significant at the 5 per cent level.

[3] Significant at the 0.1% level.

cases being concentrated into very few time periods; one which moves more slowly through a population might be expected to have a flatter, more regular distribution. Table 18.2 shows the results of a test of this hypothesis for a single English county. Measles cases were analysed for 27 recording areas over a 222-week period. Spacing of population was calculated by the formula in (12), using total population (P) rather than the estimated susceptible population (S). For each of the three measures of peaking shown in Table 18.2, detectable differences were found between the rural (low-density) and urban (high-density) areas. Regression studies showed in each case an inverse relationship between concentration and spacing; the more widely spread the population, the less peaked the incidence of cases. If the regression results were found to hold over a wider range of population densities, they would suggest the existence of a spacing level at which the cases are not concentrated but form a random distribution.

Further extensions

So far we have considered extremely simple extensions of the basic Hamer—Soper model in which spatial complexities affect the values of the coefficients (notably the β and μ values). Although emphasis has been placed on symmetrical spread processes extending regularly from a single source, other and more realistic approaches are possible. Tinline's (1970) work on irregular spread fields and Haggett's (1974) exploration of diffusion through graph structures illustrate some of the directions which can be followed.

Discussion

In our concern to explore the simple structure of a model, the problems of actual calibration have been left on one side. We now turn to two aspects of this question: estimating the coefficient values and selecting an appropriate model.

Estimating the model coefficients

In the illustrations shown in Figures 18.2 and 18.5, arbitrary values for the infection, recovery and birth rates were chosen. But to make the model operational in practice we need to replace the algebra of β, γ, and μ by specific values, i.e. data relevant to the epidemic under consideration. Two of the values are relatively straightforward. The recovery rate (γ) is specific to the characteristics of the disease under consideration and is a matter of clinical observation. For measles the average incubation period is a fortnight and we might expect γ to have a value of around 0.5 where t is reckoned in weeks. Similarly, the birth rate (μ) is a matter for demographic observation and will tend to be proportional to P, the size of the population under study (although modified by considerations of fertility, migration, etc.)

The most difficult parameter to estimate is β, the infectiousness of the disease. There are grounds for assuming that this is partly related to the epidemiological character of the disease but also to the degree of mixing and contact probabilities within the population. One indirect method of assessment is to use:

$$\beta = \gamma/\overline{S} \tag{13}$$

where the *average* number of susceptibles in a population $(\overline{S})$ is used as a surrogate for the equilibrium level, S^* (Bartlett, 1972, p. 72).

Hamer himself suggested some values for the open model based on a study of measles epidemics in London; $\beta = 0.0000033$, $\gamma = 0.5$ and $\mu = 2200$. Using the formula

$$\Delta = 2\pi/\sqrt{\beta\mu - \tfrac{1}{4}\beta^2 \mu^2 /\gamma} \tag{14}$$

where Δ is the wavelength of the epidemic, Hamer's values would give a measles epidemic recurring in cycles with a wavelength of 74 weeks or 1.42 years. This estimate is in reasonable agreement with the average period of somewhat less than two years observed by Bartlett (1957) for large towns in England and Wales. Such approximations are only likely to be useful where a particular disease has a very regular temporal pattern. Over the last few years the impact of vaccination programmes on incidence has tended to blur such regularities.

Closed or open model?

Empirical work by Bartlett (1957) and Black (1966) throws light on the question of whether a 'closed' or 'open' version of the model is appropriate. For example, Black (1966) considered the question of disease persistence in insular populations. Using monthly measles case reports from 19 island communities over periods of up to 15 years, he found breaks in the continuity of measles transmission for all communities of less than 500 000 population. In terms of the Hamer—Soper model, this implies that I falls to zero in all cases where P is below this size threshold.

As Figure 18.7c indicates, there is a rough linear relationship between the proportion of months with notified cases and the population of the islands. The islands of Guam and Bermuda form exceptions to the pattern. Their above-average proportion of months with notifications may be due to their large and transient military populations. Hawaii (550 000) was the only island group where fade-outs in measles epidemics were not recorded. From the overall relationship we should expect the threshold population where measles can remain in an endemic state to be around 650 000 people. In interpreting the graph, it should be noted that the completeness of case reporting varied greatly from one island population to another. Estimates of completeness were made by comparing the average number of cases reported with the number of children reaching their first birthday; where the reporting level dropped below 6% the island was excluded. All populations were exposed to measles infections on at least four occasions during the 15-year study period.

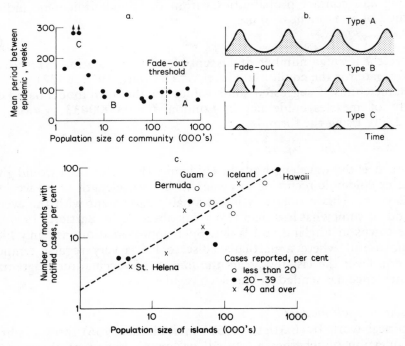

Figure 18.7   Population size and the shape of epidemic paths. (a) The relationship of spacing of measles epidemics and population size for 19 English communities. (b) Characteristic epidemic paths for the three types indicated in (a). (c) Fade-out of measles epidemics in relation to population size for 18 island communities. (Source: Bartlett, 1972; Black, 1966.)

Black's work on insular populations is a direct extension of the earlier work by Bartlett (1957, 1960) on fade-out in urban areas. Data for reported cases from British and American cities suggested that 4000 to 5000 cases of measles per year were needed to prevent fade-out and maintain continuity of disease transmission. On this basis, Bartlett calculated that fade-out would occur in any city with less than 250 000 to 300 000 inhabitants. The contrast between these figures and 550 000 for Black's study may be related to the greater isolation of islands, reducing the frequency of reintroduction of the disease from outside. Also, the reporting level for the British and American cities was well above that of the island populations.

Bartlett's findings for British cities are shown in Figure 18.7a. These suggest three typical epidemic profiles, shown schematically in Figure 18.7b. The largest cities have an endemic pattern with periodic eruptions (Type A) while cities below the threshold have an epidemic pattern with fade-outs. A distinction can be drawn between urban areas above about 10 000 people with a regular pattern of epidemics (Type B) and those where occasional epidemics may be missed, giving a more irregular pattern (Type C).

In terms of the Hamer—Soper models, the work by Black and Bartlett suggests the 'closed' model is indicated for smaller values of P (say, P below 250 000 to 650 000) where I will drop to zero. Above this threshold, we should expect an open version of the model to be more appropriate.

Conclusions

In this essay, we have taken a very simple and deterministic model of an epidemic and tried to see how certain geographical elements might be built into its structure. Some limited advances have been noted, though all depend on a much fuller development than has been attempted here. Extensions from mononuclear to polynuclear diffusion models, to more complex distributions of susceptibles, and to directional vectors which themselves vary over time, are also indicated.

Two final questions of strategy remain. First, why do we choose to look at a simple and deterministic epidemic model when more elegant stochastic versions have been subsequently developed? Here the chief rationale is a pedagogic one. Given the simple structure of the Hamer—Soper model, the effect of adding spatial components one at a time or in combinations can be readily monitored and compared. Sensitivity tests can be very simply conducted and the experience gained extended where justified to the more advanced models.

Second, what kinds of gains would we expect to see from more sensitive geographic tuning of existing epidemic models? The main benefits would be improved prediction and control. If a model is a reasonably faithful imitation of a real-world system, we should be able, given knowledge of its past and present state, to give conditional estimates of its future states. For example, a modified Hamer—Soper model might be used to estimate the likelihood of a major epidemic in one locality next month given what we know now about the present state of the system in another locality. We may also use a model to ask what action can be taken to influence a system so as to achieve desired states. For example, Tinline (1973) used his model of probable directions and rates of spread around a focus of foot-and-mouth disease to suggest selective areas for quarantine measures. Such efforts to quantify the spatial relationships which lie at the heart of a model throw up insights and understandings in the overall process of model building itself.

ACKNOWLEDGEMENTS

I should like to acknowledge the help of Mr. J. Long of the Geography Department and Mr. C. D. Hall of the Computer Science Department, University of Bristol, for developing and running a computer version of the Hamer—Soper models.

REFERENCES

Bailey, N. T. J. (1957). *The Mathematical Theory of Epidemics*, Griffin.
Bartlett, M. S. (1956). 'Deterministic and stochastic models for recurrent epidemics', *Proc. Third Berkeley Symposium on Mathematical Statistics and Probability*, 4, 81—109.
Bartlett, M. S. (1957). 'Measles periodicity and community size', *Journal of the Royal Statistical Society, Series A*, **120**, 48—70.
Bartlett, M. S. (1972). 'Epidemics', in Tanur, J. M. *et al* (Eds.), *Statistics: A Guide to the Unknown*, Holden-Day, 66—76.
Black, F. L. (1966). 'Measles endemicity in insular populations: critical community size and its evolutionary implication', *Journal of Theoretical Biology*, **11**, 207—11.
Cliff, A. D., P. Haggett, J. K. Ord, K. A. Bassett and R. B. Davies (1975). *Elements of Spatial Structure*, Cambridge University Press.
Denmark, Udgivet af Sundhedsstyrelsen (1972). *Medicinalberetning, I for Kalenderaret*, 1968, Kobenhavn.
Dietz, K. (1967). 'Epidemics and rumours: a survey', *Journal of the Royal Statistical Society*, Series A, 130, 505—528.
Gilg, A. W. (1973). 'A study in agricultural disease diffusion: the case of the 1970—1971 fowl-pest epidemic', *Institute of British Geographers Publications*, **59**, 77—97.

Gustafson, S. A. and K. O. Kortanek (1972). 'Analytical properties of some multiple-source urban diffusion models', *Environment and Planning*, 4, 31—41.

Haggett, P. (1972). 'Contagious processes in a planar graph: an epidemiological application', in McGlashen, N. D. (Ed.), *Medical Geography: Techniques and Field Studies*, Methuen, 307—24.

Haggett, P. (1974). 'Testing alternative diffusion hypotheses in graphs', *Institute of British Geographers Quantitative Conference*, Leeds, Oct. 1974.

Hamer, W. H. (1906). 'Epidemic disease in England', *Lancet*, 1, 733—739.

Long, J. (1974). *Testing the Response of Elementary Epidemic Models to Changes in Critical Parameters*, Project Paper, Department of Geography, University of Bristol.

Pyle, G. F. (1969). 'Diffusion of cholera in the United States', *Geographical Analysis*, 1, 59—75.

Soper, H. E. (1929). 'Interpretation of periodicity in disease prevalence', *Journal of the Royal Statistical Society*, 92, 34—73.

Tinline, R. R. (1970). 'Linear operators in diffusion research', in Chisholm, M. D. I., A. E. Frey and P. Haggett (Eds.), *Regional Forecasting*, Butterworth, 71—91.

Tinline, R. R. (1973). *A Simulation Study of the 1967—8 Foot-and-Mouth Epizootic in Great Britain*, unpublished Ph.D. thesis, University of Bristol.

United States Public Health Service (1972). *Morbidity and Mortality, Annual Supplement, 1972*, Center for Disease Control, Atlanta, Georgia.

Wilson, A. G. (1970). *Entropy in Urban and Regional Modelling*, Pion., London.

Chapter 19

Spectral Techniques and the Study of Interregional Economic Cycles

Leslie Hepple

The principal focus of applied economic and econometric analysis probably lies in the fields of macroeconomic model-building, short-term forecasting and fiscal and monetary policy analysis. Yet in the disciplines of regional science and economic geography there is no parallel concentration on the regional and spatial aspects of short- and medium-term economic activity. Instead, research centres on the longer-term, glacier-like movements of industrial location and physical planning.

This essay examines some of the reasons that have prevented the intensive development of interregional models of economic fluctuations and cycles, and suggests ways in which frequency-domain or spectral techniques may be employed to edge round, if not through, some of the difficulties. After describing spectral techniques and their relevance to the study of interregional economic cycles, illustrations are given from two studies undertaken by myself; fuller, technical reports of these studies will be published elsewhere.

Interregional business cycle models
The basic Keynesian relationships between production, consumption, investment, imports and exports that lie at the core of most macroeconomic models, even in these days of 'money supply determinism', may fairly readily be extended to an interregional economic system. Several models have been constructed, the most notable being that of Airov (1963). The structure of the models is of the standard multiplier-accelerator form. For example, Airov constructs a multiplier-pure accelerator model as an extension of Hicks' model

(1950), which is a second-order difference model. Allowing inter-regional trade in both consumption and capital goods, the interregional model

$$Y(t) = (M + B)Y(t - 1) - BY(t - 2) + \bar{A} \qquad (1)$$

is obtained for a set of n regions. Y(t) is the n x 1 column vector of regional incomes at time t, M and B are n x n matrices of consumption and capital coefficients and Ā is an n x 1 column vector of constant autonomous expenditures.

The algebraic extension of the single-region, national models to the multiregional case is straightforward. However, the multiregional models do not, in general, facilitate qualitative deductions about the properties of the system, whereas the national models do (e.g. Samuelson, 1939), and as a result, the emphasis in interregional models is on numerical simulation to determine the nature of the time-paths. Airov has explored the time-paths of two-region systems of type (1), and van Duijn has extensively used numerical simulation to explore various interregional structures (van Duijn, 1972).

For these interregional models to have practical relevance, it is important that the numerical coefficients correspond to those of the real world, and for this to be so empirical estimation is vital. However, there has been no econometric implementation of these interregional business cycle models. This omission springs from two causes: (a) lack of relevant data—series and (b) identification problems. At the sub-national level there are few time—series available of income, invest-ment, etc. Where such series are to some extent available, as they are partially for the states of the U.S.A., they are annual series, whereas for an interregional model data for shorter periods is necessary to capture the dynamics and time-lags of the system. At the national level, early econometric models were annual (e.g. Klein and Goldberger, 1955), but increasingly they are estimated in quarterly (or even monthly) form in order to capture the dynamic effects (Duesenberry, 1969).

Apart from the lack of relevant data, there is the problem of identifying the econometric model. This is a technical issue, the essence of which is that it is not possible to estimate the interregional models without either introducing arbitrary time-lags or constraining many of the coefficients to be zero; otherwise there is no unique set of estimated coefficients that fit the data. In the current state of regional analysis it is difficult to know how to do this: the pattern of interactions and time-lags is one of the things we wish to find out.

The result of these two difficulties — data and identification — has resulted in the separation of interregional cycle analysis and econo-metric model-building. Regional econometric models are single-region models related to the national economy, without an interregional component, and Klein (1969) has forcefully argued that this is the best way at present. In interregional terms the result has been either crude *ad hoc* methods for the study of particular effects (e.g. studies of the multiplier effects of regional policy), or highly empirical studies based on the regional time—series available, mainly annual employment series used to chart regional cyclical amplitudes and turning-points (e.g. Engerman, 1965). More recently, attention has turned to monthly and quarterly data of unemployment series, and regression methods have been employed to study the degree of response of regions to national economic fluctuations. The literature is reviewed in Hepple (1974) and Haggett (1971). However, these methods are by no means ideal for the study of direct interregional linkages and the determination of the time-paths of regional responses.

The problems of studying interregional economic cycles with these available indicator series, which must be used by themselves as proxies for economic fluctuations, may be clarified by setting out a simple model of the interacting regional series. Consider a set of n regional unemployment series. These regional series interact with each other through the mechanics of the multiplier-accelerator model and the relationship of level of production and the demand for labour. The level of unemployment in region j at time t may be represented:

$$y_j = b_1(L)y_1 + \ldots b_n(L)y_n + c_1(L)x_1 + \ldots + c_k(L)x_k + u_j \qquad (2)$$

where each of the $b_i(L)$ and $c_i(L)$ are vectors of coefficients in the lag-operator L, so that y_j is a function of a whole set of lagged values of each endogenous series. The whole system may be written:

$$B(L)Y = C(L)X + U \qquad (3)$$

for time t, where Y, X and U are vectors of the current state of the variables and B(L) and C(L) are now matrices of coefficients in the polynomial lag-operator L.

If the n endogenous regions completely fill out the national system, then X can only be the effects of international trade and linkage, and, for the empirical series available, it is difficult to incorporate this term. If, however, the n regions only map out part of the national system, X then represents the series for the other regions of the national system. The structural form (2) may then be re-arranged to give the reduced-form:

$$Y = \frac{C(L)}{B(L)} X + B(L)^{-1} U \qquad (4)$$

so that each endogenous series is specified as a function of the exogenous series.

Standard time—domain statistical procedures are essentially designed for the estimation of specific and highly structured sets of relationships. In this instance, neither the forms of the distributed lag structure in (3) and (4) are known, nor the patterning (specification of zeros) in the matrices of coefficients. It is almost impossible to trace the full causal links in the structural form (3). It should be possible to make progress with the reduced-form (4), but this is a complex and unknown distributed lag, and the errors, even if they are independent in the structural form, are certainly autocorrelated in the reduced form. The methods of Box and Jenkins (1970), based on identifying the forms of C(L) and B(L) by studying the autocorrelation and cross-correlation functions of the series, offer one avenue into this maze. An alternative and more general approach, perhaps more suitable for cyclical models, is to transform the analysis into the frequency-domain and use spectral techniques.

Spectral techniques

The techniques of spectral analysis consist of studying the structure and properties of time—series in terms of sine—cosine waves with different frequencies. The power spectrum of a time—series is a decomposition of the variance of the series into the relative contributions of waves or frequencies of different lengths. In a perfectly periodic series, only a finite number of waves would be needed to explain the series. Since economic time—series are not periodic in this way, an infinite number of wave-lengths may be necessary to decompose the structure of the series exactly. In spectral analysis it is assumed that all these possible wave-lengths are present, and the power spectrum measures the relative contribution not of individual wave-lengths but of groups of waves in a certain range, or frequency-bands. Similarly, the cross-spectrum between two (or more) time—series is a decomposition of the covariance between the series into frequency-bands together with the relative timing of waves of that frequency in the two series.

The spectrum and cross-spectrum may be estimated in several ways. The classical method is to go through the auto- and cross-covariances. These are often of interest in themselves and provide a time—domain decomposition of the variance structure of the series at various lags. By projecting these covariances onto sets of sine—cosine waves and calculating the relative amplitude of the resulting waves, the spectra may be estimated. Sine—cosine waves at frequency λ may be represented by the complex series $e^{-i\lambda l}$, and the spectrum is then:

$$f_x(\lambda) = (1/2\pi) \int_{-\infty}^{\infty} c_{xx}(l)e^{-i\lambda l}dl \tag{5}$$

which, for a finite series is:

$$f_x(\lambda) = (1/2\pi) \sum_{-M}^{M} c_{xx}(l)e^{-i\lambda l} \tag{6}$$

where $c_{xx}(1)$ is the autocovariance at lag 1. (5) and (6) in fact represent the spectrum or 'periodogram' for a periodic series, and for a stochastic series it is necessary to smooth this function into frequency-bands, either by direct smoothing of $f_x(\lambda)$ or through weighting the Fourier transform itself:

$$f_x(\lambda) = (1/2\pi) \sum_{-M}^{M} c_{xx}(l)w(l)e^{-i\lambda l} \qquad (7)$$

where $w(l)$ are tapering weights specified in various texts (Granger and Hatanaka, 1964; Hannan, 1970).

A second and more recent approach avoids the necessity of calculating (and storing on a computer) the auto- and cross-covariances, by directly projecting the data–series onto sine–cosine waves and assessing the relative amplitudes of these waves:

$$a(\lambda) = (1/N) \sum_{-M}^{M} x(m)e^{-i\lambda m} \qquad (8)$$

with periodogram:

$$f_{\hat{x}}(\lambda) = \frac{N \mid a(\lambda) \mid^2}{2\pi} \qquad (9)$$

and the spectrum of a stochastic series is (9), again smoothed and grouped into bands. An excellent discussion of both these approaches, and others, is given by Cooley, Lewis and Welch (1970).

In these estimation procedures there are several design decisions to be made: the number of lags of $c_{xx}(l)$ and the number of frequency-bands, λ, both of which depend upon N, the length of the series, so that the methods are most reliable for long series. Also, since the spectrum is a frequency-domain analysis-of-variance, the techniques will only be meaningful for stationary series, i.e. series in which the second-order (variance) properties do not change over the time-period of the series. To satisfy this assumption for economic time series it is usually necessary to filter the series by various techniques known as pre-whitening (see Fishman, 1969).

The cross-spectra may be similarly obtained, either from the cross-covariances $c_{xy}(l)$ and $c_{xy}(-l)$:

$$f_{xy}(\lambda) = \frac{1}{2\pi} \sum_{-M}^{M} c_{xy}(l)w(l)e^{-i\lambda l} \qquad (10)$$

or from equation (8) for various series:

$$f_{xy}(\lambda) = \frac{N}{2\pi} a_x(\lambda)a_y(\lambda)^* \qquad (11)$$

where $a_y(\lambda)^*$ denotes the complex conjugate of $a_y(\lambda)$. If equation (11) is used this estimate must then be smoothed over adjacent frequencies.

This cross-spectrum is a complex function (i.e. composed of a real and imaginary part) and is not itself the focus of interpretation. A series of derivative statistics provides a frequency-domain picture of the relationship between the series. The coherence between the series at frequency λ may be defined:

$$co(\lambda) = \frac{|f_{xy}(\lambda)|}{\sqrt{f_{xx}(\lambda) \cdot f_{yy}(\lambda)}} \qquad (12)$$

and is analogous to the correlation coefficient. The phase—statistic

$$\phi(\lambda) = \arctan \left\{ \frac{- \text{ imaginary part of } f_{\hat{x}y}(\lambda)}{\text{real part of } f_{\hat{x}y}(\lambda)} \right\} \qquad (13)$$

is a measure of the degree to which the λ frequency component of series y is out of phase with that of series x. This may be converted into a time-lag at frequency λ by

$$L(\lambda) = \frac{\phi(\lambda)}{\lambda} \qquad (14)$$

However $\phi(\lambda)$ is only determined relative to cycle length, so that the time-lag could also be:

$$L(\lambda) = \frac{\phi(\lambda)}{\lambda} \pm n\lambda \qquad (15)$$

where n is an integer. This ambiguity is easy to resolve for phase at low-frequencies, but more difficult for high frequencies.

These frequency-domain statistics have the advantage over the time-domain auto- and cross-correlations that the estimates for the various frequencies are (approximately) orthogonal or uncorrelated. This means that in discussing the interactions between a whole set of regional business-cycle series, such as equation (3), although we cannot estimate matrix B(L), we can separate out the various frequencies and study the correlations and time-lags between the regions at the chosen frequencies, and this cross-spectral matrix analysis is illustrated in a later section. In contrast, it is extremely difficult to interpret the non-orthogonal sets of cross-correlations.

A second advantage is that these spectral measures set out in (5) to (15) facilitate ready estimation of linear systems under very general assumptions. Consider an output series or waveform, y_t, which is viewed as the result of an input waveform going through a filter or linear system, plus some random noise (Figure 19.1). This process may be represented:

$$y(t) = \int_{-\infty}^{\infty} b(u)x(t - u)du + e(t) \qquad (16)$$

and if y(t) is only influenced by past x-values, the integral can run from zero to infinity. To estimate distributed lag models of type (16) it is necessary to make many assumptions about the form of the set $\{b(u)\}$

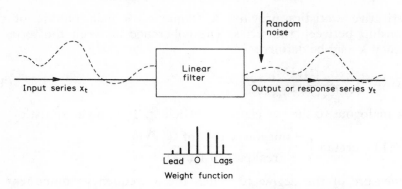

Figure 19.1   A simple linear system.

and the autocorrelation structure of $e(t)$. However, by transforming to the frequency-domain, the linear system may readily be estimated.

The Fourier transform

$$z(\lambda) = \int_{-\infty}^{\infty} b(u)e^{-i\lambda u}\,du \qquad (17)$$

defines the linear system in terms of a series of regression slopes. The transformation represented by the frequency response $z(\lambda)$ involves two distinct modifications: an amplification or attenuation of each frequency component as it passes through the filter, and a phase-shift translating the frequency component along the time axis. $z(\lambda)$ may be estimated from the cross-spectrum, as can its two components, the gain (amplification) coefficient and the phase-shift (already defined in (13) and (14)).

These techniques may be used to examine whether, in the transmission of economic cycles from one region to another, certain frequency components are being amplified. The frequency response structure reflects the stability of the regional economy. Unstable industrial structures will have responses that amplify certain waveforms, whilst stable systems will damp down the larger fluctuations. The associated methods of 'band-spectrum regression' (Engle, 1974) may be used to test whether there are real differences in response at different frequencies.

It is also possible, once $z(\lambda)$ is estimated from the cross-spectrum, to use an inverse Fourier transform to obtain the time-domain weights $\{b(u)\}$, so characterising the linear system in time-lag and response terms (Hannan, 1967, 1970).

In the next section these spectral approaches to linear systems are employed in an empirical study of the reduced-form (4), and in the succeeding section cross-spectra are employed to illustrate direct interregional estimation.

Regional response estimation

The application of these spectral techniques, and particularly response estimation, to the study of interregional cycles and fluctuations may be illustrated from a study by Hepple (1974).

Consider again the reduced-form expression for regional unemployment response in equation (4). If the system represented by the endogenous variables is small relative to the national system, then the series formed by aggregating all the external sectors will be closely equivalent to the national series. If, however, the model is expressed in this way, the lags in the response may be negative as well as positive, for some of the endogenous regions may lead the national cycle, so that each row of (4) may be written as a linear system as in equation (16). These linear systems, in both time-domain and frequency-domain, may be estimated for each region by spectral techniques.

In the present case, the regional system consisted of 39 local labour market areas covering north-eastern England. For each of these regions monthly Department of Employment unemployment returns were available. The period used for estimation was January 1961 to December 1966. After 1966 there is considerable evidence of shifting relationships in British labour markets, and these initial estimates could be used as base relationships against which to test post-1966 responses and forecasts. Because of the short length of the series, the number of lags and frequency bands to be established had to be kept small. After experiment, 24 was chosen as the number of bands. All the series were prewhitened by quasi-differencing (Fishman, 1969) before estimation began.

The national series of unemployment values, forming the exogenous series in the model, had a spectrum of the typical J-shape for an economic variable, with power concentrated in the low frequencies, declining to the high frequencies without any peaks indicating periodicities (Figure 19.2). The 39 labour market regions comprise several different employment structures, and as a result the spectra of some of the regions do not reproduce the national curve. The major industrial regions reproduce the J-curve but agricultural regions have much flatter spectra, often with the largest power at seasonal frequencies. The resort zones of Whitby and Scarborough in North Yorkshire have strong concentrations in these seasonal frequencies.

These univariate spectra produce some evidence that the national waveform is considerably altered in its impact in different regions. Cross-spectra were calculated for each regional series against the national series. The concentration of power in the low-frequency bands of the spectrum means that it is these frequencies in the cross-spectral statistics that are of greatest importance. Relationships in the few lowest frequencies determine most of the behaviour of the series.

The coherences between the national cycle and local areas are generally high, particularly at low frequencies, but the graphs of

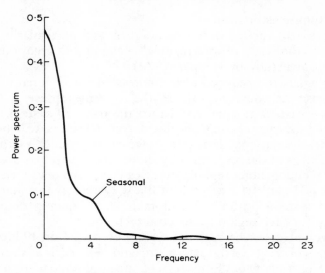

Figure 19.2 Spectrum of national unemployment series.

coherence against frequency show a ragged pattern and no smooth decline. These results parallel those obtained for south-west England by Bassett and Haggett (1971). Rural regions such as Hexham, Haltwhistle or Alnwick tend to have dips in the coherences at low frequencies. The phase-lag statistics produce much greater interregional differentiation. For most of the frequency bands, $\phi(\lambda)$ oscillates close to zero for all the series, but this is to be expected as the wavelengths are very short and the frequency-bands of little significance. In the important 48-month and 24-month bands there are quite pronounced leads and lags (Figure 19.3). Thus at the 48-month frequency, Wearside

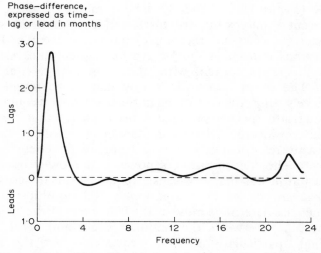

Figure 19.3 Wearside: graph of phase, expressed as time-lag.

lags the national cycle by 3 months, Tyneside lags by 1.5, Teesside by 0.5, Ashington by 6 months, whereas Guisborough leads by 1.6 and Prudhoe by 4 months. In general the rural zones and industrial zones specializing in chemicals or steel manufacture lead or parallel the national series, whereas the shipbuilding and coal-mining regions lag the national cycle.

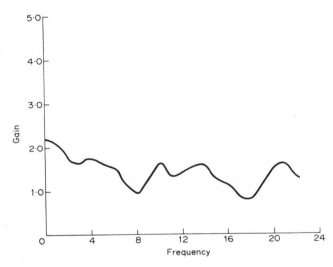

Figure 19.4   Tyneside gain graph.

The gain coefficients — the regression slopes at each frequency — show, as in Figure 19.4 for Tyneside, some increases in the lowest frequencies for the main industrial areas, and some dip at these frequencies for the rural areas, but in general they are erratic and difficult to interpret. If, however, these spectral estimates of gain and phase are used in an inverse Fourier transform to obtain estimates of the time-domain weights $\{b(u)\}$, known as the impulse response function, the different waveform filters corresponding to different industrial structures become clear. Hepple (1974) has shown that direct time-domain estimation of these weights $\{b(u)\}$ produces very poor and erratic estimates. Figure 19.5 shows the impulse response function for the Hartlepools, an industrial area. The weights are significantly non-zero for both short leads and lags. In none of the 39 regions are the weights significant for long leads and lags, and this means that an excessive number of parameters (49) is being estimated. Hannan (1967) has shown that this method is still efficient under certain conditions, but has also developed a more general but more complicated estimated procedure (still based on spectral estimation) for a restricted range of leads and lags (Hannan, 1970). Both approaches produced similar response functions for the regions but the latter set is to be preferred. The impulse response functions may be classified into a number of

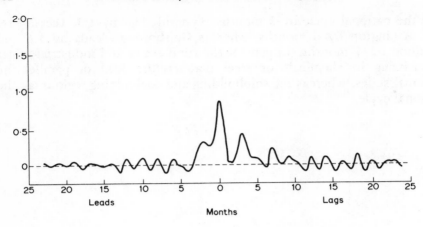

Figure 19.5   Impulse response function, Hartlepools.

types, in terms of (a) the total amplitude of the response, (b) the shape of the response-curve, and (c) the timing of the curve.

The sum of the coefficients {b(u)} represents the long-term response or 'steady-state gain', the value attained by the regional series if x rises from zero to one in a step-function and remains at this value. The steady-state gain for some of the rural series is less than one, representing a damping response, but for most regions it is greater than one, reflecting the instability of the employment structure in north-east England; in some industrial zones it is extremely high, e.g. the Hartlepools 4.7, Guisborough 4.8 and Wearside 3.5.

The second facet is the shape of the response curve. Several idealised forms are given in Figure 19.6. We assume the curves are standardised

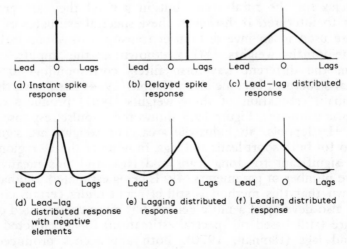

Figure 19.6   Idealised impulse response functions.

for each to have the same steady-state gain. Figure 19.6a, a simple spike at zero lag, represents a pure instantaneous response: the filter { b(u) } does not alter the shape or timing of the input waveform, but simply amplifies or damps it. Only a very few of the regions are of this type, such as Durham city. Nor are any of the regions of form 19.6b, the delayed spike function. This is interesting since most of the regression models of unemployment response assume either form 19.6a or 19.6b.

The curve of 19.6c represents a drawn-out distributed lag response to national fluctuations, with both positive lead and lag coefficients, Regions of this type feel the ripples of longer-term economic fluctuations before they are reflected in the national series, and the multiplier effects continue longer than in the national economy. The regional or output waveform becomes more autocorrelated in its path through the filter, lower-frequencies being differentially amplified. Many of the regions fall into this group, mainly complex manufacturing and heavy-industrial zones, such as Tyneside, Teesside, Loftus and the Hartlepools. The curves are, however, not symmetric, and may be skewed towards either lead (Loftus) or lag (Wearside) effects.

A rather different curve is represented by 19.6d, with negative lead and lag coefficients. For a spike input wave this would give negative outputs, but for continuous, highly-autocorrelated series, such as the national input series, this represents a response in which the current state of the national economy is emphasised at the expense of adjacent months: the lag-structure is trying to transform the input wave into a higher frequency, more erratic output curve. This form is typical of rural regions, which respond more to sudden ups and downs in the economy, such as a bad January and February in 1963, than to longer-term business cycle fluctuations. Finally, there are categories 19.6e and 19.6f, which represent forms in which the response is either behind or ahead of the national series. Areas of lighter manufacturing industry, such as Spennymoor and south-west Durham have form 19.6e and the chemical town of Prudhoe and the steel town Consett have form 19.6f.

This use of spectral techniques as a way of estimating sets of regional responses can also be employed on highly restricted structural equations. So the output series for a region like Darlington could be estimated as the result of both input waves from the national economy and from neighbouring Teesside. But it would be difficult to extend this, and an alternative spectral approach for this problem is illustrated in the next section.

Cross-spectral matrices
Whilst it is extremely difficult to model the entire network of causal reaction paths and waveforms between all the regions of the structural system, it is possible through the use of spectral techniques to build up

a detailed picture of the co-variations and lead-lag relations amongst all the regions in the system. This may be achieved by extending the cross-spectra previously discussed to the notion of a matrix of cross-spectra for each pair of a set of k regional time—series. For each frequency-band, λ, there is a k x k matrix, $C(\lambda)$, with a typical element $c_{ij}(\lambda)$ measuring the cross-spectrum at frequency λ between regions i and j. If k is at all large there are formidable computational problems in estimating such matrices by classical methods, but the advent of direct Fourier transform methods has meant that large matrices focussing on particular frequency-bands may be calculated.

From the cross-spectral complex matrix, $C(\lambda)$, matrices of the coherences and phase-differences between each pair of regions may be derived, and it is on these that interpretation is based. A small cross-spectral matrix was estimated by Granger (1969) in a study of unemployment series at the standard region scale in the United Kingdom, and a large matrix (k = 39) was used to trace the linkage and reaction-paths in a detailed network of regions in north-east England (Hepple, 1974). These techniques are particularly valuable for the study of historical interregional cycles, where there is no possibility of new data being collected for direct modelling of input-output or production-consumption relations, and where at present very little is known of links between regions. Thus Granger and Elliott (1967) estimated a small set of cross-spectra to assess the linkages between regional wheat price series in eighteenth century England, finding greater evidence of interaction between the regional markets than many economic historians have suggested. Here we illustrate these techniques from a study of trade-cycles in early Victorian England.

For nineteenth-century Britain a number of indicator series are available at a regional level to study the pattern of interregional cycles, such as agricultural price data and monetary series (country bank-note circulation), but a particularly valuable one is that for bankruptcies. Gayer, Rostow and Schwartz (1953), in their classic study of fluctuations in the national British economy during the first half of the nineteenth century, found that the bankruptcy series very closely followed their composite business cycle reference series, providing a good barometer of the health of the economy. Details of individual bankruptcies are given in the *London Gazette* for the period, and those for the years 1838 to 1846 have been aggregated into monthly county series and listed in the *Journal of the Statistical Society*. On the basis of these series a detailed image of interregional linkage in the early Victorian economy may be constructed.

For many of the lesser agricultural counties, the bankruptcy series form more of a point process than the continuous series necessary for the spectral techniques discussed here; the extreme case is Rutland, with only one bankruptcy in the period, in February 1846. Spectral methods are available to incorporate many of these point series, but for the short illustration here, attention is focused on the manufacturing, urban-commercial and main agricultural counties, where the series are continuous.

The spectra for these county series have the typical shape for economic time series, with power concentrated in the low-frequency bands. Since these are the economic fluctuations of interest, the inter-county cross-spectral matrix was calculated for low-frequency variation. The estimates, averaged over the three lowest frequencies but excluding the zero frequency, were centred on a cycle length of 35 months. All the series were prewhitened before the estimation. The coherency matrix for these low-frequency cycles reveals some interesting linkages and the most important of these are shown in Figure 19.7. The Midlands counties and Yorkshire are closely integrated, but in the North-West, Lancashire, one of the major series, is closely linked only to Yorkshire. The north-eastern series of Northumberland and Durham are more closely linked to the Midlands group than to Lancashire. The two southern series of Somerset/Bristol and London and Home Counties are only weakly linked with the manufacturing areas and have particularly poor coherences with Lancashire and Yorkshire. Certainly there is evidence that the interregional economy was much less closely

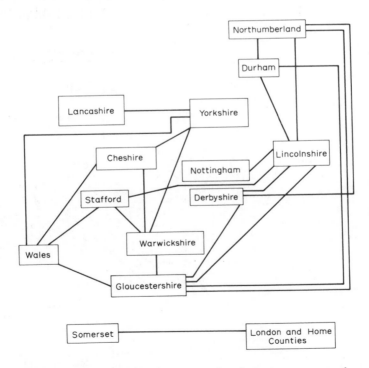

Figure 19.7   Inter-county links with squared coherences greater than 0.8 at 34-month frequency band.

integrated than today, if these results are compared to Granger's regional unemployment cross-spectra (Granger, 1969).

The phase matrix provides evidence of considerable leads and lags in the economy. Phase estimates are only reliable for highly coherent series, so initially only leads and lags between closely linked regions are considered (Figure 19.8). For this subset the phase-differences are consistent; that is the estimated time-difference between two regions A and B does not contradict and is very similar to that of A → C plus C → B. Lancashire, Lincolnshire and the East Midlands emerge as the leading areas, with economic fluctuations then travelling to Yorkshire and up into the North-East and down into Gloucestershire through the West Midlands. This is consistent with the historical evidence that the major depression of these years was mainly due to a textile-led slump imported from the United States and fuelled by the fall in home demand owing to bad harvests (Matthews, 1954). Although coherences are low, it would be valuable to fit London and Somerset into this picture. Coherences with Lancashire are very low (with London, squared coherence 0.08; with Somerset, squared coherence 0.04), but are higher with some other counties: Somerset–Derby 0.69; London–Derby 0.59; Somerset–Gloucestershire 0.47. Using these linkages as guides to the more reliable phase estimates, Somerset and London may be fitted into the time-reactions. Somerset leads London, but both

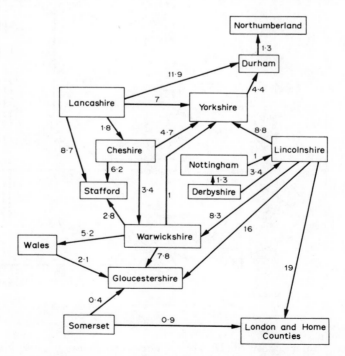

Figure 19.8   Phase-difference, expressed in leads and lags in months, based on high coherence linkages and best estimates.

considerably lag behind the northern and midland counties at these low frequencies. Gloucestershire and Wales lag Somerset but lead London.

These are only the preliminary conclusions to be drawn from such an analysis, which may be extended in many ways, but they serve to illustrate the value of spectral techniques for the study of interregional systems. One particular extension is worth noting. The coherency matrix may, like a normal correlation matrix, be used in a cluster analysis to provide a regionalisation, or as a basis for multivariate techniques such as principal components analysis. The more dominant the principal eigenvalue of the coherency matrix is, the more closely integrated is the interregional system: one component or 'reference cycle' can explain most of the variation. If cross-spectral matrices for different time-periods are compared in this way, the changing degree of integration of the space—economy should be revealed. The coherency matrix clearly contains no phase information, but multivariate analysis incorporating leads and lags may be undertaken on the complex cross-spectral matrix $C(\lambda)$ in ways similar to those for real symmetric matrices (Brillinger, 1969; Hannan, 1970). This allows detection not only of the importance of the 'spectral reference cycle' but also the leads and lags of individual regions with respect to it. An example of this technique is given in Hepple (1974).

Conclusion

These spectral methods have not resulted in the estimation of the structural system of equation (3), still less a full interregional economic model. That was not to be expected. What they do achieve is deeper penetration into the structure of relations that go to make up such a system. They illuminate facets of interregional economic cycles that are left hidden by both time—domain regression analysis and by traditional descriptive methods. The illustrations given here, regional response estimation and cross-spectral matrix analysis, represent only two possible applications, and the recent development of spectral methods for a variety of model-structures (Hannan and Nicholls, 1972) suggest that they have many other possibilities for interregional analysis. It is to be hoped that these spectral techniques, together with other approaches, will lead to a greater focus on short-term monitoring of the space—economy in regional science and economic geography.

REFERENCES

Airov, J. (1963). 'The construction of interregional business cycle models', *Journal of Regional Science*, 5, 1—20.

Bassett, K. A. and P. Haggett (1971). 'Towards short-term forecasting for cyclical behaviour in a regional system of cities', in M. Chisholm, A. E. Frey and P. Haggett (Eds.), *Regional Forecasting*, Butterworth, 389—413.

Box, G. E. P. and G. M. Jenkins (1970). *Time Series, Forecasting and Control*, Holden-Day.

Brillinger, D. R. (1969). 'The canonical analysis of stationary series', in P. R. Krishnaiah (Ed.) *Multivariate Analysis II*, Academic Press, 331—50.

Cooley, J. W., P. A. W. Lewis and P. D. Welch (1970). 'The application of the fast Fourier transform algorithm to the estimation of spectra and cross-spectra', *Journal of Sound and Vibration*, **12** , 339—52.

Duesenberry, J. S. (Ed.) (1969). *The Brookings Model: some further results*, Rand McNally.

Engerman, S. (1965). 'Regional aspects of stabilization policy', in R. A. Musgrave (Ed.), *Essays in Fiscal Federalism*, Brookings Institution, 7—62.

Engle, R. F. (1974). 'Band spectrum regression', *International Economic Review*, **15**, 1—11. .

Fishman, G. S. (1969). *Spectral Methods in Econometrics*, Harvard University Press.

Gayer, A. D., W. W. Rostow and A. J. Schwartz (1953). *The Growth and Fluctuations of the British Economy 1790—1850*, Clarendon Press.

Granger, C. W. J. (1969). 'Spatial data and time series analysis', in Scott, A. J. (Ed.), *Studies in Regional Science*, Pion, 1—24.

Granger, C. W. J. and C. M. Elliott (1967). 'A fresh look at wheat prices and markets in the eighteenth century', *Economic History Review*, **20**, 257—65.

Granger, C. W. J. and M. Hatanaka (1964). *The Spectral Analysis of Economic Time Series*, Princeton University Press.

Haggett, P. (1971). 'Leads and lags in inter-regional systems: a study of cyclic fluctuations in the South West economy', in Chisholm M. and G. Manners (Eds.), *Spatial Policy Problems of the British Economy*, Cambridge University Press, 69—95.

Hannan, E. J. (1967). 'The estimation of a lagged regression relation', *Biometrika*, **54**, 409—18.

Hannan, E. J. (1970). *Multiple Time Series*, Wiley.

Hannan, E. J. and D. F. Nicholls (1972). 'The estimation of mixed regression, autoregression, moving average, and distributed lag models', *Econometrica*, **40**, 529—547.

Hepple, L. W. (1974). *Econometric Estimation and Model-Building with Spatial Series*, unpublished Ph.D. thesis, University of Cambridge.

Hicks, J. R. (1950). *A Contribution to the Theory of the Trade Cycle*, Clarendon Press.

Klein, L. R. (1969) 'The specification of regional econometric models', *Papers and Proceedings of the Regional Science Association*, **25**, 105—115.

Klein, L. R. and A. S. Goldberger (1955). *An Econometric Model of the United States, 1929—1952*, North-Holland Publishing Company.

Matthews, R. C. O. (1954). *A Study in Trade Cycle History*, Cambridge University Press.

Meyer, R. A. (1972). 'Estimating coefficients that change over time', *International Economic Review*, **13**, 705—710.

Samuelson, P. A. (1939). 'Interactions between the multiplier analysis and the principle of acceleration', *Review of Economics and Statistics*, **21**, 75—78.

van Duijn, J. J. (1972). *An Interregional Model of Economic Fluctuations*, Lexington Books.

PART VII

Postscript

Chapter 20

The Department of Geography, University of Bristol, 1925—75

Ronald Peel

It is an interesting, and perhaps a significant, reflection, that in Britain major wars seem to stimulate an interest in Geography as a subject worthy of serious study. Lagging well behind Germany and France, in the period prior to World War I Britain offered facilities for the study of Geography at only two of its universities, London and Oxford. Its acceptance at other universities came in the early 1920s, apparently largely in response to the demand from returning ex-Service men who had no doubt experienced something of its value under severely practical conditions. A somewhat comparable boom in the popularity of Geography followed World War II, in the great expansion of higher education that occurred in the 1950s and 1960s. Today, a degree in Geography can be taken in over 40 of Britain's universities and polytechnics, and about a thousand students graduate in the subject each year. Through the post-war expansion period Geography has consistently maintained a high place among all subjects in the number of university applications received, and has experienced a considerably greater proportionate expansion in higher education than many other subjects with longer university roots. With the current growing awareness of the interdependence of all countries and peoples, of the progressive depletion of terrestrial resources, and of the growing dangers of environmental deterioration, there seems to be little likelihood of the demand decreasing; and although the traditional subject-matter of Geography is now being studied at least in part under new labels like 'Environmental Science', it remains very central to man's interests. In this concluding chapter, a brief summary is given of the history of the subject in the University of Bristol.

Origins of the university

Public interest in a local centre of higher education in Bristol goes back to the early eighteenth century with fitful attempts to introduce medical education in the city. The passing of the Anatomy Act of 1832 found two recognised Medical Schools already in existence in Bristol, which were thereupon combined into one. Subsequent years saw the emergence of proposals for a College of Literature and Science for the West of England, proposals which eventually resulted in the foundation, in 1876, of the University College of Bristol, with which the existing Medical School was incorporated in the early 1890s. Thus strengthened, the University College applied for and received its Royal Charter in 1909, to become one of the small number of new Civic Universities. In 1959 it celebrated its Jubilee, having by this time grown to accommodate some 3000 students. Today this figure has expanded to about 6500, a growth which has created severe problems of congestion in the mid-city site to which the University has adhered. Among the Universities and comparable institutions in Britain, Bristol thus appears in the middle ranks in both antiquity and size. Its original civic character is still apparent in its relationships with the city, and in its legacy of dignified stone buildings in the Gothic style, but growth has inevitably transformed the University into a national institution, drawing students from all parts of Britain and from many countries overseas.

The introduction of geography

Like a number of other British universities, Bristol introduced Geography in 1920, placing it initially under the care of the Department of Geology, but making it available in the Faculty of Arts as well as the Faculty of Science. W. W. Jervis, B.Sc. (later D.Sc.) Dunelm, was appointed to teach the new subject in collaboration with members of the Geology staff, among whom Professor S. H. Reynolds played an active part. Professor Reynolds, the first holder of the Channing Wills Chair of Geology, was keenly interested in the new subject, and it was largely owing to his encouragement and help that it blossomed so well that in the session 1924–25 the University decided to establish a separate Geography Department and to introduce honours degrees in the subject, available in both its Faculties. Jervis was appointed Lecturer-in-Charge, with O. D. Kendall to assist him. Jervis had been only 28 when first appointed; he remained in Bristol until his retirement in 1957, being elected Reader in 1926, and Professor in 1933 when a Chair of Geography was instituted. For thirty-seven years Jervis thus directed the fortunes of Geography at Bristol, and its steady growth owed much to his wise guidance and personal standing. It equally owed a great deal to O. D. Kendall, who also spent his whole working life in Bristol after a degree course delayed by service in World War I. S. J. Jones, now recently retired from the Chair of Geography at Dundee, joined the initial nucleus of staff in 1927, and P. Pilbin in 1934, he being succeeded after three years with the Department by F. Walker. At the outbreak of World War II, the total staff thus numbered four.

The growth of the department

1925—39

In harmony with the modest pre-war size of the University and the slow tempo of change, the new Department of Geography remained small throughout this period; its limited staff, like those of other departments of the period, had to work hard to cover all the necessary teaching between them. The first class graduated in 1927 and through the 1930s the annual student intake was about one dozen. Accommodation was severely restricted, being limited to a few rooms in one of the older University buildings, cheek-by-jowl with Geology and Anatomy; but the Department had the distinction of being allotted the original Council Chamber of the University, together with the former Registrar's Office and the former Strong-Room, rooms which, incidentally, it still possesses. The degree curriculum in these early days presented a fairly normal mixture of systematic and regional courses, but the arrival of Kendall witnessed a strong development of geomorphology together with the introduction, as a third-year option (the only one), of a more advanced course in topographical surveying. Thus Cambridge, whence Kendall had come, and Bristol were the only two universities offering such a course, with the result that prior to the 1950s the majority of Survey Officers in the various Colonial Survey Departments had received their training at one or other of these centres. Professor Jervis taught regional courses and the history of discovery; Jones specialised in economic geography, and Walker in historical geography. An interesting feature of the period was the development of collaboration with the Faculties of both Law and Medicine; the former because Professor Jervis was a barrister as well as a geographer, gave lectures in the Law Faculty, and arranged for his students to attend a course in International Law. The records do not reveal the nature or extent of contacts with the Medical Faculty, but the interweaving of accommodation with the Anatomy School may have had something to do with it. Small staff numbers and heavy teaching loads left little time in this period for research, but Jervis published a book entitled *The World in Maps* (1938), Kendall some papers on his physiographic researches on the Somerset coast, and Jones papers on subjects of local economic geography.

1939—45
The war years saw the Bristol Department, like others, stripped of most of its staff, Jervis being away for much of the period in varied employments, Kendall commanding a Survey Regiment in the Army, and Walker joining the R.A.F. in photo-intelligence. The trickle of students merged with those of King's College, London, who were evacuated to Bristol under the charge of Professor S. W. Wooldridge. The University, including the section housing Geography, suffered severe damage in the air-raids on Bristol, one of the present Departmental buildings (then occupied by Anatomy) being gutted by fire. After repairs, lodgement was given in the basement rooms of the South Building to the Spelaeological Society with its important library and collection, a site which it still occupies.

1945—57
The early post-war years witnessed a period of high pressure. Student intake jumped with the return of ex-Service men and women, and with the influx of those whose university careers had been postponed by the war, while no sooner had this 'bulge' passsed through than the rapid expansion under the Robbins Plan began. Jervis, Kendall and Walker returned from the wars, but were hard-pressed, and new appointments had to be sought to cope with the rapidly-rising numbers. F. G. Morris (historical and regional interests) joined in 1946, together with F. G. Hannell (climatology); A. M. Graves (regional geography and surveying) in 1948; J. W. Birch (economic geography) in 1950; A. E. Frey (geomorphology and, later, economic geography) in 1952; and L. F. Curtis (pedology and aerial photography) in 1956. By the end of this period the staff had thus grown to eight (having lost Morris by death in 1952), but the annual student intake had risen to 30 or more, giving a student total, including those taking General degrees, of over 100. The degree curriculum remained without major changes, and the pressures of teaching so large a number continued to restrict post-graduate developments and staff research. Nevertheless, by the time that the British Association for the Advancement of Science met in Bristol in 1955, research was actively under way in a number of fields, some in conjunction with the University's Reconstruction Research Group and the Nature Conservancy. Internally, despite the acquisition of some extra space from the Geology Department on its removal to other quarters, accommodation continued to be a pressing problem.

1957—75
In 1957 Professor Jervis retired, and R. F. Peel was appointed to succeed him. In 1959 Kendall also retired, and, as Jones had left Bristol in the war years, Walker remained the only representative of the pre-war staff, other than H. Freke, the Chief Technician. D. Ingle Smith replaced Kendall, but the continuing growth in student numbers

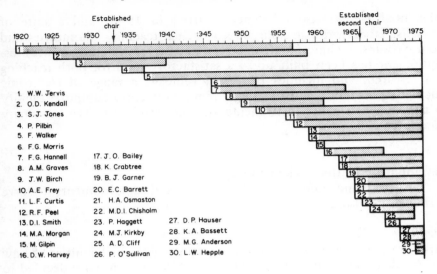

Figure 20.1   Staff appointments, 1920—75.

brought with it an accompanying growth in staff, and in the period 1959–69 nine additional posts were acquired, bringing the teaching staff to its present strength of 17. A second Chair was created in 1966 and filled by the appointment of P. Haggett, while M. D. I. Chisholm, who joined the Department in 1965 and was elected Reader in 1967, was given a personal Chair in 1972. The present staff of the Department is displayed in Figure 20.1, which also includes all teaching staff since the establishment of the Department. Additional to the full-time staff, the single Demonstratorship held in 1957 had been increased by 1970 to five; student intake increased from about 30 each year to the current level of between 60 and 70; and the solitary research student in residence in 1957 has been replaced by a group which in any one year now averages between 20 and 25. Current supporting staff comprise two Administrative Assistants, one Secretary, and seven Technical staff. The Department has thus rather more than doubled in size since 1957, and could have expanded much more but for continuing constraints on both Departmental space and student residential accommodation. As regards the former, plans for a complete new building agreed in 1960 had then to be deferred for lack of a suitable available site, and are yet to be implemented. However, the rehousing of two adjoining Departments, Anatomy and Chemistry, offered opportunities during this period for substantial space accessions, and the Department now possesses total space reasonably adequate for its present numbers, although severe pressures remain in some sectors. Some parts of the Department have been thoroughly reconstructed. The accommodation currently available totals some 2300 m² of working space, including a substantial Departmental Library (started in 1958) and a suite of specialist laboratories in addition to normal teaching laboratories and lecture-rooms, technical staff quarters, and secretarial and staff rooms. Equipment has been built up to a satisfactory level for both teaching and research, and includes two field vehicles, a range of electronic calculating machines and a P.D.P.11 remote job entry computer facility to supplement smaller instruments and the terminal to the University Computer.

Developments in the academic field
In the academic field, several changes and developments deserve particular mention.

Faculty position
Early in the period 1957—75 the connections with the Faculties of Law and Medicine were terminated, while in 1966 the University decided to divide its former large Arts Faculty by separating off appropriate Departments to constitute a Social Sciences Faculty. Geography elected to move into the latter, so that it is now equally in Science and Social Sciences. First degree students enter one or other, but in the present degree structure they may, after the first year of study, and without change of Faculty, specialise in either the physical-biological or the human-social aspects of Geography. Both Faculties award the B.Sc. degree.

First degree curriculum
The curriculum for the first degree has been revised twice since 1957. The first revision, in the late 1950s, replaced virtually all the existing regional courses with courses organised on a systematic basis, and re-built the third year of the Honours course to comprise two compulsory courses (Regional theory and Political geography) together with three optional specialisms selected from a range of seven. The second revision, introduced in 1965, was more radical. Students entering in both Faculties now take a common first-year course in Geography on a systematic basis (physical geography, human geography, technology and environment, plus 10 hours laboratory work a week) which takes two-thirds of their time, together with an appropriate second subject according to Faculty (one-third). On completion of the first year they take no further supporting subjects but are offered a choice of three two-year programmes in Geography; one specialising almost entirely in physical-biological geography, a second with an equal specialisation in social and economic geography, while the third offers a combination of selections from both the first two, plus appropriate additions, for those who do not wish to specialise. A sound grounding in statistical methods was built into the new first-year course and more advanced methods are used in

subsequent years, while the physical-biological speciaiisation incorporates a considerable amount of laboratory and field work. Field-camps
are conducted, at home and abroad, in the first year, and for the
physical-biological group in the second. Topographical surveying, for
which the demand has markedly declined, remains as an available
option in the third year in substitution for certain other courses.

Additional to the above curriculum for the Single Honours degree,
which is available in both Faculties, the Department collaborates with
other Science Departments in offering Joint-Honours degrees in Botany
and Geography, and in Geography and Geology. Various special courses
are provided for students taking these degrees, whose entry numbers
must be currently restricted to a maximum of 10 for each course. Some
12 to 15 Science Faculty students also attend the first-year course as a
supporting subject for their main studies.

The curriculum for the Single Honours degree which requires
students to undertake a substantial individual study in the second
summer vacation, and also one or more individual pieces of project
work during the third year, was decided upon in the belief that it was
time that Geography began to concentrate on developing a more
thorough and advanced knowledge of selected parts of this very wide
subject, together with a more thorough training in techniques and their
application. The innovation has proved popular with students and it is
interesting to note that curricula in various other universities have been
modified in the same direction. Experience has shown that about equal
numbers select the three options available.

Research
The period since 1957 has been marked by a great increase in research
activity. Over 50 post-graduate students have completed M.Sc. or Ph.D.
degrees in this period, and a high percentage of them have proceeded to
posts in other universities in Britain or overseas. Several research grants
have been secured, from the S.S.R.C., N.E.R.C. and from other sources,
various research symposia have been organised by the Department, and
most of its teaching staff have undertaken overseas visits, either for
research purposes or to take up shorter or longer teaching invitations at
other universities.

Conclusion
The period from 1920 to 1975 has witnessed not only the physical
growth of the Department but also an important shift in emphasis.
Building on the foundations laid in the inter-war period, the past
twenty years have seen the development of considerable research
activity on several fronts, and much of this research is closely linked to
the teaching programme. The present volume manifests this change by
presenting a collection of essays that, as indicated in the *Preface*, report
original work and/or review developments in an active research field.